SAGES LEAVE YOUR CONTEMPLATIONS;
BRIGHTER VISIONS BEAM AFAR;
SEEK THE GREAT DESIRE OF NATIONS;
YE HAVE SEEN HIS NATAL STAR.

JAMES MONTGOMERY

BECAUSE OF THIS, EVERY TORAH
SCHOLAR DISCIPLED TO THE DOMINION OF HEAVEN
IS LIKE THE ONE WHO IS HEAD OF A HOUSEHOLD,
WHO TAKES OUT FROM HIS STOREROOM
WHAT IS NEW AND WHAT IS OLD.

MATTHEW 13:52

THE
JESUS QUEST

THE THIRD SEARCH
FOR THE JEW OF NAZARETH

SECOND EDITION

BEN WITHERINGTON III

InterVarsity Press
Downers Grove, Illinois

InterVarsity Press® is the book-publishing division of InterVarsity Christian Fellowship®, a student movement active on campus at hundreds of universities, colleges and schools of nursing in the United Sates of America, and a member movement of the International Fellowship of Evangelical Students. For information about local and regional activities, write Public Relations Dept., InterVarsity Christian Fellowship, 6400 Schroder Rd., P.O. Box 7895, Madison, WI 53707-7895.

All Scripture quotations, unless otherwise indicated, are from the New Revised Standard Version of the Bible, copyright 1989 by the Division of Christian Education of the National Council of the Churches of Christ in the U.S.A., and are used by permission.

Cover photograph: Giraudon/Art Resource, N.Y. John Metropolitos, Christ Redeemer.
ISBN 0-8308-1544-9 (pbk.)

Printed in the United States of America

Library of Congress Cataloging-in-Publication Data

Witherington, Ben, 1951-

   The Jesus quest: the third search for the Jew of Nazareth/Ben
Witherington III.

     p.   cm.
   Includes bibliographical references and index.
   ISBN 0-8308-1861-8 (cloth: alk. paper)
   ISBN 0-8308-1544-9 (pbk.)

   1. Jesus Christ—Biography—History and criticism.　2. Bible. N.T.
Gospels—Criticism, interpretation, etc.—History—20th century.
3. Jesus Christ—Historicity.　I. Title
BT 301.9.W58   1995
232.9'08—dc20   95-43648

                                                       CIP

23	22	21	20	19	18	17	16	15	14	13	12	11	10	9	8	7	6	5	4	3	2
16	15	14	13	12	11	10	09	08	07	06	05	04	03	02	01	00	99	98	97

This study is dedicated to two scholars
who have labored long and hard
in the vineyard of Jesus and Gospel studies
and equally hard in the service of God
and God's people—
Raymond E. Brown and John P. Meier.
May their tribe increase.

Abbreviations

Classical and Hellenistic Sources
Epictetus
   Disc.   *Discourses*
Josephus
   Ant.   *Antiquities of the Jews*
   J.W.   *Jewish Wars*
   Life   *Life of Flavius Josephus*
   Ag. Ap.   *Against Apion*
   PGM   *Papyri Graecae Magicae*
           (Greek Magical Papyri)
Philo
   Flacc.   *In Flaccum (To Flaccus)*
   Sac.   *De Sacrificiis Abelis et Caini*
           (On the Sacrifices of Abel
           and Cain)
Tacitus
   Ann.   *Annals*
   Hist.   *History*

Early Christian Texts
Gos. Pet.   *Gospel of Peter*
Gos. Thom.   *Gospel of Thomas*
P. Oxy.   Oxyrhynchus Papyrus

Dead Sea Scrolls and Related Texts
1QapGen   *Genesis Apocryphon* from
           Qumran Cave 1
1QS   *Manual of Discipline* from
           Qumran Cave 1
1QSa   Appendix A, *Messianic*
           Rule, to 1QS from Qum-
           ran Cave 1
1QSb   Appendix B, *Rule of Bene-*
           diction, to 1QS from
           Qumran Cave 1
4Q174   *Midrash on the Last Days*
           from Qumran Cave 4

4QFlor   *Florilegium* or Eschatologi-
           cal *Midrashim* from
           Qumran Cave 4
4QTestim   *Testimonia* text from
           Qumran Cave 4
11QPs   *Psalm Scroll* from Qumran
           Cave 11

Apocrypha and Pseudepigrapha
Bar   Baruch
1-2 Esdr   1-2 Esdras
4 Ezra   4 Ezra
Jdt   Judith
1-2-3-4
   Macc   1-2-3-4 Maccabees
Pss. Sol.   *Psalms of Solomon*
Sir   Sirach (or Ecclesiasticus)
Tob   Tobit
Wis   Wisdom of Solomon

Mishna, Tosepta and Talmud
Same-named tractates in the Mishna,
Tosepta, Babylonian Talmud and
Jerusalem Talmud are distinguished
by *m., t., b.* and *y.* respectively
'Abot   *'Abot*
B. Bat.   *Baba Batra*
Ber.   *Berakot*
Beṣ.   *Beṣa (= Yom Ṭob)*
Kel.   *Kelim*
Pes.   *Pesaḥim*
Qidd.   *Qiddušin*
Sanh.   *Sanhedrin*
Soṭa   *Soṭa*
Ta'an.   *Ta'anit*

PREFACE

THE FIRST TWO QUESTS

In the middle and late nineteenth century in Europe, as one of the final effects of the Enlightenment, historical-critical scholarship began to be applied in earnest to the Gospel narratives.[1] Various scholars and lay persons began writing new summaries of the life of Jesus, some of them sensationalistic, not because any new or surprising data had surfaced but because the canonical Gospels were being reread in new ways.[2] One of the first, and certainly one of the most influential, of these lives of Jesus was David Friedrich Strauss's large work *Das Leben Jesu* (1835-1836). This work was a clarion call for "unbiased" historical research to be done on the life of Jesus, a call based on the assumption that the Gospels could no longer be read straightforwardly as unvarnished historical records of what Jesus actually said and did. Strauss argued that one must recognize the use of myth in the Evangelists' retellings of the story of Jesus.

Strauss's work was followed by many others, including the notable work by Joseph Ernest Renan *Vie de Jésus*, first published in the 1860s. Yet by the end of the century various scholars, especially Albert Schweitzer, had come to the conclusion that most of these fresh attempts to say what we could *really* know about the historical Jesus actually told us more about their authors than about the person they sought to describe. The authors seem to have looked into the well of history searching for Jesus and seen their own reflection.[3]

This last observation, which Schweitzer's important work *The Quest of the Historical Jesus: A Critical Study of Its Progress from Reimarus to Wrede* (1906) had prompted, in effect put an end to the so-called First (scholarly) Quest for the historical Jesus. What Schweitzer had shown was that these nineteenth-century lives had one and all neglected, or wrongly minimized, the eschatological and apocalyptic dimensions of Jesus' life, teachings and actions. Because these were not marginal or minor aspects of Jesus or his teachings, the result had been significant distortion rather than clarification of what the historical Jesus was like.

Schweitzer himself became persuaded by an extreme form of the "apocalyptic" explanation of Jesus, namely that Jesus and all his teachings (his so-called interim ethics) had been radically conditioned by a mistaken belief that the end of the world would happen during or shortly after his own lifetime. Schweitzer concluded that all such historical research about Jesus had reached an impasse, making further research pointless. Jesus had been deluded about something that was central to his life and teaching—the timing and nature of the end things.[4] In due course Schweitzer gave up the world of biblical scholarship and became a medical missionary to Africa.

If Schweitzer put a damper on the First Quest in terms of the substance of what could be discovered, Martin Kähler effectively silenced its by his critique of its methodology and the limits of historical inquiry in a famous and still influential work, *The So-Called Historical Jesus and the Historic Biblical Christ*, first issued in 1896. Kähler's work is remarkable in many ways, not least because it seems to have appealed equally to conservatives and liberals. On the one hand, Kähler argued it was quite impossible to separate the Jesus of history from the Christ of faith, not least because we only know the former through documents written about and exalting the latter. Kähler believed that the Christ who is now preached and worshiped is the one who has influenced history. In other words, this is the only Jesus in whom scholars should be interested.

On the other hand, Kähler repudiated the attempt to make faith dependent on historical research. This last conclusion had great influence, notably on Paul Tillich and Rudolf Bultmann, who largely separated the Jesus of history from the Christ of their faith.[5] The problem with this bifurcation is that despite numerous attempts in this century to turn Christianity into a philosophy of life, it is and has always been a historical religion—one that depends on certain foundational events, particularly the death and resurrection of Jesus, as having happened in space and time.

A faith that does not ground the Christ of personal experience in the Jesus of history is a form of docetic or gnostic heresy, for it implies that what actually happened in and during Jesus' life is inconsequential to Christian faith.

The result of the double salvo by Schweitzer and Kähler was that for much of the first half of the twentieth century the scholarly quest for the historical Jesus was assumed to be dead. As it turned out, this was not the case. In 1953, in a gathering of Bultmann's former students, Ernst Käsemann gave a famous lecture, "The Problem of the Historical Jesus."[6] In this lecture he argued against his mentor that, while the Gospel traditions were certainly interpreted by believing followers of Jesus, this did not mean they could not preserve authentic historical memories. Bultmann's skepticism about what could be known about the historical Jesus had been too extreme.

In the wake of Käsemann's lecture various scholars produced significant works, but the most influential and enduring was Günther Bornkamm's life of Jesus, published in German in 1956 and in English in 1960 as *Jesus of Nazareth*. This work reflected the newfound confidence that we can know something about the historical Jesus by fully implementing the tools of critical inquiry. "Quite clearly what the Gospels report concerning the message, the deeds and the history of Jesus is still distinguished by an authenticity, a freshness and a distinctiveness not in any way effaced by the Church's Easter faith. These features point us directly to the earthly figure of Jesus."[7] In 1959 James M. Robinson chronicled this Second Quest in *A New Quest of the Historical Jesus*, a work whose numerous reprints showed the keen interest in the subject.

One of the characteristics of the Second, or New, Quest was its focus on the present relevance of Jesus' teaching. In many cases Jesus came off sounding like an existentialist philosopher, an emphasis that may be seen as the residue of Bultmann's appropriation of existential philosophy in interpreting the New Testament. It is fair to say that as the towering influence of Bultmann and the enthusiasm for existentialism began to wane, so did the enthusiasm for the Second Quest,[8] leaving the movement dead in the water by the early 1970s.

One of the abiding lessons to be learned from a critical evaluation of the contributions to the first two quests for the historical Jesus is that it is important to distinguish between what Jesus actually did, said and was two thousand years ago and what the historical-critical method can discover and conclude about it. While Christian faith must be grounded in the historical Jesus and his ministry, this is different from claiming it should be based on the ever-shifting tides of New Testament scholarship. What is true about the historical Jesus and what the *historical method* can demonstrate are not one and the same. The latter will always be at best a truncated version of the former.

Thus we must recognize at the outset, *before* examining the Third Quest, that the most the historical-critical method can accomplish is to establish a good *probability* as to whether or not a certain saying or action reported of Jesus did actually originate with him and whether or not a given interpretation of Jesus has some historical basis. This is necessarily a minimalist approach and does not result in the sort of full-orbed picture of Jesus with which an orthodox Christian believer is familiar and fully comfortable.

What this methodology *cannot* do is prove beyond a shadow of a doubt that Jesus did *not* say or do this or that. All historians dealing with ancient subjects necessarily work in the realm of probabilities and not certainties. New Testament scholars can no more *prove* Jesus did or did not do or say something than Roman historians can prove that Nero did or did not have some responsibility for the great fire of Rome in the 60s of the first century. They can only hope to show good probability one way or another.

Furthermore, just because one cannot establish the authenticity of some particular saying or event with the historical-critical method does not mean that it absolutely did not happen or was not said. In various cases the fault may lie (1) in the limitations of the methodology itself, (2) in the paucity of the evidence at hand or (3) in the bias or limited skills of the one handling the data. The upshot of the first two quests, as much as anything else, was to reveal the frustrating limitations of the historical study of any ancient person.

In what follows I hope to give the reader an introduction to and analysis of some of the more noteworthy and celebrated aspects of what has been hailed as the Third Quest for the historical Jesus. A new impetus to discover the historical Jesus has produced a plethora of monographs and even a few attempts at something like a life of Jesus, and of course there is the famous, or infamous, Jesus Seminar. This Third Quest began in the early 1980s, fueled by some new archaeological and manuscript data, some new methodological refinements and some new enthusiasm that historical research did not need to lead to a dead end.[9] It is my hope that the reader will sense the flavor and variety of the discussion and be prompted to go back to the text of the canonical Gospels and compare what the scholars are saying with what the Gospels claim. I also hope this book will prompt readers to set out on or continue their own pilgrimage toward Jesus—toward both the Jew from Nazareth and the exalted heavenly Christ of Christian faith.

Ben Witherington III
Christmas 1994

CHAPTER 1

GALILEE & THE GALILEAN
JESUS IN HIS
SOCIAL SETTING

As one scholar has put it, *the Third Quest for the historical Jesus of Galilee has threatened at various points to become the quest for the historical Galilee. Nevertheless, it is one of the distinctive and more important contributions of the Third Quest that it seeks to place Jesus more firmly in his historical context, and this has shed fresh light on his words, deeds and character. The historical context of Jesus is sharply illuminated when we learn the degree to which Galilee was Hellenized, the influence of Rome on Galilee, the social level of Jesus and his disciples, the extent to which synagogues and Pharisees were present (or absent) in Galilee, the nature and burden of taxation, the shape and transformation of family structures, the androcentricity of society and the religious practices of Galileans. In addition to showing how Jesus' world was very different from that of the late-twentieth-century West, the emerging picture of first-century Galilee suggests a social agenda in Jesus' words, actions and movements that has frequently been overlooked.*

IN 1986 WHILE I WAS VISITING EGYPT, THERE CAME A MOMENT WHEN CULtural vertigo struck. I was standing in the great temple at Luxor, and the nearby loudspeakers were broadcasting in Arabic the Islamic call to prayer. Most of the people around me were not Westerners and were speaking neither English, nor German, nor French, the spoken languages I know. Tour guides were giving long discourses on ancient Egyptian religion and the relationship of the temples on the east side of the Nile to the tombs on the west side of the Nile. It was a religion and a culture very different from anything I had experienced growing up in North Carolina. The sense of being a stranger in a strange land struck me forcefully, and it dawned on me that if I had been transported back in time to ancient Galilee, I would surely have felt no less estranged.

The Jesus I learned about as a child spoke King James (or Revised Standard) English and seemed to fit without great difficulty into modern Western culture and values. But the historical Jesus spoke Aramaic, a Semitic language, and lived in a nondemocratic world very different from modern North America. This sense of cultural distance is important and must always be kept in mind if we are not to remake Jesus and his world in the image of our own thoughts and world. As the British novelist L. P. Hartley once put it: "The past is a foreign country. They do things differently there."[1]

Thus this book begins with a portrait of the social environment in which Jesus was born and lived, drawing on the research of various people who have contributed, directly or indirectly, to the Third Quest. This sort of "thick" description of Jesus' social, economic and religious world is characteristic of the Third Quest and reflects a reaction to the Second Quest, which had a certain culturally detached way of analyzing Jesus.

The impetus behind this aspect of the Third Quest is captured in John K. Riches's words: "Out of the many religious groups and movements that flourished in the Mediterranean in the first century, only two [Judaism and Christianity] would survive in any substantial institutionalized form, and both had their roots in the crisis in first-century Palestine."[2] On the other hand we must bear in mind the warning of Sean Freyne that the quest for the historical Jesus "is rapidly in danger of becoming the quest for the historical Galilee."[3] Having painted a picture of the life setting of Jesus, we will be in a much better position to evaluate current attempts to reenvision the Jesus of history.[4] To understand the Galilean it is crucial to understand the context of Galilee.

PALESTINE UNDER ROMAN RULE

Social and Political Volatility
Though many scholars have been quick to cite the dictum of Tacitus that during the reign of the emperor Tiberius (A.D. 14-37) "all was quiet" in Palestine (*Hist.* 5.9), this was a judgment made by a Roman looking at things from the top down with the memory of the tumultuous times before and after Tiberius's reign. No doubt the view from the bottom up appeared quite different. Both before and after the ministry of Jesus there were in fact some significant Jewish revolts against foreign domination.[5]

First, there was the temporarily successful revolt by the Maccabees against the Seleucids, leading to a century of Jewish self-rule from 167 to 63 B.C. In A.D. 6 there was something of a revolt against the census and taxation enforced by Quirinius. Then there was a major Jewish revolt in A.D. 66 to 70, leading to the destruction of the temple and of Jerusalem. Finally, there was the Bar Kokhba revolt in the early second century A.D.[6] If we add to this the symbolic actions of self-appointed prophets and messianic figures during the New Testament period,[7] various acts of sabotage and banditry recorded by Josephus,[8] the brutal acts of repression and murder committed by Herod the Great and his offspring (including the execution of John the Baptist by Herod Antipas), the atrocities of Pontius Pilate and other Roman rulers, as well as the acts of murder Jews and Samaritans committed against each other, it is not difficult to reach the conclusion that Jesus lived in a time that was dangerous for Jews.

Even if things were not always bellicose during Jesus' time, they were nonetheless far from bucolic. If they were not invariably violent, they were nonetheless volatile. The image of a gentle Jesus, meek and mild, going about Galilee offering entertaining stories called parables or engaging in abstract academic debates about various religious notions fails to convey the sensitive and sometimes hostile atmosphere in which Jesus operated and the *effect* his teaching would have had on those who lived in this environment. It was an atmosphere in which politics and religion were almost always mixed, and messianic claims, actions or ideas were normally viewed by those in power as threats to the political status quo.[9]

Two examples will illustrate the realities. According to Josephus (*Ant.* 18.60-62; *J.W.* 2.175-77), Pontius Pilate at one point during his rule of Judea, desiring to solve the continual problem of supplying Jerusalem with adequate water, decided to confiscate funds from the temple treasury in order to build an aqueduct. He anticipated some protest over this action, but in fact it was seen not merely as theft but as sacrilege. So when he next visited the city and was surrounded by a crowd of shouting and complaining Jews, he had soldiers dressed like ordinary citizens leap forth and beat every Jew within reach, protestors and bystanders alike. A second incident took place near the end of Pilate's rule in Judea (about A.D. 36). A group of Samaritans was ascending sacred Mount Gerizim in Samaria, led by a prophet who promised to reveal the sacred vessels Moses had reputedly buried there. But they were met by a detachment of Pilate's heavily armed troops. The troops seem to have expected an insurrection and attacked the crowd, killing or injuring many Samaritans and later executing a number of others (cf. *Ant.* 18.85-89). It was this sordid episode that led to the removal of Pilate from rule in Judea, but only after various Samaritan emissaries had taken their protest to Rome. With this sort of track record of brutal insensitivity to the religious beliefs of the people in the land, it is not hard to believe Luke's report that Pilate on one occasion slaughtered Galileans on pilgrimage to the temple and mingled their blood with their sacrifices (Lk 13:1).[10] Nor is it difficult to comprehend that he would have executed Jesus during a Jewish religious festival.

Roman Prefects and Client Kings

Fergus G. B. Millar informs us that Judea became for the Romans a new sort of province. For them, it was a province of second rank that was to be ruled almost exclusively by auxiliary units, not legions, except in times of extreme trouble, when the Roman governor in Syria who oversaw the entire area would send in troops. It also did not rate highly enough to be ruled as a senatorial province; its citizens had to suffice with Roman prefects of equestrian rank.[11] Many of these prefects lacked the competence to handle the delicate set of circumstances that existed in the Holy Land during the first century A.D., and even when an able man was sent by Rome, he would not have had the experience or education to deal with the mix of religion and politics in Judea with cultural sensitivity.

It must be borne in mind that Rome, as a rule, preferred to govern the East from a distance and to allow the local elites and regimes to carry out its dirty work. As E. P. Sanders says: "Rome generally governed remotely, being content with the collection of tribute and maintenance of stable borders; for the most part it left even these matters in the hands of loyal local rulers and leaders."[12] As long as a region was stable and the tribute kept flowing in, Rome generally left it alone. This is important for understanding the situation in Galilee, which throughout Jesus' adult life was ruled by the client ruler Herod Antipas, not directly by Rome.

While Pilate and other Roman rulers could be brutal and repressive, so also could local client kings. Herod the Great, whose rule ended shortly after the time of Jesus' birth,[13] was a client king of the Romans and a very effective one by their standards. In fact, in A.D. 6 the political situation changed in Judea from client king to direct Roman rule by means of prefects or governors because of the incompetence of Herod's son and successor in Judea, Archelaus. Thus throughout the adult life of Jesus, Judea was a Roman province, although Galilee continued to be ruled by client kings, in particular Herod Antipas (from 4 B.C. to A.D. 39).

Herod the Great is a familiar figure to Gospel readers. The episode in Matthew 2, which led to the slaughter of the infants in Bethlehem, is not recorded elsewhere, but we can say unequivocally that it would have been totally in character for Herod to have performed such an act. He did not scruple to kill even members of his own family, including some of his own children. Indeed, he did not stop at killing family and ordinary citizens but showed the same disregard for the sacred traditions of the Jews that Roman rulers like Pilate demonstrated. He is known to have killed members of the Sanhedrin and perhaps even dissolved that council for a time (cf. Josephus *Ant.* 14.175—15.5). As James D. Newsome puts it: "Jewish hatred of Herod was not confined to any one sect or party. The Sadducees despised the king because of his suppression of their allies, the Hasmonean family. And as for the Pharisees, . . . their enmity was insured by Herod's disregard for Torah and for other sacred traditions of Judaism."[14] We must also bear in mind that Herod and his offspring, though of Jewish descent, were not pure-blooded. They were from Idumea (earlier known as Edom), and to judge from their building programs they were thoroughly Hellenized Semites who were committed, as were the Romans, to a program of introducing Greek culture (with its hippodromes, theaters, gymnasiums and the like) into the Holy Land.

In terms of winning the hearts of the populace, Herod Antipas fared little better in Galilee than did his father in Judea. He continued the Hellenizing agenda of his father, even to the extreme of building the town of Tiberias by the sea of Galilee on top of a Jewish graveyard. This made it perpetually unclean for Jews, and many of the devout refused to enter it, for in Jewish law a corpse and thus a graveyard was the most unclean thing of all. It is probably no accident that we have no record of Jesus ever visiting Tiberias, or for that matter Sepphoris, another of Antipas's creations, even though Tiberias was in the very region where Jesus ministered and Sepphoris was within a few miles of Nazareth.

In view of the political situation we have recounted, it is not surprising that various flare-ups and violent incidents, often with a religious motive or component, took place throughout the New Testament era. In fact, it is surprising that there were not more of them. As Martin Goodman stresses, since the principal means of governing Palestine throughout this period seem to have been fear and brute force and in view of the fact that Jews had developed a taste for self-rule as recently as the first century B.C., it is no wonder that "hostility to Rome was shown from the foundation of the province"[15] or that there was longstanding hostility between Jews and those Gentiles who lived in the land and collaborated with the Romans in trying to set up a Greco-Roman society there.[16]

The Aristocracy

Matters were made worse by two factors. First, the Roman principle of provincial self-rule not only enlisted local client kings whom Rome could control by patronage and other means, it also counted on the local aristocracy to help govern by giving them authority to collect taxes and implement policy. The problem with this was that the Romans simply assumed that there *was* an aristocracy in Judea and Galilee with enough popular respect to gain the consent of the people to Roman policies.[17] Unfortunately for the Romans, as Goodman notes,

> Finding no natural landed elite in Judaea but needing the cooperation of local rulers of some kind for their administration to work successfully, the Romans elected to entrust power to those Judaean landowners who did exist, *regardless of whether such men could command any popular prestige.* These men were the creatures of Herod who had been granted land and position within the state since 37 B.C.[18]

Much the same could be said for Antipas's rule in Galilee. Mark 6:14-29 tells us of the infamous birthday party Antipas celebrated, gathering around himself "his courtiers and officers and . . . the leaders of Galilee" (Mk 6:21). But who were these "leaders of Galilee"? They were surely not popular local elders from the various villages of Galilee but were those whom Antipas had set up in power in places like Sepphoris and those thoroughly Hellenized Gentiles and Semites of some wealth who had no scruples about dining in a palace where images of animals were present, in a city partially built over a Jewish graveyard. It was Antipas's retainers, perhaps coupled with certain allies from the region, who witnessed the grisly dispatch of John the Baptist. Not without reason did Jesus call Antipas a fox, for he was not to be trusted. The point is that there was a gulf between the governing and the governed in Judea and Galilee which was not bridged by mutual respect or trust, nor by many intermediary figures who could have instilled confidence on both sides.[19]

Taxes

The second major problem was the tax burden. The Romans believed that a province or governed territory should not merely be self-supporting, by which was meant that it should support the Roman apparatus of government and troops in the region, but that it should also send taxes back to Rome in support of the emperor and his empire. Remembering that we are not dealing with governance by consent, much less by the freely chosen representatives, of the governed, it is not hard to imagine the reaction to a census, the purpose of which was a head count for purposes of taxation (cf. Lk 2:1-3), and then the administration of the taxation itself.[20]

The attempt to take a census in A.D. 6 was met with a revolt, and Tacitus records another major Jewish complaint in A.D. 17 regarding the tax burden (*Ann.* 2.42). Goodman notes that "taxation was, or felt, excessive under the procurators' rule; it is debated whether taxes were heavier after A.D. 6 than they had been under Herod."[21] But there is evidence of increases in demands as the empire's needs grew, particularly during the reign of Nero, and a special levy on Judea is known to have been exacted under the procurator Albinus in the early 60s. Adding insult to injury, the Romans "farmed out" their tax collection, granting collection rights to the highest bidder, a practice that led to all sorts of graft and corruption. So long as the local tax collector paid the government the agreed amount, Rome, and for that matter the Herodians, seemed willing to turn a blind eye to whatever extra amounts they might extort from the local populace. Thus tax collectors were often viewed by Jews as turncoats, Jews who helped the Romans or Herodians suck the blood from their own people.

This background sheds light on the Zacchaeus story and explains why he would have been generally despised and shunned by Jews. They would be shocked at Jesus' dining with such a "sinner" (cf. Lk 19:1-10). Likewise, Jesus' telling the story of the vindication of a tax collector and the rejection of a pious Pharisee's prayer (Lk 18:9-14) is revealing. Jesus' social agenda, in a somewhat oppressive environment, did not amount to a simple ignoring or endorsing of the status quo. Having a (former?) tax or toll collector as one of his inner circle of disciples would have raised eyebrows and objections.[22]

Economic Realities

In his account of the Jewish War given in his *Life of Flavius Josephus*, Josephus deliberately distinguishes between "the Galileans," that is, the peasants and others who did not dwell in the Hellenistic cities, and those whom they despised, namely the residents of Sepphoris and Tiberias, on whom "the Galileans" turned when the opportunity arose.[23] This animosity between the rural and small-town people and the more cosmopolitan city dwellers was probably of long standing, and Josephus's terminology suggests that the rural people did not see the latter as one with them, in other words as true Galileans.

In his helpful study of the politics and economics of Galilee, Sean Freyne has stressed that during Jesus' lifetime Galilee was beginning to change from a reciprocal or barter economy to a market and money economy, with resulting stress being placed on the peasants and small landholders.[24] Freyne proposes that Jesus was offering an alternate value system to both the traditional one and the new market-economy one, namely the creation of a new family and family values based on adherence and not kinship or marital ties, one that involved sharing in the new community of Jesus' followers (cf. Lk 8:1-3). By contrast, Sanders argues that "Galileans in Jesus' lifetime did not feel that the things most dear to them were seriously threatened: their religion, their national traditions and their livelihoods."[25] It is on this last score especially that Freyne would disagree with Sanders in regard to the effect of the Herodian regime, and he believes the Jesus movement itself would have created tensions.[26]

It is worth remembering that Jesus drew his first disciples from among fishermen, who already depended on a market economy for their livelihood. Since their catch had to be sold rapidly, their assets tended to be in money rather than in goods, making them a ready target for moneylenders, tax collectors and the like. Jesus may have been asking them to leave behind not just their livelihood but the economic system of which it was a part.[27]

Whatever else we might say, Jesus was certainly a devout Jew who was deeply aware of Jewish sensibilities. It was one thing to believe God was giving his people a new covenant that changed various of the ritual requirements, but it was quite another to simply trample on the Mosaic law in order to fulfill one's dreams of grandeur, as did Antipas. In general the impression we get from the Gospel tradition is that Jesus viewed with suspicion both Herod Antipas ("that fox") and the retainer classes that supported him and inhabited his new cities of Tiberias and Sepphoris, avoiding contact with the latter and having nothing good to say about the former.

The Religious Leadership

An important dimension of the power structure of Palestine during Jesus' day was the religious leadership. The high priest performed both political and religious roles, not least because he was the head of the Sanhedrin, the Jewish high council. Under Roman occupation, the one group of leaders we might expect Jews to have held in high regard would be the priests, Levites and other religious leaders. To some extent they were so regarded, but not without qualification. The Qumran community living on the shores of the Dead Sea, for instance, believed that the temple and its leadership was hopelessly corrupt and would soon be judged by God. Then too, John the Baptist, according to Matthew, anathematized both the popular Pharisees and the Sadducees when they came to be baptized, calling them the offspring of snakes (Mt 3:7-10). At the very least the reaction of various Jews to some of the religious leaders can be characterized as ambivalent.

The high priests had been chosen and installed by the Herodians and the Romans ever since the time of Herod the Great. The family that held the office during most of Jesus' lifetime was that of the formerly unknown Ananus b. Sethi (*Ant.* 18.26). "Roman rule plucked him from obscurity on the grounds of his priestly birth and, presumably since he would otherwise have been ineligible in Roman eyes, his wealth."[28] His family was to dominate the high priesthood for the next sixty years: he was himself high priest for nine years, and all five of his sons, including Caiaphas, held the position (*Ant.* 20.198).

Not only did none of the priests chosen by Herod the Great win any prestige with the Jewish people in their own right, neither did the family of Ananus, although they dominated both temple and Sanhedrin. As Goodman stresses, "Their right to lead the Jewish nation rested . . . entirely on the whim of the Romans, or in later cases Herodian princes, who appointed them."[29] He points out that "the [Jewish] rulers of Judaea were thus in a sense marginal within their own society."[30]

This does not mean that the temple, the priesthood as an institution, the sacrifices or the festivals, to which thousands of Jews made pilgrimage every year, were not held in high regard by most Judeans and Galileans. But it does mean that during Jesus' lifetime there was no great trust in

or enthusiasm for the particular individuals who administered these institutions. Many Jews were much more likely to respect local elders, Pharisees, sages, prophets or holy men, or even messianic claimants, than they
were such official leaders. It was into this environment, with its absence
of national religious leaders who could inspire widespread confidence,
that reformers and radicals like the Pharisees and Jesus came.

JESUS, THE PHARISEES AND THEIR RELIGIOUS MILIEU

In investigating the historical Jesus we must understand the role the
Pharisees played in their society in both Judea and Galilee and their relationship to Jesus. We can hardly read the Gospels without noticing how
often the Pharisees and Jesus encounter one another, sometimes as dialogue partners and sometimes apparently dueling in the presence of the
crowds and attempting to win their support. Historically, the Pharisees
are the spiritual forefathers of all three forms of modern Judaism, and
from Jesus and the Jesus movement came forth the church. Thus knowledge of Jesus and the Pharisees is imperative for understanding contemporary Jewish-Christian dialogue and Jewish and Christian religious history.

Who Were the Pharisees?

In an earlier work, I investigated the Pharisees at some length. Here I can
only summarize the conclusions of that study. "Pharisaism was, at least
for many in the pre-A.D. 70 period, the religious vox populi as well as the
group most revered by the people."[31] There were more and less strict
Pharisees, as the controversies between Shammai and Hillel show, some
of whom (the ḥᵃberîm, who were ultraorthodox) seem to have even lived
in community, much as the Essenes of Qumran did, and were very strict
in practicing ritual purity and following dietary laws. It is important also
to bear in mind the variety of people involved in the Pharisaic movement—ordinary laypeople, scribes who were the biblical interpreters and
scholars of the movement (the "scribes of the Pharisees") and ḥᵃberîm. Jesus
in all likelihood was confronted by a variety of Pharisees whose views on
the law, and especially ritual purity, varied in severity.

It seems clear from the discussions between Jesus and the Pharisees
that the Pharisees were not nationalists focusing specifically on the land,
the temple or the political state.[32] "Politics certainly was not the dominant

concern of the Pharisees of Jesus' day except insofar as it affected their ability to carry on their religious movement as they saw fit. Their agenda was the hallowing of everyday life in all its aspects within the existing structure of society, not apart from it, as was the case with the Qumranites."[33] It is both interesting and surprising how Hellenized some Pharisees could be in some regards, such as in the mode of dining.[34] Apparently a certain amount of Hellenization was not seen as at odds with the Pharisaic interpretation of the law.[35]

I remain unconvinced by the arguments of E. P. Sanders, who seeks to minimize the presence of Pharisees in Galilee. Even if it was the case that the Pharisees were primarily based in Jerusalem and Judea, there is evidence that authorities in Jerusalem would send Pharisees to Galilee to investigate ongoing developments there (cf. Josephus, *Life,* 197ff.).[36] The Pharisees, particularly those who were also scribes, were the acknowledged experts in matters of Jewish law and life. If, for example, new views of Torah or temple or territory were being promulgated in Galilee, the Pharisees, who wished to extend their influence to include all Jews in the Holy Land, would be concerned and likely to investigate.

Jesus and the Pharisees
In the course of this book we will see that Jesus and the Pharisees had many things in common and certain notable differences. Both Jesus and the Pharisees were deeply concerned about the Jewish people and focused their ministries on those who lived within the land. Neither set out to convert Gentiles in other lands. Jesus' activities seem to have been mostly centered in Galilee, while the Pharisees' activities seem to have been predominantly centered in Judea.

Unlike the Qumran sectarians, neither Jesus nor the Pharisees believed that withdrawal into the desert from a corrupt society to wait for its imminent end was the way forward. Rather, both Jesus and the Pharisees saw it as their task, borrowing a phrase from my own Wesleyan heritage, to "spread Scriptural holiness throughout the land."

In other words, Jesus and the Pharisees were concerned with the renewal and redemption of the Jewish people, who under foreign occupation had become acculturated, tainted and in some cases even lost. The Jesus tradition is quite explicit at this point, stating that Jesus was sent specifically to the "lost sheep of Israel" (Mt 15:24), though whether this meant all Israel or the lost among Israel has been debated.[37] It seems clear however that Jesus and the Pharisees disagreed on who was lost and needed redemption and who did not, and perhaps even about who was redeemable. They also disagreed on the proper means for hallowing or sanctifying God's people. The Pharisees seem to have wanted all of Israel to become like Levitical priests, keeping all the purity laws, both ritual and moral, as found in the Levitical code in the Old Testament. Jesus' view of holiness and purity seems to have been rather different.[38]

Another striking similarity between Jesus and the Pharisees was that they shared some common theological beliefs regarding angels, resurrection and new oral teachings not found explicitly in the Torah. They seem to have agreed that the Torah was the foundation of their Jewish faith and that there was a need for fresh, even novel, interpretation of it, as well as the addition of some teachings it did not explicitly contain. Yet Jesus was perceived as a threat by at least some of the Pharisees because he refused to accept *their* oral expansions of Torah at various points, calling these oral traditions the traditions of humans and not the Word of God. The Pharisees "by claiming to have the correct interpretation and ability to explain (and expand) the law according to oral tradition to meet new situations, . . . asserted implicit and sometimes explicit authority over all Jewish people. Not surprisingly, they did not easily tolerate anyone who *threatened the assumptions upon which that authority was based.*"[39] Jesus presented a threat because he claimed that his authority came directly from God, not through the accumulated knowledge of human oral traditions.

Apparently, neither Jesus nor the Pharisees were committed to going the route of the Zealots in advocating armed resistance and the ultimate violent overthrow of the occupying forces. This does not mean that either Jesus or the Pharisees were quietistic and advocated total withdrawal from the fray, like the Qumran sectarians, nor does it mean that their teachings had no social or political implications. Rather, both Jesus and the Pharisees believed that the way forward was to renew or redeem the populace as the means of changing the social situation in the land and create a holy community. But what amounted to holiness? What did God require of the chosen people in this new situation? How were they to react to the inroads of Hellenization and Romanization, of Greco-Roman culture? On these subjects Jesus and the Pharisees disagreed, indeed they disagreed strongly.

Jesus bound his followers to himself, and it was his person, his teaching and his actions that were the essence and heart of the matter. For the

Pharisees, no one teacher, scribe or, in later days, rabbi had this function. Nor did any one set of teachings by one Pharisee ever assume the status that the Jesus tradition did for his followers. Why this different outcome in two somewhat similar Jewish reform movements? In anticipation of later discussion, I would suggest it is because the Jesus movement was a messianic one that believed and consciously acted on the assumption that God's dominion was already breaking into the midst of God's people in the person and work of Jesus.

Some Pharisees might have believed that they were preparing the way for the end times, not unlike the way John the Baptist seems to have done, but they did not have the sort of realized eschatology that we find in the teachings of Jesus and his followers. The Pharisees did not see themselves as inaugurating a new covenant, but rather they were bent on fully implementing the old Mosaic one.

SOCIAL AND ECONOMIC LIFE IN GALILEE

Galilee

The region in which Jesus was raised and undertook most of his ministry had various features that distinguished it from Judea. Politically speaking, Galilee was never under direct Roman rule during this period, though Jesus may well have been followed about by Herodians, the eyes and ears of Herod Antipas, during his ministry (cf. Mk 6:14-16; 8:15; 12:13). Geographically, the region of our particular focus is what is called lower Galilee, which includes the vast majority of places mentioned in the Synoptics as having been visited by Jesus during his ministry. As Eric M. Meyers describes it,

> The hills of Lower Galilee present no effective barrier to communication. Indeed Lower Galilee is closely tied to the busy trade of both the Mediterranean and the Sea of Galilee. . . . On the other hand, Upper Galilee . . . is a self-enclosed area defined by the awesome slopes of the Meiron massif.[40]

There were in fact four major valleys that provided relatively easy access from lower Galilee to the cities and ports on the coast.

Jesus certainly grew up in the more fertile, cosmopolitan and developed area of the two Galilees. Given the region's openness to trade and travel, the residents were likely to know at least enough Greek to do business with the many Gentiles in the area. Even Galilean fishermen like Peter would have needed to know some Greek to be successful at their trade. We will return to the issue of how Hellenized Jesus and his followers were likely to have been when we discuss the idea of Jesus as an itinerant Cynic philosopher,[41] but for now it is sufficient to say that Jesus and his followers probably knew some Greek, though their primary language was surely Aramaic, as Mark's Gospel suggests (cf. Mk 5:41; 7:34).[42]

The Changing Economy

An important factor in understanding the dynamics of life in Galilee, as well as in Judea, is the relationship between the villages and the larger cities of the region, as well as the relationship between its poorer and its more well-to-do inhabitants. It is fair to say that during Roman occupation, Judea, and Galilee as well, experienced gradual integration into the wider Mediterranean economy.

But this integration entailed a widening gap between rich and poor,[43] a situation that was exacerbated by other factors, including famine, population growth (without comparable growth in arable land) and small farmers' loss of land to the wealthy who had held it as collateral against loans.[44] In such a situation parables about unlucky tenant farmers, day laborers in vineyards, absentee landlords, unscrupulous middlemen and the like would hardly have sounded like pious platitudes. They would have rung true to the realities of life, a social commentary on how the coming Dominion of God could ultimately change the situation.

Jesus had a great deal to say about marriage, family, children and the roles of women,[45] and it is important to note that he spoke in a context where Jewish society was experiencing the breaking down of the extended family into more nuclear family units, caused by the rapid growth of the population.

This process was inevitable. A father has a farm and several male children. He gives a double portion of the land to his eldest son and the rest to the other sons as an inheritance. All these sons marry and have families. Now the land that originally supported one extended family must support several families, and this it will not do. The result is that at least some of the brothers must move elsewhere, take up a trade or become a tenant farmer on someone else's farm.

In the worst cases they resorted to banditry. Archaeologists have found numerous caves in both Judea and Galilee that were used by the marginalized as bases from which to raid the well-to-do, often with the complicity of villagers who may have seen them on occasion as Robin Hood-like figures who were trying to tip the scales of the economy in a more equitable direction. Freyne cautions us in speaking of banditry during the time of Jesus in Galilee, since the evidence does not suggest that in the period A.D. 26-33 this problem was endemic there. Nonetheless, the changing economic situation was providing a climate for such activity during Jesus' day.[46]

Moreover, the values and views of any Gentile overlords and the Jews in the region would have differed in regard to matters of charity and the poor. As Goodman summarizes the situation, "Charity in the Jewish and Christian sense was unknown to the pagan world. Pagans did not notice the very poor at all except when they became politically threatening. Assistance was almost always confined to citizens. Slaves and outsiders were ignored when in distress."[47] Of course, among Jews and Christians it was an important moral duty to help the poor. Jesus not only blessed the poor (cf. Lk 6:20), but stressed how hard it was for a rich person to enter God's kingdom (Mk 10:23) and urged his disciples to help the needy (Mt 25:39-46).[48]

Jesus' teaching on a variety of such subjects was at odds with the values of those who ruled and owned much of the land—the political and economic overlords. Not only so, but his model of leadership seems to have amounted to a flat rejection of the power-and-patronage, domineer-and-dominate, might-makes-right approach (cf. Lk 22:24-27). This required that he identify particularly with the least, the last and the lost and seek their redemption.

From an economic, but not always from a cultural, point of view, the small villages in Galilee seem to have been significantly dependent upon the larger Herodian cities for marketing their goods and wares. At the same time, the cities were also dependent on the small villages and rural inhabitants, for Galilee's economy, like that of most of the ancient world, was agrarian-based. Typically, one of the larger cities would serve as a marketplace for the surrounding villages, and there goods and services could be bought, sold or exchanged. This economic interdependence may have overcome some measure of the cultural differences and disagreements.[49]

The economic importance of Galilee extended well beyond the region itself, for there is evidence that vegetables, grains, olive oil, raw materials (such as Galilean rushes for rope making), dried figs, fig honey and wine were exported.[50] Who then in Galilee were the main beneficiaries of this export trade? The more well-to-do landowners and business owners who had the capital and facilities to profit from such abundance. In other words, on the whole the abundance of fertile Galilee only helped exacerbate the distance between the haves and the have-nots. These factors come into play in the teachings of Jesus, as we shall see.

Social "Class" and Social Tensions in Galilee

It is hazardous to assume that economic and social realities in Jesus' Galilee would have been much like those of our own world. For one thing, the sense of social *class*, much less the existence of something called the middle class, did not exist in Jesus' world.[51] Not even artisans, such as carpenters or stonemasons, formed anything comparable to our middle class. What Goodman affirms about Judea was just as true of Galilee:

> There were no social categories to correspond to the function of different groups in economic production. Neither free peasants nor tenant farmers nor craftsmen, nor indeed landowners and rich merchants, used such labels to identify themselves or recognized that as groups they were separate classes with identifiable interests and rights. Important social categories for them were based on religious status: a man felt himself to be an Israelite, a Levite or a priest, a proselyte or a natural-born Jew. He felt no tug of solidarity with others in his economic class. The resentment of the poor at exploitation by the rich remained unfocused.[52]

The loyalties of Galileans were likely to be first to their extended family, then to their fellow villagers of whatever means, then to Jews in general and then to the religious institutions and its leaders in particular, not to fellow members of the same economic status or income, much less to their economic or political overlords. Freyne has stressed that "Galilean peasant loyalties appear to have been firmly anchored in Jerusalem" and this in spite of the Roman oversight and ultimate control of the administration in the temple.[53] These loyalties ran deep as they were based in religious faith and often were at odds with the values of the Gentiles and highly Hellenized Jewish city dwellers who lived in Galilee.

Cities: The View from the Village

No city in Galilee held the attraction for most Galilean Jews that Jerusalem did, no matter how beautifully it may have been built. Galileans were not making pilgrimages to see the sparkling new Sepphoris, but they flocked in large numbers to Jerusalem during the festivals.

And Jerusalem is the one city Jesus speaks of with some regularity. It appears that he identified with the smaller villages and their loyalties rather than with the Hellenized Galilean cities. Yet it is also true that he made forays into regions around Galilee (near Tyre, or in the region of the Decapolis, or Samaria), and there are reports of people from outlying regions coming to him for healing. These features of Jesus' ministry would likely have been seen as provocative to conservative-minded Jews in the region, and they provided yet another reason for Jesus to come under the surveillance of the Herodians, Pharisees and others.[54]

Some rural animosities toward Greco-Roman cities in Galilee seem to have been deep-seated and long lasting. Josephus's *Life of Flavius Josephus*, written near the end of the first century A.D., reveals continued hostility by Galileans toward Sepphoris, Tiberias and Gabara, the three great cities of the region. Yet these animosities should not be overplayed, as if there were pure Semitic enclaves in Galilee in the midst of a few decadent Hellenized cities. Hellenization had long since affected the whole culture, and we must speak in terms of less Hellenized and more Hellenized. Not even the urban regions accepted Greco-Roman culture wholesale. It is well said that "the Galilee, like the Greek East, did not accept Roman control unaltered; the people interpreted it through their own particular traditions, thus allowing themselves a modicum of control."[55] This was true even of Herod Antipas who, to stay in power for as long as he did, knew the expedient of demonstrating *some* regard for Jewish sensibilities.

In the ancient world, while only ten percent or less of the population were rulers or belonged to the class of wealthy retainers and collaborators, they nevertheless regularly received and consumed up to two-thirds of the income of society. Agrarian societies were marked by huge differences in economic conditions between the haves and the have-nots.[56] There were no labor unions for poor workers, no labor negotiators or arbitrators attempting to improve the lot of the underprivileged majority. In most respects the society Jesus lived in was one that few modern Westerners would want to endure for very long, especially if they were not members of the ruling elite, or if they were women, children, slaves or members of a subjugated ethnic group.

For the general population, life in lower Galilee was all work and very little play, and often yielded little return or reward for labor. As Riches summarizes the archaeological evidence,

> The land in the Galilean mountains was intensively farmed and parceled up into very small lots. The methods of farming were often very laborious: damming streams to stop the top soil running off, the use of a form of terracing, and so forth. All this indicates that farming was difficult and that pressure of population made it imperative to get as much from the land as possible.[57]

Since most land and almost all markets and wages were in the hands of a few, it is easy to see why many slipped from being landowners to being tenants, or even to slavery or a life of begging or banditry (cf. Mk 10:46; Jn 9:8; Lk 14:21).

RELIGIOUS LIFE IN GALILEE

Synagogues in Galilee

Scholars have debated when the institution of synagogues as specifically religious buildings began, and the presence of synagogues in Galilee is particularly disputed.[58] This matter is of importance for the discussions of the historical Jesus because it will help us understand the setting in which some of his major teaching and miracles took place. Was it merely in homes, or was it in homes or multipurpose buildings used on occasion as synagogues, or was it in buildings which had a specifically religious function?

It is easy enough to find references in rabbinic literature to second-century religious leaders speaking of or using synagogues. For example Abba Benjamin remarked: "One's prayer is heard only in the synagogue" (*b. Ber.* 6a), and R. Judah I and R. Yohanan are mentioned as having studied in front of the large synagogue in Sepphoris (*y. Ber.* 5.1.9a). The problem with this evidence is that these sources were not compiled until much later than the second century, and so it can be argued that the terminology used in these sayings is anachronistic, perhaps deliberately so. The evidence from the Diaspora synagogue in Corinth, the lintel of which reads "synagogue of the Hebrews" and seems securely dated to at least as early as the second century A.D. seems more certain, but this still does not give us clear first-century evidence.[59]

We may then work our way back to the evidence in Josephus, who had spent considerable time in Galilee and elsewhere in the Mediterranean crescent and was in a position to know whether or not there were synagogue buildings in these places. In *Jewish Wars* 2.285-91 Josephus refers to a *synagōgē* adjoining a plot of ground owned by a Greek person in Caesarea Maritima. This must be taken as a reference to a place, not an "assembly" of people, a meaning the word can also take. The same may be said about the reference in *Jewish Wars* 7.43-44, which speaks of a synagogue in Syrian Antioch. Since this work in even its Greek form was available by A.D. 80 and the Aramaic version was written earlier than this, Josephus provides us with first-century evidence of a place called a *synagōgē*. Even earlier, and perhaps more impressive, is the Jewish inscription from the African city of Berenice dated A.D. 56, which speaks of the repair of the synagogue, clearly not a reference to a group or assembly of people!

The chief archaeological evidence for first-century synagogues in Palestine comes from Masada, the Herodium and Gamala. The last of these in particular has features suggestive of a building specifically constructed for religious purposes, including (1) a ritual bath adjacent to it, (2) the presence of second-temple Jewish iconography on a lintel found with the synagogue (a rosette), and (3) the size and design of the building, the main hall of which is about sixty feet by forty-eight feet, which are not the dimensions of a household room. One may also point to the thoroughgoing Jewishness of the city throughout its brief history.[60] I would submit that the conclusion of Lee I. Levine is fully warranted, that in Gamala we have a first-century synagogue specifically set up for religious purposes, whatever other uses it may also have had.[61] Luke-Acts, like other portions of the New Testament, also provides good first-century evidence for the existence of synagogues as places and not just as gatherings of people, and for the use of the term *synagōgē/synagōgos* of these places.[62]

Social Values

1. Patriarchalism. To understand the Galilee of Jesus' day we need to be reminded of the social values and structures that undergirded religious life. First, Galilee, like the rest of the Mediterranean world, was a patriarchal and androcentric society. It was not merely male dominated de facto, but was set up so that males *would* dominate, assuming almost all the power and leadership roles in the society, both political and religious. In first-century Palestinian Jewish society there were, of course, no high priestesses in the temple of Jerusalem, no female messianic figures, and even when there were occasionally female rulers (like Alexandra during the Hasmonean period), they ruled in such a way as to preserve the existing patriarchal structure.

By androcentric I mean that this society viewed life from a man's point of view. Decisions were made, property was bought and sold, and marriages were contracted in ways that promoted male interests, ideals and views about society. It was in almost every respect a man's world.

A woman was usually passed from her father's to her husband's sphere of influence without her own consent.[63] Marriages were arranged and were to a significant degree property transactions. The evidence suggests that women were being betrothed at twelve or thirteen years of age (the men were a little older), and at that age a daughter was unlikely to try and overturn the arrangement her father had made for her. In most cases a woman was not entitled to inherit from her family, because through marriage she would be leaving her own family to become part of another. Because most families had very little property in any case, it was thought better to leave it in the male heirs' hands so it would stay in the family. The evidence also suggests that a woman could not divorce her husband in Jewish society in the Holy Land, though she might be able to precipitate a divorce through a variety of actions. A Jewish wife, like a Gentile slave, could still be acquired (in this age and even later) by intercourse, money or writ (*m. Qidd.* 1.1). The woman's sphere of influence was assumed to be the home, which sometimes also meant she would be involved in the family business. Actually, few farming families could afford not to have their women help in the planting and harvesting of crops, but in addition to this, cooking, cleaning and child rearing were seen as essentially the provenance of women.

Moreover, as Goodman puts it, "Jews took seriously the injunction in Genesis 9.1, 'Be fruitful and multiply.' . . . Contraception was also avoided."[64] Children, especially male heirs, were prized and tended not to be abandoned. All of this meant that the essential roles in life for almost all women except elderly widows, the deformed, the demented or the barren were the roles of wife and mother. The highest blessing for a woman was being the mother of a great holy man or prophet, or even more impressive, being the mother of the Messiah (cf. Lk 11:27-28). In such a society being a single woman was not seen as a viable or valued option for anyone of sound mind and body.

2. *Honor and Shame.* Within this system of values certain ideas about honor and shame applied. Males advanced the honor of a family or family grouping by their public activities and accomplishments, which garnered

them respect and a "name" in the city gate (cf. Prov 31:23), while women were meant to protect the inward life of the family or community and prevent it from experiencing shame. Women accomplished this latter task chiefly by maintaining their virginity before marriage and by remaining faithful to their husbands after marriage. In such a society a righteous and honorable man would at the very least divorce his betrothed if she was found pregnant, and he could even subject her to public disgrace and punishment (cf. Mt 1:18-19). A man was expected to defend the honor of his name and that of his family, which included defending the honor of his wife. Her honor was embedded in the family's honor, as is shown by the fact that her highest honor was seen as bearing a male heir to the family. As Bruce Malina has put it:

> Honor stands for a person's rightful place in society, his social standing. This honor position is marked off by boundaries consisting of power, gender status, and location on the social ladder. . . . The purpose of honor is to serve as a sort of social rating which entitles a person to interact in specific ways with his or her equals, superiors, and subordinates, according to the prescribed social cues of the society.[65]

One must also add that this hierarchical society was strongly inclined to place its trust in those who were older. Being young and inexperienced was not seen as an asset. Rather one looked to the "elders" in the society for wise counsel and legal rulings. The wise old man was often the most revered person in a village or town.

3. Purity and Impurity. Another striking thing about ancient Palestinian Jewish society is that it was a society that operated with an elaborate purity system. People, places and things were labeled holy, unholy or common. There was both a sense of sacred space and of sacred time.

If we ask how purity was defined, it was Torah that set the fundamental rules by which all things were evaluated. A pure person was one who observed the purity laws, or did not inherently or otherwise partake of conditions which made one impure. A nonobservant person was impure.

In such a system purity not only had to do with the moral observance of the Ten Commandments and other ethical requirements of the law, it also had to do with being whole or well. A person with a skin disease was unclean and thus impure and was to be set outside the boundaries of the community, becoming in effect an outcast. A woman during her menstrual period was temporarily unclean and could not attend synagogue services. A chronically ill or maimed person or one with crushed testicles was permanently unclean. Wholeness was assumed to go with purity.

It is easy to see how in such a culture sickness and sin were regularly associated. The question asked by the disciples about the man blind from birth, "Who sinned, this man or his parents, that he was born blind?" (Jn 9:2), and Jesus' rhetorical question about the Jews whom Pilate slaughtered and whose blood he mingled with their sacrifices, "Do you think that because these Galileans suffered in this way they were worse sinners than all other Galileans?" (Lk 13:2), are understandable in such a society. To be sick meant to be outside of the purity norm, and since sin was also viewed as deviance from a purity norm, the two were often associated as cause and effect.

One of the most radical things that Jesus did in the context of his society was to redefine the whole notion of purity and impurity. He argued that only the impurity which comes from the human heart makes a woman or man unclean (Mk 7:20-23).[66] This meant setting aside a whole purity system that suggested that certain foods, clothing, places (such as graveyards) and conditions (such as sickness or deformity) could make a person unclean. Jesus demonstrated these radical new values by joining in table fellowship with sinners, tax collectors and others marginalized by his society's purity system. This meant setting aside a significant portion of the Mosaic law, declaring it, at least implicitly, as no longer applicable or determinative now that God's perfect Dominion was breaking into space and time. One can see how by this decision Jesus came into significant conflict with the Pharisees. They wanted more purity rules and a stronger application of them. Jesus disagreed.

4. *Corporate Solidarity.* Another factor which determined the worldview of early Jews in Galilee and elsewhere was the relationship of individuals to society. While we in the West are inclined toward radical individualism, this was far from the case in ancient Jewish society. In Jesus' world, people were important because of who they were related to, or even where they came from, not so much because of who they were in themselves. Take for example Peter, or to use his Jewish name, Simon bar Jonah (cf. Mt 16:17). He is identified and singled out by whose son he is.[67] It may not be accidental that Jesus' preferred term of self-reference was "the Son of Man," which implies a relationship. In such a society paternity or even communal origin was often thought to determine one's destiny. The question "Can anything good come out of Nazareth?" (Jn 1:46) fits naturally into such a setting.

The sort of personality this kind of corporately oriented society creates is called a dyadic personality, meaning a person who sees and evaluates himself or herself through others' eyes.[68] A "meaningful human existence depends upon a person's full awareness of what others think and feel about oneself, along with one's living up to that awareness."[69] As Malina explains, such a person needs others in order to grasp his or her identity:

> Thus the honorable person would never expose his or her distinct individuality. One's unique personhood, one's inner self with its difficulties, weaknesses, confusions, and inabilities to cope, and one's distinctive, individual realm of hopes and dreams are simply not of public concern or comment.[70] Rather, persons of such enculturation know how to keep their psychological core hidden and secret . . . with a veil of conventionality and formality, ever alert to anything that might lead to their making an exhibition of themselves, to anything that would not tally with the socially expected and defined forms of behavior that have entitled them and their family to respect.[71]

Could this explain why it is that Jesus sought in various ways to silence the public proclamation of his true identity (cf. Mk 8:30)? Could it be that he was seen as a serious threat precisely because he did not conform to the expectations of behavior in such a corporate society where boundaries and taboos, in-groups and out-groups, are rather clearly defined? Could it be that he was viewed with hostility because he did not fit into people's preconceived ideas and formulas about what was appropriate in a society that sought to uphold the ideas behind corporate personality? Could it be that Jesus was viewed as an overly Hellenized person, a "sinner," because he was too much of an individual?

5. *Limited Good.* One final social concept that must be mentioned is that of limited good. Living as we do in a culture with so much material abundance, where we can always go to a store and get another package of this or another can of that, it is hard for us to imagine living in a world where things, even necessities of life, were not readily available to all. Yet most ancient people who were not part of some elite ruling group would have seen their existence as *determined* by the limited natural and social resources of their village or town. The modern notion of progress or of the self-made person who rises through the ranks and becomes prosperous was alien to them. As Malina stresses, it was believed that "all the desired things in life, such as land, wealth, prestige, blood, health, . . . friendship and love, manliness, honor, respect and status, power and influence, se-

curity and safety—literally all goods in life—exist in finite, limited quantity and are always in short supply."[72]

This in turn meant that the only way individuals or groups could improve their social status or economic condition was at the expense of others, since there was only a limited amount of these good things to go around. One might then expect the whole society to become highly competitive and come up with aphorisms like our modern saying, "The early bird gets the worm." This is not, however, how most ancient people approached the matter. Instead they went into a defensive mode, seeking to protect what honor or status or goods they did have by maintaining the status quo. They used a variety of means, including making alliances and oral contracts with other honorable people in ways that provided for reciprocal aid or benefit, such as two families helping each other harvest their crops.

An honorable person neither allowed himself to be exploited or challenged by others, nor did he seek to take advantage of his neighbor. When a favor was done for an honorable person, he or she had to return the favor, and the same applied to gifts. "To accept an invitation, a gift, or a benefaction with no thought to future reciprocity implies accepting imbalance in society. Such an action would damage the status quo."[73] The honorable person was to mind his or her own business in such a way as to be sure no one else infringed upon him or her. "In sum he does not seem to be outstanding, but he knows how to protect his rights to his inherited status."[74] In this sort of society people try to blend in with the crowd, not stand out.

People who live in such a society believe deeply that whether they are male or female, they have a right to fulfill *their inherited roles,* which implies a right to have the social and economic means to continue maintaining those roles. In an agrarian society this normally meant that the only time a peasant or villager was likely to revolt was when their subsistence, their means of continuing to live the roles they inherited, was taken away. In Jesus' day, this latter condition was a growing reality for various small farmers and villagers. The result was that some resorted to banditry, and the potential for open revolt was a real one. All of these factors must be kept in mind as we evaluate the religious life of Galilee.

Religious Life
1. *Degrees of Sacred Space.* One of the major factors affecting Galilean life was

the very fact that Galilee was not Judea, and the temple was not nearby. The Holy Land was seen as a series of sacred zones radiating out from Jerusalem, with the temple being the center and most holy zone, Jerusalem being a somewhat larger zone, Judea being a yet larger zone further out, and Galilee seen as part of the outermost sacred zone (cf. *m. Kel.* 1:6-9).[75] Daily religious life in Galilee could not revolve around the temple and its sacrifices. While Galileans lived within the sacred zone, the Holy Land, they could not reach its epicenter unless they went on pilgrimage. Pilgrimages to festivals and on special personal occasions (cf. Lk 2:41-52) became a very regular feature of Galilean religious life. In some respects life must have been somewhat like being part of a Diaspora Jewish community, because of the distance from the temple and the considerable percentage of Gentiles living in Galilee, though of course Jews were still in the majority in most regions.

2. *Religious Education.* Though there is little hard evidence to go on, religious education seems to have been important for Jews in Galilee and elsewhere. According to most scholars, there were two conditions that had to be met if a young boy was to receive religious training: (1) a synagogue in the town or village where he lived, and (2) pious parents who wanted him to be trained in this manner. Both of these conditions seem to have been met in the case of Jesus, and probably in the case of many other Galileans. We have at least the evidence of the Gospels that there was a synagogue in Nazareth (cf. Mk 6:1-6; Lk 4:16-30), though the site has yet to be discovered, and we also have evidence of the piety of Jesus' family. For example, the tradition indicates that Jesus' family went up to Jerusalem on pilgrimage (cf. Lk 2:22-40; Jn 7:1-13). A synagogue education entailed at least being taught how to read and perhaps even to expound the Hebrew Scriptures. There is, however, no evidence of Jesus' pursuing higher learning at an urban center like Jerusalem (compare Lk 2:47 to Mk 6:2-3).[76] There was also at least rudimentary religious education undertaken in the home when the parents were devout, observant Jews.

In regard to the piety of Galilean Jews in general, Freyne and Riesner have set forth evidence suggesting that Galilean Jews tended to be conservative in their faith, supporting basic institutions like circumcision, Torah and the temple, but that they were not necessarily "devoted to a Judaism of Pharisaic niceties developed by way of oral tradition."[77] This may explain why Jesus seems to have enjoyed a more enthusiastic hearing in Galilee than in Judea.[78]

3. *Conversion and Jewish Identity.* One further factor about religious life in Galilee deserves our attention, the matter of conversion. While religious conversion seems to moderns a familiar topic, in the first-century Jewish world it was something rather new, especially the conversion of Jews. Most Jews of that age were likely to ask why a person would speak of conversion at all, if what was being offered as an alternative was in fact just another of the many forms of contemporary Judaism. And in fact, when Jesus went around in Galilee calling for repentance and belief in the good news of the kingdom, he was not calling Jews to a totally new religion which had no basis or foundation in Torah or contemporary Judaism. More accurately, Jesus was calling Jews to accept reform and renewal and so to participate in the fulfillment of Old Testament promises to God's people in the dawning messianic age.

Yet surprisingly enough, conversion is an appropriate term for describing a first-century Jewish context, even when the subject is one group of Jews trying to convict and convince another group of Jews. As Alan F. Segal says, "Prophetic religions such as Judaism and Christianity stimulated conversion, raising commitment far above simple adherence."[79] In part this may be due to the effect of Hellenization on both these religions, which led to a great emphasis on the individual and his or her religious life.

Jews in Jesus' day were very familiar with the idea of converting Gentiles to Judaism. In fact there were two categories of converts—Godfearers, who were synagogue adherents not yet prepared to accept circumcision, food laws and the whole burden of Jewish ritual requirements, and full proselytes. Yet Segal is right to point out that a Jew could in effect be radicalized by converting to one of the more sectarian groups within first-century Judaism. In particular, conversion, including some sort of ritual immersion in water, was required in order to become a full member of the Essenes of Qumran. The essential assumption on the part of sectarian Jews such as these was that Judaism had become so corrupt or apostate that a full conversion to true Judaism was necessary.[80]

Did Pharisaism and the Jesus movement also regard their task as converting Jews? It would seem that the answer to this question is yes. While neither Jesus nor most of the Pharisees in general absolutely required a follower to live in a cloistered community with them,[81] they nonetheless called for a very high level of commitment and a significant, sometimes even a radical, change of lifestyle (cf. Mt 23:15). Such a call of course went directly against the flow of the culture which we have outlined above, a culture in which honor meant attempting to preserve the status quo and one's inherited roles and lifestyle. It is a measure of how seriously awry both Jesus and the Pharisees saw the religious situation in Israel that they called for conversion among Jews.

In the case of Pharisaism, conversion meant joining a new ethnic group (if the subject was a Gentile) or rejoining one's old one with new fervor and commitment. There was an ethnic and cultural component to Pharisaic Judaism that was inescapable. This seems to have been somewhat less the case with Jesus, since he was not requiring circumcision or the strict keeping of food and Sabbath laws in order to be one of his followers. Jesus' teaching seems to have demanded less conformity to certain markers of ethnic identity than did Pharisaism.

Yet it would be a mistake to see Jesus as inaugurating some sort of generic or universal religion denuded of all characteristically Jewish elements. Jesus' message was about the coming of God's Dominion, God's divine saving activity, in the present and near future. He had discussions about Jewish theological subjects like resurrection, angels, the law, marriage and divorce. He referred to himself as the enigmatic Son of Man of Daniel 7 and the Enoch literature. He presented himself as the embodiment of God's wisdom, Wisdom come in the flesh.[82] In all these regards Jesus was presenting a religious worldview thoroughly grounded in the Hebrew Scriptures.

Jesus then was not offering to Jews a non-Jewish alternative. He was offering to his audience some form of what I call a messianic, eschatological and sapiential Judaism.[83] Segal reminds us that "within sectarian and apocalyptic Judaism, conversion was an important aspect of Jewish cohesion . . . many varieties of both Judaism and Christianity proselytized, each using a method that was uniquely suited to itself."[84] Jesus made demands using familiar concepts and scriptural ideas, but in new combinations and with different points of strictness and leniency than the Pharisees.

Most, or at least many, first-century Jews would have regarded the following characteristics as essential for true Jewishness: (1) birth to a Jewish mother or father, (2) circumcision (for the male), (3) observance of certain days and festivals (Sabbath, Day of Atonement, Passover, Tabernacles), even if travel was necessary, (4) observance of certain rules of purity and impurity with regard to food, clothing, people and places, (5) belief in one God who (6) had chosen and eternally covenanted with a people, the Jews, (7) belief in Torah, the Scriptures, and (8) the practice of prayer, fasting and tithing, including payment of the temple tax.[85] Not all Jews would have agreed with the importance of all these points, and some would have wished to add a belief in Messiah or resurrection to the above list. And in the case of some sectarian Jews, such as the Qumran community, election was not something simply transferred by physical descent. Rather it was conveyed to Jewish individuals whom God had singled out from the Jewish nation. In other words, a concept of remnant, or salvation by grace *within the broader context of Judaism*, was already a living idea by the time Jesus came on the scene.[86]

As this study proceeds it will be important to keep firmly in mind what has been said in this first chapter, for it will serve as one tool for evaluating the various new proposals in the Third Quest for the historical Jesus. One thing is clear—a non-Jewish Jesus is a non sequitur. Jesus must make sense within his historical context, even if in certain ways he stood out from most of his contemporaries. Journeying toward Jesus involves more than just having a deeper relationship with the living Christ of faith, the exalted Lord in heaven. It means being committed to historical inquiry, to studying the life of Jesus in its first-century setting.

CHAPTER 2

JESUS THE TALKING HEAD

THE JESUS OF THE JESUS SEMINAR

The Jesus Seminar has received *a tremendous amount of attention as a result of its contro-*
versial procedures and results and its concerted marketing campaign. This chapter looks closely at
the intent of the founders, the makeup of the Jesus Seminar, its decision-making process and its
results. A critical examination reveals serious flaws in all these areas. In particular, Jesus is denuded
of his historical context, and his sayings are stripped of their literary settings. The very procedures
followed guarantee that too little of the relevant data will be allowed to speak to the issue of what
Jesus said or did. The seminar itself is almost exclusively made up of North American scholars,
and it is founded and dominated by a few of the more radical Jesus scholars in the U.S. Many
of the major university religion departments, graduate schools and seminaries are not represented
at all. A close look at the intent of the founders shows that the purpose of this seminar is to discredit
fundamentalist and traditional images of and ideas about Jesus. The very process of voting on the
sayings of Jesus leaves little room for nuances or probabilities, and, more importantly, yields a
picture of Jesus with which no one scholar fully agrees. This composite picture leaves us with Jesus
the talking head,[1] *a Jesus who does not fit well into the context of early Judaism and whose story*
we cannot discern.

LONG AFTER THE THIRD QUEST FOR THE HISTORICAL JESUS IS OVER, THE ONE
enduring image that will be left in the minds of many will be a group of
biblical scholars using colored beads to cast votes on the sayings of Jesus:
a red bead to indicate "Jesus surely said this," pink for "he probably said
that," gray for "he probably didn't say this" and black for "it is very
unlikely that he said anything like that." The final conclusion reached by
this approach was that only 18 percent of the Gospel sayings attributed

to Jesus were actually spoken by him.

Judging from the reaction in letters to the editor and special articles appearing in newspapers and magazines across the country, the devout layperson of whatever denominational affiliation finds this entire enterprise to be presumptuous. A great deal of heated debate has been generated and not much light shed on what is going on. In this chapter I will discuss the Jesus Seminar, its intents, its methodology and its results. One thing is certain—this seminar reflects the intense renewed interest in the 1980s and 1990s in finding out what the historical Jesus was really like. It shows that the Third Quest for the historical Jesus is fully underway.

The Jesus Seminar: Its Composition and Leaders

In its statement of purpose, found conveniently in the back of its red-letter edition of the parables of Jesus,[2] the steering committee indicates that the members of the Jesus Seminar are all critical scholars, by which is meant they adhere to the historical-critical approach of examining ancient historical sources. This however is not the whole story. It also means a commitment to newer approaches to the Bible, such as the social-scientific method and computer science. What is rather striking about this last remark is that it leaves out many older scholars, including many from Europe and the Third World.

One of the notable characteristics of the Jesus Seminar is its largely North American composition.[3] It is not a group sponsored by either of the two major scholarly guilds, the Society of Biblical Literature (SBL) or the group that originated in Europe and now, like the SBL, is an international organization, the Society for the Study of the New Testament (SNTS). Rather, it is a group sponsored, as Richard B. Hays says, by "[Robert W.] Funk's maverick entrepreneurial venture, the Westar Institute, located in Sonoma, California," the same venture that has a self-perpetuating publishing organ, Polebridge Press.[4]

From an examination of the list of Jesus Seminar fellows, it would appear to me that they are indeed a very carefully self-selected group, including none who could be labeled fundamentalists and only three or four who could be labeled conservative or evangelical.[5] But this is not all. As Hays points out, if one examines even the most recent list of seventy-four fellows,[6] "not one member of the New Testament faculty from Yale, Harvard, Princeton, Duke, University of Chicago, Union Theological Seminary, Vanderbilt, SMU, or Catholic University is involved in this project. . . . Nor are any major scholars from England or the Continent."[7] In short, this is hardly a representative sampling of critical scholars, even if one leaves evangelicals and conservative scholars out of the equation altogether.[8]

The statement of the steering committee makes clear that the fellows of the Jesus Seminar *could* not include any fundamentalists, for it contrasts the judgments of critical scholars like those on the Jesus Seminar with those of fundamentalists.[9] It also says that television evangelists inhibit conservative institutions and scholars from participating more fully in the critical debate. Near the close of this statement we find the remark, "Unless biblical scholarship wants to lose its credibility—and it has come dangerously close to doing so because of its identification in the popular view with Sunday Schools and TV evangelism—it must adhere to the canons of research and publication that govern the physical sciences, the social sciences, and the humanities generally."[10]

Even on a charitable interpretation of things, one must conclude that the steering committee of the Jesus Seminar had as one of its major agendas the presentation of a "critical" portrait of Jesus that must necessarily be distinguished from the fundamentalist or traditional portraits.[11] The we/they language is unmistakable, and it calls in question the claim to be taking an unbiased approach. In fact in personal conversations with some of the members of the Jesus Seminar, I have been told that one of the major intentions of some of the prime movers in this group was to attack and discredit American fundamentalism and the images of Jesus it offers.

Hays is also right to point out that publications like *The Five Gospels* must be seen for what they are—imaginative and creative books "produced by a self-selected body of scholars who hold a set of unconventional views about Jesus and the gospels." Hays concludes, "Their attempt to present these views as 'the assured results of critical scholarship' is—one must say it—reprehensible deception."[12] I would suggest that the results are at least interesting in that they reveal how and what a certain subset of North American scholars think about the sayings of the historical Jesus.

Only in a thoroughly democratic society where the assumption that the majority view is likely to be right and to reflect a true critical opinion on the "truth" could the idea of voting on the sayings of Jesus have arisen.[13] There are however major methodological problems with this assumption, especially when the test group of scholars is self-selected and represents only one portion of the spectrum of scholarly opinion. While the voting may make the process *appear* democratic, the preselection of the fellows, the exclusion of the majority of scholars, the disregard for the vox populi and, perhaps most tellingly, the disregard for the opinions of scholars of previous generations, shows that we are dealing ultimately with an elitist and not a democratic approach.

A Majority of the Minority

Let us suppose however that this group's views do represent the views of the *majority* of critical New Testament scholars. It does not take much historical memory to realize that very often the majority is wrong on significant matters of truth. Truth often is precisely what makes the majority edgy and leads to the suppression of the minority. The case of Galileo, to which Funk and others appeal, is a very good example. But to argue that the Jesus Seminar is *like* Galileo, a voice for truth crying in the wilderness of ignorance and blind faith, is another matter. The question is why we should believe that the majority of this *small* representation of New Testament scholarship has achieved greater clarity regarding the historical Jesus than other capable, competent and critical scholars who strongly disagree with them.

In fact, it will not do to suggest that the majority of the Jesus Seminar was in agreement with the results of the various votes taken, for the results were much more ambiguous than they appear at first glance. For example, if we take the votes on Matthew 25:29 ("For to all those who have, more will be given, and they will have an abundance; but from those who have nothing, even what they have will be taken away"), a full 25 percent of the scholars voting on that occasion thought that Jesus surely said it. Another 11 percent gave this saying a pink rating, affirming that Jesus probably said it. Thus a total of 36 percent voted some shade of red for this saying. The rest however gave it a gray or black vote, and thus it is placed either in the black category, in the earlier record of voting,[14] or in the gray category, in the new volume on the five Gospels. But if one takes *only* the black vote on this particular saying, those who are convinced that Jesus did not say it, *that* group is in the minority compared to the other three groups who (1) think it is possible but unlikely, (2) think it is likely and (3) think it is virtually certain! What this shows is not just the divisions among even this group of scholars but that a saying like this can receive substantial votes in all four categories, indeed almost as many red votes as black votes, and yet can end up in the black or gray category rather than within the 18 percent of authentic sayings of Jesus or in the "probably authentic" category.

Criteria of Authenticity

Perhaps even more important is the fact that while the editors state that all the scholars participating in this seminar affirm the use of the historical-critical method, they do not tell us whether they all agree on *how* the method should be used and what weight should be given to which tool of evaluation. For example, some scholars place a great deal of emphasis on what is called the criterion of dissimilarity. This criterion basically states that a Jesus saying which stands out both from its Jewish historical background and from its early church foreground is likely to be authentic. In other words such a saying is under no cloud of suspicion of having been invented by the early church or of being simply a quotation of something various early Jews, and not Jesus in particular, might have said.

If one uses this sort of criterion as an ultimate or final litmus test, one is bound to end up with only the distinctive or unique sayings and a Jesus who has nothing in common with either his Jewish heritage or his later Christian followers. Of course the idea of Jesus being totally idiosyncratic, without any analogy, is highly improbable. There never has been such a person in all of human history. What the Jesus Seminar people do not tell us is what weight was given to the criterion of dissimilarity and by whom.

While the criterion of dissimilarity can be used to help us discern what is apparently distinctive about Jesus' teaching,[15] it can hardly be used as the sole determinant of what is authentic among his sayings. If it is used as the only criterion it leads to a very distorted picture of Jesus, a Jesus who is both non-Jewish and has little or nothing in common with his Christian followers!

There are other criteria, such as the criteria of multiple attestation. Most Gospel scholars argue that the similarities between Matthew, Luke and Mark are explainable on a theory of mutual relationship. Typically, Mark is regarded as the first Gospel to have been written, with its influence being discernible in Matthew and Luke. The material that Matthew and Luke have in common that is not dependent on Mark is attributed to a hypothetical source called "Q" (from the German *Quelle*, "source"). The material that is distinctive to Matthew or to Luke, material that cannot be attributed to either Mark or Q, is posited as having come from sources "M" or "L" respectively. Thus the criteria of multiple attestation pertains to a saying that appears in more than one of these Synoptic Gospel sources, to which may be added John or some other independent source such as Paul. If this criterion were brought into play it would probably provide a more well-rounded and authentic picture of Jesus.[16] As Ben F. Meyer has put it, we cannot decide "historicity questions . . . in peremptory fashion by a single acid test . . . dealing with the data atomistically. . . . On the whole it is rare that a solid judgment of historicity can be made prior to and apart from a large frame of reference."[17]

Unfortunately we are not told whether the Jesus Seminar used a broad enough spectrum of criteria to reach their conclusions. In view of the fact that some of the sayings they rule out *do* meet important historical criteria but not the criterion of dissimilarity, we must conclude that some of their results might be explained by their overreliance on the criterion of dissimilarity.[18] As Hays has expressed it, "The Jesus who emerges from this procedure is necessarily a free-floating iconoclast, artificially isolated from his people and their Scripture, and artificially isolated from the movement that he founded."[19]

A further methodological problem arises from the assumption that, having stripped the sayings of Jesus from their narrative context, we can still know what they mean and decide whether Jesus is likely to have said them or not. Jesus was not just a talking head nor a sage who merely tossed out timeless aphorisms to the crowds. Rather, his sayings must be related, if possible, not only to their narrative contexts in the Gospels, but also to the *events* of Jesus' life, including the deeds he performed.[20] This the Jesus Seminar did not even attempt to do, so far as I can see, and this oversight also helps to explain the idiosyncratic results. We can make an aphorism mean whatever we want it to mean if we denude it of both its literary and its historical context.[21]

Yet another methodological problem is the apparent presumption of many members of the seminar that Jesus' sayings *must* be regarded as inauthentic unless they can be proved to be authentic. This is assumed to be *the* critical point of view. But in reality it is a perspective steeped in a negative bias, not a neutral or open stance. Behind this attitude lies the basic assumption that the early church recreated Jesus in the image it preferred, inventing many sayings and placing them on Jesus' lips. Indeed this seminar would lead us to think that as much as 82 percent of the

Gospel sayings fall into this category of ecclesiological invention.

Many critical scholars, both Christian and Jewish, and some of no religious affiliation at all, would simply reject this negative bias as neither historical nor scholarly. Too often scholars fail to be critical of their own motives and theological biases. Too often they assume they know better than the early Christians who preserved and collected the sayings of Jesus and composed the Gospels what Jesus was or was not likely to have said. This assumption is founded on hubris.

In contrast, James D. G. Dunn, on equally critical grounds, concludes that:

> The earliest tradents within the Christian churches [were] preservers more than innovators, . . . seeking to transmit, retell, explain, interpret, elaborate, but not to create *de novo*. All of which means that I approach the Synoptic tradition with a good deal more confidence than many of my New Testament colleagues. Through the main body of the Synoptic tradition, I believe, we have in most cases direct access to the teaching and ministry of Jesus as it was remembered from the beginning of the transmission process (which often predates Easter) and so fairly direct access to the ministry and teaching of Jesus through the eyes and ears of those who went about with him.[22]

In view of the fact that the earliest conveyors of the Jesus tradition were all, without exception, Jews, we would naturally expect them to treat the teachings of their master with as much respect as did the disciples of other Jewish teachers such as Hillel and Shammai. This is all the more likely if, as happened with Jesus of Nazareth, the teacher suffered an untimely and unexpected end and was highly criticized by some Jews. The need to remember, preserve and defend him against false charges would be acute.[23]

The Ascendancy of *Thomas* and Q

A further methodological problem is that the seminar seems to be overly optimistic not only about the antiquity of the sayings found in the *Gospel of Thomas* but also about its independence from the canonical Gospels.[24] Polebridge Press continues to publish volumes about Q and *Thomas*, most recently *The Gospel of Thomas and Jesus*,[25] as part of an overall attempt to force scholars and others to place the material in *Thomas* on equal footing with what we find in the Synoptic Gospels. This is problematic on several grounds.

First, we must remember where the *Gospel of Thomas* was found—at Nag Hammadi in Egypt, along with a very eclectic set of ancient documents.[26] If one can judge a document by some of the company it keeps, there is little encouragement to see *Thomas* as providing access to the early Jesus tradition or as giving us many clues about the authentic Jesus tradition. The document, it seems, actually originated in the region of eastern Syria (Edessa?). Other documents connected with *Thomas* come from this region (the *Book of Thomas*, the *Acts of Thomas*), and only in this region was Thomas known as Judas Thomas, as he is identified in the *Gospel of Thomas* and these other *Thomas* works.

Furthermore, the only firm evidence for dating this document is its earliest Greek fragments (P. Oxy. 1), which were written no later than about A.D. 200. The first reference to the document by name occurs no earlier than Hippolytus, who was writing between A.D. 222 and 235. Nothing in any of this evidence gives us good reason to think this was a first-century document.

The balance judgment of Richard J. Bauckham is worth repeating:

It seems that the tradition of the sayings of Jesus on which *Thomas* drew was Jewish Christian in origin, . . . but had developed in a gnosticizing direction. Some sayings of clearly Gnostic origin had entered the tradition and the editor of *Thomas* selected from the tradition sayings which were compatible with his own Gnostic theology. . . . The most probable opinion is that *Thomas* is dependent on a tradition substantially independent of the canonical Gospels, though influence from the canonical Gospels cannot be ruled out. . . . *Thomas* can therefore provide useful evidence for the study of the origins and development of the traditions behind the canonical Gospels, *provided that due allowance is made for its greater distance (both theologically and probably chronologically) from the historical Jesus.*[27]

Bauckham is probably right: of the sayings in *Thomas* that have no parallels in the Synoptics, a *few* may be authentic. But in view of the Gnosticizing and ascetic tendencies of the document, whether they are due to its editor or to the creator of the material, even where *Thomas* records sayings that are parallel with the Synoptics, the burden of proof lies on those who would maintain the authenticity of their *Thomas* form. It is my own judgment that only very rarely does *Thomas* provide an earlier form of a saying that is also found in the Synoptics. The argument by John P. Meier and others that *Thomas*'s frequent dependence on the canonical form of various sayings can be demonstrated is likely correct.[28]

But there is more to say about the *Thomas* mentality of some scholars. It assumes that because *Thomas* is a collection of almost solely sayings material, we can then hypothesize that such documents came from communities where a "sayings Gospel" was the only or main form of Gospel in use. In view of the other *Thomas* documents mentioned above, this is a doubtful conclusion. If it is doubtful of *Thomas*'s community it is equally if not more doubtful for the community in which the hypothetical Q document originated.[29] It seems highly unlikely that there ever was a "Q community," if by that is meant a Christian community that possessed as their sacred tradition only the Q collection of Jesus' sayings, without some form of passion and resurrection traditions.[30]

Thus it is right to be skeptical of using *Thomas* as a major source for reconstructing the teaching of the historical Jesus, not least because of the document's theological tendencies. These tendencies, especially its Gnosticizing agenda, are not found in the Synoptic Gospels and should be seen as telltale signs that the *Gospel of Thomas* likely arose, at least in its present form, in the second century when Gnosticism was well developed.[31]

On the other hand, scholars are right to insist that in principle we must be open to all possible sources of information about the historical Jesus, both canonical and noncanonical. For example, if fresh evidence at Qumran does in fact speak clearly about Jesus, we must pay careful attention to it. But *all* such sources must be evaluated with critical scrutiny. It is not reasonable to be highly skeptical about the canonical Gospels and highly receptive to the noncanonical Gospels. Earlier documents are on the whole likely to be more faithful and closer to the source and its original form than later ones, and the vast majority of critical scholars still believe the canonical Gospels, especially the Synoptics, are our earliest resources for learning about the historical Jesus.[32]

I have pointed out several quite serious methodological flaws in the approach the Jesus Seminar seems to have taken with the Jesus material, and these must be borne in mind as we begin to examine the results of the seminar. We are about to see that the Jesus Seminar paints us a picture of a Jesus who is a sage, but not a very Jewish one, and, perhaps most notably, a noneschatological sage.

The Demise of Markan Authority

Throughout this century it has been a commonplace of Gospel scholarship that Mark's Gospel is the earliest of the four and was written around A.D. 68-70. Matthew and Luke are said to be later and to have used Mark, so that most scholars would argue that in the so-called triple tradition (the stories and sayings shared by all three Synoptic Gospels) the Markan form should be seen as the earliest of the three, unless there are extraordinary reasons for thinking that one of the others had an independent earlier version. One might then expect that the sayings material in Mark would be one of the sources, if not the primary source, the Jesus Seminar would turn to in reconstructing Jesus' utterances. This expectation, however, is not met.

Amazingly enough, only *one* saying in the whole of the Gospel of Mark is deemed fully authentic and deserving of the red-letter treatment: "Give to the emperor the things that are the emperor's, and to God the things that are God's" (Mk 12:17). Almost none of the Markan material in Mark 10 about children or marriage. or divorce, or the eschatological material in Mark 13, escapes the heavy-handed ax of the Jesus Seminar.[33] One may properly ask why not, and I think the reason is not hard to discover.

We are told in some of the commentary material, presumably written by Funk and the other editors, that the first written Gospels were not Mark, Matthew and Luke, but rather Q and possibly an early version of *Thomas*.[34] To this conclusion is added the remark that when Q and *Thomas*, taken as necessarily independent sources, both include a given saying, this is to be taken as strong, early *documentary evidence* for the genuineness of a saying. In other words, the criterion of multiple attestation does finally show up, but for some reason *Thomas* is given precedence over even Mark![35] This approach not only assumes that Q was a document, even though we have no extant copies of it, it also assumes that *Thomas* was an early, pre-70 document. Now this whole procedure, which deals with Mark so cavalierly and grants *Thomas* so much reverence, can only be called radical. Hays is right to stress the problem as he does:

> Many scholars regard it [*Thomas*] as literarily dependent on the canon-
> ical gospels, though this remains a debated issue. No hint of these
> debates, however, is allowed to appear in the pages of *The Five Gospels*,
> which unhesitatingly treats the hypothetical Q and a hypothetical "ear-
> ly version of Thomas" as the crucial sources for locating authentic Jesus
> tradition. Here some suspicion begins to arise about the candor of the
> editors of the book. They claim that they want to make the results of
> the best critical scholarship available to the public, but their working

method trades upon a controversial and implausible early dating of *Thomas*, without offering the reader any clue that this is a shaky element in their methodological foundation.[36]

The Jesus Seminar also assumes something else about Q. The material that makes up Q is embedded in, even laced throughout, the text of Matthew and Luke and has to be ferreted out, leaving behind whatever editorial revisions the First or Third Evangelists may have made. Yet these scholars are more confident in *their* reconstruction of Q as representative of the early Jesus tradition than in Mark's presentation of sayings material, *even though we have a well-established Greek text of Mark, and have no such text for Q.* One can only label this approach presumptuous at best. While I am optimistic that we can know a good deal about the early form of Q, to rate it so much more highly than the source material in Mark is clearly unwarranted. This is especially so since Q's reconstruction involves fine judgments and inevitable uncertainties, with the result that no two scholars agree completely on the shape of Q!

The Parables of Jesus
What then of the Q and *Thomas* material that escapes the ax? We will concentrate here on the parable material since it is very familiar to most readers and because the other results of the seminar do not yet reveal any crucial additions to the picture it paints. We are told that there are only five parables that certainly go back to Jesus: (1) the parable of the leaven (Mt 13:33; Lk 13:20-21), which received 60 percent red votes and no black votes, the highest rating, (2) the parable of the good Samaritan (Lk 10:30-35), (3) the parable of the dishonest steward (Lk 16:1-8), (4) the parable of vineyard workers (Mt 20:1-15) and (5) the parable of the mustard seed in its *Thomas* form (*Gos. Thom.* 20.2).

All of these parables are of course familiar and draw by analogy on true-to-life situations. What could we deduce if this was all the Jesus material we had? For one thing it would be clear that Jesus had a rather radical critique of ethnic prejudice (the good Samaritan), for another we might conclude that he was bitter over the brutal social injustices in the land (the vineyard workers). Both the parable of the mustard seed and that of the leaven might suggest taking some sort of action that would eventually produce change in the midst of God's people. The parable of the dishonest steward might be understood to indicate that in a fallen world one should take an opportunistic approach to life. All of these conclusions have some merit. They suggest Jesus was an old-fashioned social commentator and perhaps an advocate of change, but they overlook the fact that these stories are about the kingdom of God, about what God was doing in and through the ministry of Jesus, rather than simply advocating human actions or attitudes.

There are an additional twenty-one parables that receive pink ratings, but some of these are alternate versions of the five listed above (for example, the *Thomas* version of the leaven parable (*Gos. Thom.* 96.1), or the Synoptic version of the mustard seed (Mt 13:31-32; Mk 4:31-32; Lk 13:18-19). Two other parables made it into the pink category only in their *Thomas* version—the empty jar (*Gos. Thom.* 97) and the parable of the tenants (*Gos. Thom.* 65). In addition, we have the following familiar parables in some form: (1) the parable of the sower (Mk 4 and parallels), (2) the three parables of the lost coin, sheep and son in Luke 15, (3) the unjust judge (Lk 18:2-5), (4) the pearl (Mt 13:45-46; *Gos. Thom.* 76.1), (5) the Pharisee and the publican (Lk 18:10-14), (6) the unmerciful servant (Mt 18:23-34), (7) the treasure (Mt 13:44; *Gos. Thom.* 109), (8) the feast (Lk 14:16-23; *Gos. Thom.* 76.1), (9) the rich farmer (Lk 12:16-20; *Gos. Thom.* 63.1), (10) the barren tree (Lk 13:6-9) and (11) the entrusted money (Mt 25:14-28; Lk 19:13, 15-24). Other parts of these parables could be mentioned separately, but we will leave these out.

What does one learn from the above list? First, that the *Thomas* version of some sayings is preferred over canonical versions, though the rationale for this is doubtful. Second, that there is a decided preference for Luke's parables and the Lukan version of parables. This last point comports with certain trends among Q scholars and deserves questioning.

There is no disputing that Matthew's version of various sayings and parables is more eschatological and often more Jewish than Luke's (using, for example, the phrase "kingdom of heaven" rather than "kingdom of God"). How are we to account for this? There are two avenues of approach. One could argue that the First Evangelist or his source introduced Jewish and eschatological elements *into* the sayings of Jesus that originally were not in this form and that Luke or *Thomas* presents the earlier version. On the other hand, one can suggest that Luke, probably the only Gentile of any of the New Testament writers and one who moreover probably wrote for a Gentile audience, is likely to have put things in a more generic form, a form more understandable to Gentiles who were not familiar with Jewish eschatological and apocalyptic forms of expression. In this case,

Matthew's version of these sayings may at various points be closer to the original, more Semitic version.

One example of this Lukan approach may be given. In both Mark and Matthew, when the centurion speaks from beneath the cross at the point of Jesus' death, he says, "Truly this man was God's Son" (Mk 15:39; Mt 27:54), while in Luke 23:47 he says, "Certainly this man was innocent," (literally, "righteous"). Now the latter declaration would make very good sense in the Greco-Roman world, where it was widely assumed that the character of a person would be revealed in the way he or she handled death. The version in both Mark and Matthew is surely more Semitic and likely to be earlier. There is no sound scholarly basis for formulating a general rule that Luke's form of sayings is more likely to be original than Matthew's. Each saying must be judged on a case-by-case basis. I would argue, as do various Lukan specialists, that Luke also *tends* to deeschatologize his source material or focus on realized eschatological aspects in accord with his salvation-historical perspective.[37]

If we take the seminar's pink material as a whole, what else do we learn about Jesus? We hear a good deal about imploring God to act through prayer, about surprising discoveries, about planting seeds and about how injustice is finally rectified and wrongs are righted. We also learn about the mistake of assuming one is going to live forever. Furthermore, we read about using the resources one has, investing them and making more, and seizing one's opportunities. Of course all of this advice or commentary once again sounds like the kind of thing even the sages who contributed to Proverbs could have said, except for one thing. Jesus says these things about change, opportunities and even saving the lost precisely because he believes God's divine saving activity is at work in these ways and with these sorts of opportunities and results. The Dominion of God certainly has social effects, but Jesus is not simply talking about the effects, he is also speaking of the divine causes of such changes and their surprising results.

Unless we are careful to note that all these parables are parables of God's *inbreaking* kingdom, the net effect of the Jesus Seminar's choices is a somewhat less Jewish Jesus, certainly a less eschatological Jesus. Funk's summary of the results of the seminar is instructive. He concludes:

1. Jesus' sayings were short, provocative and memorable.

2. Jesus' best-remembered forms of speech were aphorisms and parables.

3. Jesus' talk was distinctive.

4. Jesus' sayings and parables cut across the social and religious grain of his society.

5. Jesus' sayings and parables surprise and shock; they characteristically call for a reversal of roles or frustrate ordinary, everyday expectations.

6. Jesus' sayings are often characterized by exaggeration, humor and paradox.

7. Jesus' images are concrete and vivid, and his sayings and parables are customarily metaphorical and without explicit application.

8. Jesus does not as a rule initiate dialogue or debate, nor does he offer to cure people. He rarely makes pronouncements or speaks about himself in the first person.[38]

The Omissions of the Jesus Seminar

By and large the problem with these conclusions is not what they affirm but what they omit, which is a very great deal. In particular the teachings of Jesus that are not parables or aphorisms are omitted, as are the controversy dialogues and presumably various of the pronouncements in the so-called pronouncement stories.[39] The latter is apparently thought to be too direct for Jesus, the ever elusive and allusive sage.

Also omitted, almost altogether, is the theological and eschatological matrix out of which all this teaching operates. For example, it has long been the consensus of most scholars that if there are two things Jesus certainly spoke about they are the Son of Man and the kingdom of God. Yet these subjects hardly surface in the Jesus Seminar's discussions of important topics.

The Jesus Seminar's approach to Jesus the sage yields a Jesus who was too self-effacing and modest to speak much about himself or about his mission and purpose in life. It is very difficult on the basis of Funk's conclusions to imagine why Jesus would ever have gathered twelve disciples, and yet most scholars, including as critical a scholar as E. P. Sanders, are convinced he did.[40]

Perhaps most tellingly, *nothing* of real consequence from the passion or resurrection narratives that might present us with any clues about who Jesus was and why he died is found to be authentic. This is of course because *Thomas* has no such material, and Q has precious few hints in that direction. If one starts with *Thomas* and a very Lukan version of Q, it is hard to arrive at the picture of Jesus that one finds in Mark in general and in the passion narratives in particular.

To arrive at the minimal results that Funk enumerates requires that we dismiss a good deal of the early evidence in Mark, but we have seen that this seminar was prepared to take that step. The Jesus this seminar repeatedly maintains *did* exist was a traveling sage who traded in proverbial wisdom. While this is one legitimate angle from which to view Jesus— clearly much of his teaching takes on the form of wisdom in parables, aphorisms and riddles[41]—it does not tell the whole story. It certainly does not account for Jesus' use of eschatological language about the Son of Man and about God's eschatological saving activity breaking into the present and culminating in the future.[42]

Jesus Without a Story

What is perhaps most striking about the work of the Jesus Seminar is that while each participating scholar no doubt has a story about the life of Jesus in mind into which he believes these various sayings of Jesus fit, this framework is never discussed. Ultimately the determination of what is authentic or inauthentic among the sayings of the Jesus tradition must be checked against not merely the broader historical matrix in which Jesus operated (the historical Galilee of the early first century) but against the particular narrative, as we can reconstruct it, of Jesus' life. The judgment, "Jesus couldn't have said or done that," presupposes knowledge about what comports with the facts of Jesus' life and with Jesus' character and ministry. This is why scholars like Sanders have rightly stressed that we need a framework of facts about Jesus' life into which we can try to place and interpret his teachings (and actions).[43] The story of Jesus is the matrix out of which his words and deeds must be understood.

The seminar goes on to suggest that Jesus was not a controversialist, never initiated debates or controversies, and was passive until someone questioned or criticized him or his followers. He was not a prophet or a radical reformer. He is seen as a person who never spoke of himself or claimed to play any decisive role in God's final plans for humankind, never claimed to be the Messiah.

So we might ask how anyone as inoffensive as this could have generated so much hostility, much less get himself crucified. The Jesus of the Jesus Seminar could never have ended up on Golgotha nailed to the cross. Yet the crucifixion of Jesus is one of the basic historical givens of what we know about Jesus, as even Rudolf Bultmann agreed! Since Jesus is characterized by the seminar as a man with a laconic wit given to exaggeration, humor and paradox, he seems a much better candidate for a late-night visit with David Letterman or Jay Leno, or for an appearance in "Stand Up Spotlight." At the end of the day the seminar rejects the majority of the evidence (82 percent) in order to come up with a portrait like this. I will leave the reader to decide whether it is a truly scholarly and unbiased approach to reject the majority of one's evidence and stress a minority of it. In a court of law, where there is plenty of critical scrutiny, point and counterpoint, this sort of approach would never stand up.

We simply add that this seminar Jesus will not preach, did not come to save and likely will not last. It may be a new Jesus, but it is doubtful this portrait will ever represent *the* scholarly consensus that will lead us into the next century. More likely it will go the way of the various literary portraits painted by the nineteenth-century biographers of Jesus.[44] It probably tells us more about various members of the Jesus Seminar than about Jesus. Perhaps they wish to see themselves as sages offering countercultural wisdom.

CHAPTER 3

JESUS THE ITINERANT CYNIC PHILOSOPHER

One of the most distinctive and publicized portraits of Jesus is that of a type of wandering Cynic preacher. In this chapter I will give a brief sketch of the Cynics and then an analysis and critique of the work of F. Gerald Downing, Burton Mack and John Dominic Crossan. I will concentrate on the latter, whose work has made the largest impact and has the most to commend it. Nevertheless, it ignores major portions of the Jesus tradition, especially the material in Mark, and in the end produces an essentially non-Jewish Jesus, a Jesus that does not deal with issues like Corban or Sabbath, marriage or divorce, resurrection or Messiah. In part this is due to the methodological flaw of only dealing with material that is attested in more than one source, which leaves out an enormous amount of the Jesus material. Instead of fitting his Jewish milieu, Crossan's Jesus sounds suspiciously like an advocate of modern egalitarian notions. Neither the term Cynic *nor the term* peasant *fit the historical Jesus very well. Crossan's concept of "open commensality" turns out to be based on very little evidence, and even more suspect is his notion that Jesus approached meals this way in order to avoid being a broker or mediator of God's kingdom. Finally, the attempt to envision an ongoing Jesus movement that became Christianity without placing any real importance on the death and resurrection appearances of Jesus does not make sense of either the existence or the preaching of the earliest church.*

THE PORTRAIT THAT HAS RECEIVED THE MOST VISIBILITY IN THE MEDIA AS revealing the distinctive Jesus of the Third Quest is the image of Jesus as a wandering Cynic pundit. In large measure this is because of the enormous publicity and sales of John Dominic Crossan's rather pretentiously titled book, *The Historical Jesus.*[1] In this chapter we will undertake a detailed analysis and critique of that influential work, which has now been followed by a smaller, popularized version which Crossan calls his "baby Jesus book."[2]

THE CYNIC JESUS: DEFINITIONS, DISTINCTIONS AND EVIDENCE

One of the earliest pictorial renderings of Jesus is found in Rome. It is on a fourth-century sarcophagus, and it shows Jesus sitting on a rock, appearing like a Cynic philosopher. He has long hair, a beard, one shoulder bare, and he is holding a papyrus roll in his left hand and gesturing with his right, like some sort of rhetorician or orator.[3] Is this a fair representation of the real historical Jesus, or is it the sort of image that was first conjured up when the gospel went forth from Palestine into the wider Greco-Roman world and encountered Cynic and Stoic ideas?

The Cynics

The sarcophagus picture of a wandering Cynic peasant orator or preacher gives us an idea of what such a figure looked like, but what of the proclamation and aims of a Cynic preacher? Bearing in mind that not all Cynics were exactly alike in their lifestyles and views, we can nevertheless say that there are certain features and ideas which typified them, beginning with Diogenes of Sinope (400-325 B.C.), who was credited with founding the Cynic movement.

First, and perhaps most important, Cynics stressed *autarkeia*, the idea of self-sufficiency, or being independent from society and its entangling alliances. This aim was accomplished by living simply, even out in the open air, and on occasions begging in order to survive. In a sense, the Cynics were the "back to nature" movement of their day and stressed the goodness of acting naturally, indeed acting without shame even in public.[4] The word *Cynic* comes from the fact that Diogenes was called the dog (*kyōn* in Greek) because of his acts of public defecation and immodest, public sexual behavior.

A second notable feature of Cynics was their *parrēsia*, or "free speech." They spoke boldly and bluntly, sparing no one and showing no respect to those in authority or those with wealth. For instance, Diogenes is said to have been visited once by Alexander the Great, who asked him if there was anything he could do for him. Diogenes' reply was, "Stand out of my light" (Diogenes Laertius *Lives* 6.38).

Third, the Cynics were noted for their aphorisms and perhaps also for their telling of *chreiai,* those apt, well-aimed accounts of sayings or actions associated with Diogenes or other famous figures that carried some sort of moral. Then, too, they are said to have developed the diatribe style (a dialogue with an imaginary interlocutor) and to have engaged in symbolic actions.

Cynics were known to travel widely through many countries. They were not noted for calling or collecting disciples. Dio of Prusa, for example, advises, "If someone starts following you, claiming to be your disciple, you must drive him away with your fists . . . he is either a fool or a knave" (35.10). With this thumbnail sketch readers will be aided as they read through the following critique of the Cynic proposal.

Crossan's discussion of the Cynic movement is somewhat helpful.[5] He argues that the Cynics should be seen as examples of the introversionist approach that abandons the world as irredeemably evil. This underlies the Cynics' seeking freedom from all cares of society—food, clothing, shelter, home, marriage, children—their emphasis on *autarkeia* and the fact that by and large they did not start communities but were the radical individualists of antiquity. Poverty or the absence of possessions led to freedom, which in turn led to royalty. Epictetus said of himself, "Who when he sees me, does not think that he sees his king and master?" (*Disc.* 3.22.49). In other words, he sees himself as occupying the moral high ground that demands respect and reverence. The Cynics' ragged clothing, their unshaved and unkempt appearance, their begging and their itinerant lifestyle symbolized by the ever-present staff were the practical embodiment of their philosophy to live as nearly as possible according to nature.

It must be remembered, however, that their poverty was a *chosen* lifestyle, not one they were necessarily born into, as were peasants. Indeed, on the whole most Cynics appear not to have come from a peasant background but were people of some means and often educated, people who had become "cynical" about Greco-Roman society. The question is whether this portrait suits Jesus.

Was Jesus really an ascetic or an advocate of a back-to-nature philosophy? Was Jesus an introversionist, or was he a reformer and a conversionist in his approach? Do we know anything about Jesus' appearance that suggests that he would have appeared or represented himself to others as a Cynic philosopher? Did Jesus advocate self-chosen poverty as a way of life for his followers?

Cynics and the Hellenization of Galilee

The proposal that Jesus was a Cynic calls for a close look at Jesus' words, deeds and lifestyle. But first we must revisit the question of the Hellenization of Galilee. Burton Mack, another advocate of a Cynic Jesus, is quite clear about the net effect of accepting the Cynic hypothesis: "The Cynic analogy repositions the historical Jesus away from a specifically Jewish sectarian milieu and toward the Hellenistic ethos known to have prevailed in Galilee."[6]

Mack's statement begs a number of issues, not least of which is the assumption that a Hellenistic ethos prevailed in Galilee and, more to the point, that it prevailed in the small villages like Capernaum or Nazareth which Jesus frequented. The evidence for this last conclusion is weak at best. A distinction must be made between the ethos of the villages and that of the cities which Herod Antipas built.

I have already noted in the first chapter that Jesus seems to have avoided the very cities in Galilee, like Sepphoris or Tiberias, where Hellenization was most clearly in evidence. This casts serious doubts from the very outset on the theory that Jesus was some sort of Cynic philosopher. Hans Dieter Betz has also pointed out that the presumed presence of Cynics *in* Galilee itself is for the most part conjecture. There is indeed evidence for Cynic influence in Gadara and Tyre, but these were Hellenistic cities outside Galilee, and there is no evidence that Jesus actually spent any time there or sought to convey his message in these places.[7] In his seminal essay Betz stresses that to establish that Jesus was a Cynic, one must show that he shared their modes of conduct, their external appearance, their forms of speech and their central ideas. Since the Gospels never describe how Jesus looked or dressed, the criterion of external appearance cannot be met; but what of the other criteria? I will pursue this matter in the discussion of Crossan's approach to the issue. First, however, something must be said about the nature and date of the Cynic literature.

Dating Sources and Defining Distinctives

Throughout this discussion we must always keep in mind that evidence of Hellenization in lower Galilee is by no means evidence of Cynic influence. If there is any probability that Jesus was influenced by specifically Cynic ideas, it must be demonstrated. Furthermore, as I have argued elsewhere, "In order to make a strong case for Cynic influence on Jesus one must not only point out certain parallels at the level of linguistic phenomena or at the level of ideas, but one must also show that such traits are unique to or at least characteristic of the Cynic tradition, and not to other traditions to which Jesus might have been indebted."[8] In other words, a criterion of dissimilarity should be applied to the historical evidence of the Cynic tradition before comparing it to the Jesus tradition, so that we will recognize distinctively Cynic traits.

The problem of dating the Cynic material is also a serious one. F. Gerald Downing and others indiscriminately produce evidence from Epictetus, Seneca, Musonius Rufus or Dio, and occasionally from the Cynic epistles. Almost all of this evidence as we now have it postdates the lifetime of Jesus, with the exception perhaps of some of the material from the Cynic epistles. One can of course argue that people like Dio or Epictetus are quoting earlier sources, but this cannot simply be assumed, it must be demonstrated, otherwise the danger of an anachronistic picture of the Cynics is acute.

A further complication is that the Cynic movement displayed a spectrum of views, sometimes overlapping with Stoic and other philosophical perspectives. For example, whether we are speaking of Seneca or Epictetus, it is hardly adequate to simply call them Cynics. The most one could argue is that Cynic thought influenced them at points, and that they no doubt modified and adapted whatever Cynic ideas they may have accepted to fit into their own larger and different worldview. In other words, we cannot uncritically cite statements from a Seneca or Epictetus as examples of Cynic thought.

Downing has gone to the greatest lengths to compare in detail the Jesus tradition with the Cynic tradition.[9] But several criticisms may be leveled at his methods and conclusions, and may in fact be applied in general to the various proposals that Jesus was influenced by Cynic thought and practice. (1) While Downing shows that there are some similarities between the Cynic and the Jesus tradition, often these similarities do not reflect Cynic-specific traits or teaching. In other words, Jesus could have been influenced at these points by someone other than the Cynics. (2) Some of the Jesus tradition plainly clashes with the Cynic tradition. For example, the tradition in Mark 6:7-11 and parallels seems deliberately to distinguish Jesus and his followers from itinerants who went around begging (the "bag" that the disciples were not to take was probably a "beggar's bag"). The Cynic approach was different from that of relying on the system of standing hospitality in small Jewish villages.[10] (3) The motivation for the behavior of Jesus and that of the Cynics seems entirely different. The Cynics stressed independence and self-sufficiency, Jesus stressed God-dependency. (4) While some Cynics seem to have used aphorisms and parables in a manner comparable to Jesus, the fact remains that Jesus' use of this species of wisdom speech is closer to that of other early Jews than it is to the Cynic material.[11] (5) As Everett Ferguson points out:

> The Cynics carried to an extreme the Sophist's contrast between custom and nature. . . . They sought to free themselves from luxuries and so inure themselves to hardship by ascetic practices. In order to excite censure they exposed themselves to scorn by deliberately acting against the conventions of society; using violent and abusive language, wearing filthy garments, performing acts of nature (defecation, sex) in public, feigning madness.[12]

Very little of this sounds like Jesus. For example, Jesus had a reputation as one who dined and celebrated with all sorts of people, including tax collectors and sinners. In the Gospel tradition he is contrasted with the Baptist and his followers who fasted (Mk 2:18-22). (6) Boldness in speech is not a trait exclusively characteristic of Cynics; indeed it is characteristic of both the Jewish sapiential tradition of counterorder wisdom as it is found in Ecclesiastes and of the Old Testament prophets.

In reading the works of the three major advocates of the Cynic Jesus—Downing, Mack and Crossan—certain differences in emphasis become evident. Mack, for example, sees Galilee as deeply Hellenized and views Jesus as a Hellenistic-type Cynic sage. Borg ably sums up Mack's position of Jesus:

> An itinerant teacher, without a home, on the road, one who has deliberately abandoned the world by becoming homeless. As such Jesus taught a kind of wisdom that mocked or subverted conventional beliefs. Jesus was a scoffer, a gadfly, a debunker who could playfully or sarcastically or with considerable charm ridicule the conventions and preoccupations that animated and imprisoned most people.[13]

Crossan, on the other hand, takes a somewhat different view of the matter. He sees Jesus as a Jewish Cynic peasant. Thus Crossan sees Jesus as having at least tenuous links to Judaism. He understands that a totally non-Jewish Jesus is highly improbable. Perhaps this is one reason why of these three portraits of a Cynic Jesus, Crossan's proposal has gained both wider publicity and wider assent.

CROSSAN'S JESUS: A MEDITERRANEAN JEWISH PEASANT

The Crossan That Spoke[14]
Clearly another significant factor in Crossan's popularity is his eloquence.
It is easy to be taken in by his persuasive art:

> He comes as yet unknown into a hamlet of Lower Galilee. He is
> watched by the cold, hard eyes of peasants living long enough at sub-
> sistence level to know exactly where the line is drawn between poverty
> and destitution. He looks like a beggar, yet his eyes lack the proper
> cringe, his voice the proper whine, his walk the proper shuffle. He
> speaks about the rule of God, and they listen as much from curiosity
> as anything else. They know all about rule and power, about kingdom
> and empire, but they know it in terms of tax and debt, malnutrition and
> sickness, agrarian oppression and demonic possession. What, they real-
> ly want to know, can this kingdom of God do for a lame child, a blind
> parent, a demented soul screaming its tortured isolation among the
> graves that mark the edge of the village? Jesus walks with them to the
> tombs, and, in the silence after the exorcism, the villagers listen once
> more, but now with curiosity given way to cupidity, fear, and embar-
> rassment.[15]

Crossan's basic proposal, as this passage begins to unveil, is that Jesus was
a Mediterranean, Jewish, Cynic peasant whose real aims are revealed not
simply in his teachings but in his offering free miracles and in his dining
freely with anyone and everyone. Jesus proclaimed and sought to institute
a brokerless and egalitarian kingdom, a kingdom without any mediators
between individuals and God, not even Jesus himself. We will soon see
how these constructive proposals work themselves out. In reverse order
of Crossan's book *The Historical Jesus*, we will first examine what Crossan
says about Jesus and look at the more technical issues of definition, methodology and historical context that occupy the first portion of his book.
In this way from the outset we will form a clear idea of what is entailed
in his portrayal of a Cynic Jesus.

Jesus and the Brokerless Kingdom of God
Readers must forge their way through 224 pages of text before arriving
at the "Brokerless Kingdom," part three of *The Historical Jesus*. Here Cros-

san finally begins to discuss Jesus in some detail. It becomes evident before too many pages that Crossan, though he knows of overlap in the data, would have us choose between a Jesus who is a sage and a Jesus who is an apocalyptic seer, between a Jesus who is more like a Cynic and a Jesus who is more like John the Baptist. There are other options, of course, but they are not offered. It is important to bear this in mind in evaluating Crossan's portrayal of Jesus.

The End of the Apocalyptic Jesus
Crossan first, quite appropriately, discusses the relationship of Jesus and John the Baptist. He agrees with almost all scholars that Jesus was baptized by John and that because this was a baptism that focused on sin and repentance, later Christian tradition would have found this somewhat embarrassing. He then argues that John's message focused on God's coming in a final apocalyptic consummation, not on the coming of Jesus or some other human figure. But is this an either-or matter? John's question from prison, whether Jesus is the "one who is to come" (Mt 11:2-19; Lk 7:18-35), is arguably a historically reliable tradition and would suggest that John at least considered it possible that Jesus might fit this description.[16]

Crossan concludes that Jesus' remarks about John in Luke 7:24-27/ Matthew 11:7-11 and in Luke 7:28/Matthew 11:11 can be traced back to the historical Jesus. The former affirms John as a great prophet, indeed more than a prophet: the final prophet announcing the Coming One. In the latter saying, however, Jesus classifies even the least of those in the kingdom as greater than John, the greatest human being. Crossan takes this to mean that between uttering the first and the second saying (which he assumes are derived from separate occasions and artificially juxtaposed in the Gospels) Jesus changed his mind about John; whereas the first saying simply echoes the Baptist's message, the latter reveals Jesus' distinctive teaching about the Dominion of God.[17]

But clearly the second saying still reflects great admiration for John. It is a typical wisdom utterance, meant to startle by contrast. By stressing the second half of the saying ("yet the least in the kingdom of God is greater than he"), Jesus indicates that however great a prophet John may be, this status pales in comparison to being in God's Dominion. The point was not to devalue John, but to highlight the significance of being in God's Dominion, and perhaps also to encourage the crowd not to judge by human standards but by those Jesus would exhibit and proclaim. Crossan's interpretation results from an overly literal reading of a type of contrast typically found in wisdom sayings.

Crossan goes on to make distinctions between eschatology and apocalyptic, the former being defined as "the wider and generic term for world-negation extending from apocalyptic eschatology, . . . through mystical or utopian modes, and on to ascetical, libertarian, or anarchistic possibilities. . . . In other words, all apocalyptic is eschatological, but not all eschatology is apocalyptic."[18] While Crossan rightly points out that apocalyptic is a subset of eschatology, he surely stretches the term eschatology well beyond its natural bounds. Eschatology involves not just a particular view of a world gone wrong. It also entails ideas about how it can and will be set right in the end, including resurrection, kingdom, last judgment and the like.

Apocalyptic is a particular subspecies of eschatology that takes on a highly metaphorical and pictographic form, usually in response to a crisis or persecution of the believing community (cf. the book of Revelation). Apocalyptic eschatology has a greater tendency to emphasize imminent judgment and the like, but this is not always the case. It may, as in the *Parables of Enoch*, focus on the vertical solution of an otherworldly journey rather than on an end-time rectification of the world's problems. In both eschatology and apocalyptic there is often a belief expressed in a resolution of the issues of justice and salvation in a concrete manner, *in space and time*. In other words, eschatology should not be radically divorced from apocalyptic since both normally entail concrete results from God's intervention in human history. Cynic-like social reform movements, focusing on the present, would not normally be called eschatological.

Crossan's discussion of Jesus' Son of Man sayings is brief. This is not surprising since he thinks only one Son of Man saying actually goes back to Jesus.[19] It is in this section that we especially feel the weight of Crossan's decision to adhere strictly to the criterion of multiple attestation in reconstructing Jesus' sayings, for in this way he can dismiss most of this Son of Man tradition. But his application of the criterion is inconsistent. At the end of this section,[20] when he encounters sayings that contrast Jesus and John (Mk 2:18-20), but are not multiply attested, he is willing enough to retain this material in the discussion of authentic sayings because he finds the same *idea*, though not the same saying, in Q (Lk 7:31-35/Mt 11:16-19). This, of course, is special pleading and violates his earlier stricter application of the criterion of multiple attestation.

Why, we must ask, is this more generous approach allowed in the case of sayings regarding Jesus and John and not in the case of the Son of Man sayings? It is perfectly possible to find the *idea of the future coming of the Son of Man* independently attested in more than one source, though not in identical sayings. Why should this important idea be methodologically omitted from the authentic evidence of Jesus and other important ideas that are multiply attested included?

Crossan is even willing to argue at points that Luke introduces into his source material the phrase "Son of Man" where it originally read "I" (cf. Lk 12:8-9/Mt 10:32-33),[21] a view most Lukan specialists would reject. But Crossan, who on other matters hedges his bets, is dogmatic on this issue: Jesus "never spoke of himself or anyone else as the apocalyptic Son of Man."[22] This heavy-handed approach shows the lengths to which Crossan will go to eliminate from the earliest Jesus material all sayings that speak of the future Son of Man.

Open Table Fellowship

More positively, Crossan sees one of the keys to understanding Jesus to be his "open commensality," his willingness to have table fellowship with anyone. This practice clearly implied a rejection of certain Jewish purity taboos and implicitly redefined honor and shame in that social setting.[23] But even in this important matter Crossan draws some implications that may not be warranted.

In antiquity, eating was not only seen as one of the most intimate and relation-building acts in which one could engage, but meals were a micro-cosm of the values of the society of which they were part. The social ranking that existed in society was replicated at meals, with guests of the highest status being seated next to the host and receiving the best food, and the other guests being seated further from the host according to their status. What one did not want was people of varying ranks, classes and genders (the guests at most banquets consisted of males only) to be seated indiscriminately. Yet Jesus tells a parable where the host, after being rejected by the invited guests, invites off the streets anyone who will come, thus violating social conventions (cf. Lk 14:15-24/Mt 22:1-14). One of the more radical aspects about Jesus' ministry and of his following is that it included the down-and-out as well as the up-and-in: tax collectors and sinners, men and women, including women who were notorious and women who were notable in society (Lk 8:1-3).

Radical Egalitarianism

But Crossan moves beyond this to conclude that because Jesus would eat with anyone and accept anyone as a follower, he must have advocated a radical, egalitarian structure for his movement and other social groupings, such as families; he says Jesus was in principle opposed to any sort of human hierarchy.

To draw this conclusion, Crossan must not only ignore or reject Jesus' sayings about honoring father and mother, his choice of twelve male disciples as the inner circle of his followers and the radical effect of the prohibition of divorce,[24] but he must also reinterpret some of Jesus' sayings about the effects of belief on the physical family to mean that Jesus was deliberately setting children against parents (Lk 12:51-53/Mt 10:34-36): "Jesus will tear the hierarchical or patriarchal family in two along the axis of domination and subordination."[25] In order to arrive at this conclusion Crossan once again must dismiss many sayings in order to cling to a few, and even the remaining few he often reinterprets in unconventional fashion. One may also wonder, if Jesus really was opposed to any sort of hierarchical notions, why he repeatedly spoke of the Dominion of God, for surely God's rule over humankind is a hierarchical concept of the first order.[26]

A further example of special pleading may be seen in Crossan's discussion of the Lord's Prayer, which he does not think goes back to Jesus despite the fact that it is found in two independent sources: Luke 11:1-4/Matthew 6:9-13 and *Didache* 8.2.[27] The apparent reason for this special pleading is that the Lord's Prayer includes, among other petitions, "Your kingdom come," which implies a futurist view, and Crossan does not believe Jesus spoke about either a future coming kingdom or a future coming Son of Man. Only sayings indicating a present kingdom or Son of Man escape his scalpel.

A Kingdom of Nobodies

We may readily agree with Crossan when he concludes that Jesus had a high regard for children, who were the most vulnerable of all in an oppressive society. Likewise, it is true that the child most perfectly symbolizes that even the most humble, perhaps especially the lowliest and most humble of all, have a place in God's dominion. The child is also seen in

Jesus' teaching as a model of discipleship, something not found in other early Jewish teaching (Mk 10:13-15; Mt 18:1-4). But Crossan concludes that the child is fundamentally a symbol of a nobody, and thus Jesus offers a kingdom for nobodies. This view of children hardly comports with early Jewish views of children as one of God's highest blessings.[28]

This in turn leads Crossan to the discussion of the Beatitude "Blessed are you who are poor" (Lk 6:20; cf. Mt 5:3).[29] He rightly points out that the term *ptōchoi* does not refer only to those of low income or resources but to those who are destitute, so poor that they must beg. Luke 6:20 ("Blessed are you who are poor") should be read closely together with Luke 6:21 ("Blessed are you who are hungry now"), and the implication is that in God's dominion basic human needs are or will be met (as Luke 6:21, "for you will be filled," suggests). Both of these Lukan Beatitudes and the Lord's Prayer reflect, as Crossan says, a Jesus who is deeply concerned for those who lack even the basic human necessities and who must pray today for bread for tomorrow, since they have no surplus.

The gospel Jesus preached was not simply a spiritual gospel disengaged from everyday realities; it clearly had a social component as well. Perhaps most importantly, as Crossan is fond of saying, since Jesus believed he was already in part bringing in this dominion of God (the divine saving activity), these sayings are a program to be performed, not just a message to be proclaimed. In short, Jesus expected that basic human needs would be taken care of by, and in, the community of his followers, as a sign of the kingdom's coming. Riches were an enormous encumbrance if one wanted to enter this kingdom, not least because they led a person to find his or her security in their possessions and not in God (cf. Mk 10:23-27).

The closely related parables of the mustard seed (Lk 13:18-19 and parallels) and of the weeds or darnel (Mt 13:24-30) receive interesting interpretations from Crossan. Basically, Jesus likens the kingdom to an uncontrollable weed that people would like to keep within limits but have a hard time restraining. The same applies to the leaven in the bread, according to Crossan. The leaven was impure, but was a necessary evil which made bread rise. "It's there, it's natural, it's normal, it's necessary, but society has a problem with it."[30] Any allusions in these parables to Jesus' ragtag bunch of followers are probably intentional. They would have been seen as unwashed and unclean, traipsing about Galilee and multiplying in numbers; but in God's view they were the evidence and examples of the reign of God. Jesus did indeed set forth a new view of honor and shame, clean and unclean. It was a view that held up a woman's honor as highly as a man's by regarding the sexual infidelities of husbands as of equal gravity as those of wives.

Crossan's view is that Jesus draws on Wisdom ideas about a present kingdom as a state of being and power, not a future destination. I would suggest that this is not necessarily an either-or matter, as is also shown in the Pauline epistles, where we find both present and future kingdom sayings.[31] Jesus' teaching combines insights from both the prophetic and the sapiential literature of Judaism.

Jesus, the Man of Meals and Miracles

Crossan clearly states that his argument essentially stands or falls with chapter thirteen, "Magic and Meal"; if he is wrong about a conjunction of miracle and table fellowship in Jesus' teaching, his book must be redone.[32] Through "magic" and "meal" Jesus seeks to deconstruct an old world and build a new one.

1. Magic. Crossan spends some time clarifying what he means by *magic:* while many would refer to it as miracle working, he prefers the term *magic* because this connotes the idea of power operating outside the official and regular religious channels. In other words, magic is what Jesus' opponents were likely to call it, a collusion with the powers of darkness (cf. Mk 3:22).

While the term is frequently used in studies of Jesus, it suffers in our modern context from the drawback of connoting illusions, or drawing on the powers of darkness, or the use of spells or curses to try to cure a person, none of which characterized Jesus' deeds.[33] The closest we ever get to Jesus acting like other ancient miracle workers is that occasionally he uses spittle or clay in the process of curing someone (cf. Mk 8:22-26). Otherwise he heals by a word or a touch, even touching an unclean person (Mk 1:40-45). The frequency, immediacy and approach of his cures distinguish them from a number of other ancient miracle stories.[34]

The question posed by Crossan's interpretation of miracles is whether they should be seen as an act of religious banditry, with Jesus deliberately trying to act outside the normal religious lines to annoy or challenge the religious authorities, or whether his miracles should be seen as not directed against anyone, but rather as acts of compassion performed in conjunction with his eschatological mission. That Jesus' miracles were seen as a threat seems sure, but that does not settle the issue of Jesus' intent.[35]

2. Exorcisms and Healings. Regarding demonic possession, Crossan has pointed out that in societies where there is an occupying colonial power, possession is not uncommon.[36] If the leadership of the society is seen to be possessed, it is not surprising that individuals under duress and stress might also be viewed that way. From an anthropological standpoint, the way one views the body politic and its boundaries is interrelated with the way one views the human body and its boundaries. As various scholars have put it, the physical body is seen as a microcosm of the social body, with the two sharing maladies, taboos and boundaries.

For example, the Qumran community viewed Jewish society under Roman occupation, and even the temple and its apparatus, as demonized, infected with evil. On the macrocosmic level their world had been invaded by the powers of darkness, which had even penetrated the inner sanctum of Judaism, the most holy place, the temple. What was the response of the Qumran community? First, to withdraw from the sin-infested world and retreat into the desert, and second, to make sure evil, sin and impurity did not infect or invade their microcosmic world, the world of Essene individuals and the community. The latter end was accomplished by adhering to very strict purity laws, repeated ritual ablutions and the like. They would cleanse and control the portals and parts of the human body, even if they couldn't do the same for the body politic or society as a whole just yet. The Pharisees and Jesus adopted different purification approaches, but they too believed their society was full of sin and sickness and proposed holiness agendas, as did John the Baptist.

The famous story of the Gerasene demoniac (Mk 5:1-17) takes on new and fascinating dimensions as read through Crossan's eyes. It is not just a story about an individual but about a society gone wrong. Notice that the dark power exorcised from the man is called Legion, the name for a large military unit of the Roman occupying power. Notice also that the miracles end with possessed pigs rushing headlong into the sea, precisely what every Jewish Zealot hoped would happen to the unclean "animals" (Romans) occupying their land. Jesus is asked to leave the region because he is seen as both a personal and a social menace, not just because he was hard on swine herders. One suspects that Mark portrays the story as he does to show how Jesus chose to confront evil in his society—head on, but personally and one person at a time. Jesus was about the reformation of society *primarily* by the transformation and rescue of individuals.

There are six exorcism stories, seventeen healings and eight nature miracles in the Gospel tradition. The variety as well as the numbers should be noted carefully, for it meant that Jesus, as part of his program of reform, confronts supernatural evil, nature gone haywire and human nature that is sick. This means that his mission is about more than just the salvation of individuals, for the coming of the kingdom means a world set right, in the fuller sense of the term *world*. But this is accomplished only in part during Jesus' earthly ministry.

In regard to sickness and sin, in the prevailing paradigm of Jesus' day, the one who cures the sickness also deals with the sin, for it was assumed that people were sick because they had sinned. Jesus breaks this nexus, not only because it is not universally valid, but in Mark 2:1-12, where he assumes or concedes the connection between sin and paralysis, he demonstrates that his power to heal the one indicates healing of the other as well. Crossan points out that Jesus puts his opponents on the spot (because they assume a connection of sickness and sin) by healing the paralytic, for that ought to imply he also has the power to forgive the sin which was thought to cause the disease.

The Itinerant Strategy of Jesus

Crossan's discussion of the attire of Jesus and his followers comes as something of a surprise, since he is arguing for a "Cynic" Jesus.[37] He admits that the material in Mark 6/Matthew 10/Luke 9, the mission charge to the disciples, calls for the disciples to take no beggar's bag or bread with them but rather to eat in homes wherever they go to spread the Word. The Cynics took with them both bag and food, as it was given to them, as a mark of their independence. This suggests, if anything, a reaction by Jesus against the Cynic modus operandi. Thus Crossan must be content to argue that Jesus was a Jewish Cynic who modified the custom to suit his own agenda and setting. But such an argument, coupled with the other flies in the ointment,[38] is evidence of how the case for a Cynic Jesus dies the death of too many qualifications.

As we have said, the very heart of Crossan's case is his argument about miracles and meals. The disciples, like Jesus, were to go into villages, to help and to heal people, and to accept the hospitality of those healed and helped—a sharing or exchanging of spiritual aid for physical aid, something he calls "open commensality." He believes that the miracles and then the meals were vehicles for establishing a more egalitarian way of life for peasants and those who dwelt in small villages. They were to share with each other what they had.

The problem with this argument is that when Jesus or the disciples ate in the homes of those they had healed or taught, whether it was a peasant, a Simon the Pharisee or a Zacchaeus the tax collector, they did so *as guests, not as hosts*. They were not in a position to set the protocol for the meal, but rather the host did. Thus in the story of Luke 7:36-50 it is Simon who chooses not to perform the normal welcoming functions for Jesus his guest, washing his feet and the like. The meals Jesus and his disciples shared surely followed the normal patriarchal protocol that the hosts knew and customarily followed. It may be that the meals Jesus shared with his disciples while on the road or while visiting in their homes *were* different, but this has nothing to do with what happened when the disciples shared a meal with those they had just helped, healed or convinced.

At the end of the day Crossan's notion of open commensality, oddly enough, is not based on *any* Gospel stories about meals that either Jesus or his traveling disciples initiated.[39] Apparently it is based on: (1) the stories of healings by the disciples, and apparently by Jesus, to which it is assumed grateful peasants responded with food, and (2) on the famous parable about the host who brings in anyone from the highways and hedges to the banquet, since the invited guests had rejected the invitation (cf. Lk 14:21-23). This last parable however says nothing about the protocol the host would follow when these guests actually came to dinner, nothing about a rejection of all societal notions about seating and the like.[40] These are simply ideas Crossan assumes are present in, or implied by, the story.

While I quite agree that Jesus had both a vision and a social program that involved the reforming of various patriarchal ideas and customs in the context of his community,[41] the idea that Jesus sought to reform peasant society in general does not comport with the Gospel data we have. Where is the evidence of Jesus confronting village officials, patrons, landlords or owners of tenant farms and arguing for a new vision of society? The confrontations and conversations Jesus has are with religious figures and authorities ranging from Pharisees to Sadducees to John the Baptist. Where is the evidence that the meals Jesus shared with those he healed or helped instantly reflected a new egalitarian agenda?

Crossan does not like the notion of mediators or, as he calls them, brokers, and he rejects the idea that Jesus saw himself as a mediator between God and God's people. He argues that both Jesus and his disciples had to be itinerant so that they would not become "the religious brokers" or the establishment in any one town that all would look to for help and healing. In other words itinerancy was not a missionary tactic so much as an avoidance technique.[42] Egalitarianism is only possible if one keeps moving and never becomes a localized religious broker. Crossan adds to this conclusion the argument that Jesus was rejected in Nazareth because he refused to set up shop there and make it his religious base where he performed his miracles. This is of course not what the Gospel tradition says—it says he was rejected because his message was found offensive.

The Marginalized Message

If Crossan's book stands or falls with his case for "meal and magic," there is a further problem. What is notably absent in his discussion is a third M—the message. Indeed all four Gospels suggest that for Jesus the transforming message was primary. The miracles were in the main secondary acts performed along the way as acts of compassion, though they too revealed that the kingdom was breaking in. Meals were somewhere lower down the line of priorities, though I would not wish to overlook or minimize the importance of Jesus' dining with sinners as well as with his followers. Jesus did intend to break down some of society's purity barriers by eating with all sorts of people. But the overemphasis on meal and miracle to the neglect of message leads to a distorted picture of Jesus.

Crossan admits that Jesus spoke about taking up one's cross and following him, about making sacrifices to be his follower.[43] But what was the content of Jesus' kingdom message? What did he offer beyond a one-time healing or the occasional meal that attracted a follower? It is often overlooked that other early Jewish teachers, while they had disciples, did not seek them out and did not have itinerant followers. Disciples went to Jerusalem or elsewhere to study with such teachers, they were not sought out by the teachers as Jesus sought his followers, and the teachers were not itinerant as Jesus was.

What was the content of Jesus' missionary message? To judge from Crossan, Jesus had little or nothing to say about the future of Israel, the law, the covenants, eternal life, resurrection, last judgment or salvation as more than just a social adjustment. In short, Jesus did not address the issues that most deeply concerned many early Jews. Crossan allows that Jesus may have foreseen his death, even on a cross, but not that he saw in it anything redemptive, for Jesus in Crossan's view did not see himself as a mediator, a broker of God's grace or salvation. Rather Crossan sees

Jesus as an example of inclusive Judaism, accommodating to the Hellenism that had long since penetrated the land. This is at best a half-truth, for Jesus was no advocate of pluralism, relativism, or a naive universalism that draws no lines between God's people and the world and requires very little of one's followers in terms of the religious content of their commitments.[44]

The Cross and the Resurrection

The last two chapters of Crossan's book prove to be less stimulating and more disappointing than the rest. Once again Crossan insists on subscribing to opinions that only a distinct minority of scholars would agree with, this time regarding the passion and resurrection narratives.

1. *The Abandoned Jesus.* Most scholars would argue that the passion narrative achieved a rather fixed form well before the actual writing of the Gospels. This took place because of the crucial nature of these accounts and because of the number of witnesses who had something to say about what had happened during the remarkable last week of Jesus' life and its sequel.

Crossan by contrast argues that the earliest Christians only knew that Jesus died on the cross. They had all abandoned him, apparently even the women, and they had no clue where or by whom he was buried. He even suggests that Jesus' body may have been thrown by the Romans onto the garbage dump, where it was eaten by jackals and scavenging birds! Needless to say, this also means that the stories about women visiting the tomb and seeing him alive are pious fictions or visions not grounded in historical fact, a conclusion that is no doubt an unpleasant surprise to feminists in his audience.

If a resurrected Jesus was seen, in Crossan's view, it was as an apparition or a vision some time later (as in Paul's case), not as someone walking about with a resurrection body that was physically tangible. In a later work Crossan states flatly that various disciples never lost their faith in Jesus and consequently never required nor experienced an Easter Sunday. Crossan's theory is that some early Christians, like Paul, talked about resurrection but others simply spoke about the living Christ, who had never ceased to live (for example, those who wrote the *Gospel of Thomas*). Some saw apparitions of the risen Jesus perhaps, but it was not the basis of Christian faith. He flatly states: "My thesis . . . is that Christian faith is not Easter faith."[45]

2. The Fiction of Passion and Resurrection. Crossan also wishes to argue that, rather than Jesus' death and resurrection leading the early Christians to search the Scriptures to find an explanation and scriptural validation for these remarkable events, these stories were almost entirely created out of the Old Testament prophecies and are not based in history. As Crossan puts it, "Hide the prophecy, tell the narrative, and invent the history."[46] They "are not history memorized, but prophecy historicized."[47] For example, the story of the trials of Jesus, especially the Jewish one, he takes as entirely fictitious.

Jesus got himself crucified by threatening to destroy the temple (the *Thomas* version of Jesus' words, "I will destroy this house utterly beyond repair," is seen as authentic), and then symbolically carrying out the threat by turning over the tables and disturbing the vendors in the outer part of the temple precincts. Jesus was not trying to cleanse the temple but to do away with the very seat of Jewish hierarchical and patronal authority, the temple, in the name of his egalitarian agenda.

Crossan is able to come to these radical conclusions in part because of his radical methodology. He favors a *Cross Gospel*, which he has extracted from the *Gospel of Peter*, and which he argues is more primitive than Mark's Gospel. This "other," supposedly earlier, version speaks of Jesus being buried by his enemies. Hence the stories about visits to tombs and women at the cross must be fictions. Even offensive canonical stories about the mocking and abusing of Jesus before his crucifixion are said to owe their origin to *Gospel of Peter* 3:6-9 ("And others who stood by spat on his eyes, and others slapped him on the cheeks, others pricked him with a reed, and some scourged him saying, 'With this honour let us honour the Son of God' "[48]). This account is thought to have originated in Old Testament prophetic texts that were combined perhaps with a story like we find in Philo *Flaccus* 32-39, about a lunatic who was abused, mocked and dressed as royalty in Alexandria in Egypt! Not only does Crossan see Mark as highly creative, he sees his sources as equally creative and fictitious.[49] As if all this were not enough, Crossan also thinks that the Last Supper traditions, and in particular the reinterpretation of the Passover elements and the saying, "Do this in memory of me," are also early Christian fabrications.[50]

It is unfortunate that Crossan too often allows himself to engage in such wild and insupportable conjectures and arguments, because for many critical readers this leaven will leaven the entire lump, and even the better parts of his work will be dismissed as the views of one who has intentions of undermining traditional views of Jesus, not as the views of a scholar of history. If, as Crossan maintains, all of Jesus' followers deserted him and were ignorant of the sequel other than that Jesus was crucified, it is frankly unbelievable to me that there would have arisen a continuing Jesus movement at all. There would have been no church without Easter.[51]

Crossan's Sources and Method

Crossan devotes a great deal of space to his methodology and his use of sources. This is such an important issue that it calls for our attention. Crossan begins his methodological discussion with his characteristic acuteness. In view of the tremendous diversity of portraits of the historical Jesus appearing in books written in the 1980s and now in the 1990s, historical Jesus research is becoming a bit of a scholarly bad joke. "It is impossible to avoid the suspicion that historical Jesus research is a very safe place to do theology and call it history, to do autobiography and call it biography."[52] Crossan is of course right. There are almost as many portraits of Jesus now available as there are scholarly painters, a testimony to acute scholarly subjectivity.

1. *Sources and Layers of Tradition.* How then, in Crossan's view, do we deal with this problem? His answer is to use a broader scope of scholarly approaches on the one hand and to use a wider variety of source material on the other, without favoring the canonical Gospels over the extracanonical material. Indeed, the person embarking on reading Crossan's magnum opus who is familiar with the canonical Gospels and not with the *Gospel of Thomas* or *Gospel of Peter* will wonder about the origin of the many unfamiliar sayings and parables that Crossan has assembled in his list of authentic Jesus traditions presented at the outset of the work.[53]

Crossan uses an analogy between archaeology and source, form and tradition criticism. The Jesus tradition is to be seen like an ancient Near Eastern tel with many layers, say Megiddo, which has over twenty such levels. One must carefully separate the Jesus tradition into its various strata—from the original strata through various intermediate ones, and at last to the final form of the text. Yet, one may properly ask, how is it possible with any degree of objectivity to accomplish this task when we do not have the texts of the earlier layers of the Gospel tradition? All we have are the Gospels. In part Crossan's answer is that we do have a text of some of the earlier levels, namely in the *Gospel of Thomas* and, in some cases, in the *Gospel of Peter*.

In view of his analogy from archaeology, it is remarkable that Crossan stresses that we must start with the earliest strata and work our way to the later ones. This is certainly not how an archaeologist normally works. The archaeologist begins with the mound as it is and then carefully digs down into what lies beneath. There is also another problem with the stratigraphic analogy. In the sayings tradition there may be considerable continuity between what Jesus said and the final edited form in which it appears in a Gospel.[54] If one divides the Jesus tradition into horizontal layers, say, for example, a wisdom layer and then a later eschatological layer, one may in fact be severing a real connection between what Jesus said and its later edited form.

At the conclusion of the epilogue to *The Historical Jesus*,[55] Crossan gives what amounts to a defense not only of his own attempt to reconstruct the historical Jesus but also of the entire enterprise undertaken by the Jesus Seminar,[56] including the voting on the Jesus tradition and the placing of it into the four categories on the scale of authenticity or inauthenticity. He draws an analogy with the textual criticism which stands behind our present-day editions of the Greek New Testament. In one standard published Greek text of the New Testament, the United Bible Societies' edition, textual scholars have ranked various ancient manuscript variants into four categories according to the probability of each representing the original reading. However, this analogy contains a major flaw.

The textual scholars are dealing with actual manuscripts and are trying to reconstruct the original text from objective data. The Jesus Seminar, however, which relies so heavily on Q and *Thomas*, must engage in reconstruction *before* they can even consider the issues at hand, for there is no documentary evidence for Q. There is furthermore no truly objective evidence whatsoever for supposing that *Thomas* and *Peter* are earlier documents, and/or that in almost all cases they preserve earlier traditions than does Mark. There is, however, the objective testimony of early church fathers such as Papias about the origins of Mark, however critically we must evaluate such testimonies. Such testimonies are nowhere found for *Thomas*, or *Secret Mark*, or the *Gospel of Peter*, or a variety of other documents on which Crossan and the Jesus Seminar rely so heavily.

While it is true enough that all historical inquiry into the life of Jesus involves reconstruction, there is a difference between reconstruction built purely on scholarly conjecture and reconstruction built on viable textual evidence. At least the traditional approach to Jesus has the merit of starting with the objective evidence as we have it, with the archaeological mound of the Jesus tradition, not starting with a flawed stratigraphic theory that presupposes not merely that we must find the earliest layer, which in itself is laudatory, but that to be counted a "critical scholar" one must from the outset *dismiss the majority of the canonical data* as misrepresentations of the historical Jesus.

As Robert W. Funk, the founder of the Jesus Seminar, once said, methodology is not an indifferent net—it catches what it intends to catch.[57] Just so, and Funk, Crossan and their kin have engaged in a method that casts a net with large holes into the canonical ocean, while casting and recasting a net of fine mesh into the apocryphal sea. The result is they have caught what they were looking for—a radical, countercultural Jesus, a magician with little or no Jewish flavor but more like a wandering Cynic, espousing the modern politically correct notions of radical egalitarianism and a world with few if any boundaries between sinner and saint, good and bad, in and out, believer and infidel. It is appropriate to ask whether this portrait is accurate characterization or inaccurate caricature.

2. The Gospels and Their Literary World. A troubling aspect of Crossan's approach is his failure to take seriously that the Gospels, *and their composition,* must be compared to other ancient documents and the way they were composed, in particular to ancient biographies and historical works. The old Bultmannian argument that the Gospels are sui generis, a category unto themselves, is seldom taken for granted these days and has received very serious challenges, for example, in the excellent and detailed study on the Gospels as ancient biographies by Richard A. Burridge.[58]

Many if not most scholars acknowledge the evidence in the New Testament, presented in the past by C. H. Dodd, C. F. D. Moule and others, that there was a certain biographical interest and thrust that first led to the formation of the Gospel material. The Synoptic Gospels do not appear to be the kerygma or preaching of the early church itself, but rather to be the story about origins that stands behind the early Christian preaching we find summarized in Acts and in brief statements in Paul's letters. Because we have four canonical Gospels that provide different versions of similar or the same material, at various points we can certainly talk about source material and its redaction, or editing, by the Evangelists, but to speak of multiple strata is to build castles in the air, with no hard data to go on. It also requires us to believe that the Jesus traditions underwent a great deal of creative manipulation during a very short span of time (twenty years in the case of the Q material, and thirty-five to forty years in the case of Mark).[59]

Crossan seems to subscribe to the theory that the experience of the living Christ and the Spirit after the resurrection soon led the early church to invent Jesus traditions indiscriminately and clouded its memory about what he actually did say. In the enthusiasm of the post-Easter period they became more creative than Jesus himself, so that only a distinct minority of the Jesus sayings actually go back to Jesus. To the contrary, what the Gospels themselves suggest is that the experience of the Spirit after Easter led the earliest disciples to *remember* what Jesus had previously said and done, and have greater reverence for and understanding of his earthly life and teachings. Thus the pithy and dogmatic statement "Jesus left behind him thinkers not memorizers, disciples not reciters, people not parrots"[60] is clever, but it is also a caricature.

Disciples in early Jewish settings were learners, and, yes, also reciters and memorizers. This was the way Jewish educational processes worked. In fact it was the staple of all ancient education, including Greco-Roman education.[61] Since all Jesus' earliest followers were Jews, it is a priori probable that they would have handled the Gospel tradition the way other early Jews treated the teachings of their master teachers. There would of course be some additions and subtractions and editing, and variant versions of a saying or story would develop along the way. This is what happens when oral tradition is passed down and then set down in writing. But those who handed on the tradition would not have seen themselves primarily as creators but as preservers and editors.

3. *The Secret Gospel of Mark.* A good example of Crossan's eclectic and questionable critical judgment is shown in his discussion of the raising of Lazarus, a story found in John 11 but also in part within a document known as *Secret Mark.*[62] This latter document is known only from quotations made by Clement of Alexandria in a letter written somewhere around A.D. 200, of which there is only one fragmentary copy appended to an entirely different document, a collection of letters from Ignatius of Antioch. The date of this unusual document, found at the Mar Saba monastery, located between Bethlehem and the Dead Sea, is the mid-eighteenth century. Furthermore, the manuscript is not available in the public domain for our inspection. We only know of it from photographs

taken by Morton Smith, who claims to have discovered it.

When the discovery and contents of *Secret Mark* were first announced, it caused a sensation. In part this was because it speaks of the youth whom Jesus raised coming to Jesus, being instructed while wearing nothing but a linen cloth over his naked body and remaining with Jesus for the night while Jesus taught him "the mystery of God's kingdom." This was presumably in preparation for baptism, which in various quarters of the early church appears to have been carried out with the baptized in the nude. It is Crossan's view that this story was found in the original version of Mark *(Secret Mark)* but not in the second, censored edition which became our canonical Mark, and that John 11 is a markedly transformed version of the story we find in *Secret Mark!* We may rightly ask at this point, What's wrong with this picture?

First, we have a fragment (P52) of the Gospel of John from the second century A.D., perhaps even from early in that century, and most scholars would date the Fourth Gospel at least as early as the last decade of the first century. Needless to say, we have no such evidence for *Secret Mark*. Second, the version of the story in *Secret Mark* comports with what we know about certain second-century sectarian and heretical groups such as the Carpocratians. It does not correspond with any Christian documents that can reasonably be argued to go back to the first century A.D., nor with the extracanonical ones like the *Didache* and *Shepherd of Hermas*, nor even with the *Gospel of Thomas*, if it can be dated that early. Finally, the story as we have it in Clement's letter reflects a knowledge of several earlier Gospels, for example of Mark. In *Secret Mark* Mary (or Martha) appeals to Jesus saying, "Son of David, have mercy on me," a cry found in Mark 10:47 and in Matthew 15:22 but not in John 11. Also, the disciples rebuke the woman in *Secret Mark*, an action much like that found in Mark 10:13, but not like the John 11 story. In short, the number of scholars who think it likely that *Secret Mark* provides an earlier version of the story we find in John 11 can be numbered on one or two hands. Some would call Crossan's argument pure fantasy, but as we have already stated, the real tragedy is such eccentric judgments lead scholars to ignore many of Crossan's other arguments, some of which are more worthy of close consideration. It is interesting that in his review of Crossan's book, Robin A. Scroggs points out that for all of Crossan's use of the apocryphal Gospels it does not appear that anything significant is gained by this procedure or added to Crossan's picture of Jesus.[63]

4. *The Quest for Rigor and Honesty.* Crossan at the outset of his work stresses the criterion of multiple attestation over all other criteria for identifying what Jesus is likely to have said. In this regard his approach would seem on the surface rather different from that of the Jesus Seminar, in which he plays a leading role. He also chooses to leave out any tradition, no matter how strongly he feels it may be authentic Jesus material, if it occurs only once in the Gospels. This leads to his jettisoning crucial material such as the parable of the good Samaritan, but it also gives his work at least the appearance of great scholarly rigor.

Crossan stresses early on, "I am concerned, not with an unattainable objectivity, but with an attainable honesty."[64] Yet surely Crossan *is* concerned with striving for *some form* of objectivity, or else an openly subjective, reader-response approach to the data would have sufficed, and we could have left off the book title *The Historical Jesus* altogether.[65] As Ben F. Meyer writes in his review of Crossan's book, honesty is not enough.[66] What we require is strenuous efforts to attain objectivity by scholars who should be at least as critical of themselves and their own presuppositions as they are of the Gospels and their authors. The quest for the historical Jesus is not just a quest to be honest about what one thinks about Jesus and why, it is a quest for the truth about Jesus and his words and deeds. Nothing less will do. In fact Crossan is being disingenuous in his disclaimer because at the end of the day he believes he *is* giving us a picture of the real and historical Jesus as a result of all his strenuous labors. He is not simply staring at an inkblot and stating what he thinks he sees in it.[67]

Jesus in His Social Setting and the Issue of Peasantry

The traditional disciplines of source, form and redaction criticism are far from the only approaches Crossan wishes to take to the text, even though he admits that any study of the historical Jesus stands or falls on how one handles the literary levels of the text.[68] Crossan wishes also to bring into play two other things: (1) crosscultural, crosstemporal anthropology and (2) Hellenistic or Greco-Roman history.

1. *Mediterranean History.* In part one of his book, entitled "Brokered Empire," Crossan seeks to sketch in broad strokes the macrostructure of the social world of the Mediterranean, providing a great quantity of data, some of it very relevant, some of it irrelevant or of little relevance to the situation in lower Galilee in Jesus' day. The most helpful of all the chapters is the first, entitled "Then and Now." Yet even here there is need for

caution and critical appraisal. In general one should be very wary of broad generalizations about "Mediterranean culture" when speaking not just about "now" but also "then," all the more so when "then" is two thousand years ago.

Consider for example Crossan's key quotation of D. Gilmore's listing of the sociocultural constants within "the Mediterranean construct."[69] These constants include (1) a strong urban orientation, (2) a disdain for the peasant way of life and for manual labor, (3) sharp social, economic and geographic stratification, (4) political instability, (5) a tendency to rely on the smallest possible kinship units (nuclear families), (6) an honor-shame syndrome involving both sexuality and personal reputation, (7) intense parochialism of the villages and intervillage rivalries and (8) belief in the evil-eye concept. In addition to these traits, in subsequent chapters Crossan goes on to talk about some first-century constants such as the system of slavery and patronage that made the Roman Empire work. How much of this is relevant to the situation Jesus confronted in lower Galilee?

First, as Goodman has pointed out, one cannot assume either class solidarity or the usual patronage system whereby the elite served as brokers to and for the less well-to-do.[70] Patronage certainly must have existed, especially among the elite and the retainers who kept company with or worked for Herod Antipas in Galilee, but it is very striking how little Jesus' parables ever refer to this sort of economic system. We hear a great deal about day laborers, sons who are heirs, small-time farmers, fishermen, women who worked in the home and occasionally of servants who have other servants in their debt, but in general Jesus' parables do not describe a "you scratch my back, and I'll scratch yours" world. It is a mistake to ascribe the sort of Greco-Roman patronage system we find in Rome or Corinth (or other Roman colony cities)[71] to lower Galilee. Yet Crossan quotes at length from Roman literature to convey the feel for the larger world in which Jesus lived.

Second, it is worth stressing that most first-century Jews, no doubt as a result of their Hebrew scriptural heritage, had very different ideas about slavery from those of most Gentiles. Jesus, unlike Petronius, tells no tales about rich freedmen who became wealthy after their masters died.

2. *The Eclipse of Jesus the Jew.* One of the salient flaws and omissions in this whole study is that Crossan, apart from dealing with Josephus and Philo, makes too little effort to examine the teachings of Jesus in light of early Jewish literature, much less in light of the Hebrew Scriptures. For

example, Crossan makes no significant comparisons between Jesus' parables and those of other early Jewish sages.[72]

With rare exception, the same can be said of his evaluation of the social and economic situation in Galilee. On the basis of archaeological finds from the period, Crossan admits that Nazareth must have been a very Jewish village in Jesus' day,[73] but he does not develop this insight. Rather he stresses that Nazareth was in the shadow of the major administrative city, Sepphoris, and therefore it must have felt the influence of the latter's Hellenized cultural traditions. This suits his Cynic proposal, which he introduces at the end of part one of this work.

While it is right to stress that small villages like Nazareth were in economic contact with the more significant urban areas and that lower Galilee was a small region[74] that was densely populated, it does not follow from any of this that the smaller Jewish villages were taking their main social or religious cues from the Hellenized cities Herod had built. Proximity does not necessarily connote strong influence. The diversity of response to the Jewish revolt in the 60s, with Sepphoris holding out for peace, unlike the other areas in lower Galilee, and the deep hatred shown by the more rural Galileans toward these cities during the revolt (cf. below) should warn us against assuming cultural homogeneity in this region.

In regard to Gilmore's previously cited list, we must note briefly that some of these points (e.g., the last three) are probably on the mark for lower Galilee, but some do not fit that setting at all. For example, negative attitudes toward manual labor and the peasant way of life certainly characterized Roman aristocrats and wealthy Gentiles in general and perhaps were true of the ruling elites in Palestine who aped the values of Greco-Roman society, but this was certainly *not* the view held by the Jewish populus, even where the simplest manual tasks were concerned.[75]

In addition, we may certainly debate how much political instability there was in lower Galilee in Jesus' day. While the situation was probably volatile,[76] there are no recorded examples of insurrection or tax revolt in the region during Jesus' youth and adult life, and Galilee did not change leaders during this entire period. Furthermore, as Crossan is forced to admit, Josephus does not indicate that banditry was a problem between about 30 B.C. and A.D. 30, the very period with which we are concerned.[77]

But Crossan, by painting with broad strokes the history of banditry from before and especially after the time of Jesus, seeks to set Jesus in a milieu where he must address situations and concerns that produced such banditry. This however begs the question of whether in Jesus' day peasants and the poor (or even Jesus) already saw themselves as pushed below the subsistence level such that they were ripe for revolt, be it social, political, religious or some combination of the three. We cannot assume that conditions in Jesus' day were the same as during the period A.D. 50-70.

By drawing on modern anthropological studies, Crossan is also sometimes guilty of anachronism and irrelevance. As Scroggs writes in his review of *The Historical Jesus:* "Mediterranean studies may be *au courant*, but it is not entirely clear . . . that they are always relevant to the time and space of the historical Jesus."[78] In fact it seems rather clear that much of the discussion about class struggle, Western European revolutions and Melanesian cargo cults sheds little light on the Jesus tradition.

3. *The Elusive Peasant Jesus.* Another troubling aspect of this whole section of Crossan's work is his failure to define early on what he means by a peasant. One is left wondering if he means someone who has no skills or trade. This does not fit Jesus. Does he mean someone who is actually or functionally illiterate? This also probably does not correspond with Jesus, for he is depicted in the Gospels as being able to read the Scriptures (cf. Lk 4). Does he mean someone with a small-town, village or farm mentality who cannot relate to the culture of larger cities? This does not seem to be an entirely accurate picture of Jesus. Does he mean someone who is a day laborer, a tenant farmer or a small farmer? None of these descriptions fits Jesus. Does he simply mean someone who is destitute or nearly so? This might fit Jesus on various occasions in his life, but it is a strange definition of the term *peasant.* A person who may be temporarily homeless and sometimes itinerant is by no means necessarily a peasant.[79] Indeed Crossan's beloved Cynics fit this description of homelessness and itinerant lifestyle, but calling them peasants seems hardly appropriate, especially if we are speaking of someone like Diogenes or, even much later, Dio.[80]

Finally Crossan does define peasants. They are the rural poor who are basically powerless but still control and cultivate the soil. They depend on markets in villages or towns to sell their crops, and, due to exploitation, for them money, power, security and safety are always limited.[81] But the definition fits Jesus so poorly in some regards, one wonders why Crossan insists on calling Jesus a Jewish peasant. Jesus did not live on a farm, did not cultivate the soil, did not try to eke out an existence from the land and was not land-bound, since his trade would have allowed him to work in a variety of places. Nor is there any evidence that he lived in relationships where he was oppressed by merchants or businesspeople who would not give him a fair price for his work. Finally, from all accounts he was far from powerless, being a person of the Spirit and a miracle worker.

If the reader feels he or she is being set up in this section for a Jesus who appears suspiciously like Gandhi (a leader of nonviolent social actions and revolt for lower-caste people), or the Jesus of the social gospelers of the early twentieth century, or even a countercultural Jesus like the hippie Jesus extolled in the 1960s in the United States, one has correctly intuited where some of Crossan's arguments are going.[82] The attempt to argue that Jewish peasantry was *a*, if not *the*, dynamic force in Jesus' movement is at best a half-truth.[83] Jesus seems to have drawn his most intimate circle of followers from a mixture of people, including fishermen, toll collectors, former Zealots, women, including some women that were relatively well off (like Joanna in Lk 8:3), and a variety of others. These followers were indeed mostly common people, but they were not mostly peasants, on the definition offered above. The evidence does not encourage us to romanticize about egalitarian peasantry either, especially in view of the way women seem to have been treated in first-century peasant societies, including those of Galilee.[84]

Responses to Rome

In part two, "Embattled Brokerage," Crossan paints a broad panorama of the Greco-Roman world and the Roman Empire's domination system as well as some of the general responses to it. He then focuses on Jewish responses to the imposition of Roman authority. The culmination (part three), as we have already seen, is Jesus' response to the situation. There are considerable merits to some portions of Crossan's long discussion of social, economic, political and religious matters in Palestine from about 100 B.C. to A.D. 70.

After carefully sifting through part two, one is impressed with the degree of Crossan's indebtedness to the models and results of Horsley's various sociological studies of Jesus' era. These studies are quite valuable at many points, and we will say more about them in a later chapter,[85] but for now it is important to note that Crossan, like Horsley, rejects what was for many years a standard theory: that prior to, during and after

Jesus' day, a Zealot movement existed. This thesis has been strongly defended by Martin Hengel and is still maintained by many scholars, but Crossan ignores their arguments throughout the book.[86] He suggests the idea was a fabrication of Josephus.[87]

Crossan rightly paints a picture of a wide variety of types of people who had influence on the Palestinian masses, ranging from prophets, to self-designated kings or messianic figures, to bandits, to charismatic holy men. With the exception of some of the bandits, who did not undertake their lifestyle for religious or spiritual reasons, this evidence shows that Galilee was subject to influence from people who could assert some sort of divine claim or religious power. The residents, weary of immoral and secularized rulers, looked to others for leadership, in particular to those who seemed comparable to the great religious figures of the Old Testament.

It may be, as Vermes and Crossan have suggested, that there was a long-standing tradition in the north, going back to Elijah and Elisha, continuing with Honi and Hanina ben Dosa, and with Jesus, of miracle-working holy men of independent and charismatic power and authority. If so, Galileans may have related to Jesus as this sort of person.[88] It may be no accident that the Synoptics, and especially Mark, paint a picture of a Jesus who does not wish to be confined by the label "miracle worker" but wishes to be known as a man of words and preaching. Perhaps he was seeking to outrun popular typecasting.

Jesus Revisited

Crossan's newest addition to the burgeoning list of Jesus books, *Jesus: A Revolutionary Biography,* deserves comment. This book is in many ways an improvement over its parent volume so far as the general reader is concerned. Crossan in this volume leaves out the bulk of his cultural analysis and anthropological background. The result reads much more like a biography of Jesus. A second improvement is that Crossan neither offers up a dismembered corpus of Jesus sayings, sprinkled heavily with seasoning from *Thomas,* nor, for the most part, overplays the importance of *Thomas* or the *Gospel of Peter.* Third, the book is more complete in that Crossan gives more effort to analyzing a broader selection of the Gospel data, including the birth narratives and the passion and resurrection narratives. Crossan says he has benefited from debates and reviews of his earlier work,[89] and there is reason to believe him. The claims are, on the whole, less outlandish, at least until his discussions of the death and resurrection stories.

1. *Problems New and Old.* This is not to say that Crossan's Jesus has been domesticated this time around. The portrait of Jesus is basically the same. What Jesus was really all about was free healing and open eating, and portions of the book are simply a condensation of the earlier volume. Unfortunately, the problems of anachronism and misappropriation of data continue, as the following examples will show.

In his analysis of the birth narratives, and in particular Matthew 1— 2, Crossan makes much of parallels between this narrative and material found not merely in Philo and Josephus but in a work entitled *sēpēr haz-zikrōnôt*, or "the book of remembrances." He argues that the story of Moses' life as told in that volume, and in the form in which it appears, is the model for Matthew's account.[90] Unfortunately for Crossan this document is a medieval Hebrew manuscript found in Oxford, and it contains a version of the Moses story that has no earlier attestation. If there is any likelihood of dependency here, it is surely the other way around, since the Gospel of Matthew, as is widely known, was the most popular and familiar Gospel in medieval times. But of course Crossan wishes to treat the birth narratives as simply legends without historical substance, literary compositions meant to introduce Jesus to the reader, and, in the case of Luke's Gospel, to place John in Jesus' shadow. When one is talking about a legend it is easy and sometimes necessary to look for fictional literary parents.

Crossan continues to apply non-Jewish models to Jesus' situation, and they do not seem appropriate. For example, he continues to make much of the notion that children were seen as nobodies in antiquity and that therefore when Jesus sets up a child as a model for the kingdom, he is advocating a kingdom of and for nobodies.[91] Greco-Roman views of manual labor are again enlisted in describing the social situation of Galilee, a procedure that is open to the same criticisms I discussed earlier.[92]

Crossan continues to base his conclusions on some very dubious, though familiar, assumptions: (1) that 95 to 97 percent of all the Jewish state was illiterate[93] (the very amount of evidence of literacy from papyri, potsherds, inscriptions, epitaphs and whole libraries like that at Qumran suggests this figure is erroneous); (2) that Jesus was illiterate, despite the fact that the only concrete evidence we have suggests the contrary (cf. Lk 4 to Lk 24); (3) that the *Roman* patronal network defined the way relationships worked in Galilee,[94] despite the fact that there was no significant

Roman presence in Galilee in Jesus' day, especially not in the small villages and towns Jesus frequented;[95] (4) that Jesus' family did believe in him and his power and were simply annoyed that he would not set up shop in his hometown and let them be brokers of his cures (an argument not only based on silence, but in fact running against the little evidence we do have on the subject, i.e., cf. Mk 3:21 and Jn 7:5); and (5) that we must see Jesus as a peasant.

2. *Jesus the Cyniclike Peasant.* But Crossan seems to have modified his position in light of the heavy criticism his "Jewish Cynic peasant model" has received since his first Jesus book appeared. In one of his more candid moments he admits:

> We have in the final analysis, no way of knowing for sure what Jesus knew about Cynicism, or whether he knew about it at all. . . . Maybe he had never even heard of the Cynics and was reinventing the Cynic wheel all by himself. But the differences as well as the similarities between Jesus and the Cynic preachers are instructive even if not derivative. Both are populists, appealing to the ordinary people; both are life-style preachers, advocating their position not only by word but by deed, not only in theory but in practice; both use dress and equipment to symbolize dramatically their message. But he is rural, they urban; he is organizing a communal movement, they are following an individual philosophy; and their symbolism demands knapsack and staff; his no-knapsack and no-staff. Maybe Jesus is what peasant Jewish Cynicism looked like. . . . What Jesus called the kingdom of God and what Epictetus might have called the kingdom of Zeus must be compared as radical messages that taught and acted, theorized and performed against social oppression, cultural materialism, and imperial domination in the first and second centuries.[96]

This is as much as to say that both Jesus and the Cynics were radicals of a sort who were somewhat similar in what they opposed but not at all similar in what they sought to construct. This being the case, there is no good reason to continue to call Jesus a Cynic, any more than we should call Spartacus a Cynic simply because of what he opposed.[97]

3. *The Radical-Egalitarian Historical-Critical Method.* I have wondered for some time why Crossan insists that Jesus did not choose an elite group of twelve male disciples[98] despite the fact that the Twelve are clearly attested in two independent traditions (i.e., in 1 Cor 15 and in the Gospels). Furthermore, why does he continue to insist, despite the majority

opinion of scholars, that neither the passion nor the resurrection narratives contain any significant historical data other than that Jesus died on the cross? Here again, traditions such as the Last Supper meet the criterion of multiple independent attestation.[99] Crossan's second Jesus book offers some insight into these radical conclusions. Behind them seems to lie the same logic that requires Crossan to insist that Jesus attacked the familial "axis of power" between parents and children.[100]

The reason, as I discern it, is that Crossan simply cannot bring himself to accept the idea of a Jesus who might not be politically correct on issues of egalitarianism, who might have attempted to reform rather than simply reject the standing patriarchal system of his day. Thus the idea that Jesus chose Twelve, much less that he reconstituted the Twelve after his death, must be rejected. The stories of Jesus' death and resurrection must be seen as fictions created by Mark and other early Christians in order to legitimate a hierarchical leadership structure already in place.[101]

This commitment to radical egalitarianism, since it calls for the rejection of the passion and resurrection narratives, also drives Crossan to insist dogmatically that if Jesus was buried at all he was buried by his enemies in a shallow grave and his body was likely unearthed by scavenging dogs ("Those who cared about him didn't know where he was buried, and those who knew did not care" is his aphorism on the matter). It also drives him to insist that the Last Supper did not take place, for even this might conflict with the cherished paradigm of "open commensality." "This is my body given for you" is about mediators and brokerage, and Crossan cannot accept the historical Jesus having anything to do with that hierarchical notion. It is this same cherished paradigm which causes him to deny any historical substance to the one ministry miracle of Jesus attested in all four Gospels, the feeding of the five thousand, for there Jesus uses his disciples as mediators of blessing and miracle for the masses.[102]

It is also the commitment to radical egalitarianism that causes Crossan to insist that Jesus used itinerancy as a tool to oppose brokerage. This requires that he reject the Gospel traditions that suggest that Jesus set up a home base in Capernaum, because if he did brokerage would result. No, Jesus must always be poor, always be traveling, always without a place to rest his head, rather like a wandering Cynic philosopher.

At this point it is worth recalling the fact that almost no destination of Jesus in Galilee was a full day's journey away from either Nazareth or Capernaum and that it would have been quite feasible to regularly return to a home base in either town. But this is unthinkable to Crossan, for "the equal sharing of spiritual and material gifts, of miracle and table, cannot be centered in one place because that very hierarchy of place . . . symbolically destroys the radical egalitarianism it announces. . . . Neither Jesus nor his followers are supposed to settle down in one place and establish there a brokered presence."[103] Thus Crossan must reject the idea of nonitinerant disciples of Jesus such as Mary and Martha, whose circumstances are multiply attested in Luke 10 and John 11—12.

We must agree with Crossan that Jesus associated with all sorts of people, even at the cost of violating the laws of purity, but there is nothing in this commitment that requires us to accept the implications Crossan draws.

Lest we hope for a more supernatural Jesus, Crossan is, if anything, in this latest book even more dogmatically against such an idea. There was no virginal conception (in fact 'almâh/parthenos is argued to mean a virgin just married and not a virgin of marriageable age),[104] no raisings of the dead,[105] no demons and hence no actual exorcisms,[106] and indeed there are no miraculous healings of disease: "I presume that Jesus, who did not and could not cure that disease or any other one, healed the poor man's illness by refusing to accept the disease's ritual uncleanness and social ostracism."[107] Jesus was a therapist who could offer healing of the social and psychological effects of disease but could not deal with the physical aspect of the problem. But which is more difficult to say, "Thy mind is healed," or, "Thy body is well"?[108]

We have already noted that for Crossan the resurrection stories tell us "nothing whatsoever about the origins of Christian *faith* but quite a lot about the origins of Christian *authority*. They tell us about power and leadership in the earliest Christian communities."[109] Crossan then posits that Paul is the one responsible for setting up the idea of resurrection appearances as the normative basis of the Christian community and Christian leadership.[110] While Crossan admits that the disciples abandoned Jesus when he was taken captive, he does not think this led them to abandon hope or faith in him, nor that it required an Easter event to renew their faith.

Rather, there were Christians who relied on Jesus' power and presence both before and after his death and simply continued to do so. Crossan envisions Galilean peasants having a very different form of Christian community, one based not on the death and resurrection of Jesus but on his sayings (the ever elusive Q community, for which we have no historical evidence).[111] "What happened historically is that those who believed in Jesus before his execution *continued* to do so afterward. Easter is not about the start of a new faith, but about the continuation of an old one. . . . It is a terrible trivialization to imagine that all Jesus' followers lost their faith on Good Friday and had it restored by apparitions on Easter Sunday."[112]

In a recent and telling critique of Crossan's (and Borg's) Jesus, Leander E. Keck of Yale, who himself has written about and studied extensively the various quests for the historical Jesus, concludes that we are in essence receiving modern romantic notions superimposed on the historical Jesus:

> For Crossan (and to some extent Borg), the Jesus of history was the center of a Galilean Camelot, the halcyon days when Jesus and his band roamed the countryside, disregarding societal structures, defying hierarchical patterns, irritating elites and confounding the powerful, creating a grass-roots movement with nobodies while at the same time refusing to be its leader or mediator of the New because that would be brokering the kingdom. Ironically, the brokerless Jesus is himself thoroughly brokered by this biographer.[113]

Readers must decide for themselves which is trivialization—to believe in a Jesus who looks and sounds more like the Jesus of the *Gospel of Thomas* than the Gospel of Mark, a nonmessianic Jesus of "miracle and meal" who nonetheless performed no *actual* physical miracles and certainly never rose from the grave, but who nevertheless spawned a movement that has lasted two thousand years, *or* to believe that if Christ did not rise the church would never have existed at all.

For my part, I do not for a minute believe that the Gospel writers were badly mistaken when they concentrated half or more of their Gospels on the last week of Jesus' life. Nor do I doubt that most if not all that Jesus said or did prior to Passover week would have been long forgotten if it had not been for the events of that week.[114] Nor do I doubt that Acts has it right when it insists that the early Christian preachers focused on the death and resurrection of Jesus and, like Paul, rarely quoted Jesus' parables or aphorisms so far as we can tell.

In the end we are entirely justified in being cynical about the Cynic Jesus, in doubting most of the *Gospel of Thomas*, and in placing more weight on the variety of New Testament witnesses to the character of Jesus and his movement and their explanation of why the movement continued after the crucifixion of the carpenter of Nazareth.

CHAPTER 4

JESUS, MAN OF THE SPIRIT

This chapter deals with *three related proposals for understanding Jesus as a man of the Spirit, one who was very intimate with God, who saw visions and received revelations "in the Spirit" and who experienced the Spirit's power and used it to heal and cast out demons. We will focus on the work of Marcus Borg,[1] but we will also discuss the work of Geza Vermes,[2] who takes the view that Jesus was a Galilean ḥᵃsîd, a charismatic Jewish holy man, noted for his prayer life that produced dramatic results. Borg's proposal is seen to have some merit, though it only tells a part of the story, as even he admits. Under close scrutiny Vermes's proposal of Jesus as ḥᵃsîd proves to have some serious flaws. In particular, the material about Honi and other such figures is found in the Talmuds and other Jewish literature that comes from a much later time than the Gospel material. In addition, the ḥᵃsîdîm do not seem to have been particularly associated with Galilee, and they were extremely observant of Torah in a way that Jesus does not seem to have been. As a counterpoint to Borg and Vermes we will look at the more narrowly defined contribution of Graham H. Twelftree,[3] who also stresses Jesus and the Spirit, particularly in his role as an exorcist. We begin by discussing a significant feature of some of the more publicized portraits of Jesus: a noneschatological Jesus, or at least a Jesus who had little interest in futurist eschatology.*

THE NONESCHATOLOGICAL JESUS

One of the clear trends among Third Questers is to deemphasize the eschatological nature of Jesus and his message. This may be observed not only in the proposal of a Cynic Jesus but in others as well, and it is so evident that Marcus Borg can speak of the breakdown of the old consensus of an eschatological Jesus.[4] How is it that a variety of scholars reached such a conclusion? Should it be seen as a reaction to the enormously influential work of Albert Schweitzer,[5] Johannes Weiss and William Wrede, who in the early twentieth century put the eschatological Jesus back in the center of scholarly discussion? Or is it perhaps an attempt to salvage a Jesus to whom moderns can relate, one who does not bear the stigma of mistaken eschatological hope?

As early as 1987 Borg was speaking of "An Orthodoxy Reconsidered: 'The End-of-the-World-Jesus,' "[6] though at that time he found the "end-of-the-world-Jesus" to be well entrenched in scholarly orthodoxy. In his most recent essay on the subject (1994), however, he proclaims the breakdown of the old eschatological consensus.[7] In Borg's case at least one might be tempted to trace his views to his scholarly mentor, George B. Caird of Oxford.[8] Yet this would not be an entirely correct interpretation of Caird.

What Caird was combating, as I understand him, was the Jesus of Schweitzer, Jesus the apocalyptic seer who was convinced of and proclaimed that the end was *necessarily imminent*, due to occur during or shortly after his own lifetime. On this score I would quite agree with Caird: the ghost of *that* Jesus needs to be laid to rest once and for all.[9] However, there is no need to throw out the eschatological baby with Schweitzer's apocalyptic bath water. The options are not limited to Schweitzer's Jesus the apocalyptic seer and a noneschatological Jesus.

Borg first argues that the fruitful sociological studies of Jesus and the Jesus movement by Gerd Theissen, Richard Horsley and others[10] have generally led to a picture of a Jesus who intended the transformation of Israel, not the preparation of a community for the imminent end of the world.[11] This conclusion, as Borg himself admits, does not require us to abandon an eschatological Jesus. Eschatological seers can also be reformers, even if they believe the end is near at hand, as some at Qumran seem to have thought.

The more crucial basis for Borg's argument has to do with the rejection of the authenticity of any of the future Son of Man sayings (e.g., Mk 14:62). Though this argument is not unusual, it is in many ways extraordinary, for it requires one to hurdle several major obstacles.

First, various sayings of Jesus about a future coming Son of Man meet the criterion of dissimilarity. Early Jews before or during Jesus' day seem not to have envisioned a *coming* of the Son of Man. The closest one gets is in the *Parables of Enoch*, but there Enoch goes on a heavenly journey and is himself identified with, or as, the Son of Man. There is no emphasis on the eschatological *coming* Son of Man in that material.[12] If we turn to the non-Gospel canonical literature, we look equally in vain for evidence of proclaiming the coming of the Son of Man. Paul never mentions the phrase *Son of Man*. In Acts we do hear about a heavenly Son of Man (Acts 7:56), as we do in Revelation (cf., e.g., Rev 1:13-16, where it is a matter of an analogy), but not about his future coming to earth as the Son of Man. A search of the rest of the non-Gospel canonical literature does not provide us with any strong hints that the coming Son of Man was a key or regular feature, or even a rare but noteworthy component, of early Christian theology.

What Borg and others must argue is that this emphasis on the coming Son of Man, particularly in Matthew and Mark, is the result of the Evangelists' editorial activity. In other words, these Evangelists added eschatological emphases to a rather noneschatological Jesus tradition. This argument of course has the strength that it cannot be completely disproved, since we do not have access to the teachings of Jesus except through the Gospels. Beyond that evidence we must speculate. But we should remember that the general course of development in early Christian theology was from a more Jewish and eschatological message to one that was less Jewish and eschatological.

Second, the claim must be substantiated that even if Jesus did use the phrase *Son of Man*, it had little or nothing to do with the eschatological material in Daniel 7 and in the *Enoch* literature. *Son of Man* must be reduced to a casual form of indirect personal reference, an oblique synonym for "I" or perhaps a generic term meaning "one" or "a person like myself."

Certainly there are authentic Son of Man sayings that focus on Jesus' "present" ministry, but it is well argued that the reason Jesus felt free to use *Son of Man* in this way was that he saw God's eschatological activity already occurring in and through his ministry. He saw himself as the agent bringing that activity into his Galilean world. Thus even in the "present" Son of Man sayings, the context of Daniel 7 stands in the background. It is surely significant that the *only* place in the Hebrew Bible where the motifs of Son of Man and kingdom of God appear *together* is in Daniel 7, and these are the two most frequent and important phrases (and, we would argue, theologically loaded phrases) in the Synoptic Jesus tradition.

Third, it should surely be an obstacle for Borg and others that future

Son of Man sayings as a *general* category meet the criterion of multiple attestation. They are found, for example, in Mark, Q and special M material, to mention but three sources. This ought to be taken seriously, for multiple attestation is seen by almost all scholars as a *key* criterion for establishing authenticity. Yet this too is swept aside by those who argue for a noneschatological Jesus.

Borg in his earlier essay works through what he calls the Synoptics' "threat" material, including four important sayings from Q that speak of final judgment (Lk 10:12/Mt 10:15; Lk 10:13-14/Mt 11:21-22; Lk 11:31/ Mt 12:42; Lk 11:32/Mt 12:41). If even one of these sayings is accepted as authentic, it shows that Jesus did have eschatological concerns and spoke about the final judgment. Borg is willing to allow this conclusion, but he stresses that these sayings do not speak of judgment as *imminent.* This is true, but I would add that even the coming Son of Man sayings do not have to be read as proclaiming a *necessarily* imminent end, only a *possibly* imminent one. In other words, Borg in the end is willing to allow that Jesus may have had an eschatological message, just not the sort that Schweitzer imagined. I would agree, but then Borg has given up his argument for a totally noneschatological Jesus.

More attention must be given to Mark 13:32: "But about that day or hour no one knows, neither the angels in heaven, nor the Son, but only the Father." It is quite unbelievable that the early church would have fabricated this. And if this one saying is authentic, it can only mean one thing: Jesus did not proclaim that the end was *necessarily* imminent. At most he could only have spoken of its possible imminence, something which I believe he did do.[13]

Borg realizes, of course, that if the future Son of Man sayings didn't come from Jesus, he must explain where they originated. His theory is that Easter, the resurrection of Jesus, is what led the early church to invent future Son of Man sayings. This however is a very weak argument. It is true enough that early Jews who believed in resurrection saw it as an eschatological event. But belief in the rising of the dead from their graves, so far as the Jewish evidence goes, does not suggest that they ever thought of it as implying the coming of a Son of Man from heaven.

If Borg is right that there was little speculation about the Son of Man prior to or during the time of Jesus and that Jesus never clearly addressed the matter, it is hard to understand why the church would have created the idea even after Easter. Daniel 7 is a difficult text. In fact, in the view of many readers, it seems to speak of a Son of Man going up into the presence of God, not of a Son of Man coming down to earth.[14] This is certainly how the *Enoch* literature takes it. It is the Jesus tradition that interprets the Danielic Son of Man in fresh ways.

At the end of the day, the one fully adequate explanation for the unique sayings of the future, coming Son of Man material is that Jesus actually spoke along these lines and that this was remembered by the early church after Easter and recorded in the Gospels, despite the fact that it might, and apparently did, lead some Christians to the erroneous conclusion that Jesus had spoken of a necessarily imminent end. To be fair, Borg finally is willing to concede that Jesus may have had some sort of eschatological message, but he says it was not central to his thought.

Once the point about eschatology is conceded, however, there is no reason to think that Jesus could not have used the Son of Man material in ways at least partially similar to what we find in other Jewish eschatological literature such as *1 Enoch* or the later material in *4 Ezra*.[15] In fact, I believe that the Daniel 7 material was foundational for Jesus' understanding of who he was and what God wished him to do and proclaim.

Finally, contemporary discussion of the end-of-the-world language in the Synoptic Gospels raises the issue of whether Jesus meant the end of *the* world, or simply the end of *his world as it was*. It is true enough that some of the material in Mark 13 speaks of the "birth pangs," or events preliminary to the destruction of the temple-centered world of early Judaism. In these instances the annihilation of the cosmic order is not being signified, but rather the end of a particular world order.

But the coming of the Son of Man for judgment is said to be heralded and accompanied by cosmic signs (darkened sun and moon, falling stars, shaking of the powers of heaven, Mk 13:24-25) and leads to the gathering of the elect "from the four winds, from the ends of the earth to the ends of heaven" (Mk 13:27). One is hard pressed to regard this simply as apocalyptic embroidery of coming "earthshaking" events in Jerusalem. And while this language does not imply the total destruction of the world, much less of the universe, it does entail a cosmic end.

Thus on the whole one must say that Jesus, like various other early Jews and early Christians (cf. Dan 7—11; Is 60—66; Rev), believed that ultimately not just the world order as he knew it but the world itself and all its inhabitants would be radically changed when God chose to bring human history to a close. Within the Jewish worldview this would mean a radical transformation of *the* world, which includes human beings, and thus the language of *end* is appropriate when speaking of Jesus.

JESUS AS SPIRIT-FILLED PERSON (MARCUS BORG)

Charisma and Charisma

Webster's New World Dictionary defines *charisma* as "a special quality of leadership that captures the popular imagination and inspires unswerving allegiance and devotion."[16] This is perhaps the most common way the term is used in English-speaking cultures, with the focus on a person's *qualities*. The term however has a long history. It is originally a Greek word which Paul and others use to mean literally "a grace *(charis)* gift," "a gift from God" (cf. 1 Cor 7:7). In the Third Quest for the historical Jesus the term has been used with yet another nuance, one that draws on sociological and anthropological insights.

In this latter context *charisma* means a social relationship, not an attribute or mystical quality of individual personality, involving a situation in which a leader strikes responsive chords in his or her audience, acting as a catalyst to convert latent feelings and ideas into actions by the audience.[17] This definition is helpful in that it emphasizes the relational aspect of charisma: one has it or is perceived to have it in relationship to others. It involves one's *effect* on other people. While not minimizing this social side of charisma, in this chapter we will be focusing more on the source of that charisma in Jesus' life, in particular what it means to say he was a man of the Spirit.

According to Marcus Borg, Jesus should be seen as an example of a well-known type of religious personality. A "Spirit person" has two primary defining traits: (1) he or she has vivid and frequent experiences of another level of reality, the realm of God or of the Spirit, to such an extent that we might call this person a mystic or a visionary, and (2) by virtue of these experiences this person becomes a channel or conduit through whom the power of God or the Spirit flows into our mundane lives. Characteristically such persons are healers, and they have a deep and personal relationship with God. As Borg puts it, they not merely believe in God, they know God in their own experience.[18] Thus Jesus, unlike other early Jews, used the word *abba*, a term of personal intimacy that a child used with a father, when he addressed God. In a culture where one avoided even saying God's name, but instead used circumlocutions (e.g., "I swear by heaven" instead of "I swear by God"), this would probably have been viewed as shocking familiarity with the Almighty.

Borg has rightly complained that too often in modern Western civilization beliefs in another world or a spiritual realm, as well as claims about visions, dreams or miracles, are largely ignored or explained in purely psychological terms.[19]

But the reality of the other world deserves to be taken seriously. Intellectually and experientially, there is much to commend it. The primary intellectual objection to it flows from a rigid application of the modern worldview's definition of reality. Yet the modern view is but one of a large number of humanly constructed maps of reality. . . . To try to understand the Jewish tradition and Jesus while simultaneously dismissing the notion of another world or immediately reducing it to a merely psychological realm is to fail to see the phenomena, to fail to take seriously what the charismatic mediators experienced and reported. For many of us, this will require a suspension of our disbelief.[20]

I think that this model of understanding Jesus sheds important light on an aspect of who he was and is certainly preferable to the "magician" model.[21] For one thing, we have concrete evidence that the early followers of Jesus had such spiritual or "mystical" experiences (cf. 2 Cor 12:1-7 and the entire book of Revelation, especially Rev 1:10-12: "I was in the spirit [or *Spirit*] on the Lord's day and I heard . . . and I saw"). There is no reason to assume such experiences began with early Christians.

Indeed, as Borg suggests, we have signs that Jesus had such experiences as well. For example, in Luke 10:18 Jesus speaks of seeing Satan fall like lightning from heaven, and a careful reading of Mark 1:9-11 suggests that on the occasion of his baptism Jesus saw and heard things others did not. We may call both of these experiences apocalyptic visions if we like, but they show Jesus was in contact with another realm or world.[22] On the occasion of his baptism, by means of contact with the realm of God, Jesus' identity was confirmed and his life-task set, and he was empowered to undertake the tasks God had in mind for him.[23]

Yet it must be added that while this picture does seem to capture something true about the historical Jesus, it does not account for all that we learn about him. Borg realizes this, and so he supplements the image of Jesus as a Spirit person with several other models, namely, that Jesus was a subversive sage (a teacher of alternative wisdom), a radical social prophet who strongly critiqued the purity and domination system of his culture and a movement founder, one whose purpose was not to try and start a new religion but rather to transform Judaism. But one senses that for Borg the first proposal underlies and undergirds the last three. What his work shows, I think, is that any one model for characterizing Jesus is likely to be inadequate, a fact which makes his proposals much stronger than those like Crossan's that focus on only one paradigm.

The Politics of Holiness

Borg's earliest work, *Conflict, Holiness and Politics in the Teachings of Jesus*, is a technical and more scholarly monograph than his subsequent works, and it is in this volume that some of his most important work comes to light. What this first volume shows, as N. T. Wright has observed,[24] is that Jesus' prophetic words clearly had a political dimension. A great deal, though not all, of what he foresaw and spoke was in regard to the end of *a* world, the world of temple-centered early Judaism, not the end of *the* world, with cosmic signs and wonders. In short, much of the eschatological material in Mark 13 and elsewhere was for Jesus about events that would transpire within the short term, a forty-year span (a generation), and would include the destruction of the temple and apparently much of Jerusalem as well (cf. Mk 13:30). Jesus saw these imminent events as the judgment of Israel's God on unfaithful Israel, and he sought to establish a new and transformed Judaism. Jesus then was indeed political, not in the sense of being a Zealot seeking to stir up a military revolt but in the sense that much of what he said about Israel's future and its heart, the temple, would have been seen by Jewish leaders as a threat. Such prophecies eventually led to Jesus' execution.

Borg sees Jesus as opposing the purity systems of his Jewish world because they set up a we/they conflict in early Judaism between Jews and Gentiles, including the Romans. This system of exclusive holiness also set Israel up against the diseased and outcasts among the Jews. This meant that Jesus necessarily came into conflict not just with the Zealots, who wished by force to cleanse the land of unclean Gentiles, but also with the Pharisees, who had a different holiness agenda.[25] Borg sees Jesus as advocating the practice and politics of mercy as the true form of holiness, in contrast with establishing holiness by ritual cleansing and drawing lines between clean and unclean people.

This is a strong proposal that explains a great deal of the Jesus tradition, but by no means all of it. While Borg admits that Jesus probably did say some things about the end of the world, in particular about a last judgment,[26] he does not think that Jesus spoke of a coming Son of Man, a parousia, especially not one that could possibly be imminent. In addition Borg argues:

In all likelihood, the pre-Easter Jesus did not think of himself as the Messiah or in any exalted terms in which he is spoken of. Second, we can say with almost complete certainty that he did not see his own mission or purpose as dying for the sins of the world. Third and finally, again with almost complete certainty, we can say that his message was not about himself or the importance of believing in him.[27]

Since we will later have occasion to deal in detail with the suggestions that Jesus was a social prophet and a Jewish sage,[28] we will confine our remarks here to the more distinctive of Borg's proposals. First, only a small amount of the Jesus tradition suggests that Jesus was what we might call a mystic. The evidence suggests that at certain key junctures in his life (baptism, transfiguration), Jesus had such visions, but it is a mistake to paint him as a sort of Julian of Norwich or, for that matter, a John of Patmos. The fact is, the Jesus tradition does not carry that much apocalyptic imagery, though there is plenty of eschatology, both of the already and the not-yet variety. In short, the Spirit-person model provides *a* window on who Jesus was and how he lived his life during his earthly ministry, but it by no means tells the whole tale.

Second, we have already spoken in this chapter about the limits and problems entailed in a noneschatological Jesus or, perhaps better said in Borg's case, a Jesus for whom eschatology is all a matter of things realized in his own lifetime or shortly thereafter. As we have argued, the idea of the coming of the Son of Man appears, though in slightly different forms, in a variety of sources. I do not think this material can be dismissed. A more balanced approach to Jesus' eschatology is necessary, including recognition of the already and the not-yet dimension of Jesus' eschatology. In other words, Jesus did indeed speak of the end of the world, but quite naturally he spoke of it in conjunction with the end of the temple-centered world of early Judaism. For him, the two events were connected, for they would both be brought about by God the Savior and judge of the world.

Finally, while Borg affirms numerous aims and actions of Jesus—mediating the Spirit, starting a movement to reform Judaism, cleansing the temple, seeking to do away even with Torah-sanctioned approaches to holiness—he denies that this suggests an exalted self-consciousness or any sort of messianic self-understanding. If Jesus was indeed a social prophet, subversive sage, movement and community founder and Spirit person, it is difficult to see how Jesus would *not* have had an elevated sense of his identity. In particular, if we insist on Mark 1:9-11 as a portrait of an experience Jesus actually had, there is no reason to dispute that he could have believed himself to be God's Son, in some sense destined for a special purpose on this earth. Surely his distinctive use of the term *Abba* also reinforces this picture of his self-understanding.

Furthermore, with all that Borg maintains is true about Jesus, how could Jesus not have seen himself in messianic terms, *especially in view of the fact that other comparable figures in first-century Palestine with less distinguished qualifications saw themselves in that fashion?* Why should we think that the Samaritan, or later Theudas or the Egyptian, (all known to us through Josephus[29]) had a higher or more exalted self-concept than Jesus, when they undertook less impressive actions and yet saw themselves in messianic terms?[30] In short, Borg's portrait of Jesus is accurate as far as it goes, but it is inadequate to explain important parts of the Jesus sayings tradition, and especially many of Jesus' actions.

Meeting Jesus Again

Aware of some of these shortcomings in his earlier work, Borg seeks in a more popular work, *Meeting Jesus Again for the First Time*, to explain further what he means, without shifting paradigms. This particular book is more confessional in nature, beginning as it does with a recounting of his own spiritual pilgrimage, from a conservative Lutheran background to alienation from the Christian faith and to a return to the church, but now with a very different image of Jesus. From the outset of this book Borg seeks to drive a wedge between having a personal relationship with and experience of Jesus or God and believing certain things about him. This leads to a further dichotomy between a Jesus who advocates compassion and a Jesus who makes moral demands.

Behind all of this lies a fundamental conviction that the Christ of faith and the Jesus of history are by and large very different, if by *Christ of faith* one means the Son of God who came and died for our sins on the cross and rose again from the dead. For instance, we hear repeated statements like, "The contrast between the Synoptic and Johannine images of Jesus is so great that one of them must be nonhistorical. Both cannot be accurate characterizations of Jesus as a historical figure."[31] This of course requires that Borg denude the Synoptics of all christologically focused passages or nuances, declaring them later accretions to the Jesus tradition. Doubtless, the Jesus of the Jesus Seminar does not match up with the Jesus of the Fourth Gospel, but then the Jesus Seminar deliberately chose not to play with a full deck of Synoptic playing cards. Yet it must be admitted that there are *some* arguably authentic passages in the Synoptics where Jesus sounds very much like the Johannine Jesus (e.g., the Q material found in Mt 12:25-27 and parallels).[32]

Compassionate Jesus

It becomes clear in this latest book that Borg sees compassion as so central to Jesus' teaching that it is categorically impossible to contemplate a Jesus or even a Paul who might demand moral purity. For example, in one of the more risqué parts of the book, Borg contemplates a Paul who might have said, in the spirit of the radical and compassionate Jesus, "In Christ there is no gay or straight." This of course flies in the face of what Paul actually does say about homosexual behavior in texts like Romans 1:24-32 or Galatians 5:19-21,[33] and there is nothing in the Jesus tradition even remotely like this.[34] Instead we hear startling teaching about being a eunuch for the sake of the kingdom (Mt 19:12), a teaching that unquestionably implies sexual purity.[35]

Let us consider the claim that compassion was the central characteristic of Jesus to the neglect or even denial of various demands for moral purity. The basis for this claim rests on Luke 6:36, which parallels Matthew 5:48. Borg quite naturally prefers the Lukan form of the saying, which speaks of being compassionate, as opposed to being perfect, especially since the latter might carry a connotation of moral purity. In other words, only one version of this saying takes the form "Be compassionate," and Borg dismisses the other form as an example of Matthean redaction since "the use of the word *perfect* is a demonstrable characteristic of Matthew's redaction."[36] The same, however, could be said for the concept of compassion in Luke's Gospel, for he has more stories and sayings about God's compassion than any other Gospel (cf., e.g., Lk 15). In other words, using Borg's logic, there is no reason to prefer the Lukan form of the saying over the Matthean, since in both cases the concept involved is a favorite one of the Evangelist. More importantly, using the standard historical criteria for authenticity, the saying "Be compassionate" is much more poorly attested than various teachings of Jesus about moral purity.

Consider, for example, Jesus' teachings about marriage, divorce and adultery (the pericope on divorce has been called "the best attested tradition in the gospels").[37] Here we find material that appears in a variety of forms and sources, not only in the Sermon on the Mount but also in Mark 10 and parallels, as well as being partially attested in 1 Corinthian 7. By all normal historical criteria the authenticity of Jesus' teaching on marriage, divorce and adultery is more secure than the saying "Be compassionate." These teachings reveal a Jesus who at the very least intensifies the demands for sexual purity found in early Judaism and limits sexual expression to the context of husband and wife within marriage. Of this pericope Borg has nothing to say, and we might wonder whether it is because it conflicts with his view that Jesus, in his advocacy of compassion, was opposed to purity systems of all sorts.

I would maintain that Borg has made the classic error of mistaking the part for the whole. Clearly Jesus did set aside, or at least saw as no longer applicable in light of the coming dominion of God, the laws about ritual cleanness and uncleanness (cf. Mk 7).[38] It does not follow from this that he rejected all demands for holiness or purity. Rather, I would suggest that Jesus substitutes a more strenuous moral holiness system for one that includes both ritual and moral dimensions. This is precisely why Jesus fell into conflict with various Pharisees—both offered new visions of holiness, and they were to some extent conflicting visions. Had Jesus really been an advocate of what Borg suggests, an ethic that makes few or no demands about sexual behavior, he would not merely have been in debate with the Pharisees, he would have been at war with them.[39]

As do the members of the Jesus Seminar, Borg tends to wrench certain sayings, particularly aphorisms, from their literary contexts and make them say something very different from what the Gospel author had in mind. Consider, for example, Borg's handling of Matthew 23:9: "And call no one your father on earth, for you have one Father—the one in heaven." Borg argues, following some feminist scholars, that this saying "may very well be directed against the patriarchal family."[40] There are several problems with this conclusion: (1) if Matthew understood the saying in that sense, it is unlikely that he would have included it in his Gospel, since elsewhere he portrays Jesus as one who is concerned with honoring parents (cf. Mt 15:1-6),[41] and (2) the context of Matthew 23:9 has to do with teachers (cf. vv. 8 and 10), whom we know were sometimes called *abba*, or "father," by their disciples.[42] Jesus is suggesting in Matthew 23:8-10 that teachers should not be called *rabbi* ("my great one"), or *abba*, or even "teacher," and in particular that his own followers should avoid such titles being applied to themselves. Jesus' sensitivity about appellations of regard for teachers is clear from elsewhere in the Jesus tradition (cf., e.g., Mk 10:17).[43] In other words, all the contextual indicators suggest that it is highly unlikely that Matthew 23:9 had anything to do with members of the physical family at all.

Another example is Borg's misreading of the parable of the prodigal son (Lk 15). He wishes to see the story as a parable about the religious life that is opposed to the conventional wisdom about duties, requirements and rewards. It is seen as a story about compassion that makes no such requirements but simply accepts the son as he is.[44] While no reasonable reader would deny that compassion is a major feature of this parable and an important characteristic of God as envisioned by Jesus, this parable is not about accepting what is unclean or immoral in the son's life. Indeed, the parable is about the son's *turning* from such a lifestyle and *returning* to the father and the family he had left behind. The son's full contrition is evident in his cry when he returns, "Father, I have sinned against heaven and before you" (Lk 15:21).

It is the recognition of his state and his need for change that enabled the son to make the return in the first place, and it is hard to doubt that the father's acceptance of the son implies a recognition of this contrition, for the father says that the son was lost but now is found (v. 24). How very different the parable would have looked if, for example, the son had come home and brazenly requested a job or more funds so he could continue his dissolute lifestyle. But Borg wishes to offer us a no-fault religion as the essential teaching of Jesus, and this requires a rejection of traditional readings of various parts of the Jesus tradition.

Is then the parable in Luke 15 a rejection of the traditional wisdom that faithfulness, loyalty or hard work is rewarded by God? Consider how the parable ends. Borg argues that the elder son represents the voice of conventional wisdom, and to some extent I think this is correct, but what is crucial is the father's response to the elder son. He does not say, "You've got it all wrong, your long service and faithfulness are meaningless and have gained you nothing." Instead he says, "You are always with me, and all that is mine is yours" (Lk 15:31). That is, he is no more rejected than is his brother; both are implored to partake of the banquet. In short, compassion is important, but it does not cause the Father to reject the value of faithfulness or hard work.

The Sacred Center of Existence

More disturbing than these attempts to reread the Jesus tradition in light of modern notions of compassion or fairness is what Borg says about the nature of God. In Borg's view,

> God does not refer to a supernatural being "out there" . . . [r]ather . . . God refers to the sacred at the center of existence, the holy mystery that is all around us and within us. God is the non-material ground and source and presence in which . . . "we live and move and have our being."[45]

One may be forgiven for concluding that this sounds altogether very similar to what we hear from modern advocates of New Age philosophy. God as a power or force or source of energy that suffuses all things is substituted for God the personal and transcendent Being who created the universe and all that is in it.

Borg apparently does not go as far as New Age philosophy, which affirms pure pantheism or the deity of the individual, for he argues that God is *more* than everything and is not to be identified with any particular thing. What he does want to say however is that "everything is in God."[46] In other words, he wishes to deny the sense of God as "Holy Other" and affirm a God who is around and within us all, apparently without regard to our beliefs or behavior.[47]

At the heart of Borg's affirmation is the experience of the sacred in nature, human and nonhuman. This, in his view, seems to be the essence of having a relationship with God. Beliefs and behavior requirements are for those who only experience a secondhand or second-level faith.[48] But if true religion amounts to only experience and does not also include understanding and belief, how can one tell the difference between a heart-warming experience and heartburn? What would count as a bad or even evil experience? Borg provides no answer to these sorts of questions.

When God is depersonalized, the possibility of a real relationship with God is removed. If God is an "it" or a "force," the possibility for an "I-Thou" relationship is eliminated. We cannot pray to a ground of being and expect a personal response or dialogue in the way the Bible envisions between God and God's people.

For Borg there is no such thing as a definitive revelation of God, only a collage of metaphorical images (both within and without the Christian tradition), none of which can be taken literally. Thus, for example, calling God *Father* does not really say anything definitive about God because, Borg argues, God could also be called *Sophia*, and, after all, these are all human approximations born out of human culture.[49]

Whatever else one may say about the flat denial of the possibility that there might be a God who gave a definitive revelation to some group of people, it certainly eliminates the need for accountability to any one sacred book or set of sacred traditions. Individuals are free to pick and choose as they wish. Truth claims rarely enter the picture, because the possibility of Truth with a capital *T* has been ruled out from the start. This sort of a priori means that Borg is far removed from Jesus and his early followers, all of whom seem to have manifested a clear belief not only in the concept of divine revelation but in the definitive revelation of God's divine character in the Hebrew Scriptures in sayings like, "Be holy, as I am holy."

We should be immediately suspicious of any portrait of Jesus that suggests that Jesus might have been an advocate of modern notions of relativism.[50] One thing is clear about the message of relativism, if it is accepted any particular message quickly becomes passé, outdated, irrelevant and unimportant, rather like the passing fads of modern pop culture.

Yet at the end of the day, Borg does not really fully wish to plunge into the abyss of complete relativism. He does not really want to say that there is no timeless truth to be learned about Jesus as a person and as a teacher. In fact, the ostensible reason for writing *Meeting Jesus Again for the First Time* is to suggest otherwise, indeed to urge others to go on pilgrimage and find and even experience Jesus.

If one is going to argue that contemporary faith should indeed be based on the historical Jesus, then in the end one must be very concerned about truth claims, in particular about what Jesus really said, did and was like. At points Borg is downright dogmatic about what Jesus really did or didn't say or do, or what he was like, especially when it comes to the issue of compassion, or Jesus as a Spirit person.

Once we admit to the possibility of the quest for truth, we have also admitted to the nonviability of the gospel of relativism, for truth by its nature is particularistic. It means affirming this rather than that about Jesus. And, not incidentally, it involves affirming some things about God and rejecting others. One cannot have faith without beliefs any more than one can have truth without particularism.[51]

Borg's portrait of Jesus, like Crossan's, is deliberately provocative and evocative, and he is to be commended for reminding us of the spiritual dimension of Jesus' life. Unfortunately, too many aspects of Borg's presentation rest on both questionable exegesis of crucial texts and equally questionable a priori assumptions about the nature of God, truth and the like. It is now time to turn to another, and in some respects less shocking, portrait of Jesus as a Spirit person.

JESUS THE HASID (GEZA VERMES)

Geza Vermes is on any showing an interesting figure in the historical Jesus debate. Having begun life as a Catholic in Eastern Europe, Vermes eventually recognized he was of Jewish origins and in due course returned to the faith of his ancestors.[52] How much this transformation affects Vermes's evaluation of Jesus is difficult to say, except that it is clear that he attempts to place Jesus in a category that says something less about Jesus than Christians have traditionally wanted to assert. Vermes's heuristic category for Jesus is that of the Galilean holy man, or hasid (ḥᵃsîd).[53] A hasid was a pious Jew who as a charismatic figure worked wonders and operated outside the channels of usual religious power and authority. The basis for establishing hasid as a "type" is the material found in the Talmuds about Hanina ben Dosa and Honi the Circle Drawer.

There are problems with this approach in several regards: (1) As Crossan points out, a hasid, according to later rabbinic literature, was an ultra-pietistic person of prayer known for ethical and ritual works of supererogation. He was the ultrastrenuous observer of the law: the Pharisaic vision of what a person of true piety looked like. On this showing neither the revered Honi the Circle Drawer nor Hanina ben Dosa nor Jesus should be called members or forerunners of the hasidim; rather, they were all known as miracle workers.[54] (2) Though it is true that sonship language is used of Honi, who was a first-century B.C. figure, it is not the same sort of sonship language as is used of Jesus.[55] Honi is called a "son of the house," which, though connoting closeness to God, has no such messianic overtones as has the sonship language in the Synoptics. (3) Vermes's discussion of the abba material[56] is also inadequate.

All of the hasid evidence as we have it is clearly later than the New Testament, and in none of this material do hasids address God as abba as Jesus does. The most promising example Vermes can produce, *Targum* of Malachi 2.10, involves not a *ḥᵃsîd* but the Davidic king being told he would call on God as *abba*. If we are to follow the lead of this example, it suggests, not that *ḥᵃsîdîm* would or did pray to God using *abba*, but rather that a messianic figure, a king who was thought to be in a special sense God's son, would be able to do so. As I have said elsewhere, "This text, if it is early, would lead us to precisely the opposite conclusion from Vermes's that various people of Jesus' era likely addressed God as *abba*. On the contrary, this text could suggest that Jesus' use of *abba* counts as evidence that he saw himself as the Davidic Messiah!"[57] Equally important, it is an argument from silence to maintain as does Vermes that the use of *abba* of God comes from lower-class Palestinian piety. We have no evidence of ordinary Jews addressing God or praying to God as *abba*.[58]

Perhaps the heart of Vermes's case is the argument that Jesus was the sort of miracle worker that Honi and Hanina were. He pictures "Jesus curing the sick and overpowering the forces of evil with the immediacy of a Galilean holy man."[59] On the one hand, Vermes is perhaps right that Jesus would not have been seen as a professional exorcist, for there is no evidence he used incantations or magical formulas like those attributed to King Solomon.[60] But on the other hand, it is also true that two of the things which Vermes sees as characterizing the miracles of a *hasid* do not seem to have been characteristic of Jesus, namely the use of prayer in producing the cure and the performance of miracles of rainmaking. We have no evidence of Jesus being asked, or of his performing, the latter activity at all, and the evidence of the former is scant. One may perhaps point to John 11:41-43, but it is striking how in the Synoptics evidence of prayer before healing is absent. In particular, as Graham H. Twelftree points out, prayer seems never to have been part of Jesus' technique of exorcism.[61] Furthermore, exorcism is a prominent feature of the Synoptic portrait of Jesus, but it is rare at best in the material we have about Hanina and his kin (but cf. *b. Pes.* 112b).[62]

As Vermes points out, Jesus' miracles, which manifested his charismatic authority, seem to have been one of the main factors which set him at odds with the Pharisees. The Pharisees were probably irritated by Jesus' lack of expertise or at least his lack of interest in halakic matters and his willingness to share table fellowship with a variety of unclean people, including harlots and tax collectors.[63] If one admits however that Jesus had little interest in halakic matters, matters of the legal expansion of the

Torah to include new customs and commands, then one has classified Jesus as a non-*ḥᵃsîḏ*, for *ḥᵃsîḏîm* were certainly interested in the law and its expansion in Halakah.

One of the more interesting possibilities that Vermes raises is that because Elijah was a northern prophet who was also a rainmaker and miracle worker, it would have been natural for some in Galilee to understand Jesus, Honi or Hanina in light of this greatest of all northern prophets. This might explain why, on the one hand, Mark records that some were speculating about Jesus and his relationship to Elijah (Was he Elijah returned? [Mk 8:28]; Why did he call on Elijah from the cross? [Mk 15:35]) and why Jesus seems to have deliberately attempted to reapply such speculation to John the Baptist (cf. Mt 11:18; Lk 7:27 and Lk 1:17). What Matthew 11:18 suggests is that Jesus did not want to be identified as, or in the line and tradition of, Elijah. If there was a connection between Elijah and the *ḥᵃsîḏîm*, Jesus by disassociating himself from the former may have disassociated himself from the latter as well.

A more detailed and telling critique of Vermes's proposal has now been offered by John P. Meier.[64] Meier's critique is twofold: (1) at the level of methodology which Vermes uses, and (2) at the level of the substance of the argument. We will deal with both objections at once.

Meier argues strongly that Vermes fails to apply the same sort of critical approach to the Jewish sources that he applies to the Gospels. For example, Vermes tends to rely on the much later evidence about Honi and Hanina found in the Talmuds and less on what Josephus or the Mishnah says. In fact, many key aspects of Vermes's presentation depend on data that is only found in the later sources, and these sources are historically suspect on several grounds. For example, only Honi is mentioned in Josephus's *Antiquities* (book fourteen), and there it suggests only that Honi was a powerful man of prayer whom God responded to by giving rain. As Meier stresses, there is a difference between a person of prayer and a miracle worker, and there is nothing in this early material that suggests Honi should be seen as a miracle worker. The material in Josephus also suggests that he was from Jerusalem and not Galilee. Furthermore, Honi's fame is related to one particular incident in his life, not to a pattern of behavior.

From the end of the second or beginning of the third century A.D., we have a Honi tradition, now found in the Mishnah, that elaborates the basic story: Honi at first prays and gets no response, then he draws a circle and tells God he will not move until he gets rain. When rain comes it is in small quantities, and Honi complains until he gets the major rainstorm he needs (cf. *m. Ta'an.* 3:8). This is the only so-called miracle story about a pre-A.D. 300 religious figure in the Mishnah. But strictly speaking, this is not a miracle story, and nothing whatsoever is said about Galilee. What we find in the Babylonian Talmud version of this story is that Honi is domesticated and turned into a proper rabbi. Not only is he called rabbi in *b. Ta'an.* 23a, but his action of drawing a circle is defended as being in accord with Torah, and the Sanhedrin confirms his action. In other words, the tradition has undergone "rabbinization," having been embellished in fictional ways.

Meier is right in any case to stress that these traditions are quite late, since Honi lived in the first century B.C. Even Josephus was writing over one hundred years after Honi's day, and the Mishnah is dated over one hundred years later than Josephus. This should be contrasted to the mere forty or so years between Jesus' life and the composition of the earliest Gospel, Mark. Meier concludes of Honi that "[t]here is no basis in the early tradition for constructing a Galilean charismatic miracle-worker."[65]

This leaves us with the data about Hanina ben Dosa, who seems to have been active before A.D. 70 but not before or during the time of Jesus.[66] This is an important point, as it means that whatever else one can say, Jesus was not following in his footsteps. Josephus does not mention Hanina, the first reference appearing in the Mishnah (*'Abot* 3:10-11 and *Sota* 9:15). In the former text, Hanina is already called rabbi, and we have some sayings, though Hanina is not presented as one who debated or ruled on legal or halakic matters. In *Sota* 9:15 Hanina is called one of the "men of deed," which could mean miracle worker, but as Vermes admits, it could also mean one who performed acts of compassion (cf. *Ber.* 5:5). Since the context of the reference in *Sota* is about moral character, one would naturally expect the reference to be to exemplary ethical actions.

Most important is the text in *m. Ber.* 5:5, where we read that Hanina knew when someone would be healed or not by whether the prayer was fluent in his mouth. The text does not claim that Hanina's prayer has any special ability to heal, only that when he prayed he could know the outcome in advance by how and whether his prayer was flowing and fluent. What is miraculous then is Hanina's special knowledge that came with prayer, not his prayer per se.[67]

It is of course true that in the later Talmudic material (cf., e.g., *b. Ber.*

34b) all sorts of miracles are said to have been performed by Hanina, but most scholars recognize these as legendary, a later generation's attempt to build up the reputation of Hanina, perhaps in competition with the increasingly influential Gospel traditions. It is rather amazing how uncritical Vermes can be at times, even relying on very late traditions from the eighth or ninth century A.D., material in the *Pirque Rabbi Eliezer*, to fill out the evidence for some of Hanina's sayings. This is why Meier concludes, "Ultimately, Vermes' acritical use of sources undermines his whole argument."[68]

Even the evidence that Hanina was from Galilee is not found in any sources earlier than the Talmuds. The most one could argue about Hanina with historical probability is that as a Palestinian Jew who lived in the mid to late first century A.D., he was well known for his prayers on behalf of the sick and his miraculous knowledge of whether one or another would be healed of an illness.[69]

Meier's conclusion is that "beyond the fact that around the turn of the era there existed two Jews in Palestine named Honi and Hanina, both of whom were famous for having their prayers answered in extraordinary ways, nothing definite can be said."[70] In short, Jesus cannot be fit into a preexistent type of a Galilean charismatic or hasidic miracle worker. Only Hanina *may* have been from Galilee. Neither Honi nor Hanina appear to have been miracle workers, but rather were men noted for their effective prayer life. Neither fits the later definition of a ḥᵃsîḏ.

In conclusion, Vermes has not presented a compelling case for seeing Jesus as essentially like a Hanina ben Dosa or a Honi the Circle Drawer, who are said to be representatives of lower-class Galilean piety. There is simply too much of the arguably authentic Jesus material that does not fit this portrayal. On the other hand, we would not dispute either that Jesus was a miracle worker, or that he addressed God as *abba* and had an intimate relationship with the Father, or that his authority was charismatic and immediate, not being derived from his education or training in Torah and Jewish customs.

JESUS THE EXORCIST (GRAHAM H. TWELFTREE)

Graham H. Twelftree's analysis of Jesus provides a needed corrective for those who are tempted to ignore the exorcism material in the Jesus tradition. Jesus' exorcisms are attested in various layers and sources of the Gospel material, including the earliest material found in Q and Mark.[71] As Twelftree points out, the extracanonical data, including non-Christian data, are in agreement with the Synoptics that Jesus was a powerful and successful exorcist, though there is disagreement in the non-Christian material about whether or not the source of this power was the biblical God (cf. Mk 3 and *b. Sanh.* 43a, where the latter says Jesus was killed for practicing sorcery). There is also the evidence from the Greek magical papyri, where Jesus' name is used in an exorcism formula: "I adjure you by the God of the Hebrews Jesu" *(PGM* IV. 3019ff., cf. IV. 1227).

Twelftree ably demonstrates that while there are unique features in the stories about Jesus' exorcisms (including the absence of mechanical devices, no explicit prayers or power or external authority invoked to bind the demon),[72] there is more than sufficient evidence to show that Jesus was one among a variety of early Jewish exorcists. In particular the material in Josephus about Eleazar the exorcist *(Ant.* 8.46-49), the story of the sons of Sceva (Acts 19:13-19), the Gospel tradition of anonymous exorcists (Mt 12:27; Lk 11:19) and the evidence from Qumran in the *Genesis Apocryphon* (1QapGen col. 20), as well as a variety of material from *1 Enoch, Jubilees,* other Qumran data and Philo, provide clear enough evidence to set Jesus in a particular Jewish context. Within the Jewish tradition exorcism was especially linked to Solomon and his wisdom, in this case wisdom about secret and magical formulas by which one could perform an exorcism. As we shall see later in this book, Jesus presented himself as a sage and as Wisdom, and in that context it is not surprising that he also performed exorcisms, for "one greater than Solomon is here" (Mt 12:42; Lk 11:31).[73]

Other important conclusions reached by Twelftree include the fact that exorcism stories have not been appended to the Gospel tradition nor are the present exorcism stories in the Synoptics rewritten in the light of other such stories.[74] The exorcism stories lie in the earliest layers of the Gospel material. It is noteworthy that in the latest of our Gospels, the Fourth Gospel, we find much emphasis on Jesus' miracles, especially in the so-called book of signs (Jn 1—12), but no presentation of Jesus as an exorcist. This may serve to confirm the impression that the early church was not in the business of inventing stories about Jesus as a Jewish exorcist but rather tended to downplay or omit reference to this aspect of his ministry, perhaps because it made Jesus susceptible to charges of sorcery or even necromancy.

Perhaps the most important of all of Twelftree's conclusions is that Jesus, in distinction from other early exorcists, explicitly connected exorcism with eschatology. "It was he who associated the notion of the cosmic, supernatural battle against the kingdom of Satan in the eschaton with the very act of an ordinary exorcism. Satan was being defeated and the coming of the kingdom of the [sic] God was taking place in his exorcisms (cf. the parable of the Strong Man)."[75] The tradition found in Matthew 12:28 and Luke 11:20 ("But if it is by the Spirit/finger of God that I cast out demons, then the kingdom of God has come to you") provides strong evidence for this conclusion. Exorcisms are seen not merely as a foreshadowing but as a manifestation of the inbreaking of God's dominion in and through Jesus' ministry.

When Matthew 12:28/Luke 11:20 and the little parable of binding the strong man (Mk 3:27 and parallels) are given their due weight, it becomes difficult, if not impossible, to argue for a noneschatological Jesus. For to admit that Jesus was an exorcist and offered an interpretation of his actions along the lines suggested in these early traditions leads not only to the conclusion that Jesus believed he lived in the eschatological age, but also that he considered himself an eschatological figure bringing God's Dominion into the midst of God's people.[76] "The unique and unprecedented aspect of Jesus' exorcisms is that he gave profound meaning to a relatively ordinary event of exorcism."[77] It is also important to point out that the Q saying of Matthew 12:28/Luke 11:20 indicates that Jesus performed his exorcisms by the power of the Holy Spirit, as would his followers. Thus in his exorcisms Jesus can indeed be seen as a man of the Spirit.[78]

Twelftree goes on to argue that Jesus, like other early Jews, believed that there were two stages to Satan's defeat: first the binding of Satan and liberating of his captives and then the destruction of Satan.[79] This implies that while Jesus believed he was inaugurating the eschatological age, the coming of God's dominion or reign on earth, there would also be an ongoing period of time in which exorcisms would be necessary, prior to Satan's final destruction. In short, while the dominion had *in part* come, this was only the beginning of the end, and the timing of the close of the age was not specified. There was still considerable time for both ministry and mission, not only for Jesus but also for his followers, whom the record suggests also performed exorcisms.

CONCLUSIONS

After a review of the problems with attempts to come up with a non-eschatological Jesus, we have concentrated in this chapter on images of Jesus as a Spirit person. We have seen both the promise and the problems of such images. Borg's picture of Jesus as a visionary has a good deal to commend it, yet it provides only a small window on Jesus and is based on too little evidence to be the basis of an overall picture of what Jesus was like. Vermes's attempt to portray Jesus as a *hasid* is based on a misuse of the rabbinic *hasid* category which on the whole does not suit Jesus. That Jesus was a charismatic, miracle-working Galilean with an intimate relationship with God does not make him a *hasid*, a Jew devoted to Torah piety and scrupulous observance of the law and of Halakah. Vermes is quite right however to emphasize both the Jewishness of Jesus and his conflict with the Pharisees, not least because of his miracle-working activity *and his interpretation of it.*

Twelftree helpfully sets Jesus in the context of other early Jewish exorcists and the literature about them and even more helpfully shows how Jesus uniquely connects his exorcisms with the coming of God's dominion on earth. Here is another piece of evidence that a noneschatological Jesus will not do. Yet Twelftree too quickly dismisses the possible messianic overtones of these traditions and inadequately analyzes their connections with Wisdom traditions about Solomon. We will return to these matters toward the close of this study.

Here it is sufficient to point out that while it is accurate to call Jesus a Spirit person, a charismatic holy man or an exorcist, this is only a partial explanation of the Gospel evidence about Jesus. Even confining ourselves to the best-attested miracle traditions, there are more nonexorcism miracle stories than there are exorcism stories. Interpreters must avoid the pitfall of mistaking the part for the whole in attempting to portray Jesus. Like studying a portrait from only a few inches away, one may adequately view and describe in detail one part of the canvas, say the cheek of the person portrayed, but that is hardly a satisfactory description of the whole. In the quest for the historical Jesus, all of the arguably authentic evidence must be used in order to adequately describe the Jew from Nazareth.

CHAPTER 5

JESUS THE ESCHATOLOGICAL PROPHET

Not all the images of Jesus being proffered in the Third Quest are nontraditional. In fact, the pictures painted by E. P. Sanders and Maurice Casey bear striking resemblances to the Jesus of Albert Schweitzer, the eschatological prophet or seer. Even within these parameters, however, there are notable differences between Sanders and Casey, for instance, as to whether Jesus had significant controversies with the Pharisees, the meaning and implications of Jesus as a friend of sinners and the meaning of Jesus' action in the temple that helped precipitate his death. Sanders stresses that in order to make sense of Jesus' words they must be related to certain "facts" about his life. Casey puts considerable stress on the Markan data and thinks that Jesus did see his death as in some sense an atoning sacrifice. Both Sanders and Casey are willing to entertain the notion of Jesus as some sort of messianic figure, with Sanders speaking of Jesus as God's last envoy or viceroy and Casey of the one who undertook to fulfill the Baptist's predictions about the Coming One. In each case, however, the social dimensions and implications of Jesus' teaching are not fully appreciated. And while there is much to be gained in understanding Jesus as an eschatological prophet, the notion that he advocated a restoration theology and considered the end to be necessarily imminent are problematic.

FOR SOME MODERNS THE WORD *PROPHET* CONJURES UP AN IMAGE OF SOMEone who is all talk and little action. Yet among the Old Testament prophets we discover some prophets who seem to have been less talk and more action, and political action at that. Whether we think of Elijah confronting the prophets of Baal, Samuel anointing a king, Amos proclaiming the doom of the northern kingdom or Joel warning of a coming judgment of God, Israel's ancient prophets acted, gestured and spoke in what we would call the political arena. We would be hard pressed to find a prophet whose message was "purely spiritual." Herod Antipas was only reacting like previous nervous monarchs when he imprisoned and then executed John the Baptist.

One of the most enduring images of Jesus in Christian history is that of Jesus as a prophet. A recent book on this very subject concludes as follows:

The historical Jesus resists attempts to modernize him. He was not a modern capitalist intoning the values of individualism and free enterprise, nor was he a modern socialist calling for a bureaucratic state. He was not a militarist who believed the sword can make the world safe for his values, nor was he a pacifist who thought conflict must be avoided at all costs. He was not a freedom fighter who believed that justice can come only through violence, nor did he turn aside from the struggle for human dignity because politics is a dirty business. He was not a champion of modern women's rights, nor did he promote male power and prerogative as the bastion of civilized values. He was not a racist, hating Gentiles as foreigners, nor was he a world citizen who knew all people to be the same underneath a veneer of cultural difference. He was not a secularist who tried to establish separation of politics and religion, nor was he a fundamentalist who wished to impose a narrow, doctrinaire tradition upon all members of society. He did not intend to be the savior of the world; he intended to be a good Jew, faithfully following the path of conscience inspired by tradition and by the fresh presence of God. Above all else, he was a prophet in word and deed. He did not curry favor with the wealthy and powerful in order to garner their support for his reform movement. Neither did he pander condescendingly to the poor in order to use them in his enterprise. Like true prophets of the past, he fearlessly proclaimed God's will as he saw it, letting offense or approval be the result of his message, not the shaper of it.[1]

There is a good measure of truth in this assessment, though I would not agree with all the author suggests. Thus we must look carefully at the idea of Jesus the prophet, an idea that has a very ancient pedigree.

The Gospel writers are in agreement that at least some Jews saw Jesus as a prophet even during his ministry (cf. Mk 8:27-30 and parallels). The Gospel traditions also suggest that Jesus alluded to himself as a prophet on more than one occasion (cf. Mk 6:4; Lk 13:33). Yet, strangely, when we examine the Jesus tradition itself, we find an overwhelming amount of evidence suggesting that *prophet* is too limited a term to *fully* describe Jesus.

For one thing, exorcisms are not predicated of any of Israel's prophets, nor of John the Baptist for that matter. Then, while some prophets had followers (e.g., Elijah), they do not by and large seem to have sought out disciples. Finally, most of Jesus' sayings come in the form of aphorisms, riddles and parables, all of which are forms of wisdom speech. Though prophets apparently told parables on occasion (cf. 2 Sam 12:1-7), we find not a single instance of Jesus proclaiming, in prophetic fashion, "Thus says the Lord." He seems to have spoken on his own authority, not merely as the mouthpiece for God.

But there are still plenty of scholars who argue that *prophet* is the term most descriptive of Jesus and his ministry. I wish to stress at the outset that there is a rather large range of what *sort* of prophet Jesus is thought to be. On the one hand, in the work of E. P. Sanders we find a Jesus who is an eschatological prophet, frankly not very political and certainly not a revolutionary of any sort. He is more of an advocate of restoration theology. To this image we may compare the somewhat similar description in the work of Maurice Casey.

On the other hand, a variety of scholars, most notably Gerd Theissen and Richard Horsley, are very insistent that Jesus should be seen as a radical social reformer, if not a revolutionary subverting the existing order in various ways.[2] Some refrain from suggesting Jesus was a revolutionary but certainly see him as a social reformer, as the quote above from R. David Kaylor's book suggests. We will examine each of these major orientations in turn, beginning with the highly influential work of Sanders and following with a discussion of Casey's work. We will reserve the discussion of Jesus as a social prophet for the next chapter, where we will examine the views of Theissen and Horsley and look at the recent work of Kaylor entitled *Jesus the Prophet*.

JESUS THE JEWISH PROPHET OF ISRAEL'S RESTORATION (E. P. SANDERS)

Prior to the appearance of Crossan's *The Historical Jesus* no recent scholarly work on Jesus has had more impact in North America than E. P. Sanders's *Jesus and Judaism*. When it appeared in 1985[3] it was immediately hailed as an important study in the field and won the coveted Grawemeyer Award in Religion and a national book award.[4] It has now been followed by a more popular though substantive volume entitled *The Historical Figure of Jesus*.[5] One of the main reasons Sanders's work has received plaudits from both Jews and Christians is that he is a widely acknowledged expert in early Judaism, having published many studies about aspects of early Jewish life, practice and religion, including landmark volumes on Paul and early Judaism.[6] Thus Sanders is well equipped to evaluate whether and in what way Jesus might have fit into his Jewish environment. In Sanders's view, a non-Jewish Jesus is a non sequitur, a historical improbability, and thus the only real question is: What sort of Jew was he?

Unlike Crossan and the Jesus Seminar, Sanders approaches the search for the historical Jesus not by beginning with the sayings traditions in the Synoptics but with certain indisputable or nearly indisputable "facts" about the life of Jesus. This is in part because Sanders does not have the same confidence Crossan and others do that we can readily get back to the earliest layer of the sayings tradition by using criteria such as dissimilarity or double attestation.

The Facts of Jesus

Nevertheless, unlike Crossan, Sanders has a basic confidence in the reliability of the Gospels. They tell us a good deal about the historical Jesus: "We should trust this information unless we have good reason not to do so; that is unless the stories in the Gospels contain so many anachronisms and anomalies that we come to regard them as fraudulent."[7] It is worth setting out at this juncture Sanders's list of "facts," which vary a bit from the earlier work to the more recent one:

1. Jesus was born about 4 B.C., near the time of the death of Herod the Great (only listed in HF).[8]

2. Jesus spent his childhood and early adult years in Nazareth, a Galilean village (only listed specifically in HF).

3. Jesus was baptized by John the Baptist (both *HF* and *JJ*).

4. Jesus called disciples (both *HF* and *JJ*).

5. Jesus spoke of their being twelve (specifically listed in *JJ*).[9]

6. Jesus confined his activity to Israel (specifically listed in *JJ*).

7. Jesus taught in the towns, villages and countryside of Galilee (apparently not the cities) *(HF)*.

8. Jesus preached "the Kingdom of God" *(HF)*.

9. About the year 30 he went to Jerusalem for Passover *(HF)*.

10. Jesus engaged in a controversy over the temple *(JJ)*, and created a disturbance in the temple *(HF)*.

11. Jesus had a final meal with his disciples *(HF)*.

12. Jesus was arrested and interrogated by Jewish authorities, specifically the high priest *(HF)*.

13. Jesus was executed by the Romans outside Jerusalem *(JJ)* on the orders of the Roman prefect Pontius Pilate *(HF)*.

14. Jesus' disciples fled *(HF)*.

15. Jesus' disciples "saw" him after his death (in what sense is not certain) *(HF)*.

16. As a consequence they believed he would return to found the kingdom *(HF)*.

17. They formed a community or identifiable movement *(JJ)* to await his return and sought to win others to faith in him as God's Messiah *(HF)*.

18. At least some Jews persecuted at least some parts of this new movement, a persecution which seems to have lasted until near the end of Paul's career *(JJ)*.[10]

Two things may be observed immediately from this list. The list has grown from the earlier to the later volume, though there are no major changes or retractions, and, secondly, items fourteen through eighteen focus on the disciples' reactions to what happened at the close of Jesus' life. It is worth noting that Sanders sees as almost indisputable facts two things which Crossan dismisses: the selection of the Twelve and the Last Supper. This is not accidental, for Sanders is much more inclined than Crossan to believe that Jesus had a specifically Jewish view of life and was an observant Jew in regard to feasts and, at least to some extent, even purity laws (cf. below).

What cannot be deduced from the list of facts, but becomes clear in reading the two volumes, is that one of the major assumptions of Sanders is that Jesus was indeed an eschatological or even an apocalyptic prophet, who, as Schweitzer thought, saw the end as necessarily imminent and probably involving the destruction of the temple. This affected all of Jesus' teaching and ethical advice. Sanders is of the old German school on this matter.

In both volumes Sanders places a great deal of weight on Jesus' action in the temple as revealing what he was really about, who he thought he was, and perhaps most importantly, why he ended up on the cross.

The other side of this conviction is that Sanders does not really think the Pharisees had anything to do with Jesus' demise and he doubts the historicity of the polemical debates between Jesus and the Pharisees as recorded in Mark. Even more controversial than this last view is Sanders's argument that *sinners* in the Synoptics means the truly wicked, not merely the nonobservant Jews or "the people of the land," and that Jesus, unlike his predecessor John, associated with them and offered them places in the kingdom *without requiring repentance*. It will be useful at this point to flesh out some of Sanders's major points in each volume.

The Restoration of Israel

One of the strengths of Sanders's presentation is that he is not satisfied with simply establishing this or that about Jesus but believes and seeks to demonstrate that "there was a causal connection . . . a substantial coherence between what Jesus had in mind, how he saw his relationship to his nation and his people's religion, the reason for his death, and the beginning of the Christian movement."[11] In other words, he does not subscribe to the view that Jesus was a radical social reformer (for instance, an antipatriarchalist), who was so badly served and poorly interpreted by his followers that the Gospels deliberately obscure his real character in favor of a later, more domesticated image. He does not subscribe to this view because it does not make sense of Jesus in his Jewish setting,[12] nor does it explain why the church arose and took on the character it did.

Sanders is apt to side with Jewish over against Christian scholars on the issue of Jesus and the law:

> Those who presumably know the most about Judaism, and about the law in particular—Jewish scholars—do not find any substantial points of disagreement between Jesus and his contemporaries, and certainly not any which would lead to his death. Christian scholars, on the other hand, seem to have become increasingly convinced that there was a fundamental opposition between Jesus and Judaism and the opposition was *intentional* on Jesus' part.[13]

Sanders finds too much anti-Semitism, or at least anti-Judaism, in Christian scholarship, and he is skeptical of interpretations of Jesus that tend in such a direction. My own view is that while on the whole Sanders is right to be skeptical about non-Jewish Jesus proposals, such as the Cynic

Jesus model, he has gone too far in the other direction, denying the points where Jesus stood out from his Jewish matrix. The difficulty for any historian is in achieving the right balance between Jesus' continuity and discontinuity with early Judaism. Insist on too much discontinuity, and it becomes impossible to explain why Jesus had an exclusively Jewish following during his lifetime and why so many different kinds of Jews were interested in giving him a hearing. Insist on too much continuity, and differences of the church from early Judaism, even in the church's earliest days, become very difficult to explain.

In his earlier work Sanders begins his real discussion of Jesus with the event in the temple.[14] He regards it as definitely a prophetic symbolic gesture, not a real but feeble effort to cleanse or destroy the temple. But what does it symbolize? Sanders takes it as a symbol of attack or destruction of the temple system of Jesus' day, but with a view to its proper restoration. Jesus is seen as a prophet of restoration theology, a prophet of the coming judgment but also the coming new age, who predicted that God would destroy the temple in order to raise up a new one in its place. Sanders points to early Jewish evidence that such an idea of a new temple was extant in early Judaism, citing the *Temple Scroll* from Qumran.[15] The interpretation that the temple event was a "cleansing" is firmly rejected in favor of eschatological expectation:

> We can see that Jesus' work fits into eschatological expectation, not reform. Thus there is *no* context for understanding the symbolic action as "cleansing." Contemporary Judaism would not expect "cleansing" from an eschatological prophet or teacher; and nothing which is reliably attributed to Jesus points towards cleansing.[16]

Having sketched the Jewish background out of which eschatological restoration theology could come, Sanders stresses that early Jews who reflected on such matters regularly looked for the restoration of the twelve tribes of Israel.[17] It is into this matrix that Jesus' choice of an inner circle of twelve disciples fits. This choice reflects Jesus' commitment to restoration theology, and not just restoration of some Jews, but, as the number twelve suggests, restoration of "all Israel" in the coming eschatological action of God.[18] This argument makes considerable sense. I myself have argued that the choice of the Twelve was not for them to *be* Israel, but rather to *free* Israel. They were Jesus' emissaries to all Israel, not an alternative community that would turn its back on most Jews and be satisfied with a righteous remnant theology.[19]

Agent of the Kingdom

Certainly one of the most controverted aspects of Sanders's reconstruction is his conclusion that Jesus, unlike John, does not seem to have called Israel to national repentance in view of the coming eschaton, even though that was common in Jewish restoration theology. He dismisses the Markan summary of Jesus' preaching in Mark 1:15 and parallels, and the three other substantial passages that suggest that Jesus, like John, called for repentance on a large scale (cf. Mt 11:21-24 and parallels; Mt 12:38-42 and parallels; and Lk 13:1-5). Nor does he regard as authentic the notion that Jesus proclaimed a judgment which would weed out the unworthy within Israel.[20] He is equally convinced that not only did Jesus not call for repentance and a return to the law as a means for preparing for the end and restoration, but he also "did not look for a political and military restoration."[21] The question then becomes, What did Jesus mean by the coming kingdom of God?

Sanders argues that Jesus uses the phrase pervasively but that it is difficult to determine what exactly, beyond a reference to the ruling power of God, Jesus had in mind.[22] He concludes that it is probable that there is both a present and a future referent in Jesus' phrase "kingdom of God," and that in the present it seemed to mean that God's eschatological power was at work in the world, "but that the time would come when all opposing power would be eliminated, and the kingdom of God in a somewhat different sense would 'come'—be ushered in."[23] The temple demonstration and probably also the exorcisms show that Jesus believed he was God's agent, that God's power was working in and through him on behalf of this kingdom.

More specifically, Sanders insists that Jesus gave a good deal more weight to what was going to happen than to what was already happening in his ministry. In essence, "Jesus looked for the imminent direct intervention of God in history, the elimination of evil and evildoers, the building of the new and glorious temple, and the reassembly of Israel with himself and his disciples as leading figures in it."[24] The disciples thought concretely enough about this kingdom to ask about their places and roles in it, perhaps especially since they as Twelve symbolized the restoration of Israel.[25]

What role then did miracles play in Jesus' ministry? It could be argued that miracles drew the crowd and that Jesus then used the occasion to proclaim the coming of the kingdom of God.[26] More probable, in Sanders's view, is that Jesus and his followers saw in his miracles evidence of his status as a true spokesperson of God, one who spoke and acted with divine authority.[27] The miracles led to the conclusion that Jesus was not just a teacher, and they are compatible with the view that he saw himself as an eschatological prophet.[28] I would go further and argue that Jesus believed that in both word and deed he was bringing in the kingdom through his ministry, though there were still crucial events yet to take place before one could say the kingdom had fully come.[29]

Frankly, I find Sanders's discussion of miracles, like Crossan's, rather frustrating. He argues that some of the claimed miracles are based on exaggeration (a psychosomatic illness is seen as something more, and thus the cure is seen as miraculous), some on wishful thinking, and a few, but only a few, on the conscious wish to deceive![30] He also argues that those "miracles" that actually happened are things that we cannot yet explain because of ignorance of the range of natural causes, because of lack of scientific knowledge.[31] Presumably, then, in Sanders's view those actual miracles that Jesus performed were simply manipulations of presently unknown natural causes.

These explanations may work for some of the exorcisms, or some of the unverifiable illnesses (a person with an internal problem), but they certainly do not explain things like the healing of the blind, or of the deformed, or of those with impurities of the skin and the like, and it certainly does not explain the raising of the dead, which is one of the best and most frequently attested motifs in the Gospels. If Jesus did not really heal these people, then when they went to report to the authorities it would surely have been obvious to them that the person was not well. If on the other hand he did heal them, are we to attribute to Jesus a scientific knowledge of cures and *natural* healing principles that have escaped other doctors in the last two thousand years? Is it not easier to believe that perhaps God does intervene in human lives in ways we would call miraculous? In view of how little we know about our universe, do we really know that nothing can happen without a "natural" cause?[32]

Sanders is much more helpful when he distinguishes between miracle and magic.[33] He points out that miracle workers were charismatic individuals who in performing mighty deeds relied directly on God or God's Spirit or power, or on their intimate connection to God through prayer.

Magicians were different; they followed rules. Magic was based on a particular application of a widespread view: that there was a Great

Chain of Being in which everything is linked to something else, both above and below it. The manipulation of certain common elements (e.g., garlic, goat's urine and grass) would influence the Beings next higher on the Chain, and so up the entire Chain to the deity. The correct manipulation of the lower elements, together with the right incantations and the use of the right names, would make the higher deity perform one's desires. Magicians were for hire.[34]
Jesus by contrast was not for hire, and he bypassed the chain altogether and went directly to the source, performing miracles by the power of the Spirit resident in him.

Welcome to Sinners

Certainly the portion of *Jesus and Judaism* that has caused the most debate is chapter six, where Sanders's interpretation of the term *sinners* and his understanding of Jesus' relationship with the Pharisees come to light. In Sanders's view *hamartoloi* ("sinners") has as its background the Hebrew *rešāʿîm*, which means "the wicked," those who sin willfully and in a major way and do not repent. The negative corollary of this argument is that *sinners* does not refer to the common people.[35] Put more broadly, Sanders understands the references in the Gospel tradition to the "lost" as a reference to this same group, which would embrace tax collectors and other sinners, including harlots.

This group of people is not simply to be identified with the poor or the downtrodden or the meek, for all of whom Jesus showed concern but none of whom can simply be identified by the term *sinner* or *lost*. Jesus was not accused by his opponents of simply associating with the ritually unclean or with those common people who were not able to observe all the purity laws.

Furthermore, Sanders objects to those who argue that since at least some Pharisees were *ḥăbērîm*, and the *ḥăbērîm* separated themselves from the common people in adhering to more stringent Levitical purity laws, they must have labeled those ordinary people who did not follow their stringent regimen as "sinners." This, he argues, "debases and falsifies Judaism, and it trivializes Jesus, to understand the issue of 'Jesus and the sinners' as if it were 'Jesus and the common people *versus* the narrow, bigoted but dominant Pharisees.' "[36] In Sanders's view, even if the Pharisees were present in Galilee in numbers and did object to Jesus' association with common people, they were not in a position in Galilee whereby they could regulate synagogue practice to the extent of controlling how the nonobservant common people would be treated in synagogue and community.

Sanders goes on to argue that if Jesus had led sinners and tax collectors to repent and repay, no one, including the Pharisees, would have objected. Indeed Jesus would have been seen as a national hero![37] Sanders even objects to the suggestion that Jesus offered God's forgiveness first before requiring reformation, or put another way, that Jesus' proclamation of forgiveness was conditional and only became effective when it was followed by conversion or amendment of life.[38]

In Sanders's view the truly radical thing about Jesus is that he offered forgiveness and inclusion in the kingdom *without* requiring repentance as ordinarily understood; that is, without requiring the offering of sacrifice and, in the case of an offense against another person, providing the required restitution (cf. Lev 6:1-5; Num 5:5-7) and then keeping the law obediently. The case of Zacchaeus is said to cohere with Sanders's view: Jesus did not *require* Zacchaeus to make restitution or sacrifice. Zacchaeus chose to do the former and the latter goes unmentioned.[39]

Sanders does qualify his detailed and somewhat surprising argument that "Jesus did not call sinners to repentance" with the proviso *"as normally understood."* Thus Sanders has left an opening for some kind of understanding of repentance, implied or expressed by Jesus. However, if Jesus did act in such a way that suggested that sinners simply needed to hear his message and follow him *rather than* following the normal means of expressing repentance, this would nevertheless have been objectionable to Pharisees and Sadducees alike. It would have meant that God's acceptance could be gained *apart from the temple apparatus*, apart from sacrifice, and thus apart from turning or returning to a strict observance of Mosaic, and in particular Levitical, law.[40]

In *The Historical Figure of Jesus* Sanders further clarifies that he does not think that Jesus was opposed to repentance; rather, traditions like Matthew 11:20-21; 12:41 and 21:31-32 suggest that he did favor it, but "he was not a repentance-minded reformer."[41] The point is that Jesus' approach was different from the Baptist's. The latter preached repentance with the alternative of destruction and was an ascetic. This approach was, at best, only partially successful. Jesus, argues Sanders, preached "God loves you" and underscored the point by eating and fellowshiping with sinners. Jesus was not opposed to the law but regarded hearing and heeding his message and participating in his mission as what really mattered. The most important thing was to accept Jesus and his message, and everything else was of lesser import.

This message was offensive on two counts: (1) Jesus did not try to enforce the commandments of Jewish law that stipulated how one moved from the status of sinner to righteous (via sacrifice, restitution, turning to law observance); (2) even more offensive, Jesus regarded himself as having the right to say who would be in the kingdom, indeed suggested that the sinners who followed him would enter the kingdom ahead of the righteous.[42] Indeed, as Sanders points out, "Were he a reformer of society, he would have had to face the problem of integrating wicked people into a more righteous social group. . . . Since he thought that God was about to change the world, Jesus did not have to deal with such problems."[43]

Jesus and the Pharisees

Before addressing the shortcomings in this argument, it is worth noting that Sanders seems to have swallowed a camel and yet strains over a gnat. If Jesus did indeed fellowship with sinners, did not urge them to fulfill the law's requirements for repentance and even suggested that sinners might enter the kingdom ahead of the righteous and law-observant, this would *surely* have offended the legally scrupulous, including the Pharisees. Furthermore, if Jesus was willing to go this far, what was preventing him from striking out on an independent course in regard to the laws of purity and sabbath observance as well? Why should we assume that Jesus was only selectively maverick in the way he handled the law's requirements? To put it another way, if Jesus was willing to act and speak in a fashion that might *suggest* that the cultic means of repentance, including temple sacrifice, was not absolutely necessary for a proper relationship with God, why should we hesitate over accepting the idea that Jesus suggested that the purity laws were no longer binding either? If one grants Sanders's arguments about "sinners," the likelihood that Jesus had some serious conflicts with Pharisees seems all the more, rather than less, probable.

Consider Sanders's argument about the famous saying "Follow me, and let the dead bury their own dead" (Mt 8:21-22 and parallels). He admits that Jesus, because of the priority of following him above all other obligations, commands an exception to the rule of maintaining filial piety, that of honoring a parent by proper burial.[44] My question is, If following him could lead to an exception in as fundamental a duty as burying a parent, why should we think that he was unlikely to make other "excep-tions" in regard to purity or Sabbath observance?

Let us take an another approach to this issue. Consider the case of Honi the Circle Drawer, who was in some ways in a position rather like that of Jesus.[45] Honi was bold enough to insist that God give good and timely rain when Israel needed it. A leading Pharisee of the day objected, saying, "Were you not Honi I would have pronounced a ban against you! But what shall I do to you—you importune God and he performs your will, like a son who importunes his father and he performs his will" (cf. *m. Ta'an.* 3:8). If a leading Pharisee could object to a rainmaker like Honi and be led to the point of imposing a ban, why should we doubt that Jesus prompted similar responses when he performed miracles, or fellowshiped with sinners, or said something controversial?

Further questions may be raised at crucial points in Sanders's argu-ment. First, the Gospel traditions of Jesus' sabbath and purity conflicts with Pharisees are about as well attested as his table fellowship with sinners and his proclamations about sinners and the righteous. They should not be dismissed.

Second, the argument about the necessary imminence of the parousia is weak on two grounds. (1) Important Gospel traditions suggest that, at most, Jesus spoke only of the possible imminence of the end (Mk 13:32).[46] (2) Other Jews of the period (e.g., some at Qumran) who did believe the end was imminent nonetheless had a social program and engaged in social reforms in their extended community. That Jesus had an eschatological message does not provide a good reason for neglecting or dismissing (as Sanders does) a good portion of the material on the Sermon on the Mount because it entails a social ethic.[47]

Finally, the term *sinner* could be used by Jews to refer to Gentiles, and it could be used by one group of Jews to refer to another that held to different or less stringent views about the law. While I would consider it possible that *sinner* in the Gospels was used in a sense akin to the latter meaning, overall I am prepared to agree with Sanders that *sinner* in the Synoptics probably does normally mean the "wicked."[48] But I am prepared to accept an implication of Sanders's argument which he himself rejects: we have yet another good reason to believe Jesus would have had conflicts with the Pharisees.[49]

It is not surprising that immediately after discussing sinners Sanders takes up the subject of Jesus and Gentiles. One might expect that if Jesus were so open to Jewish sinners, he might be equally open with Gentiles. Sanders, however, unlike Joachim Jeremias and others, believes Jesus expressed no explicit viewpoint on Gentiles nor did he institute a Gentile mission. He probably, like other Jews, expected some Gentiles to be included in God's people in the last days. This, Sanders thinks, will explain why the issue was still debated in the early church (cf. Gal 2 and Acts 15). The most Sanders is willing to say is that "Jesus started a movement which *came to see the Gentile mission as a logical extension of itself.*"[50] In his later book he confesses that since Jesus was a kind and generous person, and because Jewish precedent can be found, it is unlikely that he believed that the Gentiles would be destroyed rather than converted and saved at the eschaton.[51]

The Implied Self-Understanding of Jesus

When Sanders addresses the issue of Jesus as a religious "type," it is clear he is most comfortable with the term *prophet* to describe Jesus,[52] but in his second work he is willing to go a bit further and suggest that since Jesus did not count himself as one of the Twelve, and since he probably did say they would have roles in the kingdom judging the tribes of Israel, and since he claimed to know who would be in and who would be out, who would be forgiven and who would not, presumably he saw himself as God's eschatological viceroy (or last envoy)—"the head of the judges of Israel, subordinate only to God himself."[53] But what does this mean?

Sanders believes Jesus' self-concept and implicit self-claim was a considerable one.[54] He even believes Jesus probably rode a donkey into Jerusalem and was praised like a king on that occasion. Thus he suggests that Jesus would have seen the title of king (of a sort) as not inappropriate: " 'king' yes, of a sort; military conqueror no," as was signaled by his choice of mount when he entered Jerusalem.[55]

Sanders, in analyzing the cause of Jesus' death, relates it to his words about and action in the temple. He sees the initiators of the process as temple authorities (including probably the high priest) and not the Pharisees, and he is convinced that the Romans executed Jesus for sedition or treason, not for blasphemy. I agree with Sanders that any viable interpretation of Jesus' death "must hold together his own execution as would-be 'king of the Jews' and the survival of his disciples as an a-political messianic group which was not rooted out and eliminated."[56]

This seems to mean that Jesus was not seen by the Romans, or for that matter by the priestly authorities, as a revolutionary or military leader, for had that been the case his followers would very likely have been sought out and killed. He was rather seen as a present nuisance and a potentially dangerous threat, particularly if he was allowed to continue to act or teach in the temple precincts during a festival, remembering how volatile, vibrant and massive the crowd could be in Jerusalem during festival time. This makes it doubtful that Jesus had undertaken anything so drastic in Galilee as the reordering of society, and in particular of village life, along egalitarian lines. However, within the circle of his followers he may well have reordered things to comport with his vision of the inbreaking kingdom.

An Eschatological, Not a Social, Prophet

In his more recent work Sanders goes out of his way to insist that Jesus was not really a social reformer but a theocratic and eschatological prophet. Time and again one senses that he is taking on Richard Horsley's and Gerd Theissen's views (the subject of our next chapter) of Jesus. It is worthwhile illustrating this point, for what Sanders opposes is as revealing as what he supports.

For one thing, Sanders questions the "powderkeg" hypothesis, the view that such a significant number of people in Galilee felt their livelihood threatened that they were on the verge of banditry, which in due course could lead to open revolt.[57] It seems to me that Sean Freyne has struck the balance on this issue:[58] that tensions did exist in Galilee between cities and increasingly marginalized dwellers in small towns, villages and farms. *Powderkeg* may be too strong a term if one thinks of a lit fuse, but *volatile* is about right, and certainly the social overtones of some of Jesus' parables would not have been missed. It is one of the great weaknesses of both Sanders's books that he does not come to grips in any detail with many of the parables and aphorisms, or even with the material in the Sermon on the Mount, which is arguably authentic.

On the other hand, Sanders is right to protest the reductionism of taking a saying like Luke 17:20-21 and arguing (as do Horsley and Borg) that it is Jesus' only meaningful saying on the kingdom ("the kingdom of God is among you"),[59] or by attempting to argue that *kingdom* was nothing more than a code word for a human sociological construct. Jesus was talking about the kingdom of God, which as the Lord's Prayer shows, he believed was "up there" before it was ever "down here." Even more to the point, it was "out there" in the historical future, to be brought to consummation by the coming Son of Man. It was not first and foremost a social blueprint, though I would urge it certainly had social implications if one believed God was forming a kingdom community in the present. There must be a balance between theological substance and social implications in evaluating the kingdom. For his part, Sanders points out that even Luke 17:20-21 is a preface to 17:22-37, which speaks of the future coming day of the Son of Man. "One cannot take Luke 17.20f. as cancelling the large number of sayings about the future kingdom—including those that immediately follow in Luke."[60] For Sanders, sayings like Matthew 12:28 and 11:2-6 must not be dismissed, but what they tell us is not that the kingdom was present in his exorcisms but that Jesus believed God's powerful saving activity was revealing itself even in the midst of Jesus' critics.

Sanders is surely correct in insisting that Jesus' idea of the kingdom cannot be reduced to a sociological construct; we cannot take God out of the equation. At the same time Sanders overplays the imminence of the coming kingdom, assuming that it rules out the likelihood of Jesus being a social reformer in any sense.[61] While Jesus did not say or imply that people could get together and *create* the kingdom of God, whether by open table fellowship, free healing or social, religious and political reform,[62] it does not follow that Jesus did not believe that the coming of a kingdom (divine saving activity) placed moral and ethical demands on its beneficiaries. Freely they had received, freely they should give, turn the other cheek, love their enemies and the like. Sanders admits that Jesus said that by right living some would enter the kingdom in the future, but he denies that the kingdom in the present has social implications.

The debate over the meaning of Jesus' kingdom sayings suffers from one side overemphasizing a certain reading of the "present" kingdom sayings at the expense of the future ones, while the other side lurches too far in the other direction, placing too much or exclusive emphasis on the future. As Sanders himself admits, there is no reason why Jesus could not have spoken of kingdom as both present and future.[63] I think part of the problem with Sanders's analysis lies in the conclusion that just because Jesus did not try to seize the controls of the political machinery or plot to overthrow the high priest, Jesus' ministry and his idea of the kingdom must have been apolitical.[64] I suspect that the real problem arises out of Sanders's insistence that Jesus believed in the *necessary* imminence of the end, not just its possible imminence (cf. Mk 13:32). A person who believes the end *may* come soon is still likely to say and do a good deal about the interim. This is not necessarily the case with one who sets dates in the near future for "Apocalypse Now."

Sanders's critique of Horsley and others is, in my opinion, inadequate. But this should not obscure the fact that he has made a major contribution to the Third Quest of the historical Jesus, especially in placing eschatology back in the forefront of discussion. While his denial of conflict between Jesus and the Pharisees is overdrawn, much of the rest of his analysis rings true, especially in explaining the facts of Jesus' life and why he died as he did. Sanders has sharpened our understanding of the logic of the progression and conclusion of Jesus' life.

JESUS THE JEWISH PROPHET OF ISRAEL'S REPENTANCE (MAURICE CASEY)

Though Maurice Casey has not produced full-length monographs on Jesus as Sanders has, nevertheless through his investigation of the Son of Man material in Daniel, various articles and now a book on the origins and development of Christology, Casey has made a significant contribution to the discussion of Jesus as a prophet.[65] Casey, like Sanders, insists that Jesus must make sense within the context of pre-A.D. 70 Judaism. In Casey's view, if Jesus was to obtain the Jewish following that the Gospels suggest he had, the range of options is limited. Within that context of early Judaism, Casey depicts Jesus as having a rather specialized mission directed toward the lost sheep of Israel.

Casey is notably less skeptical than Sanders about the value of the material found in both Mark and Q for reconstructing what the historical Jesus was like, and a great deal less skeptical than Crossan and other members of the Jesus Seminar about the value of the traditions in Mark.[66] The result is an image of Jesus that is strikingly different from the portrait offered by the Jesus Seminar or by Crossan, because it involves a good deal more than just the image of Jesus presented by Q. In my judgment, Casey is also right to stress that the criterion of dissimilarity is too flawed a tool to be used as some sort of ultimate litmus test to determine what can and cannot be authentic Jesus material.[67] The same could be said for the exclusive use of the criterion of multiple attestation to the exclusion of other criteria, an error of which Crossan is guilty.

Repentance in the Face of Eschatological Crisis

Casey's portrait of Jesus begins with the assumption that, far from being radically different from John, Jesus, having been baptized by John, set out to fulfill John's prophecy of a coming one (Mt 11:2-6/Lk 7:18-23).[68] Like John, Jesus affirmed that the end, including the coming of God's kingdom, was near at hand. Casey is in fundamental agreement with Sanders that Schweitzer was right in his assumption that Jesus saw the eschatological clock set to go off in the not-too-distant future. This meant it was time to gather all of the flock together, including the lost, and prepare for the final intervention of God. Casey insists that sayings like Mark 9:1 ("There are some standing here who will not taste death until they see that the kingdom of God has come with power") or Mark 13:30 ("This generation will not pass away until all these things have taken place") must be taken quite literally.[69] I would agree that they must be taken very seriously as saying something about the near future, not the distant future. But in the case of Mark 9:1, Mark seems to assume this saying is about the transfiguration (Mk 9:2-8), which is seen as a parousia preview, while Mark 13:30 seems to refer to the events which lead up to the destruction of the temple, *not* the cosmic events which follow at some unspecified time "after those days."[70]

For Casey, Jesus, like John, is a preacher of repentance to the lost sheep of Israel, calling them to "return" *(tûb)* to the Lord, which includes the idea of repentance. Casey however differs with Sanders in the identification of the "sinners." While Sanders would identify them with the wicked, Casey takes a more nuanced view, simply seeing them as "lapsed Jews," those who had fallen away from God and did not observe the law as they should.[71] He also differs from Sanders in that he thinks Jesus did call the sinners to repentance. Jesus simply did not agree with the interpretation of the representatives of "orthodox Judaism"[72] as to what keeping the law entailed.

Jesus and the Pharisees

This brings to light perhaps the most important difference between Sanders's approach to Jesus and that of Casey. Casey is convinced that there was real conflict of serious proportions between Jesus and the Pharisees, and that the Pharisees, in combination with the priestly authorities in Jerusalem, likely had something to do with Jesus' death. In essence, Casey sees Jesus as in conflict with the Pharisaic attempt to extend the priestly halakic requirements to all Jews, not least because Jesus understood that Jews in Galilee, especially those who were peasants or artisans, would then be unable to be faithful Jews. This means that Jesus was in conflict with one of the essential elements of the Pharisaic program.

To reach the sinners with the good news, "it was necessary to ignore orthodox development of the purity legislation, for this made it impossible to make contact with Jews who did not maintain a state of ritual purity."[73] Casey does not take this to mean, however, that Jesus rejected the Sabbath requirements or even the purity requirements of Judaism, but rather that he gave them his own interpretation.[74] In particular, he had to interpret the Sabbath and purity requirements in such a fashion that he would be able to reach and redeem the sinners and unclean.

In fact, Casey argues that the First Evangelist was right in insisting that Jesus intensified at least the moral demands of the law, for instance in regard to forbidding swearing of any sort or any form of retaliation.[75] But the evidence seems to demand that Casey temper his conclusion in regard to Sabbath and purity requirements. Where in the tradition is anything that suggests that Jesus accepted the purity laws and went through purification rites when he became unclean by touching a corpse, a sick person or a woman with a flow of blood?

The appeal to Mark 1:44, where Jesus sends the leper to the priest to go through the ritual of purification, can be explained as an example of Jesus making sure that this man, who was not going to become one of Jesus' traveling followers, was reintegrated into and accepted by his community. In other words, it was an act of practical wisdom and compassion for someone whose purity needed official certification for his reentry into his village. Mark's interpretation of Mark 7:15 ("There is nothing outside a person that by going in can defile, but the things that come out are what defile") must be allowed to stand and be seen as the radical critique it was. In the kingdom, new occasions taught new duties. An intensifying of moral requirements and, toward that end, a lessening of the ritual requirements of the law was the order of the New Day.

Not surprisingly, Casey sees Jesus' action in the temple as an attempt to reform practices that were seen as secular activities carried on in a sacred place.[76] This, of course, is not how Mark interprets the act, as is seen by his framing of the story with the cursing of the fig tree and in the prediction of the destruction of the temple in Mark 13. Casey does admit, however, that the debate between Jesus and the Pharisees about purity escalated into polemic such as we find attributed to the scribes in Mark 3:22 and to Jesus anathematizing both scribes and Pharisees in Matthew 23:13. This eventually led to an alliance of scribes and priests against Jesus.[77]

The Martyr's Death

Unlike most of the scholars we have reviewed so far, Casey argues that Jesus not only foresaw his own death but viewed it as an atoning action:

> We should deduce that Jesus' mind was working the same basic lines as those who meditated on the deaths of the innocent Maccabean martyrs, and who concluded that their deaths were an expiatory sacrifice which assuaged the wrath of God and enabled him to deliver Israel (cf. 2 Macc. 7.37-8; 4 Macc. 17.20-22). Jesus' death likewise was to be an expiatory sacrifice which . . . enabled him to redeem Israel despite her faults.[78]

This conclusion does not mean that Casey believes that Jesus saw himself in a messianic light, if by that one means as in some way unique or doing something more than what the Maccabean martyrs had done. Jesus' words about vindication beyond death are taken to refer to his belief that he would be raised at the general resurrection like other righteous Jews, which he assumed would take place soon after his death.[79] Casey does not, in general, think that the discussion of titles like "Christ" or "Lord" reveals anything about the historical Jesus. Not even a discussion of the arguably authentic Son of Man sayings sheds any unique light on Jesus. This is because he believes the term was used not as a title but as a generic term to say something in a self-effacing and nonexclusive manner about himself.[80] It meant something like "a man, such as myself" or "a man in my position." Sayings such as Mark 14:62, which do not seem to fit into this mold, are simply said to be inauthentic.

We observe in the work of Casey a willingness to give credence to a good deal more of the Gospel material than is true of most of the scholars whose works we have already examined. But if, as Casey seems to assert, Jesus did not in some way project a messianic identity and did not rise from the dead, it is very difficult to explain the character and tenacity not only of the movement that came forth from Jerusalem in his name, but the character of their proclamation: Jesus as Messiah and risen One. In this respect Sanders seems somewhat closer to giving an adequate explanation of the rise and character of the church and its preaching.

CONCLUSIONS

I will reserve my general conclusions about Jesus as a prophet until the end of the next chapter, but here I note that in the works of Sanders and Casey we see a much more concerted and viable attempt to place Jesus in his Jewish matrix, including the matrix of early Jewish eschatological thinking.

Casey seems nearer the mark in allowing for significant disagreement between Jesus and the Pharisees, but Sanders's discussion adds a great deal to what we can know with some probability about the historical Jesus. Sanders's focus on the facts of Jesus' life is helpful, and his over-reliance on these has been somewhat corrected in his most recent work. Both writers are persuasive in showing why many of his contemporaries may have seen Jesus as a prophetic figure, but neither scholar adequately comes to grips with Jesus' own self-understanding. If, as Sanders suggests, Jesus' action in the temple is crucial to understanding not just the outcome of his life but who he thought he was, then more needs to be said about Jesus' self-concept, and especially how he viewed his death. Casey tries to attend to this last matter, but the Maccabean analogy is not entirely satisfactory.

CHAPTER 6

JESUS THE PROPHET
OF SOCIAL CHANGE

While the last chapter concentrated *on the idea of Jesus as an eschatological prophet, this chapter focuses on Jesus as a social prophet in the works of Gerd Theissen, Richard A. Horsley and R. David Kaylor. Theissen's influential thesis is that there were three elements that made up the Jesus movement: Jesus the Son of Man, his itinerant disciples and his localized sympathizers. Theissen argues that the latter group basically stayed within the confines of Judaism, while the former group continued to itinerate and eventually developed into what we know as early Christianity. In Theissen's view Jesus subscribed to a near end of the world, but even so he set up an ongoing movement. He believes that Jesus was the instigator of a reform movement, a "peace party," in the midst of a highly volatile situation in Galilee. Finally, Theissen's most recent work draws into question the radical assumptions lying behind the idea that the Gospel traditions were not formed until the second half of the first century A.D.*

The works of Richard A. Horsley cast Jesus as an even more radical social reformer, one who began a social revolution from the grassroots up. In Horsley's view Jesus sought to transform Galilean village life by reforming the power structures in towns and in families. Jesus is said to have strongly opposed contemporary power structures, both familial (patriarchy) and societal (the imperial system, whether operating directly or through clients). In Horsley's view Jesus did not seek to bring change through setting up an alternative community but through reforming existing society. Horsley sharply distinguishes between oracular and eschatological prophets and prophets who were men of deeds like an Elijah, identifying Jesus with the latter. For Jesus, kingdom was first and foremost a social and political construct, rather than a theological or religious one.

Finally, we will look at a significant study of Jesus as social prophet by R. David Kaylor. Kaylor often follows Horsley, but he seeks to ground Jesus' social program within the context of covenant theology and its commitments to justice and mercy along the lines of premonarchial egalitarianism in Israel. Like Horsley, Kaylor maintains that Jesus' grassroots social reforms were meant to prepare for God's direct intervention in the political situation of the day. Whatever the failings of these proposals, both Kaylor and Horsley remind us that a purely spiritual interpretation of Jesus' teachings, actions and aims is inadequate.

THE SHADOW OF THE GALILEAN (GERD THEISSEN)

Though he has not written a full monograph on Jesus, there are few scholars who have had more impact on the discussion of Jesus during the Third Quest than the German New Testament scholar Gerd Theissen. This is due to a variety of important studies, including *The Shadow of the Galilean*, an innovative narrative re-creation of the ethos and setting of Jesus and his movement.[1] While he is not always acknowledged to the extent that he deserves in recent surveys of the Third Quest,[2] Theissen is important not only for his views but also because of the impact they have had on other scholars, such as Horsley and Crossan. In particular, the thesis of Jesus as a radical charismatic itinerant preacher was first forcefully advanced by Theissen in the late 1970s, a thesis which was then picked up and echoed by North American scholars.[3]

Wandering Charismatics and Local Sympathizers

Theissen's basic thesis in its original form can be described briefly. It is that the Jesus movement was socially structured by three interrelated parts: (1) the Son of Man, the bearer of revelation, who formulated ethical and religious commandments for his followers, (2) wandering charismatics who sought to model their lives after Jesus and (3) sympathizers, who in the strict sense of the term were not disciples since they did not follow Jesus around Galilee but remained located in their own towns or villages and provided material support, especially when Jesus and his followers visited there. Theissen stresses that Jesus did not primarily form local communities but called into being a movement of radical wandering charismatics. The sympathizers in local communities remained within the structure of early Judaism, and the wandering charismatics were the ones who passed along what was later to take independent form as Christianity. In particular they passed on a good deal of the Synoptic Jesus material, especially the sayings of Jesus.[4]

Theissen describes the wandering charismatic followers of Jesus as homeless, lacking family (having abandoned or renounced family), lacking possessions and lacking protection, since they traveled without staffs and operated with an ethic of nonretaliation. To this we can add the imaginative description in *The Shadow of the Galilean* of a situation in which both Judea and Galilee were ripe for revolt,[5] where Roman injustices and the murders of figures like John the Baptist were opposed by Zealots of one sort or another. In such an environment radical itinerancy by Jesus and his followers could from one perspective look like some kind of ragtag army on the march and from another appear to be a good tactic for staying out of harm's way.

In Theissen's view these two socially different groups, traveling charismatics and localized sympathizers, continued to influence the shape of the Jesus movement after Easter, with James remaining in Jerusalem while Peter preserved the tradition of the traveling charismatics.[6] During the time of Jesus the wandering charismatics were the authority figures even in the homes of the local sympathizers, but as time went on, local authority and traditions necessarily developed, producing a rather different and less radical form of discipleship that did not involve the renunciation of family and worldly goods.

Theissen sees this situation as similar to that of the Qumran community, where there were radicals who had renounced all, including marriage and property, but also those who did not commit themselves to these extremes. The analogy with the Jesus movement is not perfect, however, for it was the radicals who were located at Qumran and the moderates who traveled back and forth or lived in villages not far from Qumran, the reverse of what Theissen envisions with the Jesus movement.

Unfortunately for Theissen's theory, the idea that Jesus' traveling followers were made up of socially rootless or already homeless people[7] does not comport with the evidence we have which suggests that Jesus called people away from their *trades*, such as fishing. In the case of James and John we are told that they had hired employees, which does not suggest a marginalized situation (cf. Mk 1:20), and one of the women was the wife of Herod's estate manager (Lk 8:1-3, Joanna wife of Chuza).

Furthermore, lower Galilee was a small place. One could leave home base, travel to several villages and return by dark on the same day.[8] The evidence suggests that Jesus had such a base in Galilee, Capernaum (cf. Mk 2:1 to Mk 1:21-39). This implies that a commitment to traveling and evangelism did not necessarily mean that all of Jesus' traveling followers were committed to "radical homelessness and living without family." Indeed, the evidence further suggests that while clearly Peter continued to travel, he did so with his wife as late as the 50s (cf. 1 Cor 9:5).

What this suggests is that while some, in order to truly follow Jesus, did have to renounce or abandon a great deal, it was not a universal requirement of Jesus that everything had to be left behind to be a disciple, even for a traveling disciple of the Master. Furthermore, the stress by Peter and others on how much they gave up to follow Jesus suggests that they had considerable assets (cf. Mk 10:28-31). They were not totally marginalized peasants. I suspect Jesus asked people to give up whatever might hinder their being a true disciple, and that could differ from person to person. Of course, if you have nothing, you have nothing to lose, and so if there were homeless and rootless people who followed Jesus, we may say they gave themselves to Jesus, but we may not say they gave up much of worldly goods to be a disciple.[9] The traveling followers of Jesus, like Jesus himself, did not beg or ask for alms. They carried no beggar's bag like other itinerants, but rather seem to have relied on the system of standing hospitality provided by people like Mary and Martha and the resources provided by followers of some financial means like Joanna (cf. again Lk 8:1-3).

In fact, in the light of such evidence as I have just mentioned, Theissen has to somewhat modify his earlier conclusion. He concludes on the basis of followers like Zacchaeus, Mary and Martha, Joanna and an intimate of Antipas (Acts 13:1), that in fact "the social context of the renewal movements within Judaism of the first century A.D. was not so much the lowest class of all as a marginal middle class, which reacted with a peculiar sensitivity to the upward and downward trends within society."[10] This makes better sense of the available data and draws into question the appropriateness of calling either Jesus or most of his followers Galilean peasants (*contra* Crossan). But it surely does not explain why a "rich young ruler" or a Joanna would *want* to follow Jesus. It would appear that a purely social explanation for why Jesus generated a following, and for the sort of following he generated, is inadequate. One must factor in a variety of religious considerations as well as the social ones.

I think, however, that Theissen has struck on an important feature of the Jesus movement that made it rather like other early Jewish renewal movements. He calls it a socioecological factor and sums up what he means as follows:

The programmes of all the renewal movements suggest a detachment from the Hellenistic cities and an ambivalent attitude towards Jerusalem. They affirm the holiness of Jerusalem, but they no longer recognize it as a given fact; rather it had been surrendered, and the more they contrasted the idea of the holy city with the reality, the more radical their criticism became.[11]

This description fits very well with the ethos in which Jesus seems to have operated in Galilee, avoiding the large cities,[12] and also explains the ambivalent attitude toward Jerusalem in the Jesus tradition. On the one hand it is loved, on the other hand it always seems to kill its prophets and charismatic reformers.

Jesus and Jewish Renewal Movements

Under the heading of sociopolitical factors, Theissen stresses that there were two different types of radical theocratic movements: prophetic and programmatic. The former announce what God is doing or will do, the latter what should be the case. The former focus on a particular prophetic figure like Jesus or Theudas, who promised the Jordan would be divided again (cf. Josephus *Ant.* 20.5.1), while the programmatic seem somewhat independent of particular personalities. The Zealots and other movements that resisted Rome fall into the latter category, while Jesus falls into the former.

It becomes clear in this part of Theissen's analysis that he, like Sanders, subscribes to the theory that Jesus saw the kingdom as fully appearing within a generation and thus understandably did not need to concentrate on resistance to Rome.[13] In the Jesus movement, miracles served the function of demonstrating that the kingdom was in fact already coming, and it involved a very real change in Palestinian society, with outsiders like Peter, James and John becoming rulers in Israel (Mt 19:28), the meek possessing the earth and the peacemakers coming into their own. In short, Jesus did not counsel revolt or armed resistance to Rome, for the "Jesus movement was the peace party among the renewal movements within Judaism."[14] Yet Jesus' speaking of the coming Dominion of God reflected an ethos in which hope that a just order of society could be achieved by human action, apart from direct divine intervention, had been abandoned.

Theissen also rightly notes a characteristic of early Jewish reform movements: they involved both the intensification of some norms or laws and the relaxation of others. "While those interpretations of the law which intensified its norm were to be found above all in the social sphere [i.e., marriage, aggressive behavior, possessions], it is in the religious sphere that we find interpretations which relax these norms [i.e., food laws, washing of hands, Sabbath restrictions]."[15] This is seen as just the opposite approach from that of the Zealots.[16] Whether we are talking about the Jesus movement, the Zealots or Pharisaism, all in some respects, according to Theissen, "are a reaction to the drift towards assimilation produced by superior alien cultures."[17]

The effect, however, of the relaxation of the religious norms which made Judaism distinctive was an implicit universalism, an implicit open door to even non-Jews to enter both the community of Jesus' followers and the kingdom. Theissen does not see this breakthrough of "grace" as the abiding basis of inclusion in the saved group prior to Paul, though perhaps the impetus is present in Jesus' approach and some of his teaching.[18] The ethnocentrism of Judaism metamorphosed into ecclesiocentrism (no salvation outside the church), and the ethical radicalism of Jesus was transformed into a radical proclamation of the grace of God.[19] In part this transformation was natural since part of that ethic involved the radical notion of loving enemies and reconciliation with those who have wronged you.

I would suggest that at this point Theissen has seen as either-or that which should be both-and. Jesus proclaimed a radical ethic that had as its central tenet love of God and neighbor, even if that neighbor happened to be a hated enemy. This radical ethic was not transformed into a later proclamation of grace by Paul. Grace was already implicit in this ethic in the teaching and parables of Jesus (cf., e.g., the parable of the Pharisee and the tax collector, Lk 18:9-14), especially because all of Jesus' commandments were based on the assumption that God's divine saving activity, God's rulership, was already intervening in the world through Jesus' own ministry. The demand was grounded in the transformation already being wrought by God. The aggressiveness of the dominant society was ultimately absorbed, not resisted, through an ethic and practice of nonretaliation and finally through making the crucified carpenter from Nazareth the central symbol of the movement. Jesus took the worst violence the world could commit and triumphed over and, paradoxically, through it. This set the pattern forever for his followers who were under pressure and persecution.

There is much to commend in Theissen's essential analysis. Doubtless Jesus' radical ethic entailed a criticism of a male-dominated and sinful society. Theissen is surely right, despite the protests of Sanders, that Jesus did indeed relax some of the Jewish religious and ritual distinctives and implicitly opened the door for non-Jews to enter Jesus' community, though there is no evidence he personally sought out a Gentile following. He is also on target, in my judgment, in seeing the Jesus movement as being the peace party among the renewal movements of his day, though Jesus was highly critical of Jerusalem and saw an ominous cloud hanging over the Holy City.

Jesus operated out of a small-town setting and addressed his ministry to the variety of people he found in such places. Theissen, unlike Crossan, also realizes that the "radical itinerancy" theory can be overdone, but I would suggest that he nonetheless too narrowly defines whom Jesus regarded as disciples. Surely Mary and Martha, and many others who did not travel, also fall into this category. I suspect that the proper social distinction is between traveling evangelists and healers, and local supporters. In other words, the difference is functional and not a matter of drawing boundary lines so that only wandering charismatics truly constituted the Jesus movement. Unlike Theissen, I would argue that Jesus did indeed envision the setting up of a community of his followers in the future, after his death,[20] not least because he believed the coming of the kingdom, not the end of the space-time continuum, was imminent, and that it created community. It may come as something of a surprise that when we review the work of Horsley we will see that in his view Theissen's picture is not socially radical enough.

The History of the Synoptic Tradition

One further work of Theissen deserves some attention before turning to Horsley, namely *The Gospels in Context*. This book involves nothing less than a reenvisioning of the history of the Synoptic traditions, and it is in some ways as potentially groundbreaking as Bultmann's original work on that subject. It is important because, if Theissen is right, Crossan's attempt to make *Thomas* the earliest Gospel, while relegating the traditions in Mark and some parts of Q to a later period, is not just mistaken but badly mistaken.

Gerd Theissen's most recent offering sets out to answer the question of whether or not anything concrete can actually be said about the prehistory and development of the Gospel traditions.[21] Abandoning the traditional form-critical method used by Bultmann, which of late has fallen into disfavor, he seeks to illuminate the process by which the Gospels and their traditions were composed by examining social, geographical and political markers in the text as keys to tradition formation.[22] Basically, his theory is that Gospel materials, and eventually the Gospels themselves, were formed in response to two major crises of the first century: the crisis involving Caligula's abortive attempt to place his own statue in the temple in Jerusalem in about A.D. 40, and the crisis of the Jewish War and the destruction of the temple in 66-70.

Many of his conclusions are remarkable and include the following: (1) the oldest forms of some of the sayings traditions were already in writing *within ten years of Jesus' death;* (2) both the passion narrative and the Synoptic apocalypse (Mk 13 and parallels) were formed in the early 40s in response to the Caligula episode (not much later, as Crossan and others argue), and Q also was likely formed in the 40s; (3) the Gospels were written in the period 70-90, Mark first in the early 70s, and Luke and Matthew shortly thereafter; (4) the provenance of Mark and Matthew alike is Syria, or in any case very close to Palestine; and (5) Luke on the other hand reflects a broader, more distant and more Western perspective.

Theissen continues to hold to his theory that there were, so to speak, two groups of early Christians: the radical wandering charismatic preachers who more directly imitated Jesus' modus operandi and were responsible for much of the Q traditions, and the more sedentary Christians who met in house churches and produced narratives about things like in-house teaching, community crises and the passion story. Theissen also toys with the notion that some of the Jesus traditions, namely the miracle stories and perhaps the account of John the Baptist's death, were told and passed along, at least at first, independently of the Christian community.

In response to Theissen's *approach* many scholars will want to ask: Is it really possible to locate and date traditions on the basis of passing geographical references, knowledge of local customs or, for example, an allusion to Herod Antipas as "a reed blowing in the wind" (an image depicted on one of the coins he minted)? One could conceive of a Gospel writer who was born and raised in Palestine and thus knew the region well, but in fact wrote his Gospel for a community far removed from Palestine, for instance Rome. Mark may have been such a person. Knowledge of a locale does not necessarily mean a Gospel is addressed to people in that locale. If Mark is written to an audience in such close proximity to Palestine, why does the Evangelist have to repeatedly translate Aramaic phrases, explain local customs and the like?

Furthermore, just how far is it really possible to press the connection with the Caligula traditions, especially in the case of the Synoptic apocalypse, which Theissen argues was formed in the 40s and then re-formed by Mark around 70? If Mark had known these traditions alluded to Caligula, then he also knew that such prophecies did *not* in fact come true during the reign of Caligula. Would he really have reused such failed prophecies to speak to a different situation? Many of Theissen's problems arise because he simply assumes without argument that the Synoptic apocalypse is almost entirely *ex eventu* prophecy (i.e., "prophecy" written after the event has already occurred). It would have been more fruitful to discuss how Jesus' sayings about the end could have been redacted in one way or another by the Synoptic writers.

Nevertheless, this is a very important book, not the least because it avoids the impasse to which form criticism had come and the extreme skepticism about the Gospel traditions all too evident in recent books about Jesus and the Gospels.[23] Some no doubt will say of Theissen's book that the social and political approach is too narrow in scope, for it is possible to argue well and logically within a certain circumscribed circle without being entirely correct, since the evidence may require a much bigger circle. I would agree with this critique, but this book, even with its shortcomings, still sheds much light on the communities that handed down the traditions, the way the traditions were formed and how it is we came to have Gospels.

At some point scholars like Crossan, Borg and Mack will have to interact seriously with this study, for it makes extremely unlikely the proposition that the passion narratives and the eschatological substance of the Jesus tradition reflect later Christian theologizing. It also makes it almost impossible to believe that the preservers of such traditions were far removed from the original conceptions of Jesus held by his first followers and from Jesus' own views of himself and his mission.

JESUS THE PROPHET OF RADICAL SOCIAL CHANGE (RICHARD A. HORSLEY)

"More emphatically than any other North American scholar, Richard Horsley has made Jesus' engagement with his social world central to his portrait of Jesus."[24] Horsley, like Theissen, seeks to locate Jesus primarily in the context of his social setting, rather than his religious setting[25] as is characteristic of the approaches of Sanders and Casey. Like Theissen, Horsley sees a situation in which peasants in Galilee as well as in Judea were severely marginalized, but even more than Theissen, he is prepared to argue that Jesus chose to be a social revolutionary, taking the side of the poor and oppressed and standing over against the power elites. The latter included the temple and its hierarchy, which had turned the temple into "an instrument of imperial legitimation and control of a subjected people."[26] Jesus' response to this oppression was to organize a social revolution (from the grassroots up), rather than a political revolution (from the top down, involving the overthrow of the current regime).

The Revitalization of Local Communities

Unlike Theissen, Horsley argues that Jesus set out to reorganize village life in Galilee, with his radical ethical teaching as the basis of a new community order. This means that Jesus' ethical teaching is essentially addressed *not* to the roving band that followed him around, those who would normally be seen as the inner circle of his disciples, but rather to ordinary people as a guide for living in their local communities. Even loving one's enemy is given a new twist and taken to mean creating relationships of solidarity within one's local community.[27] Horsley will have none of Jesus seeking rapprochement with Romans or the ruling elites in Palestinian society.

A further component of this picture is that Jesus was seeking to establish a radically egalitarian society, abolishing hierarchy and patriarchy in local communities. Even the eschatological saying about the Twelve judging the twelve tribes of Israel is given a new reading. It is taken to mean that these disciples will "establish justice" for Israel. This reading is required because otherwise the saying would suggest that Jesus sought to set up a hierarchy of some sort in the newly arriving kingdom.

Not surprisingly the kingdom is seen as this-worldly and refers to a social and historical transformation of society already underway.[28] Even eschatology is seen in the light of the vision of social transformation. Jesus expected God to come and complete the social revolution by bringing about the political revolution and overthrowing the oppressive governing powers, whether Roman, Herodian or priestly.[29]

Horsley also provides a detailed paradigm of the cycle of violence which eventually led to the Jewish War. He likens the social situation to a class struggle in a colonial setting, involving conflict between urban ruling elites and economically oppressed peasants (representing perhaps 90 percent of the population). The urban elites are landowners extracting money from peasants. This sets off a process that goes from bad to worse—institutionalized and legitimized violence against peasants leads to protest, then further repression and finally revolt by the marginalized (in A.D. 66-72). Horsley does not see this ongoing process as involving Zealots, at least prior to the revolt itself, but as initiated by peasants and small-time farmers, who resorted to sporadic banditry.[30]

Jesus' role in this process is that of social prophet, proclaiming and instigating a reconstruction of village life in Galilee. Horsley handles the miracle stories in a way that comports with his overall agenda. First, they must be read as typical, not as directly historical accounts (whatever that might mean). Second, Jesus did not recruit these "healed" people but sent them back into their own communities to contribute to the ongoing reformation in the villages.[31]

Horsley is also highly critical of the proposal that Jesus was a Cynic, or even a wandering charismatic.[32] For Horsley, Jesus was not building up an army of traveling preachers but reforming local villages. His ethics were directed to that context, not to the traveling fellowship. "Indeed, Jesus' disciples were not simply supported by local households but, as catalysts of a larger movement, focused their activities on the revitalization of local community life as well."[33] The way this revitalization would happen was by the forgiveness of debts, the giving back of land that had been taken and the reorganization of the family structure in such a way that the only Father to be acknowledged as head was the heavenly One, not any earthly father or teacher.[34] The receiving of food, family and lands by the disciples "in the kingdom" was already happening because the kingdom was already coming in these Galilean villages.

Jesus Among the Prophets

In a helpful summary of his views about Jesus as a prophet, Horsley argues that Jesus was perceived by his contemporaries not as *the eschatological prophet* but like one of the prophets of old, say an Elijah or Jeremiah.[35] The "issue for Jesus' contemporaries was apparently less one of theological ideas or eschatological expectations . . . than one of concrete social-historical phenomena."[36] Horsley's approach is to first minimize the importance of the evidence of expectations for an eschatological prophet and then to posit a popular stream of prophets, some like the classical oracular prophets and others patterned after the great liberators of early Israel like Moses or Joshua. Both of these sorts of prophets arose, according to Horsley, from Palestinian Jewish peasantry and had little to do with literate, scholarly groups like the Pharisees or Essenes of Qumran.

The first step in this approach involves the argument that the idea of a prophetic Elijah figure appearing before the day of the Lord, while present in literature (cf. Mal 3 with Sir 48:10) that clearly predates the time of Jesus and apparently also present in the speculation about Jesus during his ministry (cf., e.g., Mt 11:14), was not really central to Jewish expectations in Jesus' day and thus doesn't really explain much about Jesus.[37]

Similarly with the "prophet like unto Moses," Horsley minimizes the importance of this idea for Jesus' milieu, even though he admits the idea does surface in as diverse material as the Qumran literature (1QS 9:11 and 4QTestim) and in the Samaritan literature about the coming *Taheb*, the restorer who would be Moses back from the dead or a prophet like Moses (cf. Jn 4:19, 25). His conclusion is that "expectations of an eschatological prophet do not appear to have been a prominent feature in extant Jewish literature at the time of Jesus."[38]

Horsley's critique of the more traditional approaches to Jesus' social setting is to posit a dramatic contrast between the 90 percent of the population who made up a peasant class and the 5 percent or so who made up the ruling class. Between these two classes was a small literate group, called "parties" by Josephus, which included people like the Pharisees and the Essenes. Horsley argues that in fact they had little impact on the common folk and that the common folk did not look toward them for leadership. The upshot of this is that the Gospels are seen as misleading when they suggest either that the Pharisees were leading figures in Galilee and its synagogues, or that Jesus had any notable dialogues or controversies with them. Rather this is a product of later debates and polemic between Christians and Jews after A.D. 70. The problem with this analysis is that it is probable that Mark's Gospel was written prior to or right about A.D. 70, and thus before the posited heated debates between Pharisees and Christians would have taken place in the late first century.

A further significant component in Horsley's argument is the assertion that the so-called Zealot movement is a modern scholarly construct and not an ancient historical phenomenon. I will only say at this point that this involves an overreliance on and a misreading of Josephus's *Jewish Wars*, which was intended as a propaganda piece, and it neglects the more straightforward and less polemical data about Pharisees, Zealots and others in Josephus's *Antiquities*.[39] Horsley in his analysis both of the Jesus movement and of the Zealot movement engages in what amounts to a form of reductionism. He consistently underplays, ignores or dismisses the theological component in the underlying philosophy and teachings of these groups in the interest of pursuing a social-scientific explanation. This is a very serious error, for it results in a Jesus who is little different from the other social reformers of the day. What Horsley's analysis notably fails to explain is why, if it was primarily based on a failed social experiment, the Jesus movement continued and expanded, alive and well, long after the crucifixion, while the movement that supported Theudas disappeared quickly and the followers of Judas the Galilean and the Zealots were crushed in the Jewish War of A.D. 66-70.

In his paradigm Horsley wishes to distinguish between oracular prophets, who while they perhaps had a few followers were largely men of words, and prophets who led movements and concentrated on deeds and acts of deliverance patterned after those of Moses and Joshua. These latter, for example, led their followers to the Jordan River, promising to part the waters again and lead a new entrance into (and conquest of) the land.[40] Among their number were Theudas and the Egyptian, as well as the Samaritan who sought to go up Mount Gerizim with the promise of revealing the holy vessels buried there by Moses (cf. Acts 5:36; 21:38; *Ant.* 20.5.1; 20.8.6; 18.4.1). Horsley does not think these action-prophets who led movements were violent revolutionaries.[41] He would also distinguish these prophetic movements from messianic movements, movements where peasants sought to proclaim or make someone king in the Davidic mold. Jesus, in Horsley's view, is to be seen in the prophetic not the messianic mold.

Reforming Social Analysis

There are problems with this analysis, not only in its evaluation of early Jewish history, but also as it applies to Jesus and his movement. In the first place it probably assumes too much about the social situation in Galilee with regard to the relationship of peasants to both the literate groups and the elite. In particular, it underestimates the role of the literate in Jewish religious life in Galilee and their leadership roles. A figure like Jairus was

surely important and influential in his Galilean community and synagogue (cf. Mk 5:21-43). It also underestimates the importance of the
expectations of early Jews that figures like Elijah, Moses or David would
arise again. It is not likely that Christians were the only ones who wondered if John the Baptist was the Elijah figure spoken of in Malachi. It is
probable that various people saw Jesus in that light, especially in view of
his miracles and his Galilean origins.[42]

Second, Horsley's attempt to downplay the role of the Pharisees in
Jewish society in Jesus' day is unconvincing. Paul's own life and spiritual
testimony, as well as that of Josephus, who at one point was or sought
to become a Pharisee, are important indicators of how this group inspired
an admiring following among a variety of people, including the literate.
Horsley's view fails to explain how it was that Pharisees could have dictated the way the Sadducean priests performed the sacrifices in the temple during and following the reign of Herod the Great. They were able
to do so because they had considerably more popular support, probably
in both Galilee and Judea, than did the Sadducees and the temple hierarchy.

Furthermore, the distinction between oracular and action prophets
makes no sense when applied to Jesus, since even on a highly critical
reading of the Gospels he both performed symbolic actions in the temple
precincts and offered prophetic utterances of judgment against the temple, while also generating a movement of followers.

As we have seen in chapter one, a "social class" analysis of Galilee does
not work, since there were no social classes as in modern Western society.[43] Nor is it convincing to argue that Jesus' teaching was directed primarily to villagers rather than to the circle of Jesus' disciples. Jesus was
indeed interested in creating community, but this did not involve the
direct social action of reforming existing village structures. We have no
stories about Jesus confronting local village authorities, unless one counts
the Zacchaeus episode, and even there Zacchaeus is not asked to give up
tax collecting altogether. We also have no stories about Jesus confronting
the power elites who lived in Galilean cities like Sepphoris or Tiberias,
which he would surely have had to do if those elites had already taken
over and controlled both land and social structure in the small villages to
the extent Horsley assumes.[44] In short, much of Horsley's argument is
based on silence or unverifiable assumptions about the social situation in
Galilee.

This is not to dismiss the evidence that in some of Jesus' parables we see that the elites exert social pressure and that Jesus is highly critical of the wealthy who oppress. His answer to these problems, however, was essentially a religious one, though it had strong social implications. Israel's heart must be changed, and then renewed lives and social structures would follow. But the locus of the change was within the Jesus movement, not within peasant society in Galilee at large. This meant change both on the road and in the homes of Jesus' supporters in Capernaum and elsewhere. On this score and others, we find Theissen much more credible than Horsley.

None of these criticisms should be taken as an attempt to dismiss Horsley's work. It is precisely because I do believe that Jesus' message and ministry had a significant social component and that religion and social life, and even politics, were inevitably intertwined in early Jewish society that I believe it is crucial to bring the picture into proper focus. Horsley's analysis falls short not because it pursues Jesus in his social setting but because the social dimension has swallowed up or minimized the importance of other dimensions.

JESUS THE SOCIAL REFORMER (R. DAVID KAYLOR)

Kaylor's work is in many ways dependent on that of Horsley and to a lesser degree on Crossan. Kaylor, however, brings to the discussion an emphasis less evident in Horsley's work and entirely lacking in Crossan's, an attempt to see Jesus as an advocate of the renewal of Israel by means of "a return to the covenant traditions that would produce a society of justice and peace."[45] More than Crossan, Kaylor insists on situating Jesus within the mainstream of Jewish prophetic tradition. This, in Kaylor's view, must mean that Jesus was a political figure with a political and social agenda.

A Political Jesus?

Kaylor is not renewing the older attempt by S. G. F. Brandon to argue that Jesus was a Zealot, a violent revolutionary, seeking to expel the Romans and their cronies from the Holy Land.[46] Nor is he suggesting that Jesus was trying, by political maneuvering, to place one of his followers in the corridors of power in Jerusalem or in Galilee, nor seeking to establish a political party. Rather, "One can argue that Jesus' words and actions had political implications without arguing that Jesus was primarily a political actor. . . . Jesus preached and taught a message that was thoroughly political, a message that demanded a social and political revolution."[47] As a result of this message, Jesus was executed.

In other words, in Kaylor's view it was not just the symbolic actions of Jesus in the temple or in his "triumphal entry" that led to his demise. He was executed for sedition because his message was correctly understood to be subversive of the ruling powers and their overlords. This contrasts with the more familiar notion that while Jesus made "royal" claims and spoke of a kingdom, it was a spiritual and otherworldly kingdom he had in mind, and unfortunately the Jewish and Roman authorities misunderstood him.

Kaylor further defines what he means by saying Jesus was "political" by adding that the restoration of the covenant community on the basis of the Old Testament Scriptures involved seeing the mundane things in life—food, clothing, shelter, land—as spiritual matters, just as the prophets did. For Jesus, Kaylor wrote,

> Spiritual issues concern not merely [the] internal, private, and individual relationship between a person and God. The spiritual also governs interpersonal and community relations. . . . Jesus was political in the same way the preexilic prophets in general were political: He believed that God's blessing of the people depended on their manifesting in the political sphere the justice God required of covenant people.[48]

The Palestinian Political Climate

A crucial component in Kaylor's portrait of Jesus as a political prophet is fleshing out the conditions in Palestine that could have called forth such a prophet. Like Sean Freyne, Kaylor suggests a conflict brought about by the Hellenizing cities in lower Galilee whose values were at odds with the traditional rural values of the Galilean peasants. Coupled with this is the notion that various Jews in Galilee who were more well-to-do were buying up the land of smaller farmers to create large estates. Thus small farmers in Galilee were gradually being forced off their land and becoming either tenant farmers or day laborers.[49] I suspect this analysis is correct, but some of Kaylor's additional assumptions are more dubious.

Kaylor seems to assume that the agrarian system of early, premonarchical Israel was in some sense "egalitarian."[50] We can agree that prior to the monarchy Israelite tribal and familial patterns determined how land was distributed and that a system of barter was commonly used. Further, with the establishment of the monarchy there were increasing cases of family property being bought up or seized and an increase in the practice of lending money at interest. Consequently, farmers who lived a marginal existence were being driven into poverty. But we should be under no delusions that Jewish practice, or even Jewish ideals, were in any modern sense "egalitarian." They were undoubtedly more equitable in the earlier period, but in fact they were thoroughly hierarchical and, at least in practice, also patriarchal. If Jesus was advocating an "egalitarian" approach to social relations, he was advocating something new, not renewing old systems.

To take an example of the sort of confusion involved here, Kaylor argues that the Essenes of Qumran "harked back to the more egalitarian strains in Israel's economic thinking, *even though their government was very hierarchical.*"[51] He is referring to the common ownership of all property at Qumran. This practice, however, did not prevent Qumran from being hierarchical and highly patriarchal. This equal sharing of property, or even familial patterns of ownership and barter, should not be confused with the modern notion of egalitarianism, which has both an antihierarchical and an antipatriarchal emphasis. The market economy system that was beginning to take firm root in Israel during Jesus' life indeed increased the power and property of the few males who were running the society and therefore exacerbated the problems created by patriarchy and a highly stratified society. But the economic system did not create these problems, nor did its economic predecessor prevent or rule out either hierarchy or patriarchy as a system of power and control.

Like Horsley, Kaylor is also apt to overestimate the revolutionary climate of Galilee in Jesus' day.[52] We have commented in earlier chapters on the volatile situation in Galilee, but so far as we can tell it was not a violent situation. An exception would be the incident that took place near the time of Jesus' birth, during the interregnum period after Herod the Great's death, when the arsenal at Sepphoris was attacked by Judas the Galilean.[53] There were messianic pretenders during and after the lifetime of Jesus, but they seem to have been concentrated in Judea. It is also a mistake, as Sanders has repeatedly pointed out, to assume that Galilee was overrun by Romans or Roman institutions and that Rome dominated the region. This is simply untrue, and, consequently, arguments based on Roman institutions of patronage and the like will not explain what Jesus was reacting to or against in his teaching.[54] The only political actions by Romans that seem to have directly affected Jesus and his ministry was taxation and, of course, the events that ensued during Jesus' final days in Jerusalem. Otherwise the system of Roman domination should by and large be put aside in favor of assessing the effects of Hellenized rulers like Antipas and their retainers.

The Elusive Politics of Jesus

The heart of Kaylor's case is that Jesus addressed, sometimes obliquely in parables and sometimes more directly, concrete problems and issues of his day. This in some real measure led the governing authorities to perceive him as a threat and resulted in his execution. I think there is *some* truth in this claim, but I would suggest that it is Jesus' teaching in Judea that makes this connection possible and that we have no hard evidence that Jesus, while teaching in Galilee, was being shadowed by Roman authorities, Sadducees or representatives of the high priest—*unless some scribes and Pharisees served such a function.*

No one doubts that Jesus was crucified or that crucifixion was a political act, but it must be remembered that even this extreme penalty could be and was used both in defiance of evidence of sedition as well as because of it. In particular, Pilate's record does not encourage us to think that he would have been reluctant to bend the law and execute someone unjustly (cf. Lk 13:1). Thus Jesus' execution does not *necessarily* imply that his general teaching was perceived to be politically dangerous. The stories of the trial(s) of Jesus suggest that it was misunderstood remarks Jesus made in Judea about the temple or about "rendering unto Caesar" that may have helped seal the case against him. We have no evidence that Jesus' parables or healings or, for that matter, the Sermon on the Mount led to his death. Thus Kaylor's attempt to link the end of Jesus' life with this part of his message is, I think, weak.

The case is not strengthened much by the argument that Jesus' action in the temple was aimed at the high priestly aristocracy rather than, say, against the temple apparatus and sacrificial system (a symbolic act of destruction), or against particular abuses in the temple courts (a symbolic act of cleansing).[55] The key saying in Mark 12:13-17 and parallels[56] must be set, as in Mark, within Jesus' teaching in Jerusalem during the last week of his life.

Kaylor assumes that the very fact Jesus is asked about the tribute money shows he was engaged in political activity.[57] I do not see how this follows, especially if we accept the view that Jesus' interlocutors were trying to "catch him in his speech." In other words, the question may have been raised because of its usefulness in pinning Jesus to the wall, not because of his track record as a political figure.

With Kaylor we should be critical of the notion that Jesus in commenting on "Caesar's coin" was endorsing the principle of separate spheres of influence for God and Caesar, or as we might call it, separation of church and state. This hardly sounds like the Jesus who argued that God's Dominion was breaking into human history through his ministry and who certainly would have endorsed the scriptural teaching that the earth and all that is in it belongs to God. Not even humanly manufactured coins ultimately fall outside the sphere of God's ownership.[58] Thus it is very likely that when Jesus said, "Render to Caesar the things that are Caesar's," he was saying, "Give back to Caesar his worthless coins, and give to God your whole-hearted and undivided allegiance."

It seems that Jesus is being deliberately oblique at this point, forcing his audience to ponder his reply rather than jump to conclusions that he was either for or against paying tribute money or taxes to Caesar. As Horsley observes, Jesus turns the discussion to focus on a more primary question, Who is Lord?[59] Jesus' view then would amount neither to open cooperation with Caesar or violent revolution against him, but recognizing only God's lordship and thus relativizing Caesar's claims.

A further problem with Kaylor's analysis lies in his repeated insistence that Roman domination was breaking down the family and land structures that existed in Galilee.[60] There is no evidence for the Romans doing any such thing, though one could argue that the Herodians began to do so, perhaps with permission from Rome. Again, the social setting is misrepresented in speaking of Matthew 20:1-16, the parable of the day laborers and the owner of the vineyard, as an example of patronage. Day laborers were not ongoing clients, they were hired hands, hired only for one day at a time. They were found in the marketplace and did not turn up at a patron's door looking for work or a handout. Nor is there any evidence that the landowner in the parable assumes the duties of a patron, who was obliged to help a client in exchange for the client's support.[61] Kaylor, however, is right to point out that a denarius could hardly be called a generous gift by anyone's standards. It might not even suffice for a poor man to feed his family for a day. Thus we must be careful about

insisting that this parable speaks of God's generosity even to the unde-
serving. It may rather speak of obtaining what is sufficient unto the day
(as in the Lord's Prayer). We must be equally careful in insisting that this
parable does more than "tell it like it is." There is no explicit correction
of social problems implied in the story; the equities and inequities of life
may simply be represented.

Reenter the Eschatological Jesus

In his discussion of Jesus' teaching of the kingdom, Kaylor, like Horsley,
minimizes the eschatological as well as the individual and spiritual components. His emphasis, not surprisingly, is on the community and social
components. He is right in what he affirms but wrong in what he denies.
For while Jesus' kingdom teaching had clear implications and included
explicit instructions about behavior, lifestyle and social interaction in the
present, with equal clarity it presented the coming of the kingdom as an
event involving personal and spiritual transformation as well, *in preparation
for the consummation of the kingdom in the future.*

Kaylor notably omits any meaningful discussion of the Son of Man
material. Like Crossan and others, Kaylor tries to deny that this concept
goes back to Jesus or at least to minimize the significance of the sayings.
As we noted in discussing Sanders's work, Jesus could have been an
eschatological seer, a sage *and* a social reformer—they are not mutually
exclusive options. Indeed belief in the inbreaking of God's kingdom and
its possible near consummation was capable of producing a considerable
social agenda. Nor is it adequate to argue that Jesus was speaking only of
the end of a particular political and social system,[62] though the consummation of God's kingdom would have included that.

As we have seen in previous chapters, the striking thing about Jesus'
teaching in Mark 13 is the juxtaposition of political events, seen in the
foreground as precursors to the end (cf. Mk 13:30), and cosmic events,
seen as transpiring at some undisclosed time after the preliminary events
(cf. Mk 13:32). The traditions about the future coming of the Son of Man,
the future messianic banquet, the future judgment and resurrection and
the future "judging" of the twelve tribes by the Twelve, clearly show that
for Jesus the kingdom of God was an already-and-not-yet matter. Equally
clearly these teachings show that the kingdom had an earthly and social
dimension even at the eschaton and not just in the present.

Kaylor is quite right that it is not necessary to go to either extreme of the spectrum (either Jesus the apocalyptic seer who does not address his present social realities or Jesus the revolutionary).[63] The truth must lie somewhere between these two poles. Kaylor endorses Horsley's view that Jesus was a revolutionary who argued for the transformation of society in preparation for God's action that would change the political situation and save Israel.[64] I think there is a good deal of truth in this assessment, but much depends on where one places the emphasis—on God's coming activity, or on social transformation here and now instituted by the faithful.

Politics Where We Least Expect It

The remainder of Kaylor's work seeks to show the political dimension of Jesus' teaching in the Beatitudes, the Antitheses ("You have heard it said, . . . but I say"), the parables, the Lord's Prayer and in his calling of the disciples. Here in the second half lies the real strength of the book.

For example, consider what Kaylor says about the Lord's Prayer. He argues for the likelihood that this prayer in some form goes back to Jesus and that it shows how Jesus wed spiritual and social concerns. The first part of the prayer, with its use of *abba*, shows Jesus' great intimacy with God and how he expected his disciples also to have such closeness to the Father.[65] But this closeness to God did not cause Jesus to lose his focus or concern for people and their needs, hence the prayer speaks of the provision of bread and the forgiveness of debts.

Furthermore, the call for God to vindicate or "hallow" his own name is a call, much like that of the prophets, for God to eliminate injustice and oppression and to reestablish *šālôm* among God's people (Ezek 34:25-31). The plea to bring in the kingdom and will of God on earth as in heaven is eschatological in character and shows that such concerns did not rule out a passionate desire that the hungry be fed and the burdened be relieved. Jesus' piety is not divorced from his concern for the community of God and its physical as well as spiritual and social well-being.

Likewise the Beatitudes reflect this combination of the spiritual and social concerns of Jesus. Although the two forms of the Beatitudes are rather different (cf. Mt 5:3-12 with Lk 6:20-23), in the end they seem to have approximately the same meaning. Jesus is talking about the reversal of fortune to be experienced by the poor, the hungry, the mourning and the persecuted, an event to take place presumably in the kingdom in the future. But one cannot help but notice that Jesus set about reversing these situations and problems during his ministry and sent his disciples out to do the same. It is plausible, with Kaylor, to view these Beatitudes in light of Isaiah 61:1-3, 8-9.[66] I would add that Jesus saw as part of his mission the fulfilling of that Isaianic prophecy, as Jesus' sermon in Luke 4 certainly suggests, and this explains why he gives the Beatitudes; they are being and will be fulfilled as the kingdom comes.

Jesus' social agenda was real, but it was not that of the revolutionaries who used violence, the Jewish aristocracy who sought to maintain the status quo, the Pharisees who thought that extending the ritual purity requirements to all would lead to God reestablishing his people or the Qumran sectarians who thought that asceticism and withdrawal from the world into a commune was the way forward.[67] All of these groups had social agendas, but they were not the same as that of Jesus. I would disagree with Kaylor that Jesus in the Beatitudes was addressing the powerful elites. He was rather blessing the disenfranchised and promising that God, in part through Jesus himself, would remedy things.

Kaylor sees Jesus as arguing for justice within the parameters of the Jewish law and basically only going "beyond" the law by intensifying its demands. He insists on reading the antitheses as if they are both-and statements: "You have heard it said, . . . *and I say* . . ." This is exegetically possible, but Jesus appears to be more radical than even Kaylor thinks. His prohibition of divorce or oath-taking does indeed go beyond the law, but the point is that Jesus claimed the authority to urge his followers to go beyond the law. Even more significant, he implies he has the personal authority to go behind Moses to the creational intentions of God.

The reformation of God's people would prepare for God's final intervention. Jesus does not appeal to human precedent or tradition but asserts things on his own authority. This tells us something about Jesus, and frankly Kaylor ignores the fact that this places Jesus in a category above and beyond a prophet, who is only a mouthpiece for God.[68] I would agree, however, that what Jesus offers in the Sermon on the Mount is more a vision or general principles than it is a program or legal rulings.[69] Jesus was especially, though not exclusively, concerned with those who were relegated to the margins of society, the victims of poverty, oppression, hunger, ignorance and the like.

In a helpful discussion, Kaylor argues that the parables are like mirrors that can both reveal the truth about society and life and create a wish for something better.[70] He argues they are social commentary, meant to interpret God's will for Jewish society. Kaylor dismisses the christological interpretations and applications of the parables as later allegorical accretions. This, as we shall see in a later chapter, is a dubious conclusion, since parable and allegory were closely related in early Judaism.[71]

Kaylor also offers an interesting interpretation of the parable of the weeds and wheat (Mt 13:24-30).[72] He argues that it was bad farming to leave the weeds in the wheat until the harvest, since darnel or zizania was poisonous and would endanger the crop at the end if not weeded out earlier. He then suggests that rather than seeing this as an example of God's withholding judgment on weeds until the end, it is really a comment about patterns of land tenure and use attempted by ignorant landowners of large estates, a joke that would cause small farmers to laugh at the estate owner's expense. The problem with this view is that the parable must be in some way about the kingdom. Is the point that the kingdom reveals to us our foibles, so that we see ourselves as others see us?

Kaylor argues that texts such as Mark 10:41-42 indicate that Jesus rejected explicitly hierarchical social structures.[73] But this conclusion hardly follows from such texts. Some of these texts, such as Matthew 20:16, are about reversal (first becomes last, bottom becomes top) and do not deny hierarchy at all, but involve a changing of positions within the hierarchy. Some of these sorts of texts, like Mark 10:41-42, focus on taking the lead by serving others. Jesus does not say that no one can be first, but that the way to be first is to serve all, as he has done. This does subvert conventional expectations about status and rank, and of who should be considered first, but it does not deny all hierarchy. Jesus contrasts servant leadership with other abusive and coercive models of leadership—he does not oppose all models of leadership or all social structuring.

In general we may say that Jesus, in communicating the character of the kingdom and its social as well as spiritual implications for day-to-day life, often used examples from real life with which the audience could identify. Jesus clearly enough calls for equity and justice, and he does not see abusive hierarchical patterns as a good thing. But it does not follow that he opposes all sorts of hierarchical structures. Indeed his choice of the Twelve, which Kaylor admits is likely historical,[74] suggests otherwise, even though they are called to be agents and take the lead in serving others, not follow other leadership models. Clearly a hierarchy is implied in Jesus placing himself above the Twelve as their leader and teacher.

The cumulative impact of the proposals by Horsley and Kaylor is that we are forced to recognize the social dimension of Jesus' teaching and his commitment to change the people of God into something nearer to what would please God. The kingdom means transformation both internally and externally, transformation both of individuals and of the covenant community.

CONCLUSIONS

As we have seen in this and the previous chapter, calling Jesus a prophet means different things to different scholars, though broadly speaking we can divide their proposals into two groups: those who tend to see Jesus as an eschatological prophet and those who tend to see him as a social prophet. It is worth reminding ourselves that these two categories are not necessarily mutually exclusive. At Qumran we find eschatology and, precisely because of it, a social program. It is my own judgment that we find both in the person and ministry and teaching of Jesus as well.

In his portrayal of Jesus as an eschatological prophet, Sanders seems nearest the mark, though we have taken issue with his conclusions regarding the Pharisees and sinners. Amongst the reconstructions of Jesus as social prophet, Theissen seems most helpful except in his over-insistence on wandering charismatics as being *the* disciples of Jesus who best represent all the facets of his original radical teaching. But instead of being presented with Jesus as either eschatological prophet or social prophet, we should be considering both-and.

CHAPTER 7

JESUS THE SAGE:
THE WISDOM
OF GOD

In this chapter two main proposals *about the historical Jesus are reviewed and analyzed. The first is that of Elisabeth Schüssler Fiorenza, whose influential work argues that Jesus was a prophet of God, whom he viewed as Sophia, or Wisdom, rather than Father. Jesus, Fiorenza argues, led a renewal movement that stood in continuity with an egalitarian tradition within Judaism that was critical of the dominant tradition of Jewish patriarchalism. Jesus preached and practiced a kingdom of equals and opposed patriarchy in any form, and his death is attributed to his resistance to Roman domination. Fiorenza adopts a hermeneutic of suspicion toward the Gospels and early Jewish and Christian texts. Specifically, since, in her view, the Jesus tradition underwent a long process of transmission and change, including christological transformation, the historical, egalitarian Jesus can be only critically discerned behind the veil of androcentric, patriarchal and christological overlays. In a similar way to Crossan and the Jesus Seminar, Fiorenza values the* Gospel of Thomas *and* Q *as primary sources for the historical Jesus.*

I will argue that Fiorenza's assumptions are problematic and that her use of Wisdom texts in the Jesus tradition is both selective and idiosyncratic. In the second half of this chapter I will discuss my own work and argue that it is far more probable that Jesus saw himself as a prophetic sage and as God's Wisdom come in the flesh. The merits of this proposal are shown by its ability to explain a great deal of the Jesus tradition, aspects of which otherwise seem unrelated. In addition, this perspective demonstrates the continuity between early Jewish sapiential literature, Jesus and early Christianity, and thus sheds light not only on the aims and self-understanding of Jesus, but on the perennial question of how the early church understood the continuity between the Jesus of history and the Christ of faith.

IN A WELL-KNOWN PASSAGE IN JOSEPHUS'S WORK *THE JEWISH ANTIQUITIES,* written probably in the early 90s, Josephus says the following about Jesus:

> At this time there appeared Jesus, a wise man [*sophos anēr*], . . . a doer of startling things, a teacher of people who receive the truth with pleasure. And he gained a following both among many Jews and among many of Greek origin. . . . And when Pilate, because of an accusation made by the leading men among us, condemned him to the cross, those who loved him previously did not cease to do so. . . . And up until this very day the tribe of Christians, named after him, has not died out. (*Ant.* 18.3.3)[1]

Josephus sees Jesus as a Jewish sage, a man mighty in word and deed (cf. Acts 2:22), who had an ardent following that refused to die out during the course of the first century.[2] It is interesting that when we examine the patristic evidence, none of the early Christian writers called Jesus a *sophos anēr*, a "wise man," or a "sage," indeed none of the New Testament writers use the adjective *sophos* of Jesus directly.[3] It is clear enough what Josephus has in mind by the term *sophos anēr* used in a positive sense, for this is what he also calls both Solomon and Daniel (*cf. Ant.* 8.2.7 with *Ant.* 10.11.2). In Josephus's mind Jesus fits into the stream of tradition that began with Solomon, the fount of Jewish wisdom, and continued through a host of prophetic sages like Daniel, who reflects, as does Jesus, the melding of prophetic, apocalyptic and wisdom insights into God, humankind and their interaction in history. In this chapter we will explore what prompted an important, educated Jew like Josephus, who knew Israel and its intellectual climate well, to view Jesus in this light.[4]

In the Third Quest for the historical Jesus two sorts of proposals involve wisdom. The first of these is that Jesus saw himself as a prophet of Wisdom/Sophia and addressed God as such. The most notable exponent of this view is Elisabeth Schüssler Fiorenza, though Marcus Borg, Burton Mack and others also see this as an aspect of how we ought to understand Jesus.[5] The second type of proposal is in some respects more radical and suggests that Jesus saw himself as God's Wisdom come in the flesh, the embodiment of God's wisdom, mind and plan. Only the latter proposal carries with it the implication that Jesus may have seen himself as the bearer or conveyer of the divine presence on earth in a sense that would not have been true of prophets or other charismatic figures in early Judaism.

This latter perspective is my own, though I must stress that I believe

Jesus was a complex historical figure and that the combination sage/Wisdom only gets at *some* of the most important aspects of how he viewed and presented himself. I am not suggesting that this explanation is an all-encompassing one which makes obsolete other images of Jesus and insights into his character and ministry. Both Fiorenza and I argue that Jesus saw himself as a Jewish sage standing at the confluence of the prophetic, apocalyptic and wisdom traditions. I will first examine and critique Fiorenza's proposal and address some broader issues raised by Fiorenza's work, especially the issue of Jesus' regard for and treatment of women, and the presentation of women in the Gospels.

JESUS THE PROPHET OF SOPHIA (ELISABETH SCHÜSSLER FIORENZA)

In chapters five and six we dealt with the suggestion that Jesus was a prophet in some sense of the word. In examining the work of Elisabeth Schüssler Fiorenza, the foremost contemporary feminist New Testament scholar, we must extend this theme. Fiorenza also envisions Jesus as a prophet, but of a different sort.[6] Jesus was a prophet of eschatological wisdom speaking for Sophia, the name she applies to Jesus' vision of God. Jesus is viewed as a radical prophetic figure, liberating women and the marginalized from the oppressive patriarchal structures of the day[7] and creating a movement that involved the discipleship of equals, a community where male and female had equal standing, status and roles.[8] Some of this approach will be familiar from our discussion of John Dominic Crossan,[9] but we should point out that in terms of chronology Fiorenza was already saying these things in the late 1970s and early 1980s more clearly and at greater length than was Crossan.[10] He has clearly been influenced by her work.[11]

In Memory of Her
Fiorenza's interpretation in *In Memory of Her* has been seen by many as the benchmark against which other feminist reconstructions of early Christianity must be measured. Both in terms of methodology as well as in terms of historical-critical research and exegesis, her work stands above that of others. It is thus appropriate to give it careful attention as a good representative sample of one sort of attempt to see Jesus as a prophetic liberator.

1. Working Assumptions. Fiorenza begins her analysis by making an important distinction: Jesus and his followers formed an alternative prophetic renewal movement within Israel, whereas the Christian movement led by Paul and others was a religious missionary movement within the Greco-Roman world. The Jesus movement was not an alien intrusion into Judaism but was a particular development of its religious traditions; Christianity, on the other hand, did intrude into the dominant ethos of the largely Gentile Greco-Roman world.[12] Both the Jesus movement and at least the nascent Christian movement are seen as being in tension with the dominant patriarchal ethos, though the Jesus movement is in tension with Jewish patriarchy while Christianity is in tension with Greco-Roman patriarchy. Jesus and his followers had the advantage of operating in a somewhat homogenous religious and cultural milieu, while Christianity had to address persons of widely varying cultural and religious backgrounds and orientations. It is the view of Fiorenza that women had large roles to play in both the Jesus movement in Palestine and in early Christianity throughout the Mediterranean crescent.[13]

These presuppositions Fiorenza brings to her reading of the Jesus material. In addition, she assumes that the material we find in the Gospels, even in the Synoptics, went through a very lengthy traditioning process, so that the Gospels must be read critically, not as transcripts of Jesus' life. She says, "New Testament writers were not concerned with preservation and antiquarian reading, but with proclamation and interpretative persuasion."[14] This can and has been challenged on both counts: (1) Theissen, as we saw in the last chapter, has recently challenged the argument that the Gospels went through a lengthy traditioning process,[15] and (2) many scholars would cogently argue on good grounds that the Gospel writers *were* interested in faithful preservation *as well as* proclamation of the Jesus material. It was not an either-or situation.

These presuppositions about the character of the Jesus material are very important to Fiorenza, for they allow her to take a selective approach to the Gospel material.[16] Like Crossan, Fiorenza dismisses all material that might suggest that Jesus spoke of God's judgment or wrath or the need for atonement for sins. Fiorenza's view is that Jesus envisioned God as an inclusive Creator God who does not judge people, except in the sense that God attempts to reverse conditions of oppression. Fiorenza also ignores or dismisses traditions that might suggest that Jesus was supportive of the physical family or that he chose twelve male disciples as his chief agents of the proclamation and implementation of the good news.

The major problem with Fiorenza's earlier work is that while she is often right in what she affirms about Jesus, she is wrong in what she denies about him. My essential criticism of her work is that she modernizes Jesus, making him an advocate of a politically correct egalitarianism. The Jewish feminist scholar, Judith Plaskow, is somewhat nearer the mark when she says of Jesus that while "he in no way reinforced patriarchy, there's also no evidence that he did anything radical to overthrow it,"[17] though I would want to add that Jesus was a *reformer* of the existing patriarchal system. But to see him as one who simply rejected that system and attempted to liberate everyone from it is going beyond what the historical evidence will bear.[18] Fiorenza's view, like that of Crossan, leaves out too many pieces of the Jesus tradition to make a persuasive case.

It is as important to recognize Jesus' direction as well as his position in regard to the patriarchal institutions of his day. There can be little doubt that he was seeking change in the patriarchal system. In his own day no doubt he would have been seen as radical in various ways, but when we evaluate Jesus' deeds in light of late-twentieth-century Western conventions and views of freedom and human liberation, he will seem to many radicals of our era at best a reformer and at worst too tame to make a difference today.[19]

Fiorenza is right to stress that since Jesus was a Jew, it is wrong to simply pit him against his "Jewish background," since of course Judaism figures in his foreground as well.[20] She is particularly trying to avoid pitting Jesus against Israelite patriarchal religion, as if Jesus was anti-Semitic and had a non-Jewish point of view. The way she accomplishes this feat is by arguing that Jesus was continuing one stream of Jewish tradition that was critical of the dominant patriarchal system that existed in Judaism:

> The issue is not whether or not Jesus overturned patriarchy but whether Judaism had elements of a critical feminist impulse that came to the fore in the vision and ministry of Jesus. . . . The praxis and vision of Jesus and his movement is best understood as an inner-Jewish renewal movement that presented an *alternative* option to dominant patriarchal structures rather than an oppositional formation rejecting the values and praxis of Judaism.[21]

Principally, Fiorenza sees Jesus as pursuing the sort of enlightened view of women one already finds in a book like *Judith*, which she dates to the first century B.C., and in material about the life of Jewish women in places like Egypt, Elephantine in particular. We will say more about this in a moment.

A third methodological key to Fiorenza's work is that she insists we must operate with a hermeneutic of suspicion when dealing with texts written in a patriarchal culture almost exclusively by men. In other words, we must read between the lines to determine what women's actual roles and status were in such a culture. Patriarchal texts cannot be taken at face value. Her three key methodological rules for feminist hermeneutics are: (1) the Jewish and Christian source material from the era of Jesus must be read as androcentric texts, texts that see the world through men's eyes and with a male point of view;[22] (2) the formal, codified laws are generally more restrictive than the actual relationship of men and women in a patriarchal culture; (3) women's actual social and religious status should be determined by the degree of economic independence they have and the roles we actually find them taking and not by prescriptive remarks by various Jewish males, which may not be descriptive.[23] She warns against reconstructing the roles and status of women in Judaism and Christianity by simply taking at face value the words of the patriarchal "winners" who came to dominate both of these religions after A.D. 70.

In general, I think these warnings are salutary so long as they are not taken to suggest that part of early Judaism or the early Jesus movement was somehow radically egalitarian and only later fell from that original state of grace. I see no solid historical evidence, even when the evidence is critically read, for such a conclusion.[24] It is a different matter to argue that Jesus, as a reformer of patriarchy, was working his way toward a more just and egalitarian society than had previously existed in Palestinian Judaism.

Fiorenza rightly attempts to set Jesus and his movement in the context of other early Jewish renewal movements such as Pharisaism, the Essene or Qumran movement, and the movement of John the Baptist. All of these other movements were, however, very strongly patriarchal in character. For example, by insisting on the stricter and broader application of Levitical and priestly laws, the Pharisees in effect further limited the roles women could play in their Jewish ethos and still maintain the approval of the dominant males.

Fiorenza is also right, in my judgment, that "the Jesus movement refused to define the holiness of God's elected people in cultic terms,"[25] though she goes on to conclude that Jesus redefines holiness in terms of the wholeness intended in creation. It must be added that Jesus was also very interested in ethical or moral holiness, as is shown by his teachings on adultery (cf. Mt 5).

2. *A Jewish Egalitarian Tradition?* Two things should be said about the data upon which Fiorenza bases her argument that Jesus continued an egalitarian tradition within early Judaism. First, the texts that come from Egypt must be used with very great care, for as is widely known, Egypt was a place where women, including Jewish women, had considerably broader and more varied roles than in Palestinian Jewish culture, and indeed more than in many places in the Mediterranean crescent.[26] In short, one cannot simply extrapolate from the roles Jews took at Elephantine and elsewhere in Egypt, including Alexandria, and apply those conclusions to the role of women in Israel.

The case Fiorenza mounts on the basis of *Judith* is a stronger one. Judith outwits Israel's enemies by using her femininity as a weapon, for she counts on her male foes being beguiled by her beauty and underestimating her wisdom and intelligence. She is right, and she becomes the instrument of the God of the oppressed (cf. 11:22-23). She is met and greeted by the high priests and the senate in Israel and blessed by the priests, and she goes before all Israel with other women in a victory dance, while the men of Israel followed her (15:9-13). What this story actually shows, however, is that women were from time to time, as in the period of the judges, raised up by God to perform mighty deeds, and that the Jewish culture did not suppress these events but rather seems, at least on occasion, to have celebrated them.

This does not mean that the story of Judith provides evidence for an early egalitarian movement in Judaism. Judith, unlike Jesus, does not try to change the patriarchal structure in the home or community or temple. Rather, this story shows the flexibility of early Jewish culture, that even while remaining patriarchal, it could make room for the deeds of such notable women. *Judith,* of course, is a fictitious story, but it enshrines an attitude of tolerance and greater openness than one might expect in a highly patriarchal culture. This in turn suggests that there may have been an openness to some, though not all, of Jesus' reforms when he appeared a century or so after the story of Judith was written.[27] I do not think this work provides a precedent for all of Jesus' reforms, especially some of the more controversial ones such as those having to do with the food laws.[28]

Thus I must conclude it is saying too much to argue that "the book of Judith mediates the atmosphere in which Jesus preached and in which the discipleship of equals originated."[29]

We must now turn to Fiorenza's portrait of Jesus' life and teachings. She begins by comparing Jesus to the Baptist. Her essential argument on this score is that while John announced God's judgment and wrath before the coming of the *basileia* and the eschatological restoration of Israel, Jesus stressed that eschatological salvation and wholeness for Israel was already available in and through his ministry.[30] This is true enough, but it fails to come to grips with the fact that Jesus differs from John not in omitting a discussion of judgment but in reversing the order of things—salvation offered first, followed by judgment on the temple and those who reject the Gospel. Jesus does not doubt that judgment in some form is near, and he speaks of a future and final judgment as well. For that matter, John is also calling people to repentance, which shows that he too wishes for the redemption of his people in the day of the Lord.

The contrasting of John as a prophet of judgment and doom with Jesus as a prophet of wholeness, healing and salvation is something of a caricature. The difference lies chiefly in the matter of timing. In Jesus' view the kingdom is already breaking in and redeeming people. The contrasting lifestyles of John and Jesus show that one is preparing by prayer, fasting and moral earnestness for the coming sifting by God of his people, while the latter is celebrating that God has already come and the salvific activity and the eschatological benefits are already present to be shared in and celebrated.

Fiorenza is, however, right to contrast Jesus' festive table celebrations with all and sundry, by which he foreshadowed the character of the messianic banquet, with cultic meals that maintain and reinforce the status quo. Jesus did indeed eat with sinners, tax collectors, the morally and ritually unclean, and some were outraged by this practice (cf. Mk 2:15-22). This is not because Jesus was uninterested in moral holiness, but precisely because he believed that God cared about everyone, and that even the least, last and lost were redeemable. These meals should not be seen as a tacit endorsement by Jesus that the lifestyles or activities of those with whom he dined were acceptable. For Jesus holiness meant both wholeness and moral rectitude. He was not interested in just healing the body or remedying the social situation, though these were some of his concerns. He was also interested in the moral transformation of the heart, mind and life of those to whom he reached out.[31]

3. *Jesus Against Patriarchy.* There are various key texts from which Fiorenza argues that Jesus believed in the eschatological abolition of patriarchy. One such text is Mark 12:18-27, which she reads in an intriguing way. She takes this text to mean that when the kingdom fully breaks in, patriarchal marriage will vanish.[32] While we may agree with her that this text is not about asexuality or freedom from intercourse in the kingdom,[33] it is also clearly not about marriage in general. It is a discussion of a particular Jewish form of marriage known as Levirate marriage.

Levirate marriage was solely for the purpose of raising up an heir for a deceased brother and was never treated by early Jews, when it was practiced at all, as the equivalent of full Jewish marriage. The important thing to note about this form of marriage is that it was created as an institution to overcome the intervention of death in a family's life. Jesus' response to the Sadducees, who neither believed in resurrection, or apparently in any positive form of afterlife (beyond the concept of Sheol, the going to the land of the dead), is that they do not know the Scriptures that support the idea of resurrection and the afterlife. In the afterlife, death is no more, and therefore the very reason for Levirate marriage is also no more.

If Jesus had given them a straight answer it would probably have been to the effect that the woman in question was still the first man's wife, since only he had married her in the normal way. Finally, the text speaks of abolishing any new acts of marrying, hence the language about marrying and being given in marriage. This in turn means the abolition of the patriarchal procedure of carrying out such an act in which the man chooses to marry and the woman is given by her father to the man. While one can argue that this implies the abolition of a particular patriarchal way of doing things, one cannot argue from this text for the total abolition of marriage in the kingdom. The point of the comparison is that we will be like the angels in their immortality, not in their asexuality or lack of married condition. This conclusion is made rather certain when we compare a similar note in Philo *(Sac.* 5), where he speaks of Abraham inheriting incorruption and so becoming equal to angels.

Let us, however, for the sake of argument, assume Fiorenza is right—marriage in general is seen as abolished in this saying. The question then becomes *when* this is implemented, and the answer is "in the resurrection" (cf. Mk 12:23 and 26), that is, when death is no more. This probably would tell us nothing at all about the state of marriage before the resurrection. The most one could infer is that Jesus might argue for the abolition of the patriarchal practice of Levirate marriage, now that the kingdom is already breaking in.

The material in Mark 10:2-9 is also treated by Fiorenza.[34] Here her analysis bears more fruit. She argues that Jesus' appeal to the creation order of things implies more of a partnership relationship between husband and wife, and his dismissal of divorce rules against male privileges in a patriarchal society. This is true enough. She also remarks that the quoting of Genesis 2:24 shows that Jesus is abrogating the patriarchal procedure whereby a woman becomes part of the husband's home and larger extended family. Rather, the husband is to leave his parents and cleave to his wife. The problems with this conclusion are several: (1) the Genesis text does not suggest the husband go to live with the wife but rather that he set up his own household, a possible alternative in a patriarchal culture and one that did not abrogate patriarchy, though it did modify clan and extended family structures;[35] (2) the Genesis material is quoted without any significant emendation, suggesting that Jesus was not modifying an ancient practice in this particular matter.

More controversial is Fiorenza's conclusion that Jesus equates hardness of heart with patriarchy in general. She concludes that since hardness of heart has no place in the kingdom, neither does patriarchy. But "hardness of heart" speaks of a moral condition, not a social institution or structure. While we may agree that this saying is about the reforming of the abuse of power by males, the effect of "no divorce" is to give women more security within marriage, not to liberate them from it in general. Fiorenza seems in the end to recognize this.[36]

The next aspect of the Jesus tradition that Fiorenza sees as addressing patriarchal structures is found in texts like Luke 14:26 ("Whoever comes to me and does not hate father and mother, wife and children, brothers and sisters, yes, and even life itself, cannot be my disciple"), where she finds the "a-familial ethos of the Jesus movement."[37] Fiorenza at this point is critiquing Theissen and his view that there was a group of wandering charismatic *men*, itinerant followers of Jesus who had left their wives and families at home. Fiorenza points out that Theissen relies on Luke 14:26 to reach this conclusion, which she argues reflects Luke's editorial hand and does not go back to Jesus. In her view, women also left home and followed Jesus. This is surely correct, but it is also true that there were disciples, perhaps like Peter, who did leave wives at home. Thus, this sort of saying tells us nothing about the afamilial ethos of Jesus' movement itself, but about what his followers left behind, at least temporarily and from time to time.[38]

More important is Fiorenza's argument about the Q material in Matthew 10:34-36/Luke 12:51-53 ("For I have come to set a man against his father, and a daughter against her mother").[39] As she says, this "hard" saying stresses division between parents and children, but *not* between husband and wife. She goes on to conclude that not only does this text speak of intrusion into the patriarchal household and a dividing of it, but it also speaks of "a radical a-familial ethos." But is this really the case? This saying surely develops the same theme we find in Luke 10:38-42 or Mark 3:31-35, namely that the family of faith and its agenda take priority over the agenda of the physical, "natural" family. If the latter is divided over following Jesus and obeying his teaching, then following Jesus must come first, even if children must be left at home when one or another or both parents follow Jesus. Far from establishing an "a-familial ethos," Jesus is setting up a new kind of family—the family of faith, which includes all those who do God's will.

Equally clearly, a saying like Luke 11:27-28 reveals that true or ultimate blessedness must be found in discipleship, not biological motherhood. The latter is not all God requires of a good Jewish woman, indeed it is not the primary thing God requires in terms of religious duty. Fiorenza's conclusion about this text is right: "The original saying opposes religious claims made on the grounds of motherhood but not on the grounds of discipleship."[40] Just so, but this does not imply that Jesus did not have a positive attitude toward women bearing children, so long as the end is not at hand and so long as it does not interfere with discipleship. The point of this saying is that in the new order, bearing children is not seen as *the* sign or means of religious claims or blessedness.

It is especially important to insist that the use of family language in Mark 3:31-35 makes clear whom Jesus sees as his primary or true family, his true mothers, brothers and sisters. Fiorenza rightly raises the question, Why not fathers as well?[41] Her view is that Jesus had no room for males assuming father roles in the family of faith, since it was a nonpatriarchal entity, rejecting the power and status and claims of the male as head of the family. This argument has some merit, but it overlooks two things. (1) Jesus clearly enough sets himself up over his community. They are his flock, and he is their shepherd. Notice that he does not count himself as one of the Twelve. In other words, while we may speak of the discipleship of equals in the family of faith, this does not mean there is not a hierarchical structure involved, with Jesus as the head or leader of his followers. (2) Leadership, to be sure, means servant leadership for Jesus, not the sort of abusive patriarchy modeled in the world. But it *is* a form of leadership, and a leadership structure is expected to exist in the eschaton as well (cf. Lk 22:24-30).

Equally important for Fiorenza is the material found in Matthew 23:1-12 (cf. Mk 12:38-40; Lk 20:45-47).[42] It is only in its Matthean context that we read, "And call no one your father on earth," but in all three Synoptics the issue is leadership within Jesus' community as undertaken by his disciples, in comparison to leadership and titles among other Jewish teachers. The followers of Jesus are not to desire lofty titles like "master" or "rabbi" or "father," because, as the First Evangelist explains, they have one master and one teacher, and one Father, God.

In a tour de force, Fiorenza concludes that this means, "The 'father' God is invoked here, however, not to justify patriarchal structures and relationships in the community of disciples but precisely to reject all such claims, powers and structures."[43] First we must note the context. The issue here is titles of honor in the community of Jesus' followers as opposed to those in Judaism in general. Jesus is not commenting on the physical family and its structure at all! It is perhaps true that this saying implicitly argues against a patriarchal structure being imposed on or assumed in the kingdom or in Jesus' community.

Second, the saying has a theocratic thrust, recognizing only God as worthy of such patriarchal titles or names. Thus while patriarchy *may* be ruled out at the level of the social structure of the new community, this is not taken to imply that at the theological level it is also ruled out in the way one addresses or talks about God. To the contrary, it is precisely because God is the ultimate authority, the ultimate head and Father of the chosen people, that mere human claims to spiritual fatherhood are ruled out.

It is notable that Fiorenza says nothing about the *abba* sayings or the Lord's Prayer, presumably because she wishes to argue that Jesus called and saw God as Sophia. The problem is that the Sophia idea is less well attested than Father, which is found in Q (cf. Mt 6:9 to Lk 11:2) in Matthew's special material (Mt 23:9), and in the form of *abba*/Father in Jesus' own prayer language in Mark (Mk 14:36 and parallels), as well as in early material in Paul (Rom 8:15), where it appears in the same Markan form.

Fiorenza goes on to quote approvingly the radical views of Mary Daly, that the fatherhood of God denies any father and all patriarchy the right to exist.[44] This is certainly saying a good deal more than the text either allows or suggests, since it is not talking about society in general but a specialized pedagogical form of "fatherhood" that existed in early Judaism. It is especially important to stress this latter point since elsewhere Jesus urged the honoring of both father and mother, which included providing them financial support (Mk 7:9-13).[45]

What we must conclude from Matthew 23:9 is that Jesus had no problem applying "Father" language to God, nor in light of other sayings did he object to some sort of leadership hierarchy among God's people, *but* he does oppose the honor and shame conventions involving illustrious titles and names being given to Christian leaders and teachers. There is to be a discipleship of equals, including women, and all leadership must be servant leadership. This is a reform of patriarchal notions of leadership and discipleship, but it does not go as far as Fiorenza or Daly assume.

Fiorenza offers some comments on the model of the child for discipleship in Mark 10:15.[46] She maintains that the child is held up as the paradigm for true discipleship. The issue is, In what *way* is the child a model? In what way or respect are disciples to turn and become like a child? Fiorenza uses the phrase *slave/child* here because the Greek term *paidia* can refer to either. It does not however refer to both in one text, and our context shows that Mark understands the word to refer to children. In other words, this text is not about the reversal of slave-master relationships or anything of that sort. Rather it is about the leading disciples of Jesus in some way becoming like children if they wish to enter the kingdom.

Perhaps the implication is that one does not get in on the basis of honor or status or position but by renouncing all of these and receiving the kingdom as a gift, as a child must do. This comports with Jesus' teaching about how hard it is for the rich to enter the kingdom. Mark 10:15 would thus imply a reversal of values as they sometimes were expressed in early Judaism. The first and best do not get in on their merits, but rather children and those like them get in. It may be that Fiorenza is right that this saying "challenges those in positions of dominance . . . to become 'equal' with those who are powerless," but we are talking about leaders in Jesus' circle, not masters and slaves.[47]

4. *God as Sophia.* As an alternative to a religion that worships God as Father, Fiorenza argues that Jesus held up a vision of God as Sophia. The argument is based in part on the assumption that Israel, in its Woman Wisdom material in Proverbs 1—9, had integrated language about the Egyptian goddess Isis or Ma'at into its own material as "reflective mythology," which was then used to express something about the gracious goodness of God. This conclusion is in part correct, though whether we should call the use of personification "mythology" is doubtful.[48] The further conclusion that from the third century B.C. on, Jewish wisdom theology celebrated God's goodness of allowing his gracious presence to dwell "in the female *Gestalt* of divine Sophia" in the midst of the chosen people[49] is saying more than we have evidence to support.

The more important issue, however, is whether we may conclude that Jesus used the Sophia/*Ḥokmâh* image of God to speak of God's gracious presence among the chosen people. This conclusion is based to a large extent on Luke 7:35/Matthew 11:19, and in particular on the conclusion that Luke preserves the earlier form of this saying, which speaks of Wisdom being vindicated by her children, while the Matthean form speaks of being vindicated by her deeds. The Matthean form suggests that Jesus saw himself as Wisdom, the Lukan form that Jesus saw God in this light. I will deal with the reasons why I believe the Matthean form of this saying is likely to be original shortly. Here I wish to point out that there is plenty of other evidence in the Gospel tradition that suggests Jesus may have seen himself in this light, but very little evidence apart from this saying (and possibly one other, Lk 11:49[50]) that he spoke of God that way. In texts such as Matthew 11:28-30 (cf. Sir 51:26-28) and Luke 13:34 Jesus does not speak as Wisdom's messenger, but simply as Wisdom. My point is simply this: even if Fiorenza's interpretation of Luke's two sayings is correct, it is too slender a basis to support the argument that Jesus' dominant image for God was Sophia, or Wisdom, *rather than* Father, or *abba.* The latter is better attested.

Fiorenza's arguments, though they are insufficient to justify all the conclusions that she would urge, are nonetheless sufficient to show that Jesus spoke and acted in ways that amounted to a reformation of the patriarchal structure of his society, especially by way of creating a new community of faith with greater openness structured into it. Her arguments are also sufficient to show that Jesus' view of discipleship involved both men and women as equals and both men and women as traveling disciples (cf. Lk 8:1-3). Jesus' teaching on marriage, divorce and singleness (cf. Mt 19:10-12) not only gave women greater security in marriage but opened up new roles and possibilities for single women. Furthermore, his teaching on the family of faith rather than the physical family as the basic unit of his new community (Mk 3:31-35), makes clear that a reenvisioning of the role of the physical family is in mind, both now and in the coming kingdom. Places in the family of God do not come by natural descent, but by faith and by doing God's will.

Fiorenza's argument never comes to grips with the important traditions about the Twelve and the Three (Peter, James and John), which not only are found in a wide variety of Synoptic texts but also in early material in 1 Corinthians 15 and Acts 1. Had Jesus really been like some modern feminists assume, he surely would have felt obligated to choose at least one woman, say a Mary Magdalene, to be among the Twelve and would never have spoken of the Twelve having roles in the eschaton judging or bringing justice to Israel.[51]

I think it is fair to say that while Jesus did not set out to create a modern egalitarian structure for society, it is also true that he did not intend to set up a *purely* gender-based hierarchy in his own community. Both women and men could assume important roles of proclamation and leadership as his disciples. Jesus lived within the structure of Jewish society but bore prophetic witness against its inequities both verbally and by practices such as eating with sinners. Into that patriarchal society he also injected the witness of his own community which was different, and *more egalitarian*, than the society at large. During Jesus' lifetime and the years immediately thereafter, the changes of which he spoke and urged seem to have come about mainly, if not solely, within his community and not in society at large.

Jesus: Miriam's Child, Sophia's Prophet

In her most recent work, *Jesus: Miriam's Child, Sophia's Prophet*,[52] Fiorenza is primarily concerned to further spin out the implications of her views that were already stated in her earlier work, *In Memory of Her*. In this new work she does not offer much new exegesis but rather concentrates on methodological and theological issues.

1. A Consideration of Methodology. First, we must again stress that it is crucial to Fiorenza's whole program that she must assume that the Gospel material must have gone through a lengthy process of transmission and substantive *change.*[53] This assumption is what validates a repeated and radical reconstruction of the Jesus tradition that rejects a majority of the material and gives a particular construal to a selection of a few salient passages. In this regard Fiorenza's approach is much like that of Crossan's, and the same critique applies.[54] While I agree that historical reconstruction is necessary to sort out the truth about the historical Jesus,[55] unlike Fiorenza I would argue that there is *not* a willful misconstrual or patriarchal reconstructing of most of the arguably authentic Jesus material in the Synoptic Gospels. If this is true, much of Fiorenza's argument and justification for her exegetical and theological program falls to the ground.

Second, Fiorenza seems now much more prepared than in her earlier work to take seriously the suggestion that the material in the *Gospel of Thomas* provides us an early and authentic window on the kind of wisdom Jesus proclaimed.[56] Once again the critique given previously of Crossan applies at this point. *Thomas* can be shown again and again to be a later Gnosticizing reappropriation of the Jesus tradition found in the Synoptics.[57]

Third, there is the whole matter of the ever elusive Q community, situated somewhere in Galilee perhaps. Fiorenza is inclined to accept and build on this theory as it allows her to argue that there were a variety of alternate Christian communities from the start, perhaps even with competing visions of Christ and God. The problem with this argument is that there is not a shred of solid historical evidence that there ever was such a Q community, if by that we mean a community that operated without a passion narrative, or, in Fiorenza's case, operated without a vision of God as *Abba* and Jesus as God's Son.[58]

Fourth, there is a further theological/philosophical problem with Fiorenza's approach. It is Fiorenza's assumption that all God language is simply symbolic, metaphorical and analogical since "human language can never speak adequately about divine reality."[59] Frankly, this is a proposition that ought to be debated and substantiated, not simply assumed as an axiom. No one is arguing that human language can exhaustively represent the truth about God, but the question of adequacy is another matter. Most Jews and Christians, not to mention Muslims, have always believed that it was indeed possible for God to be truthfully and adequately imaged or described in human language. Even eschewing a belief in revelation, this has been believed and cogently argued.

This theory of language that Fiorenza espouses allows her to suggest that there are no definitive images of God, for "divine reality cannot be comprehended in human language."[60] But if this is so, there is no reason to advocate alternate images or names for God, since they too must fall under the dictum of the impossibility of properly imaging God. I would argue that Fiorenza is not being entirely consistent here, for clearly enough she does believe there are more and less true images of God or else she would not be so eloquently and passionately arguing for these alternative images. But if this is so, then one must ask, By what standard do we determine which images are more or less true or revealing of God's character? Fiorenza's answer presumably would be one from experience: those images that liberate the oppressed are "true" images of God.[61] The danger here is that we re-create God in our own image and especially in the image of our cultural and political agendas. I would suggest that while human experience should not be ignored, it should not be the starting point for deciding the issue about God language.

It is my own personal conviction that God can be comprehended at least in part because God has revealed the divine character in the person of Jesus, something I think Fiorenza would at least partially affirm, or else all of her detailed attempts to deal with the Jesus tradition would have no adequate purpose or explanation. More importantly, I would add that God has revealed that character in Jesus in a true and *adequate*, and even definitive, though not exhaustive, way. If this is true, then we are not free to simply pick and choose from a smorgasbord of images for God. Before we make a claim on God, God has already made a claim on us and revealed the divine nature. This means that not just any image will do.[62]

Finally, it is hard to doubt that the driving engine behind such statements is Fiorenza's liberationist aims. As she says, "Nothing stops feminist theologians from critically assessing the kyriocentric framework of the wisdom traditions (and all other biblical traditions) *in order to rearticulate some of its discourses in such a way that wo/men can theologically claim it*," or to "open up possibilities of liberation and well-being."[63] But if this is so, it becomes clear that theology is dictating how the historical research is going to be conducted and what the outcome must be. It is one thing to assert that no historical research is value-free and to be aware of and cautious about one's own presuppositions and predilections. It is quite another to deliberately use the historical data to support or buttress one's own agendas. Unfortunately Fiorenza's own rhetoric encourages the reader to see her reading of the Jesus material as deliberately tendentious, and this will mean that many of those who most need to hear some of her very helpful historical insights into Jesus will not do so.

2. *Jesus and Judaism.* Fiorenza is especially concerned to avoid certain sorts of proposals about Jesus the "feminist," because they can be accused of being anti-Jewish. That is, if Jesus simply rejected Jewish patriarchy and its religious manifestations, he could be accused of being anti-Jewish. Fiorenza sees the emphasis on Jesus the Jew in the Third Quest as leading inevitably to seeing

> his relation to women in terms of dominant Jewish as well as Greco-Roman malestream reality. By remaining oblivious to the role of Jewish women or marginalizing it as a feminist ideological question, dominant scholarship tends to preclude a re-envisioning of the Jesus of history in line with emancipatory tendencies and movements in early Judaism and Greco-Roman cultures and religions.[64]

Fiorenza's remedy for these problems, as we have seen, is to see Jesus as following in the stream of early Jewish emancipatory tendencies or movements, however slim the historical evidence may be for such trends, and thus Jesus is rescued from anti-Judaism and anti-Semitism.

I quite agree with Fiorenza when she critiques the Jesus Seminar as guilty of "a reductionist method, which abstracts Jesus as an ahistorical artifact from the movement of his followers and separates him from his historical-religious context."[65] Unfortunately, I must conclude that to some extent she is guilty of the same methodological flaw, for while we have plenty of evidence for showing that the early church, even as early as Paul's earlier letters (written within about twenty years of Jesus' death) viewed Jesus as God's Wisdom, we have precious little evidence that they viewed Jesus' God as Wisdom/Sophia. Yet this is what Fiorenza must argue if she is to see continuity between Jesus and his earliest followers. To the contrary, the same evidence suggests that both Jesus, Paul and various others saw God as Father, in particular as *abba* (see, e.g., Gal 4:6; Rom 8:15). Furthermore, as I will argue below, the early Christians saw God as Father precisely because they were applying Wisdom insights to God and Jesus, just as Jesus had taught them to do. In short, the Wisdom stream of early Judaism is no less patriarchal in its God language than any other stream of early Jewish thinking. Indeed, it could even be said that in its *emphasis* on God as Father, it is more patriarchal.

Fiorenza then, sees Jesus and his female and male followers as part of an emancipatory movement that involved theological reflection, common meals and healing events, and were part of "the various *basileia* and holiness movements that in the first century sought the 'liberation' of Israel from imperial exploitation."[66] One could agree with much of this conclusion, but when we read that this is not simply a historical conclusion but part of "our common struggles for transforming religious patriarchy" today and that "feminist theological reflection must privilege soteriological over christological discourses and socio-cultural over individual-anthropological theological frameworks"[67] one has a right to worry that ideology is dictating methodology as well as historical and exegetical conclusions.

Fiorenza is equally concerned about another facet of what she calls Christian anti-Judaism, namely the supersessionist argument that the church replaces Israel, or that Christianity is the more perfect form of Judaism. She seeks to avoid this by arguing, "Only if we explicitly acknowledge that Judaism and Christianity are two different religions, which have roots in the Hebrew Bible and in the pluriform religious matrix of first century Israel, can we avoid reading 'renewal movement' in a supersessionist fashion."[68] As a description of how things have turned out after the first century A.D., this argument has considerable merit, but as a description of the historical Jesus and his first followers it is problematic.

It is especially problematic since many of the early Christians, including many of the New Testament authors, clearly saw Christianity, by which they meant Jew and Gentile united in Christ, as the ultimate form that the one true people of Israel's God should take. This is certainly true of Paul, the author of Luke-Acts, the author of 1 Peter, the author of Hebrews, the authors of the Gospels and the author of Revelation, and doubtless one could argue for other New Testament writers as well. In short, to arrive at the conclusion that Fiorenza reaches, one must reject the theological interpretation of the vast majority of New Testament writers.

This sort of attempt to avoid the scandal of particularity in regard to early Christianity and its claims, or even in some respects the historical Jesus and at least his implicit claims, is, I think, doomed to failure. At the end of the day, modern Jews and modern Christians will simply have to agree to disagree about Jesus and his historical claims, if indeed Jesus made unique claims that most Jews presently reject and Christians accept.

There is probably no historical Jesus that is going to be equally acceptable to all persons—Christians, Jews, Muslims and others.

It is Fiorenza's view that the Jesus movement was a resistance movement, like other early Jewish resistance movements "organized against Roman imperial domination," and thus "Jesus was not crucified because of his theological teachings but because of their potentially subversive character and because of their political threat to the imperial colonial system."[69] The problem with this conclusion is that it goes at least partially against what little evidence we have from the teachings of Jesus, namely that he was not a Zealot and did not preach resistance against the Roman authorities. It was Jewish authorities, not Roman authorities, who were, at least at the outset, responsible for Jesus being arrested and handed over to Pilate.

I would suggest that Jesus was executed for religious and political reasons, which means at least in part because of some theological differences between Jesus and Jewish leaders, and probably some implicit personal claims of Jesus. Without a doubt some of Jesus' teachings would have seemed subversive to some Jews, but this is not the same as suggesting he organized a resistance movement against the powers that be, especially if by that one means the Romans. As we have seen in the previous chapter, it is quite another matter to suggest that he rejected any and all sorts of claims that Caesar and other authorities made on Jews and planned active resistance against them.[70]

3. *The Kingdom of Equals.* As we have seen earlier, Fiorenza's essential argument is that Jesus at his best advocated a different sort of kingdom from that envisioned by Rome. It was to be a kingdom with the discipleship of equals and without the systems of domination that existed in all worldly kingdoms. It was to be a kingdom where one was free of poverty, hunger, sickness and other things that oppress human life, a kingdom in part already realized in the table fellowship and patterns of relating in the circle of Jesus' immediate followers. This political agenda was, however, subverted by the Evangelists, including Mark, who depoliticized the teaching of Jesus.[71]

Like most of Fiorenza's arguments, this one prompts a yes and a no. It is true enough that Jesus envisioned and began to enact a different sort of world and that he sought to alleviate hunger, sickness and spiritual sources of oppression. It is also true that he sought to offer women new and liberating opportunities in the circle of his followers. It does not follow from this that Jesus was opposed in principle to any and all sorts of leadership structures among his followers. He offered a different model of leadership, servant leadership, which is not in fact the negation of all sorts of hierarchical structures. It makes clear how those who lead are to do so, but it does not suggest that his disciples do not need leaders. Indeed, all the numerous texts that deal with Peter, James and John suggest that Jesus did single out some to be leaders among the disciples, but that he did not want them to follow "worldly" models of how leadership should be exercised (cf. Lk 22:25-27/Mt 20:25-28).

It is only some moderns who assume that a discipleship of equals necessarily means no hierarchical leadership structures of any sort. This sort of interpretation does not even do justice to Jesus as an individual, for clearly enough he does not see himself as one of the Twelve or as simply another follower of God. Rather he has come to model and offer a different form of leadership. In short, Jesus himself and the roles he assumed are the negation of the false equation: "Discipleship of equals means no hierarchical leadership structures of any sort."[72]

4. *The Christological Clothing of Jesus.* In her new work, Fiorenza takes an entire chapter to reiterate her arguments that Jesus saw God as Sophia, with himself as Sophia's prophet. She believes that the Divine Sophia traditions in the Gospels and elsewhere in the New Testament have been overlaid with a thick veneer of what she calls kyriocentric or christological language. This suggests that these traditions originally did not have any christological intent or content. She asks whether it is possible to "transform such a figure clothed in kyriocentric language in such a way that it can . . . have a liberating function in emancipatory struggles for a more just world."[73] It is this latter goal that Fiorenza passionately longs for and works for, and to that end she wishes to remove the christological garb with which the Gospel writers have (in her view wrongly) clothed Jesus. Of course the very metaphor of clothing suggests that there was nothing essentially christological about Jesus or his ministry. It is here on this latter point especially that I would most strongly disagree with Fiorenza.

In her discussion of the early Jewish traditions found in Proverbs, Sirach, Wisdom of Solomon and elsewhere,[74] Fiorenza is not clear as to what she means by divine Wisdom. At one moment she speaks about God being "present in the female personification of Wisdom,"[75] and she goes on to say that the biblical and early Jewish tradition struggles not to fall into di-theism, but at the next moment she is talking about Sophia as "the personification of God's saving activity in the world, of Israel's election, and of the salvation of all peoples."[76] One may properly ask which she means: Wisdom as a personification of God, or Wisdom as a personification of God's activity, or perhaps of an attribute of God? This question is never directly answered, but Fiorenza suspects that this use of Wisdom language may be a polemical reaction to "the possibility that Divine Wisdom might have been worshipped by Jewish women and men."[77]

Fiorenza considers it possible, on the basis of her reading of Philo (the Therapeutae mentioned in *De Vita Contemplativa*) and Wisdom of Solomon, that there were Jews using the language previously applied to Isis to speak of Israel's God in a form of reflective mythology.[78] It is by such tentative conjectures that she seeks to build a case for an ethos in early Judaism that led Jesus to pursue the idea of God as Sophia and a radical egalitarian kingdom that involves salvation for all peoples.

A significant feature found in all of Fiorenza's works is an attempt to elucidate an argument regarding the development of the Jesus tradition:

> The first level, which may go back to the historical Jesus himself but is barely traceable any longer, understands Jesus as messenger and prophet of Sophia. The second level of theological reflection identifies Jesus with Divine Wisdom. Jesus however is not called "Sophia" but receives "male" christological titles such as *kyrios* and *sōtēr* which also were titles of Isis-Sophia. . . . Early Christian sophialogical reflection also knows a transitional stage in which attributes of Sophia were given to Jesus [e.g., in the pre-Pauline hymns].[79]

This sort of analysis may be distinguished from my own (see below) in which I argue that Jesus presented himself explicitly as a sage and at least implicitly as the embodiment of Wisdom. This led to the various developments of applying Wisdom language to Jesus in later Christian tradition. In other words, the tradition was christocentric, at least implicitly, from the outset. It is not a case of a development away from God as Sophia to Jesus as Sophia.

I find particularly amazing Fiorenza's attempt to minimize the evidence in the New Testament's christological hymns where Jesus is already seen as Wisdom, not simply as having some of Wisdom's attributes. The same can be said of what we find in Paul's writings from the 50s, in 1 Corinthians 1—4 and 10.[80] If the argument for change is tenuous at the transitional stage of the 40s and 50s, as witnessed in the christological hymns and Paul, what about the Jesus tradition itself?

Fiorenza stakes a lot on certain key texts which she sees as revealing the earliest stages of the tradition: (1) Luke 13:34, (2) Luke 11:49, (3) Luke 7:35 (contrast the Q parallel Mt 11:19) and (4) Matthew 11:28-30.[81] It is noticeable that Fiorenza strongly favors Lukan texts or texts in their Lukan version. She nowhere faces the possibility that Luke's version of things may be the later adaptation of more Jewish texts for a Gentile audience.

Luke 13:34 ("Jerusalem, Jerusalem, the city that kills the prophets. . . . How often have I desired to gather your children together as a hen gathers her brood under her wings, and you were not willing!") is indeed a lament using female imagery, but it does not even hint at the language of agency. It does not suggest Jesus is acting as the agent of God/Sophia in speaking this way. Rather, it simply suggests that Jesus is speaking about himself and his own role in relationship to Jerusalem, the heart of Israel. It is a lament because of the personal rejection he has experienced during his own ministry, which has led him to feel like a rejected mother.[82] There is nothing here to support the conclusion that God equals Sophia in Jesus' teaching. The same may be said about the last of these texts, Matthew 11:28-30 ("Come to me, all you that are weary . . . I will give you rest. Take my yoke upon you"), which is surely a modification of material found in Sirach 51:26-28, where Wisdom is the one who offers a yoke.[83] Nothing in this text suggests anything other than the conclusion that Jesus saw himself as Wisdom or Wisdom's embodiment in the flesh and offered his yoke as Wisdom's yoke.

Luke 11:49 ("Therefore also the Wisdom of God said, 'I will send them prophets and apostles, some of whom they will kill and persecute' ") is a more difficult case. Here it is possible that God is spoken of as Wisdom, but this is not certain. Two other conclusions could be drawn. (1) In view of the reference to prophets and *apostles* and the fact that the verb is in the future tense ("I will send"), as well as the fact that the charge leveled is against "this generation" (as v. 50 makes clear), the text is probably referring to Jesus' own agents and emissaries, whom Luke has styled in later Christian terms (i.e., "apostles"). If so, this text calls Jesus God's Wisdom. (2) The phrase "the Wisdom of God" may not refer to a person, whether God or Jesus, but to a source from which this saying comes, or more probably to an attribute of God (God's wisdom) that comes to expression or is revealed in this saying. In others words, "the wisdom of God" here may refer to a thing or concept rather than a person. In any case, it is very tenuous to base a whole reconstruction of the development of Wisdom thinking about God and Jesus using this verse as the linchpin of the argument.

Finally, we come to Luke 7:35 ("Wisdom is vindicated by all her children"), and notice that Fiorenza does not mention the parallel to this saying in Matthew 11:19. She seems to assume that we may take it for granted that Luke preserves the earliest version of this saying. But this is by no means certain, and in the Matthean form of the saying ("Wisdom is vindicated by her *deeds*") it seems reasonably clear that the reference is to Jesus. I have argued in another context that the reading "children" in Luke may not be original in view of Luke 7:32, where children are the subject of the discussion at the beginning of these sayings (Lk 7:31-35).[84] Various manuscripts have the reading "children" at Matthew 11:19 (C, D, L, and a host of others), which scholars believe is an attempt to harmonize it with Luke 7:35.[85] Clearly "deeds" is the more difficult reading here and thus more likely to be original. Fiorenza's argument again hangs by the thread of a particular reading of an isolated saying about which there is contention as to its original form and meaning.

She further compounds the problematic character of her argument by insisting on a Q community that followed in Jesus' footsteps in seeing God as Sophia, with the Q prophets standing in the line of a succession of her messengers which included Jesus. But we have no firm historical evidence there ever was a Q community, so now we are mounting one very tenuous hypothesis upon another.[86]

As if this were not enough, she also follows a very dubious interpretation of the Markan baptismal narrative in which the dove in the story is interpreted as the Near Eastern love goddess, and the voice from heaven is the voice of Divine Sophia who has found her elect one. Thus Jesus is the Spirit-filled prophet of divine Sophia.[87] This interpretation simply ignores two important points: (1) the "dove" is only a metaphor in Mark for the *descent* of the Spirit and it is not equated with the Spirit or seen as the symbol of Sophia as it seems to be in Philo (*Quis rerum* 127-28), and (2) the voice from heaven speaks of Jesus as *beloved Son*, which in fact echoes Psalm 2:7. This text has to do with the coronation of the Davidic king by "the Lord" Yahweh, not by Sophia. It is right to point to texts like Isaiah 11:1-4 as providing background for the concept of a Wisdom teacher endowed with the Spirit,[88] but there as well it is connected with royal ideology and the covenant God of David, not Sophia.

I must conclude that Fiorenza's argument for Jesus (or early followers of Jesus) relating to God as Sophia has not been strengthened in her most recent work. The evidence is very tenuous at best and involves a doubtful reading of only a very few texts. What Fiorenza's work does show, however, is that there is strong evidence of sapiential material in the Jesus tradition. The question is how to interpret it properly. It is at this juncture that I suggest an alternative reading of the data that still takes into account all of the Wisdom texts and allusions that Fiorenza has rightly noted.

JESUS THE SAGE, THE EMBODIMENT OF WISDOM (BEN WITHERINGTON III)

I should repeat from the outset that I do not think any one term or title fully captures the truth about the historical Jesus. In my first study of Jesus, *The Christology of Jesus,* I made very clear that I believe that some combination of several different approaches and insights best represents who Jesus thought he was. I am quite convinced, for instance, that Jesus was indeed a healer, was seen as a prophetic figure and did prefer the term *Son of Man* to refer to himself. I also believe that he saw himself in some sort of messianic light, perhaps along the lines of what we find in Zechariah. But if we ask what heuristic category comes closest to explaining the most about who Jesus thought he was and what he said and did, what comes closest to explaining why early christological thinking about Jesus developed as it did, then we must come to grips with sages and Wisdom.

A sapiential approach to Jesus and his ministry can explain things as diverse as Jesus' work of healing, including his exorcisms, why he never uses the prophetic phrase "thus says the Lord," why he spoke in aphorisms and parables and beatitudes, why he gathered disciples, why he spoke as one with independent authority, why he used the language of Father for God, why he does not spend much of his time quoting or exegeting the Pentateuch and engaging in halakic discussions, why his message has a more universal flavor to it, why he goes back and appeals to the creation order in his discussions of marriage and its purpose, why he said there was something greater than Solomon present when he came on the scene, why the phrase "Son of David" seems to be associated with Jesus when he performed miracles and why his message seemed so positive in comparison to John the Baptist's. If the value of an approach is shown by the wide variety of puzzles and enigmas it helps to solve, then a sapiential approach to Jesus has a lot going for it. I will try to unpack a few of these suggestions in the remainder of this chapter.[89]

It is crucial at the outset not to make the mistake of assuming that Jesus or other early Jews would have simply thought in nice discrete categories of prophetic images on the one hand and sapiential ones on the other. In fact, already before and during Jesus' day we see the blending of the prophetic (and eschatological) and wisdom traditions in works like Daniel, the Wisdom of Solomon and the so-called *Parables of Enoch*.[90] Thus, for instance, in the latter work we see the blending of Son of Man speculation with Wisdom speculation, the very sort of mingling we see in the Synoptic Gospels, only now applied to Jesus instead of Enoch. Or again in the Wisdom of Solomon we see the attempt to read the salvation history of Israel as a history of how Wisdom assisted God's people throughout its development. Solomon is portrayed in this work as the great ruler imbued with the Spirit. He is even given the vision of the kingdom of God (Wis 10:10), a phrase we find almost nowhere in the Old Testament (though cf. Dan 7) but very frequently in Jesus' teaching.[91] Jesus arrived on the stage of history precisely when all these different Jewish traditions were converging, and I would suggest he drew on them in the way he presented himself.

In Solomon the royal and sapiential traditions already had come together, and when the prophets looked for some kind of messianic figure, this expectation often had a sapiential component. Thus, for instance, in Isaiah 11 the shoot of Jesse is described not only as having the Spirit of God upon him, but as having also with that Spirit the spirit of wisdom, knowledge, understanding, the fear of the Lord—the very things most touted in the early Wisdom literature (cf. Prov). In short, the desire was to have a wise royal ruler like Solomon who had the sagacity to establish Israel as a respected world power. In the *Parables of Enoch* it is Enoch as the Son of Man about whom it is said, "in him dwells the Spirit of wisdom" (*1 Enoch* 49:3) and that he is the one endowed to be the revealer of the secrets of God's wisdom (*1 Enoch* 51:3).

In my judgment some of the strongest proposals that have arisen during the Third Quest are those that view Jesus as a prophetic figure.[92] Yet at the end of the day even they leave too much unexplained. One of the things which started me down the path of examining Jesus in light of sapiential ways of thinking is the fact that Jesus seems never to have used the formulas one normally expects of a prophet. He never seems to see himself as a mouthpiece for God, prefacing his remarks with "thus says the Lord," but rather speaks on his own authority, or as Mark 1:27 suggests, as one who has independent authority. Furthermore, over and over again in the Synoptics one gets the impression that Jesus' public mode of discourse was one or another form of wisdom speech, including riddles, parables, aphorisms, personifications and beatitudes.

It became clear to me when examining the relationship of Jesus to John the Baptist that one had to account for why their styles of ministry and message were different in certain key respects. Briefly, this difference can to a large extent be explained by the fact that John stood in the line of the classical prophets, while Jesus came across as a prophetic and eschatological sage. What I would like to do now is to present a brief sketch of the evidence that leads me to the conclusion that Jesus saw himself as a sage, as one who embodied the very Wisdom of God, indeed even saw himself as God's Wisdom come in the flesh.

Let us return briefly to the Q material found in Matthew 11:16-19/Luke 7:31-35. Here we find a deliberate contrast between Jesus' lifestyle and that of John. Jesus as the Son of Man came eating and drinking, celebrating and dancing, while John came in ascetic fashion as if in mourning. Yet neither style seemed to please the audience. Jesus in particular was accused of being a drunkard and a friend of toll collectors and sinners.[93] The passage ends with the remark "Yet wisdom (Ḥokmâh) is vindicated by her deeds." In other words, though the Son of Man does not receive affirmation or confirmation from some of his audience, nevertheless his actions vindicate him as God's Wisdom. One may properly ask, How so?

At this juncture, we must consider some samples from the Wisdom tradition. First of all we note that this tradition has a good deal to say about eating and drinking, in particular about banqueting (see, e.g., Sir. 31:12—32:6). Wisdom literature in general encourages one to have a certain joie de vivre, to enjoy eating, friends and the good things in life. But even more to the point, we find traditions like that in Proverbs 9:1-6, which speaks of a feast set by Wisdom herself where she invites very unlikely guests to the table—the simple, those without sense and the immature—so that they may learn to be wise.

Meals were the occasion for teaching in antiquity, both in the Jewish as well as in the Greco-Roman world, and this is important for understanding Jesus in context. If we ask why it is that Jesus dined with unlikely clientele, just the opposite of those a respectable person might want for dinner guests, the answer must be because Jesus saw it as his mission to reach the least, the last and the lost in his society. In the context of dining he could begin to impart wisdom to them, a wisdom which, as the Wisdom of Solomon puts it, could "save" (cf. Wis 9:18). In short, Jesus is seen acting out the part of Wisdom, and thus not surprisingly he concludes with the confidence that he will be vindicated for doing so, for his actions led to the salvation of various people of God who had been given up for lost. In sum, John the Baptist came across like a great prophet of judgment of old, like a Jeremiah or an Amos, but for the most part Jesus did not. This fact must be explained.

A second tradition, which seems innocent enough on first glance, is found in Matthew 8:20/Luke 9:58: "Foxes have holes, and birds of the air have nests; but the Son of Man has nowhere to lay his head." This has often simply been taken as a statement about the nature of Jesus' itinerant ministry and the fact that Jesus did not always get a warm reception. But this overlooks the important fact that this image had been used earlier of Wisdom having no place to dwell until God assigned her such a place (cf. Sir 24:6-7 to *1 Enoch* 42:2), with *Enoch* speaking of the rejection of Wisdom ("but she found no dwelling place"). There is also the further tradition that raises the question of the credibility of an itinerant person: "So who will trust a man that has no nest, but lodges wherever night overtakes him?" (Sir 36:31). The mention of nests in both this saying and in Matthew 8:20/Luke 9:58 is striking. It once again suggests that Jesus envisions and articulates his experience in light of sapiential traditions and especially in light of what happened to Wisdom according to the late Wisdom material in *1 Enoch* 42.

The lament found in Matthew 23:37-39/Luke 13:34-35 comports with the above and further suggests that Jesus saw his rejection by Jerusalem as the rejection of God's Wisdom. Those who knew the Wisdom traditions would know the irony of this, for in Sirach 24:11 it is said that wandering Wisdom was finally given a place to dwell in Jerusalem by God, in particular in or as the Book of the Covenant (Torah).

An important tradition is found in Luke 10:21-22/Matthew 11:25-27, which in Luke's version runs as follows:

> At that same hour Jesus rejoiced in the Holy Spirit and said, "I thank
> you, Father, Lord of heaven and earth, because you have hidden these
> things from the wise and the intelligent and have revealed them to

infants; yes, Father, for such was your gracious will. All things have been handed over to me by my Father; and no one knows who the Son is except the Father, or who the Father is except the Son and anyone to whom the Son chooses to reveal him."

Marinus de Jonge rightly discerns that the relationship described in this text more nearly resembles that of the relationship of Wisdom to God as it is depicted in Wisdom of Solomon than it resembles the relationship of the righteous Servant to God.[94] De Jonge thinks that this text may express the essence of Jesus' relationship to God in a way that goes beyond all the traditional titles. I believe this is also correct.

It is thus appropriate at this juncture to remind ourselves that according to the Wisdom tradition it was Wisdom who was entrusted with the secrets or revelation of God and with the task of unveiling them to humankind (cf. Prov 8:14-36; Wis 2:13, 16; 4:10-15). By alluding to this Wisdom tradition, Jesus was suggesting that he had a uniquely intimate relationship with the Father (said of Wisdom in Job 28:1-28; Sir 1:6, 8; Bar 3:15-32; Prov 8:12) and a profound awareness of a task to reveal the divine will and manifest God's saving activity, as is said to be Wisdom's task in Wisdom of Solomon 8—9. Both the subordinationist theme in this saying (the Son must rely on what is revealed to him), and the fact that the Son is not the content of the revelation, favor the early origin and the probability that this is an authentic saying of Jesus.

This saying then draws out the implications of Jesus' use of the term *abba*, indicates that he believed he had a unique relationship with God and suggests that he was given this revelatory knowledge or wisdom for the purpose of revealing God's true nature as *abba* to those whom he chose as disciples.[95]

We have already seen in this chapter two traditions where Jesus may have identified himself directly as God's Wisdom, Matthew 11:19 and Luke 11:49.[96] These would provide clear confirmation for the view we are suggesting if the objections to the authenticity of these sayings could be overcome. I believe the arguments I advanced in response to Fiorenza go some distance toward validating their authenticity. Matthew 11:19 in particular seems likely to go back to Jesus. But the case does not need to rest solely on such explicit statements.

There are other small telltale signs that Jesus was constantly thinking in sapiential ways. For instance, Jesus' theology should be seen in light of the creation theology that we find in Proverbs. Jesus speaks of the beauty of nature and quite naturally, as a sage, compares it to the raiment of the great sage-king, Solomon (Mt 6:29/Lk 12:27). Or when he wants to talk about what marriage really ought to be like, he appeals to what God intended from the first, the creation order (cf. Mk 10:6-7 and parallels). It is also not surprising that Jesus says little about heaven. In his creation theology it is God's plan to redeem the world, re-create the earth and renew persons by means of resurrection (cf. Mk 12:25 and parallels). Even when Jesus thinks of judgment he associates it with some of the great confrontations that the great sage Solomon endured, and he suggests such seekers after Wisdom as the Queen of Sheba will bear witness on the last day (cf. Mt 12:42 and parallels).

Creation theology also involves the high valuation of children (cf. Mk 9:33-37 and parallels; Mk 10:13-16) and the enjoyment of life through feasting rather than fasting (cf. Mk 2:16-20), and it does not emphasize the punctiliar observance of rules of clean and unclean. The image of Jesus as a bridegroom feasting and of his followers as wedding guests comports with all of this (cf. Mk 2:19-20 and parallels; Jn 2:1-12). It is often argued that Jesus' unmarried status is provided a certain justification by his unique teaching on eunuchs (Mt 19:10-12). Eunuchs were not normally seen in a positive light in early Judaism, but strikingly there is a beatitude on the eunuch in Wisdom of Solomon 3:14, where he is said to have a great place in God's temple, something that he probably was deprived of in Jesus' own day.

Creation theology also has a strongly universalistic bent, which may account for Jesus' broader vision that both Jews and Gentiles would one day sit down together for the ultimate banquet in the kingdom, something Jesus himself very much looked forward to (cf. Mt 8:11/Lk 13:29 to Mk 14:25). There is a good deal more that could be said along these lines, but this will suffice to show that Jesus' theological reflections often mirror the sort of creation theology we find in earlier Wisdom literature.

Yet when we ask what *sort* of Wisdom teaching or worldview Jesus offered, one must say that it often sounds like the Wisdom of counter-order that one finds in Ecclesiastes or even Job, where the world is turned upside down.[97] Jesus speaks repeatedly of the last being first, the lost being saved, the least being greatest, the leaders being servants and the like. He clearly believes not merely that the world is askew or upside down (as Qoheleth in Ecclesiastes did) but that *God* is turning the world upside down in righting wrongs, healing the sick and the like. Jesus' message is full of statements about eschatological reversal so that finally God's justice will be done and wrongs will be righted. In the kingdom these things were and would be brought about.

This whole concern, however, for the righting of wrongs in the long run is one of the driving engines of all Wisdom literature, beginning even with Proverbs. The sage profoundly believed that God had established a moral universe and that when the righteous suffered or the wicked prospered it was a temporary aberration that God would in due course rectify. Many of the earliest sages were convinced it would always be rectified in the lifetime of the person concerned, but Qoheleth showed that this simply was not true. In due course, sages like the author of the Wisdom of Solomon incorporated the idea of everlasting life to explain when and how God would set all wrongs right.[98]

Jesus also subscribed to the act-consequence theory that pervades sapiential literature, namely that good deeds were ultimately rewarded and bad ones punished, but not so much in the form we find in Proverbs as that of Wisdom of Solomon or perhaps the *Parables of Enoch*. Thus for Jesus, the inbreaking of the kingdom meant the beginning of the process of the reversal of wrongs, the making well of the sick and the like.

Health, long life, prosperity and plenty were three of the great promises of the sages to their disciples if they would but follow their advice, fear the Lord and lead a godly life (cf. Prov 10—23). Jesus promises all these things to his followers in the kingdom, where the promises of the sages would finally come true in full, where the Beatitudes would come to fruition and hunger, mourning, strife and even death would be done away with. This worldview is certainly eschatological, but it is also profoundly sapiential in character and is not deeply indebted to the legal traditions of the Old Testament. That sages in their advice were much concerned about good health and wellness (cf. Sir 25) may explain why Jesus seems to have styled himself a physician (cf. Mk 2:17 and parallels and Lk 4:23) and was frequently found healing people.

In evaluating the proposal that Jesus presented himself as God's Wisdom come in the flesh we must recall that in early Judaism the concept of divine agency was alive and well, being applied to everything from personified attributes of God (such as wisdom), to patriarchs, to special angels.[99] There was a longstanding tradition of speculation about personified Wisdom (cf. Job 28; Prov 1, 3, 8, 9; Sir 1, 24; 11QPs-a18; Bar 3—4; *1 Enoch* 42; 4 Ezra 5; 2 Baruch 48; Wis 1—9). What is important for our purposes is that already in the time of Ben Sira, well before Jesus was born, there were attempts to identify wisdom not simply with a general attribute of God or of God's creation, but to make its locus on earth even more concrete. Thus in Sirach 24, Ben Sira clearly sees Torah as the locus where wisdom exists on earth, and of course Torah was something concrete and even material, something that could be handled, referred to and transported. It was not a far step from this to identifying a particular person instead of a thing with God's Wisdom. Indeed one can argue that in the Wisdom of Solomon we already see the transition, for there Wisdom seems almost more than a personification, more like a divine being, and in fact is identified with God's very Spirit at key points (cf., e.g., Wis 1:6-7). I am suggesting that Jesus took this step, in concert with his belief that he was God's divine agent (šalîaḥ), God's apostle or sent one, endowed with a divine commission, an intimate knowledge of the Sender's mind and purposes. This latter is how Wisdom is described in Proverbs 8, the agent of God who reflects God's very mind and will.

When we come to grips with this data, several other things begin to fall into place. Solomon of course was the preeminent son of David with whom almost the whole Wisdom corpus is identified, from Proverbs through Ecclesiastes to Wisdom of Solomon. If it is true that Jesus made a claim that something greater than Solomon was present in and through his ministry, one must ask what it could be (cf. Lk 11:31 and parallels). Surely the most straightforward answer would be that Wisdom had come in person.

Let us suppose then for a moment that Jesus saw himself as a prophetic sage, indeed as *the prophetic sage*, fully endowed with God's wisdom. This would explain the fact that his teaching takes the form of riddles, aphorisms and parables, and that he offered some eschatological wisdom teaching. But there is a great deal more that needs to be explained about Jesus to which the proposal that he was a sage simply does not do full justice. This is why in my most recent work[100] I have sought to expand the proposal to include the idea that Jesus saw himself as God's Wisdom come in the flesh, as one even greater than Solomon.

Not only did Jesus "sapientialize" all the traditions he used, including the prophetic and apocalyptic ones, he seems to have believed that he was the one to reveal the secrets of God's coming kingdom to God's people. If, as I think likely, Matthew 11:25-27 in some form probably goes back to Jesus,[101] this passage suggests that Jesus saw himself as a revealer of the very mind of God, as Wisdom is said to be in Wisdom poems such as we find in Proverbs 1, 3 and 8.

It is noteworthy however that Jesus did not merely call people to come and study or follow his teaching but rather to come and follow him. He bound his disciples to himself. The yoke of Wisdom he offered was "his yoke" (cf. above on Mt 11:28-30). Furthermore, the trajectory of his career is the trajectory of Wisdom, who goes to the heart of Judaism in Jerusalem, is rejected and returns to be by the side of the Father (*1 Enoch* 42). I have suggested in *Jesus the Sage* that Jesus may have seen the Wisdom hymns of Proverbs 8 or Sirach 24, or even Wisdom of Solomon 8—9, as the clue to his own career and its outcome. He had come from God and would return to God by way of his rejection in Jerusalem.

This is not the place to do a lot of detailed exegesis, but I want to now show the very diverse elements in the Jesus tradition that find a clear explanation if Jesus saw himself as both prophetic sage and the embodiment of Wisdom on earth:

1. Jesus' use of the Father language for God, something not characteristic of Old Testament expression at all, is explained in view of the fact that we do find such language much more frequently in Wisdom material (cf. Sir 23:1, 4; 51:10; Wis 14:3 and cf. 3 Macc 6:3, 8).

2. Jesus' use of kingdom of God language *in conjunction with Wisdom speech and ways of looking at things* is found almost exclusively in contexts like Wisdom of Solomon 10:10.[102]

3. Jesus' exorcisms could easily have led to his seeing himself as, and being seen as, the successor to or one even greater than Solomon. By the first century A.D. Solomon was believed to have been an exorcist, and his wisdom was regarded as the key to exorcisms in the present (cf 11QPs 91; *Ant.* 8.45).

4. Jesus' use of Son of Man language echoes not merely Daniel but the sort of esoteric material we find in the *Parables of Enoch*.

5. The many echoes of Sirach in the teaching of Jesus require and receive explanation if Jesus saw himself as sage and Wisdom (cf. Sir 11:18-19 to Lk 12:13-21; Sir 24:9 and 6:19-31 to Mt 11:29-30; Sir 23:9 to Mt 5:34; Sir 28:3-4 to Mt 5:22; cf. Sir 29:11 to Mt 6:19; Sir 32:1 to Lk 22:26-27; Sir 36:31 to Lk 9:58).[103]

6. Jesus' willingness to portray himself in female imagery such as we find in the lament over Jerusalem in Matthew 23:37-39/Luke 13:34-35 is also explained by this hypothesis, since this is the way Wisdom is por-

trayed in such crucial texts as Proverbs 8—9 and Wisdom of Solomon 8—9.[104]

To put things another way, the sage and Wisdom proposal is the only one I know of that makes sense of Jesus' teachings, Jesus' miracles as Son of David (i.e., one like Solomon cf. Mk 10:46-52), Jesus' self-presentation as Son of Man bringing in the kingdom of God, Jesus' yoke and binding his disciples to himself, the connection between messianic concepts, sapiential concepts and Son of Man material *and the development of Christology found in the church as early as the christological hymns* (Phil 2; Col 1; Jn 1). In short, the vast majority of all the material in the Synoptics, and especially its distinctive markers of parabolic teaching, Son of Man sayings, kingdom material and miracles can be explained by this approach.

Perhaps what is most impressive about this approach is its cumulative effect and its breadth. While one may wish to quibble about one piece of exegesis or another, even if I am only right about some of the texts mentioned above, one must take the Jesus as sage and Wisdom proposal very seriously. Notice that it allows an explanation of the character, nature and purpose of Jesus' ministry as a whole, as well as how he viewed himself, without having to resort to a wide variety of titles or disparate ideas. It also provides a reasonable explanation for the historical continuum between Jesus and his followers, both before and after Easter. A sapiential understanding of Jesus and his ministry allowed his earliest disciples to hold together their experience of the Jesus of history and the Christ of faith.[105]

CONCLUSIONS

In this chapter I have devoted a great deal of space to critiquing Fiorenza's proposal that Jesus viewed God as Wisdom/Sophia. There are numerous weaknesses in the proposal, not least of which are its reliance on problematic interpretations of a very few controverted Gospel texts and some unsupported conclusions about Judaism, the Q community and the development of the earliest christological affirmations. All of Fiorenza's major proposals are interconnected and in many cases depend on each other for viability. They are debatable at best, and most of them would be contested by the majority in the international community of New Testament scholars. Though Fiorenza is surely right to place Jesus within the context of sapiential traditions and concepts, these Jesus traditions reveal a christocentric rather than a purely theocentric focus even in their earliest stages. Jesus saw himself as the one who lamented over Jerusalem, offered his own, Wisdom's, yoke and spoke predominantly in metaphorical sapiential speech patterns.

My own proposal has been briefly outlined in the last half of this chapter. I believe it explains more about Jesus and how he viewed his own person, life and ministry than any other single proposal. It certainly explains the development and use of Wisdom traditions in the early church by Paul and others better than Fiorenza's does.

But my proposal raises provocative questions about how Jesus' followers in a post-Enlightenment age should talk about him. I must admit there is something incongruous in doing a detailed analytical analysis of a person's teaching when the form of teaching is metaphorical and is not easily reduced to propositions or principles. It was more intended to help people catch the vision and follow where the pillar of fire led, than to be dissected inch by inch.

Jesus' teaching about the kingdom, or even implicitly about himself, is grounded in a story, the story of Wisdom and its progress, acceptance and rejection among and by God's people. If Jesus saw himself as the embodiment of God's Wisdom, he envisioned himself in a storied world, and this means to understand him one must also enter and understand that storied world about Wisdom that preexisted, assisted in creation, came to earth, called God's wayward people back to God, saved some, infuriated others, was rejected and returned to the right hand of God the Father. If this story sounds rather like what we hear in Philippians 2 or John 1, or even later in the Apostle's Creed, we should not be surprised. All of these tellings of the tale are ultimately grounded in texts like Proverbs 1, 8—9 or Sirach 24.

It follows from this that if we really wish to journey on the path toward Jesus, the path leads us backward to that rich and fertile material found in the Wisdom traditions of Israel from Proverbs all the way to Wisdom of Solomon and the *Parables of Enoch*. We must immerse ourselves in this long-neglected material, and maybe then we will see more clearly, follow more nearly and love more dearly the historical Jesus who came to be revered as the Anointed Anointer of God, the Spirit-bearing, Spirit-sharing Savior, the very fullness of God on earth. Perhaps it would be sagacious if we all prayed with the author of the Wisdom of Solomon, who recognized that spiritual things are spiritually discerned:

Who has learned your counsel, unless you have given wisdom and sent your holy spirit from on high? And thus the paths of those on earth were set right, and people were taught what pleases you, and were saved by wisdom. . . . Wisdom rescued from troubles those who served her . . . she showed him the kingdom of God and gave him knowledge of holy things . . . so that he might learn that godliness is more powerful than anything else. (Wis 9:17-18; 10:9-10, 12)

In our next chapter we will turn to an examination of the work of several scholars who suggest a more traditional image of Jesus, namely Jesus as in some sense a Messiah or Redeemer figure. This chapter will show that not all traditional images of Jesus are being neglected or ignored in the Third Quest for the historical Jesus.

CHAPTER 8

JESUS: MARGINAL JEW OR JEWISH MESSIAH?

This chapter focuses on the variety of proposals that suggest that Jesus viewed and presented himself as a messianic figure. The first and perhaps most important of these is found in the massive and as yet uncompleted work of John P. Meier. Meier's work is characterized by caution and careful, detailed argumentation. He argues in the first volume for a focus on the canonical sources because the extracanonical sources offer us little that is likely to be authentic. His portrait of Jesus is in most ways a rather traditional one, and he labels Jesus a marginal Jew because in his own life he lived at the edge of the empire, traveled within a narrow range, identified with those on the margins of society and held views and performed miracles that were out of the ordinary. The second volume is chiefly devoted to a study of Jesus' relationship to John the Baptist, Jesus' kingdom message and Jesus' miracles.

The works of Peter Stuhlmacher, James D. G. Dunn, Markus Bockmuehl and Marinus de Jonge are then briefly reviewed. They demonstrate that even within the Third Quest, there are a variety of scholars, especially in Europe, who are still arguing that Jesus saw himself in some sort of messianic light.

The chapter concludes with an examination of N. T. Wright's work which, like that of Meier, is also a work in progress. Wright's program is more ambitious in that he seeks to redo the whole way we view early Judaism and in that context revise our understanding of Jesus, and to reexamine the methodology used in doing so. Wright sees Jesus in a messianic light, but makes creative proposals suggesting Jesus saw himself as Israel or the new temple or both. It is too early to do a detailed critique of either his work or that of Meier's, but both works serve as correctives to some of the more radical Third Quest proposals reviewed earlier in this study.

THE QUESTION OF METHODOLOGY CONTINUES TO BEDEVIL THE DISCUSSION
of the historical Jesus. We have already seen how the overzealous use of
only one criterion of authenticity (the criterion of multiple attestation) led
John Dominic Crossan to a very lopsided and in some regards wrong-
headed portrayal of Jesus. It is not surprising that some have thrown up
their hands at the very illogic of such portrayals. This sort of approach
leaves us, as the Cambridge scholar Markus Bockmuehl has recently pro-
tested,

> With a highly improbable scenario: a Jewish apocalyptic prophet (John
> the Baptist) is succeeded by a wandering Cynic disciple (Jesus), whose
> message of timeless wisdom is in turn corrupted by followers bent on
> apocalyptic and eschatology. This kind of approach proves in the end
> unable to provide us with a picture of either Jesus or the earliest Pal-
> estinian Jewish Christianity that is sufficiently attached to its inalien-
> able religious and historical moorings in Galilee and Judaea.[1]

But Crossan is by no means alone in his methodological eclecticism. There
has even been a recent volume espousing a whole new approach to the
Gospels, including the singular argument that John is the earliest of the
Gospels, that Mark wrote to respond to John and that the lost ending of
Mark is found in John 21![2] Two of the major figures whose work we will
be considering in this chapter (Meier and Wright), in order to avoid the
methodological pitfalls we have already noted, have devoted not just
pages, but a whole volume, or nearly so, to answering methodological and
historical questions *before* they actually discuss Jesus.[3] It will be necessary
then to evaluate not just the portraits of Jesus they offer but how they
arrived at them as well.

JESUS AS A MARGINAL JEW (JOHN P. MEIER)

The first volume of Meier's trilogy on Jesus is largely composed of discussions about methodology, presuppositions and background. Even so,
this volume is so well written and so careful and persuasive that it has
been hailed as the best and most believable of the recent books on Jesus.[4]

What does Meier mean by calling Jesus a marginal Jew? Meier says he
chose the word *marginal* to conjure up a number of aspects of Jesus' life
and ministry: (1) Jesus in his own day "was at most a blip on the radar
screen," in the estimation of the larger Greco-Roman world, as is shown
by what Josephus, Tacitus and Suetonius say about him;[5] (2) Jesus had

obviously been pushed to the margins of his own society, as his death on the cross shows;[6] (3) in a sense Jesus marginalized himself by giving up his trade (carpentry) and becoming jobless and itinerant to pursue his ministry, and he was further marginalized when this career decision led to his rejection by many, including his hometown folks and a number of his family members; (4) Jesus' teaching on such subjects as divorce, fasting, celibacy and the like was marginal in the sense that it was not mainstream, "it did not jibe with the views and practices of the major Jewish religious groups of his day";[7] (5) and Jesus' style of teaching and living pushed him to the margin so that he appeared "obnoxious, dangerous, or suspicious to everyone from pious Pharisees through political high priests to an ever vigilant Pilate."[8] What Meier does not mean is that Jesus is marginal in terms of the longer view of human history, especially Western history and culture.

One notices immediately in reading Meier's work that he is fully committed to the historical-critical method and spends a great deal of time dealing with issues of literary and redaction criticism in order to arrive at a solid core of arguably authentic data, data that ultimately goes back to a situation in the life of Jesus. This does not, however, lead him to the same sort of conclusions or methodological impasses that we find in the work of Crossan, or even in the earlier work of Sanders with its overemphasis on the "facts" as opposed to the sayings tradition.

Meier believes it is necessary to distinguish between the historical Jesus and the "real" Jesus. By the former he means the Jesus that can be reconstructed using the historical-critical method and by the latter the total package of who Jesus really was.[9] This distinction is not entirely helpful, because by calling the Jesus that can be recovered by the historical method "the historical Jesus" one can be misled into thinking that anything else that one might say about Jesus is not grounded in history. I would distinguish between the historical Jesus and the Jesus that we can recover by means of the historical-critical method, the latter being a smaller subset of the former. The distinction between historical and real is not helpful, any more than was Kähler's older distinction between "historic" and "historical."[10]

Sources and Methods for Jesus Research

One of the most helpful features of Meier's first volume is the discussion of the sources for reconstructing Jesus' life. Meier starts by saying that a historian must in principle be open to examining all sources possible, though any source must be critically sifted. I quite agree with this general principle, and it leads to the conclusion that while the canonical Gospels are not our only sources for learning about the historical Jesus, they are our primary sources, and in fact we learn very little of importance about the historical Jesus from anywhere else, including from the *Gospel of Thomas*. Meier, unlike many scholars, does not dismiss the Gospel of John as a source for historical data about Jesus, and in fact he thinks it tells us a good deal about the length of Jesus' ministry, Jesus' close associations with the Baptist prior to his own ministry, and several other important matters as well.[11]

One place where I would part company with Meier to some degree is in the assumption that we must reckon with "decades of liturgical adaptation, homiletical expansion, and creative activity on the part of Christian prophets."[12] The evidence for Christian prophets speaking words that were later retrojected into narratives about the historical Jesus is nonexistent, if we leave the reputed evidence of the Gospels themselves out of consideration. The material we find in Paul, Revelation or other parts of the New Testament may indeed provide evidence that the risen Jesus spoke to or through various early Christians, but in each case he speaks as the risen Lord, not as the historical Jesus. There is no attempt in these other documents to claim it was something Jesus said while on earth.[13] In short, the argument that there were such retrojections is an argument from silence.[14] On the other hand, there is no arguing with the fact that the Gospel writers, and probably their predecessors as well, did shape and edit the Jesus material as they have passed it along and used it for a variety of purposes. It is this latter fact that makes source, form and redaction criticism both necessary and helpful if the goal is recovering what Jesus said or did.

Meier's discussion of Josephus and the latter's testimony about Jesus is one of the most judicious ever penned. He carefully applies the historical method to the so-called *Testimonium Flavianum* in *Antiquities of the Jews* 18.3.3 and comes up with a statement about Jesus as a sage and miracle worker who gained a following, was crucified by Pilate and whose following continued on even in the 90s when Josephus wrote.[15] This is a plausible statement from the mouth of a non-Christian who held no great animus against nor interest in Jesus. We learn very little more from the minimal mentions in Tacitus and Suetonius, but it is good to have examined them closely, even if they only confirm what we already knew from the canonical Gospels.[16]

Especially telling is Meier's critique of the use of the *Gospel of Peter* and of *Thomas* by Crossan and others to come up with a nontraditional Jesus. In both cases Meier concludes that there is surely evidence of dependence on the canonical Gospels in these works, and accordingly they must be considered later than the canonical Gospels and derivative of them.[17] This is not to say that there may not be a saying here or there that we find in a more original form in *Thomas*, and Meier admits this. But as he maintains,

> Unlike the picture painted by those who want to make some form of Gnostic Christianity an equally valid manifestation of first-generation Christian experience, the mainstream picture of Christianity presented by documents and traditions that definitely do come from the first and second generations are different from some of the wilder developments among certain Christians in the 2d century.[18]

Meier makes very clear the Gnostic and mystical flavor of the *Gospel of Thomas*.[19] He also shows that *Thomas* draws on material from Mark, Q, M, L and apparently even John, showing clearly its later provenance.[20] In short, the more radical modern portraits of Jesus arise from a questionable use of later extracanonical data to provide firm historical data about Jesus. One of the prevailing impressions in reading Meier is the careful, sound judgments he makes. He is not given to quirky or trendy theories, flights of fantasy or special pleading for a pet extrabiblical source.

Meier's enumeration of the criteria he will use to sift the Gospel material provides few surprises.[21] The first is the criterion of embarrassment: sayings or traditions that would have embarrassed the early church and so would not likely have been invented by Christians (e.g., the baptism of Jesus by John, a baptism for repentance of sins!). The second is the criterion of discontinuity or dissimilarity: material that cannot be derived either from early Judaism or from the early church is likely to go back to a situation in Jesus' life (e.g., Jesus' prohibition of all oaths). Here Meier parts company with E. P. Sanders, who, when he comes to a saying like Mark 7:15, argues that since this saying is discontinuous with early Judaism, Jesus could not have said it. Meier is using the criterion in reverse from Sanders.[22] The third criterion is that of multiple attestation. This criterion is used repeatedly by Meier, but he does not use it in isolation from the other criteria, unlike Crossan. Especially important in Meier's view is double multiple-attestation: namely, sayings and deeds attested in multiple sources (Mark, Q) and in multiple forms (parables, miracle stories). The criterion of coherence is to be applied after the other criteria mentioned above are used. That is, what coheres with the critical minimum derived from using the aforementioned criteria is also probably authentic and from Jesus' mouth or situation. Meier then points to a criterion that is not usually mentioned, namely the criterion of rejection and execution: "A Jesus whose words and deeds would not alienate people, especially powerful people, is not the historical Jesus."[23] Several other minor criteria, such as the ability of a saying to be retrojected from the Greek into Aramaic are mentioned, but as Meier says, they can only be supplemental to the main criteria. For example, Jesus' earliest followers spoke Aramaic, so the ability to find an Aramaic original might only point to those followers and not to Jesus himself.

Perhaps more important than all the above is that Meier seeks in various ways to distinguish the Jesus of history from the Christ of faith. For example, he argues that the resurrection of Jesus, as opposed to the claims to have seen resurrection appearances, is not open to historical inquiry because it is not an historical event per se. By this he means it is not an event in space and time that a nonbeliever could have observed and reflected on.[24] He apparently sees the resurrection as something that happened in the spiritual realm, and thus all the resurrection appearances, and not just Paul's, took place *from heaven*.[25] Meier also affirms that the crucified, risen, reigning Lord who is accessible to all believers is the object of Christian faith and as such is not open to historical investigation.

I have some difficulties with this argument. For one thing, it seems suspiciously like an attempt to protect the object of real Christian faith from historical inquiry. For another it too readily distinguishes the Jesus of historical inquiry from the Jesus of faith. The Christian claims about Jesus involved not just what he did from Golgotha on. There were also theological claims about who Jesus was, what he said and did during his ministry (cf. e.g. Acts 2:22-36). More importantly, if Jesus himself made theological claims, even implicitly, as I have argued he did, then history and theology or history and the object of Christian faith cannot be so neatly distinguished.[26] The distinction that can be made is between historical claims and "the truth." Jesus may have claimed many things about himself, and so may his disciples, but from a historian's point of view, recognizing such claims and evaluating their truthfulness are two different tasks.

Or again, when we are dealing with Jesus' miracles it can be argued not merely that Jesus did something that he and others saw as miracles, but also that historically he made certain theological claims or evaluations of the significance of such works. The historian may be able to detect the historicity of such claims without being able to evaluate their theological or philosophical validity. In other words, the quest for the historical Jesus, while primarily the quest for the human face of Jesus, may also involve evaluating whether or not he made certain theological claims about his words, deeds and person. History and theology in such a case cannot be neatly separated.

From the middle of the first volume through the end of the second volume,[27] Meier carefully argues and sets out the conclusions about what can be known about the historical Jesus using the historical-critical method. It will be useful to summarize his results at this point, especially since his research and presentation is massive.[28]

A Basic Life of Jesus
Somewhere around 7 or 6 B.C. Jesus was born, before the death of Herod the Great (4 B.C.). According to Meier, he was most likely born in Nazareth, though Bethlehem cannot be completely ruled out.[29] In any case, Jesus grew up in Nazareth in Galilee, as his second "name" (Nazorean) shows. His mother was named Miryam and his putative father Yosef, and he had various brothers (named) and sisters (unnamed). "Jesus' family would have been imbued with an 'uncomplicated' type of Jewish piety probably widespread among the peasants of lower Galilee. Ordinary Galilean Jews . . . would have had no time for or interest in the theological niceties, the special observances, and the fierce disputes of the Essenes, the Pharisees, or the Sadducees."[30] Rather, their piety involved sticking to the basics of circumcision, sabbath-keeping, food laws and pilgrimage to Jerusalem, particularly at Passover and the other great feasts.

Being the firstborn son of his family, Jesus probably received special attention from his parents. He trained as a woodworker, and apparently Joseph died before Jesus became an adult and began his ministry, since he is not mentioned after the birth narratives. The signs of tension between Jesus and his family in the Gospels are real; apparently they were not among his followers during his ministry.

Jesus spoke Aramaic as his first language, though he may have spoken some Greek on occasion and perhaps had learned Hebrew to be able to read the Torah. There is no evidence that Jesus received higher education, though Meier is inclined to the view that he was literate. Jesus' trade of woodworker would have assured him of a modest but average living—poor by our standards, but no poorer than most Galileans of his day. His status as a woodworker and as a member of a pious family would have obtained him a certain amount of status and honor in his society, honor he would perhaps have forfeited when he abandoned his home and began his ministry. One quality that would have made Jesus stand out very clearly was his decision to remain single. This was unusual, but not unprecedented, since it appears that various Essenes and John the Baptist were celibate.

Somewhere around A.D. 28, at the age of about thirty-four, Jesus left behind his settled life in Nazareth.[31] He felt led to seek out John the Baptist, who had appeared in the lower Judean valley, living an ascetic lifestyle and proclaiming an imminent fiery judgment that was going to swallow up Israel if it did not repent and receive his baptism. "According to John the final judgment was to be administered by an eschatological figure whom John vaguely referred to as 'the stronger one' or 'the one who comes.' This mysterious figure would show his superiority to John by baptizing with the holy spirit instead of with mere water."[32]

The fact that Jesus knew John, spent time with him and, especially, submitted to his baptism suggests Jesus "accepted his eschatological message and baptism and in that sense at least became his disciple."[33] Thus, as the title of Meier's second volume suggests, he sees the Baptist as Jesus' mentor. Jesus believed in John's message that the whole nation, even the apparently pious and legally scrupulous, needed to repent and have a fresh start in light of coming judgment.

Jesus emerged from the Baptist's entourage, perhaps after a period of time (cf. Jn 3—4), and began his own public ministry. It was a ministry more wide-reaching than John's since it was not confined to one region of the country (i.e., along the Jordan).

Jesus reached out to Jews of all sorts, both the respectable and especially the sinful, both the rich and the poor, as he traveled through Galilee, Samaria, the Decapolis, Perea and Judea. His ministry likely lasted longer than one year and involved more than one trip to Jerusalem.

Jesus' message was broader than the Baptist's, though he maintained his eschatological emphasis and spoke of coming judgment. In addition, he spoke of the good news that God was coming in power to save and restore his sinful and scattered people. Jesus seized upon the rare phrase, "the kingdom of God," and used it to speak of the coming of God to rule as King among his people. The phrase did not refer to a social program or social movement but rather to God's coming in person to transform his people and rule them in the last days.

> In using the multifaceted, multilayered symbol of "the kingdom of God," Jesus conjured up in his audience's imagination the whole biblical drama of God's kingly rule over his creation and over his people Israel. . . . It was this dynamic, multivalent "salvation-history-in-a-nutshell" quality of "kingdom of God" that allowed Jesus to use it both of his pivotal ministry in the present moment and of the denouement of his ministry, soon to come.[34]

This kingdom had a future dimension (hence the prayer "your kingdom come"), but on the other hand he also proclaimed that through his actions, healings and exorcism the kingdom was in some sense already present during his ministry (Lk 17:21).

It is these miracles that especially distinguished Jesus' ministry from John's, as well as the more positive content of his message. Jesus thus was "not just another prophet uttering more prophecies about the future. He was the prophet who was accomplishing what the prophets had foretold."[35] Much of the popular excitement about Jesus came no doubt from his reputation as a miracle worker. People saw him as both a prophet of some sort and a miracle worker. Very few Old Testament prophets performed miracles—Moses, Elijah and Elisha are apparently the only notable ones—and thus it would have been natural for the people to associate Jesus with these figures. In particular the claims that Jesus raised the dead would have distinguished him from even Moses, but not from these other two northern prophets.

> Whatever his precise relationship to the Elijah of old, Jesus the eschatological prophet was acting out the role of the eschatological Elijah as he both proclaimed the imminent coming of God's rule and made the rule a reality even now by his miracles. It was this convergence and configuration of different traits in the one man Jesus . . . that gave Jesus his distinctiveness or "uniqueness" within Palestinian Judaism in the early 1st century A.D.[36]

As a preview of what he will say in the third volume, Meier mentions that he will argue that Jesus presumed to give his followers clear directives on how to observe the Mosaic law, and he even took upon himself the authority to rescind or change some individual institutions in the law, for instance in regard to divorce, oaths, vows and perhaps even in regard to kosher food laws. Jesus presented himself as a teacher, not just as a prophet or healer. "As a true charismatic, Jesus located his authority to interpret and even change the Law not in recognized traditional channels of authority . . . but rather in his own ability to know directly and intuitively what was God's will for his people Israel in the last days."[37] This convergence of features leads to a portrait of a complex historical figure. All this serves as background to the final volume, where Meier intends to deal with the question of Jesus in his relationships to others as a clue to how he viewed himself.[38]

Having discussed the basic outline, it will be well to consider some of the finer points of Meier's analysis. Meier rightly points out the difficulties in getting a fix on the chronology of Jesus' life, apart from its beginning and ending. On the latter point, we know that Jesus died while Pontius Pilate was ruling in Judea, which means between A.D. 26-36.

Is it possible to be more specific? It is almost impossible to date Jesus' death as late as 36 because of all the events mentioned in Acts which transpire before A.D. 50. Thus, a date in the late 20s or early 30s is more plausible. If one analyzes the synchronism in Luke 3:1-2 carefully, this strongly suggests that the Baptist's ministry and Jesus' contact with him did not take place before about A.D. 28. In addition, Philip, who is mentioned there, died in A.D. 33-34; this narrows the scope to A.D. 28-33 for Jesus' public career and his death. Finally, Tiberius's fifteenth year can be limited to somewhere between A.D. 26-29, depending on which calendar Luke was following. As we have noted above, Meier takes into account the Fourth Gospel when reckoning the chronology of Jesus' life, and this means at the very least that Jesus had a ministry that lasted for more than one year, something the Synoptics do not really suggest. But with Meier it seems right to conclude that the material in the Gospels leading up to the passion narrative is not much help in setting a chronology, not least because various stories have different placements in different Gospels. Apart from the baptism, none of the events in Jesus' ministry prior to the last trip to Jerusalem can be firmly dated.

Meier's work also shows that though a rough chronology is possible in regard to the end of Jesus' life, the attempt to be more specific is much more difficult.[39] This is especially the case because of the difficulty in reconciling the Johannine and Synoptic chronologies. Though it may surprise some, Meier is inclined to go with the Johannine chronology, and I tend to agree with him. The question becomes when the fourteenth of Nisan fell on a Friday between the years A.D. 29-34. A.D. 29 and 32 are excluded whether one follows John or the Synoptics, as is A.D. 28 since that is too early in view of Luke 3:1-2 and the length of Jesus' ministry.[40] This leaves us with A.D. 30 or 33. Meier, rightly I think, argues for the earlier date. All of the discussion on these very complex issues is pursued with considerable learning and care.[41]

Equally helpful are some of the lengthy discussions in the second volume which range widely from theological to historical to philosophical issues (e.g., what is a miracle?). One begins to see where the discussion will lead right from the beginning of the second volume, where Meier once again stresses that what made Jesus unique is a complex configuration of factors: he was teacher, he was miracle worker, he was prophet of the last days, and now, he adds more clearly, he was the gatherer of Israel, as the gathering of the Twelve suggests.[42] This gives a clue as to where the study will go in the third volume, and this last clue is important, as it surely means that Meier sees Jesus as some sort of messianic figure, however much Jesus eludes precise definition.

Features and Questions
1. *Jesus and the Baptist.* Meier's lengthy discussion of John and Jesus is one of the best available, and it leads to the conclusion that the view that Jesus at one time affirmed John's eschatology but later changed his mind is implausible. The attempt to play down the future eschatological element in Jesus' teaching will not work in view of likely historical sayings such as Luke 11:2/Matthew 6:10; Mark 14:25 and Matthew 8:11-12/Luke 13:28-29.[43] The discussion of the Baptist also leads to the rejection of the theory that the "stronger one" John referred to, who was coming after him, was simply God. This latter view makes no sense of John's metaphor of "tying the sandal"; it would be strange for John to say that he was unworthy to tie God's shoe! Rather, John was looking for some undisclosed historical figure who would succeed him.[44] Thus sayings like that found in Luke 7:18-23 and parallels suggest that John at least entertained the notion that Jesus might be that "stronger one." The reason for John's doubt may have been that Jesus was a healer and was proclaiming good news, and John expected imminent judgment instead. As Meier says, "Jesus was not a carbon copy of John. Yet a firm substratum of the Baptist's

message and life remained; and as far as we know it remained throughout Jesus' ministry."[45]

2. *Banqueting, Speaking and Q.* A variety of Meier's other conclusions I find helpful and correct, for example his agreement with Sanders that when Jesus dined with sinners it was not as a casual Jew who was not strict enough in his ritual purity practices, but at least in some cases he deliberately banqueted with the bad, including toll collectors guilty of extortion.[46] Though he does not analyze parables in any depth, Meier does conclude that Jesus spoke many of them and that the Jewish *māšāl* could involve both metaphor and on occasion even allegory.[47] Indeed, as Meier suggests but does not develop in this volume, Jesus' use of the Son of Man language is itself like a parable or riddle in its self-designation, and it is plausible and in keeping with Jesus' main form of public speech, which involved the use of sapiential language.[48]

Equally helpful is Meier's discussion of Q, where he is skeptical of elaborate theories of Q's development and a theology of the Q community. As he humorously puts it:

> I cannot help thinking that biblical scholarship would be greatly advanced if every morning all exegetes would repeat as a mantra: "Q is a hypothetical document whose exact extension, wording, originating community, strata, and stages of redaction cannot be known."[49]

3. *Kingdom of God.* One of the most challenging and useful sections of the second volume is the helpful overview of the whole matter of Jesus' use of kingdom of God language. As Meier points out, this terminology is found only sparsely in earlier Jewish literature, and the fact that Jesus makes it central in his teaching is remarkable.[50] Meier follows Chilton and others in making very clear that the phrase *kingdom of God* cannot simply be a cipher for some sort of humanly initiated social program (vs. Horsley, Crossan and various liberation theologians), not least because the phrase means "God in person coming in power to transform and save his people." In Meier's words, "The effect of the kingdom's coming cannot be separated from the person of God who comes as king. Thus 'the kingdom of God' is not a political movement or program for social improvement."[51] Meier especially points to the core Beatitudes, which make clear that "it is God alone who acts in the end time to establish his kingdom of justice and love; humans can only wait for it (see, e.g., the parable of the seed growing by itself)."[52] This is not to say that God's action does not call forth a human response that is similar in character and effect, but the

point is, God is the initiator.

His detailed analysis of the kingdom material leads Meier to the following conclusions: (1) Jesus expected a future final coming of God to rule as king; (2) this hope was so central for Jesus that he passed it on in the disciple's prayer as something they should long for ("your kingdom come"); (3) the coming kingdom will bring about the dramatic reversal of present injustices, including poverty, hunger and the sources of sorrow and pain; (4) perhaps the most astounding reversal the kingdom will bring is the presence of Gentiles as honored guests sharing the eschatological banquet with Jews; (5) Jesus believed, despite his impending death, that he himself would experience a saving reversal beyond death and participate in that final banquet.

The last two points especially show the discontinuity of the coming kingdom with the world as it now is and make clear that the kingdom is not just a full flourishing of something already happening in miniature.[53] Meier is convinced that neither John nor Jesus engaged in speculation about the precise timing of the coming of the kingdom in power, but both believed it could come soon.[54]

4. Eschatology. In his second volume Meier takes on the old Schweitzerian chestnut that Jesus was a prophet of the future, but very imminent, coming of the kingdom of God, a view Sanders in part revives. Meier's analysis of the key sayings that prop up this view (Mk 9:1; 13:30; and Mt 10:23) leads him to the conclusion that all these verses are a creation of the early church and do not go back to anything Jesus actually said.[55] I have argued earlier that these three verses will certainly admit of another interpretation than a necessarily imminent end, and that it is very difficult to believe that the early church would create problems for itself by inventing such sayings.[56] Thus, while I would certainly agree with Meier's conclusion that Jesus did not insist that the end, including the parousia, was just around the corner, I would arrive at that conclusion by another route.

One of the weaker and more problematic portions of Meier's analysis is his handling of Mark 13, in particular Mark 13:28 and 30.[57] He regards Mark 13:30 ("Truly I tell you, this generation will not pass away until all these things have taken place") as inauthentic, because the emphasis on "time limits" for the kingdom's arrival (as with Mark 9:1 and Mt 10:23) is a telltale sign of its origin in the early church, pressed as it was to come to terms with the passing years and the failure of the end to come.

But in his argument Meier fails to notice the rather clear structure of the discourse of Mark 13, which has an A, B, A, B pattern, speaking alternately of preliminary events and then cosmic and final events, with the preliminary events occupying the larger part of the discussion. The preliminary events are discussed in terms of "these things," "all these things" or even "those days," while the final cosmic events are referred to as happening in those days *after* the preliminary events and in particular after the tribulation (Mk 13:24). All the material in Mark 13:3-23 is about preliminary events, a subject that is revisited briefly in verses 28-31, while verses 24-27 and 32-37 refer to the final cosmic events, including the parousia of the Son of Man. Understanding this structure becomes crucial in interpreting the material in Mark 13:28-31. The reference to something being "at the gates," coupled with the reference to fig leaves ([28] "From the fig tree learn its lesson: as soon as its branch becomes tender and puts forth its leaves, you know that summer is near. [29] So also, when you see these things taking place, you know that it is near, at the very gates"), is surely a clear reference to the coming destruction of the temple, especially in view of the cursing of the fig tree, which sandwiches the story of the cleansing of the temple only two chapters previously in Mark 11. Thus Mark 13:29 must be translated "it is near, at the very gates" not "he is near or at the gates." The reference to "these things" in verse 29 alludes back to Mark 13:4 ("when will . . . these things . . . be accomplished?"), where the disciples ask a question primarily about the destruction of the temple and all the other preliminary events leading up to it. Thus Mark 13:30 also, with its reference to "all these things," which is an even clearer allusion to Mark 13:4, makes evident that the subject of Mark 13:30 is the culmination of the *preliminary events*, including the temple's destruction, not the final end with the coming of the Son of Man. This is surely how Mark understands the matter, as telltale phrases like the aside in Mark 13:14 and the final command to "watch" in 13:37 make clear. "All these things" are coming to fruition even as Mark writes to his audience somewhere between A.D. 68-70. Accordingly, there is no need to interpret Mark 13:28-30 as referring to the Second Coming.

5. *Jesus and Early Judaism.* One other critique is worth mentioning. Meier's tendency is to rely on Sanders's judgments about early Judaism on subjects such as what early Jews believed and did. It should be noticed, however, that Sanders, in attempting to defend early Jews, and Pharisees in particular, from various anti-Semitic Christian stereotypes, sometimes goes too far in the other direction and neglects the strong evidence that

Jesus and the Pharisees surely did have some major controversies over things such as the sabbath. One example will have to suffice. In Mark 3:1-6, Jesus heals on the sabbath a man with a withered hand by means of a word of command. Sanders argues that speaking a word was surely not considered work and so was not a violation of the sabbath, as Mark seems to imply.[58] The problem with this analysis, which Meier simply follows, is that it ignores the fact that according to Genesis almost all the creative work that God did was done simply by speaking words and that it is precisely this creative *speaking* from which God rested on that first seventh day, or sabbath. It is quite believable, in view of Genesis 1, that there would indeed be a criticism for Jesus speaking in such a manner to accomplish a work, a miracle on the sabbath, especially because the man could have waited since his life was in no danger and he did not fit the well-known Jewish exception that human life can be rescued on the sabbath. Meier, who is critical of many scholars' works, is surprisingly uncritical of Sanders's works in these sorts of matters.[59]

6. *Miracles of Jesus.* As with his methodological comments in the first volume, Meier once again separates historical and theological claims in discussing at great length Jesus' miracles. He does not argue for the historicity of any of the miracles per se, but does argue that some of the stories about miracles go back to historical occasions or events in the life of Jesus, which both Jesus and others interpreted as miracles. Meier writes, "[I]t is sufficient for the historian to know that Jesus performed deeds that many people, both friends and foes [and probably Jesus himself], considered miracles."[60] But Meier is equally clear in rejecting the modern a priori judgment of Sanders that miracles cannot and therefore never did happen.[61] More conservative readers of Meier's second volume will then find cause for both some frustration and some relief. As we have already noticed, even for the historian it is not always so easy or possible to separate history from theological evaluation. This is because some events may well have inherent theological content or intent, and find no explanation outside the realm of God language.

We will not enter into Meier's immense and detailed analysis of the miracle stories,[62] but as we draw this discussion to a close, it will be worthwhile to look briefly at Meier's critique of the attempts of Morton Smith, David E. Aune, John Dominic Crossan and others to categorize Jesus' miracles as examples of ancient magic. Meier's careful analysis shows that there was a sliding scale, with miracle at one end and pure magic on the other, and that the vast majority of Jesus' deeds do not come close to the sort of thing we find, for example, in the Greek magical papyri.[63] In particular, when one analyzes ancient magical practices, the following features keep cropping up: (1) complicated rituals; (2) magic spells or recipes; (3) the incantation of esoteric names for gods; (4) uttering nonsense syllables in the hope of landing on a combination that would force the god to do one's bidding; (5) extreme syncretism; (6) the attempt to manipulate divine power rather than personally relate to God; (7) coercion as opposed to request or petition of the gods; (8) the reliance on a professional technician who demands payment and secrecy, and who does not have a community around him or her. This list could be lengthened but enough has been mentioned to show how devoid are the Jesus stories of these sorts of features.[64]

Furthermore, on the positive side we often hear of faith being a key ingredient in the Gospel healing stories, faith in Jesus as a person who can heal.[65] The power that Jesus exercises in healing is never, with the possible exception of Mark 5:24-34, seen as an impersonal force to be tapped, and even there Jesus raises the woman's consciousness above the level of a magic-tainted faith to a fuller faith in the personal God.

As Meier also shows, there is no evidence at all that Jesus used magic spells or potent foreign words. The Aramaic words in texts like Mark 5, where Jesus addresses Jairus's daughter, represent language addressing a person who spoke Aramaic. The words are then translated by Mark, another clear sign that magic is not involved. The most important element in magic was the proper spell, and Jesus' terse words of command stand out in contrast.[66] Notable too is that Jesus does not waste his energy on the petty matters that magic was often used for (e.g., winning a horserace or a girlfriend's heart).[67] At most one could say that Jesus' occasional use of spittle and clay in healing reflects ancient healing practices and perhaps the ancient belief in the healing qualities of saliva. This hardly amounts to much of a case for claiming Jesus was a magician.[68]

Meier's work is still in progress, and thus it is not appropriate to render any final judgments on his efforts. One must wait and see what is unveiled in the third and final volume of the work. But if the first two volumes are any indication, Meier's work is likely to be recognized as one of the most significant contributions, if not the most significant and helpful, to the Third Quest for the historical Jesus. None of the criticisms rendered above should detract from the stature of Meier's accomplishment, not least his rendering highly improbable some of the more radical proposals of Crossan, Borg and others. I find myself in considerable agreement with Meier at point after point, though we no doubt would disagree on this or that piece of exegesis. His conclusions and his methodology are sound and cautious, and he has helped us see the historical Jesus more clearly than any of the other authors we have so far discussed. The completion of this massive project will be a welcome event, for at the very least it causes us to ask the right questions about Jesus and his story.[69]

JESUS AS JEWISH MESSIAH (PETER STUHLMACHER, JAMES D. G. DUNN, MARINUS DE JONGE, MARKUS BOCKMUEHL)

It may seem surprising to many readers that we are well over halfway through our odyssey and have not once come across any scholar who argues *at length* or in detail that Jesus saw himself as the Jewish Messiah. Readers may ask how this can be. Indeed, the vast majority of scholars do believe Jesus was crucified under the placard "the King of the Jews," and the early church was unanimous in calling Jesus "the Christ," or more often simply "Christ," as a virtual second name for Jesus.[70] The reason for the general neglect of the possibility that Jesus saw himself as the Jewish Messiah can be explained in part by the desire of scholars to say something fresh and new about Jesus. But there are also difficult questions surrounding the issue that are not apparent on the surface.

Judaisms and Their Messiahs

There is first of all the difficulty of terminology. James H. Charlesworth argues that we must distinguish between Christology, the discussion of the notion that *Jesus* was the Christ, and messianology, the ideas that arose out of early Judaism about a variety of so-called messianic figures, including prophets, priests and kings.[71] It is this variety and a lack of focus on one kind of expectation or messianic figure that leads to book titles like *Judaisms and Their Messiahs at the Turn of the Era.*[72] In fact it appears that a consensus is growing among biblical scholars that runs as follows: (1) the phrase "the Messiah" *(Ha Mashiach)* does not occur in the Old Testament per se, and it occurs only rarely in early Jewish literature in general;[73] (2) messianism or Jewish messianology really arose in a noticeable way only in the first century B.C., due to the disintegration of the Hasmonean dynasty that had begun with such promise with the Maccabean revolt and the retaking of the land by Jews; (3) one cannot claim that in Jesus' day all or the vast majority of Jews were looking for a single Messiah figure to rescue them (some were not looking for such a person at all, e.g., the Sadducees); (4) there was no *normative* concept of Messiah by which possible candidates for the office, such as Jesus, were measured, but rather there were a variety of ideas and expectations involving prophets, priests and kings, no one of which seems to have been *the dominant idea*; (5) messianic ideas and titles were fluid and often related to each other, as can be seen in *1 Enoch* 48, where Son of Man, Messiah and Elect One are used interchangeably to describe a single person and his functions (cf. Mk 14:61-62); (6) the first clear evidence for the use of Messiah as a technical term for a royal figure in the line of David is found in the *Psalms of Solomon* *(Pss. Sol.* 17—18), and the *Parables of Enoch*, both of which probably date to the first century B.C.[74] In fact some scholars like Richard A. Horsley are willing to go much further than Charlesworth and argue that there is no point at all in using *Messiah* as a generic term for agents of salvation, since many different terms were originally used and since if one means by Messiah *the* agent of final eschatological salvation, it does not fit any of the kings and prophetic figures of the first century, including Jesus.[75]

Messiah Jesus
Lest we prematurely close the book on the idea of "Messiah" in early Judaism, it is well to remember that many scholars do not agree with the assessment of Horsley. In particular we may mention Peter Stuhlmacher, James D. G. Dunn, Marinus de Jonge and Markus Bockmuehl.

1. Peter Stuhlmacher. Peter Stuhlmacher argues as follows:

Without seeing and acknowledging that the human Jesus already laid claim to being the messianic Son of Man whom God sent to Israel, one cannot make sense historically of Jesus' ministry, or of even the passion narrative. The apostles did not attribute characteristics and behavior patterns to Jesus subsequent to Easter that were not his in his humanity (nor that he claimed to possess); the Christian community's post-Easter confession of Jesus as Son of God and Messiah confirms and acknowledges who Jesus claimed to be historically and who he was and remains for faith. God's history in and with Jesus, the Christ of God, is prepositioned to the Christian faith. It maintains and determines this faith and is not merely called into existence by it.[76]

How very different this judgment seems to be from what we observed in

Meier, who severs the Christ of faith from any historical reconstructions of Jesus, though not from the historical Jesus himself.[77] Stuhlmacher is following the arguments of a predecessor of his at Tübingen, Adolf Schlatter, who also argued that the historical Jesus appeared as and made the claim in some way to be Messiah and Son of God.

Stuhlmacher argues in this fashion because he is convinced that the Gospel records are largely reliable in recounting the life of Jesus. For example, he believes Mark was indeed written by John Mark, based on material from Peter in Rome prior to the destruction of Jerusalem in A.D. 70.[78] He also believes that the Jesus tradition was handed down carefully in the church, in a manner consistent with the way early Jews dealt with important religious traditions. Stuhlmacher is a good example of the rule that the more reliable one believes the Gospel accounts to be in recording history, the more traditional one's portrait of Jesus is likely to be; on the other hand, the more one believes it is necessary to apply a hermeneutic of suspicion to the text, the more likely it is that one will come up with a nontraditional, possibly even a shocking, image of Jesus.

Stuhlmacher points to a host of factors in the text that he thinks point in the direction of a rather traditional conclusion. For example, the Gospels never characterize Jesus' special relationship to God as calling for his faith in God, and when he pronounces someone forgiven, or acts to heal or help, he seems to stand on God's side of the ledger, rather than the merely human side. Or again Jesus speaks in novel fashion about believers actually participating in the activity of God by healing and helping others through faith (Mk 11:22-24).[79] In Stuhlmacher's view, Jesus' experience at baptism, where he received the Spirit of God, was the point when Jesus fully realized or understood his messianic identity as God's Son, and from thence he acted in the light of such knowledge.[80] Stuhlmacher also draws on the work of his Tübingen colleagues Martin Hengel and Otto Betz to build up a plausible picture of an early Judaism that could have made sense of a messianic Jesus.[81]

Stuhlmacher is by no means an isolated figure in arguing for a messianic Jesus. Both I. Howard Marshall and Petr Pokorný, approaching things from very different angles, have also stressed that the historical origins of Christology must be located in Jesus' messianic claim, whether explicitly or implicitly.[82]

2. James D. G. Dunn. Likewise, James D. G. Dunn argues that the question of whether Jesus was Messiah must have come up during Jesus' ministry, as Mark 8 suggests. Dunn also sees the Gospels as largely reliable since they are the records of the memory of the early church about what Jesus said and did and claimed, and since he believes the traditions did not go through multiple redactions over a long period of time.[83] Dunn believes that there was a significant expectation of a royal Messiah who would be a military leader and that Jesus reacted negatively to such a notion.[84]

Dunn argues that there must be a historical core to the story in Mark 14:57-62, not least because 2 Samuel 7:13-14 was being read in Jesus' day as messianic prophecy (cf. 4QFlor 1:10-13) of a Son of David (royal Messiah or anointed one) who would build the temple and would be God's Son. Hence the high priest's questions, the connection with the accusations that Jesus threatened the temple, and hence Jesus' response.[85] The setting and the dialogue fit the larger historical evidence.

Dunn argues that we must allow that while Jesus rejected some kinds of messianic acclamations, particularly the more politically loaded ones, he creatively handled the issue and redefined the category of Messiah in his own terms.[86] He did not reject the idea outright when it was applied to him, though he always qualified such acclamations or questions by responding in terms of the Son of Man (cf. Mk 8:29-31 and Mk 14:61-62).

Dunn goes on to stress that to understand the Jesus material we cannot limit the discussion to the influence of messianic ideas on Jesus, since Jesus seems also to have seen himself in prophetic terms and as a righteous sufferer (possibly along the lines of 2 Macc 7:38, 4 Macc 17:22 or even Is 53).[87] Nevertheless, Jesus' use of texts like Isaiah 61:1-2 in his response to the Baptist (cf. also Lk 4) suggests that in such "implicitly messianic" texts he saw himself and his mission. Though "he adapted and molded [them] by his own conception of his mission . . . he himself must be seen as part of the stream of Jewish messianic reflection and one of the most important currents within that stream during the first half of the first century C.E., broadening the stream and quite soon becoming the occasion of it splitting into two different channels."[88]

3. *Marinus de Jonge.* The work of Marinus de Jonge on the title Messiah has already been mentioned,[89] but now he has followed up this work with a book on the historical Jesus, made up of his Shaffer lectures given in 1989 at Yale Divinity School.[90] De Jonge believes that while Jesus did not

use the term *Son of Man* as a title, nonetheless the concept of the "one like a son of man" likely influenced Jesus' thought and mission.[91] Drawing on the evidence to show that in the first century A.D. David was viewed not merely as a king but as a prophet and exorcist (cf. Josephus, *Ant.* 6.166-68; 11QPsa Dav. Comp. vv. 9-11), de Jonge suggests:

Jesus may have understood himself as a prophetic Son of David called to proclaim the Gospel and exorcise demons in order to inaugurate God's Kingdom, and destined to hold full royal power in the near future. If so, he could regard himself as the Lord's anointed like David, not only in the future, but already during his prophetic work in Galilee.[92]

De Jonge believes it is necessary to explain the use of the term *Messiah* in reference to Jesus both before and after Easter. The explanation above allows for some continuity in its use of Jesus by his followers as well as his detractors, both before and after Easter. This is necessary, since as de Jonge points out, neither the empty tomb nor the appearances in themselves demonstrated Jesus to be the Jewish Messiah. In short, the acclamation of Jesus as Messiah was not created by the passion and Easter events. "The Easter experiences affirmed earlier belief in Jesus as Christ and expectations concerning his future and that of those connected with him."[93]

De Jonge also explores the possibility that Jesus saw himself as God's Son in some special sense. He points to the use of *abba* in Mark 14:36 and the use of Father language in several different strands of tradition (Lk 11:4/Mt 6:9-13 and Lk 10:21-22/Mt 11:25-27). Regarding Luke 10:21-22/ Matthew 11:25-27, de Jonge notes:

The relationship between Father and Son depicted here goes beyond that of the truly righteous man who is called son of God in Wisd. Sol. 2.13, 16-18. It is closer to that between (female) Wisdom and God in Wisd. Sol. 8.3-4 (cf. 9.9). . . . Jesus is more than a supremely wise and righteous man or the ideal representative of Wisdom on earth. . . . Luke 10.21-22 may represent the very core of Jesus' relationship to God, which goes beyond the use of any special title.[94]

With this I agree, and if this tradition is authentic, as I have argued elsewhere, it pushes us beyond the ideas of Jesus as anointed Davidic "Son" and into a realm which I have already discussed in the previous chapter, namely it makes it likely that Jesus saw himself as sage and God's Wisdom.[95] De Jonge concludes his discussion by affirming that Jesus saw himself as the one who not merely announces but inaugurates God's kingdom on earth, which "placed him in a unique relationship to God, and he was aware of it when he addressed God as Father. It is probable that he regarded himself as the Messiah and Son of David inspired and empowered by the Spirit."[96]

4. *Markus Bockmuehl.* In a similar vein, Markus Bockmuehl makes the central contention of his recent book *This Jesus* that "the life and work of Jesus of Nazareth can be plausibly and credibly interpreted as standing in a relationship of vital continuity with the emerging orthodox Christianity that finds expression in the New Testament and the creeds."[97]

Bockmuehl argues that Jesus' life and work did have messianic connotations but that some messianic expectations were not fulfilled during his earthly life. He maintains, however, that this is not because Jesus failed in or misunderstood his mission but rather because he did not believe the messianic and soteriological mission God sent him on would be completed before the Son of Man came on the clouds of heaven.[98] In short, Jesus' earthly ministry was part of a work in progress, the beginning of the good news, which the early church believed was being continued in the present by the Holy Spirit, and it would only be fully completed at the (Second) Coming of the Son of Man.

I have taken the time to point out the examples of Stuhlmacher, Dunn, de Jonge and Bockmuehl because it is important to recognize that N. T. Wright is not an isolated example of a scholar who sees Jesus in messianic terms. It is perfectly true that early Jewish messianic expectation was so diverse that we cannot speak of a normative idea of Messiah in early Judaism. It is also true that the term *Messiah* comes up far more often in the New Testament than in other early Jewish sources, and that *māšîaḥ/ christos* was probably not a technical term until shortly before the era of Jesus. Nevertheless it is overstating the case to argue that there were no messianic ideas that might have influenced Jesus or that he might have taken up and reshaped, and no messianic expectations that people might have tried to relate to Jesus and his mission.

Messianology flows into Christology because of the way Jesus lived and used messianic ideas and gestures. It is a mistake to ignore the possibility that Jesus could have seen himself in some sort of messianic light, especially in view of the title on the cross and the way the early church persistently applied the term *Christ* to him. Wright, as we shall now see, does not make such a mistake.

JESUS AND THE RECONSTITUTION OF ISRAEL (N. T. WRIGHT)

As with Meier's work, the paint is not yet dry; indeed, Wright's portrait of the historical Jesus is not yet finished. It is another example of a work in progress, and it must be evaluated accordingly. In his recent book *Who Was Jesus?*[99] written for a popular audience, Wright says the "way to find the real Jesus is, as it were, by a pincer movement: forward from the picture of first century Judaism; backward from the Gospels."[100] This is the program he is following in his multivolume work that has only begun to take shape. In the first volume, entitled *The New Testament and the People of God*,[101] Wright does not in fact directly discuss at any length the historical Jesus but deals with introductory issues such as the character and beliefs of early Judaism and the early church, the nature of ancient literature (especially biographies), the problems of studying ancient historical figures and the limits and possibilities of what we can know about them.

Defining and Redefining a Worldview

For our purposes it is not necessary to relate a good deal of this ground-clearing discussion, but Wright's description of the hopes and beliefs of early Jews is of some importance, as is his conviction that the Gospel writers were producing ancient biographies intended to convey reliable information about the historical Jesus.[102] We will defer the discussion of the latter until toward the end of this chapter, but the former demands our attention immediately.

1. The Symbolic World of Judaism. Understanding Israel, the context in which Jesus lived, requires that we understand the structure and major symbols that dominated its national life.

Nothing was more central for Jews than their temple and all the activities that went on in it. As Wright says, Jerusalem was more like a temple with a small city around it than a city with a temple, not least because much of the industry in the city and the nearby countryside supported what happened in the temple.[103] "Allowing for the fact that the Romans were the *de facto* rulers of the country, the Temple was for Jews the centre of every aspect of national existence. The high priest who was in charge of the Temple, was as important a political figure as he was a religious one."[104]

These facts must be kept steadily in view, considering the way Jesus' life ended, especially since it included a controversial action in the temple

and a prophecy about it. Almost equally important is the fact that various
late Old Testament prophetic books (Zephaniah, Haggai, Zechariah and
Malachi) point toward the restoration of the temple under the leadership
of either a royal (Davidic) figure or perhaps a priestly figure.[105] It is
precisely this indeterminacy of expectation connected with the restoration of the temple that could lead to tensions between the high priest and
all possible messianic or charismatic figures, especially those who came
and taught, acted in and spoke about the temple as Jesus did. As Wright
stresses:

> The Temple thus formed in principle the heart of Judaism, in the full
> metaphorical sense: it was the organ from which there went out to the
> body of Judaism, in Palestine and in the Diaspora, the living and healing
> presence of the covenant god. The Temple was thus also, equally im-
> portantly, the focal point of the Land which the covenant god had
> promised to give to his people.[106]

It follows from this conclusion that any attack on or threat against the
temple, whether actual or simply perceived, would be seen as an attack
on the heart of early Judaism. Under such circumstances Jesus' death after
the events of his last week in Jerusalem come as little surprise.

But of course the belief in the temple was linked to the belief in a Holy
Land, the center of which was the holy of holies in the temple. The temple
served as a constant reminder that Yahweh should be ruling and his
people should be free throughout the land. With a Jerusalem and temple-
centered religion, there was always concern about foreign influence in the
Holy Land, especially the further one got from the temple itself, for instance Galilee. It was widely known there was a considerable pagan presence and influence there, as the new cities of Sepphoris and Tiberias
would attest. If Israel was under the thumb of a foreign power, it was at
least in part because of Israel's sin, and the way to remedy this situation
was often debated, but it always included what John the Baptist called
for—repentance and renewal of covenant to turn away the wrath of the
covenant God.

> If Israel's god claimed the whole Land, loyal Jews needed to make sure
> that they—and their compatriots—were keeping in line. This meant,
> among other things, making the appropriate tithes to show that they
> still regard the produce of their fields as covenant blessings. . . . It also
> meant, when necessary, cleansing the Land from pollution, in order to
> "turn away wrath from Israel"—and to restore Israel.[107]

But the rub came in figuring out how to accomplish this cleansing.

Jesus, the Pharisees, the Qumran community, the Zealots and the Sadducees all seem to have had different visions about how this was to be accomplished and whether it could involve the temple and its hierarchy as it now was or whether it required a drastic change at the heart of Judaism. Jesus and the Essene sectarians of Qumran seemed to think it required a drastic change, while the Pharisees wanted to create in a sense a kingdom of priests and the Sadducees were more happy with the status quo and business as usual.

Two other crucial components or symbols that configured the way Jews thought about their story were Torah and racial identity. How one approached these two matters affected the way one viewed Judaism as a whole, almost to the same degree as one's view of temple and land. The fact that Jesus seems to have said some rather shocking things about all these four symbols, or identity markers, indicates that he had a rather different vision of God's people and the way God was going to relate to them in the future.

2. Questions and Answers. Wright in my judgment is correct to say that there was a series of interrelated questions and answers that went into the makeup of the various worldviews in Israel in early Judaism. These are as follows: (1) "Who are we?" to which the normal and almost universal answer was, "We are Israel, the chosen people of the Creator God"; (2) "Where are we?" with the reply, "We are in the Holy Land focused on the temple, but paradoxically we are in a sense still in exile, still outsiders in our own land"; (3) "What is wrong?" "We have the wrong rulers; pagans on the one hand, compromised or half-breed Jews (the Herodians) on the other. We are all involved in a less than perfect situation"; (4) "What is the solution?" "Our God must act to give us the proper sort of rule again, God's own rule through a priest or a king or both, and in the meanwhile Israel must be faithful to the covenant."[108]

As Wright points out, the current high priests would not have entirely agreed with (3) and (4), and there was a wide and wild variety of views about how (4) was to come to pass, ranging from the violent overthrow of the Roman authorities by Jewish Zealots, to direct intervention by God in Jerusalem and elsewhere, to the reformation of Jewish life in the land. It was the hope about the future that was in jeopardy and how that hope was to be realized that was under debate.

3. Monotheism, Election and Covenant. Wright believes that both Jesus and

Paul set about to deliberately and radically redefine the Jewish worldview and belief system. "Jesus . . . redefined the *hope* of Israel in such a way as to call in question the normal interpretation of Jewish belief; Paul, seeing the hope thus redefined in practice around Jesus, completed in principle the task of redefinition of belief."[109] This meant that it was not just *Halakah*, the Jewish way of living out Torah, that was being challenged and reconfigured, but the very belief and hope of Israel.

Wright engages in a helpful and somewhat detailed discussion of the various forms of dualism that Israel embraced in its belief system, including epistemological dualism (ordinary knowledge versus special revelation), ontological dualism (the belief in other supernatural beings besides the one God), eschatological dualism (this age versus the age to come) and creational dualism (Creator-creature/creation distinction).[110] Of special concern is what he says about ontological dualism.

Wright stresses that the recognition of supernatural beings other than the one God is not a violation of pure monotheism but rather an attempt to deal with the problem of a transcendent God who also providentially runs the world on a daily basis and intervenes periodically in more dramatic fashion. He also stresses that monotheism for early Jews, including praying the *Shema*, did not have

anything to do with numerical analysis of the inner being of Israel's God himself. It had everything to do with the two-pronged fight against paganism and dualism. Indeed we find strong evidence during this period of Jewish groups and individuals who, speculating on the meaning of some difficult passages in Scripture (Daniel 7 . . . or Genesis 1), suggested that the divine being might encompass a plurality.[111]

Wright points to Philo's speculations about the Logos and the portrait of the Son of Man/Enoch in the *Parables of Enoch*, but one may as well point to such Wisdom material as the *Wisdom of Solomon*.[112]

It is Wright's view that "it was only with the rise of Christianity, and arguably under the influence both of polemical constraint and Hellenizing philosophy, that Jews in the second and subsequent centuries reinterpreted monotheism as 'the numerical oneness of the divine being.' "[113] This is undoubtedly a crucial argument for Wright, for it means that neither Jesus nor Paul in the particular ways they reconfigured Jewish belief could be accused of a fall from the primordial grace of belief in the numerical oneness of God's inner essence.

The discussion of election and covenant treads on familiar ground. Israel was chosen for the task of restoring creation to its natural order after it had been distorted by the forces of darkness. Evil is not seen as an essential part of creation but rather an aberration from it or a cancer on it. "The creator god has found a way of restoring his world: he has chosen a people through whom he will act. Monotheism and election, together with the eschatology they entail, form the fundamental structure of Jewish basic belief."[114] Part of this picture is Wright's view that Israel saw herself as the Creator's true humanity. The original promises and commands to Adam and Eve are regiven in different form to Abraham and his seed, such that taking possession of the Holy Land and dominion over it has taken the place of Adam's stewardship of Eden and dominion over nature or creation in general.[115]

4. *Adam, Israel and the Son of Man.* Israel is then to act under God and over the world in the role that Adam was originally to act—being a blessing and light to the world, a source of its order and harmony and life and means of relating to God. This is why the prophets used the imagery of paradise to describe the restored Jerusalem and Israel after the exile. In another crucial move, God's Wisdom is identified with, or seen to have its locus in, Torah, so that true humanity was to be had only by those who kept Torah and so fulfilled God's original vision for his human creation. This necessarily meant that the person or persons who dispensed this Wisdom were functioning in an Adamic role, whether it was the high priest wearing vestments, which according to *Numbers Rabbah* 4.8 originally belonged to Adam, or someone else.[116] Jesus' assumption of this sapiential role as the dispenser of true Wisdom not only placed him in the role of Adam or true human being but set him up as a rival to other such claimants, in particular to the high priest and other prophetic and messianic figures.

Where Wright and I appear to part company is in the interpretation of Daniel 7. Wright argues that the humanlike figure is simply a cipher for Israel as the true humanity, as opposed to the beastly pagan nations. This is a possible interpretation, but it draws on a rather dubious idea of corporate personality.[117] It appears more likely to me that the Son of Man is seen as a representative of Israel, the true humanity, just as the kings or horns were representative of the beastly nations. The people of God could not simply be the new Adam; they required a representative to fulfill this role. Wright is however correct that it was indeed seen by various prophets as the vocation of God's people to restore the whole creation, not just the Promised Land, and this meant that what happened to the Gentiles was conditioned upon what Israel was doing and what was happening to Israel.[118]

5. *Israel: Its Plight and Hope.* Even before the time of Jesus, and certainly during it, the question of theodicy was a pressing one for Israel. If Israel was God's chosen, why was it suffering so? And even more to the point, Why wasn't it ruling as it should have been? There were varying answers to this, chiefly that Israel had sinned and needed to repent, but even long before Jesus we hear the complaint, "Here we are, slaves . . . in the land that you gave to our ancestors to enjoy. . . . Its rich yield goes to the kings whom you have set over us because of our sins" (Neh 9:36-37).[119]

Because Jews were not going to abandon their notion of monotheism or election, it followed that they must grope for some sort of restoration eschatology. God must act to restore his people to their proper condition and status in the world.

> At the present time, the covenant people themselves were riddled with corruption, still undeserving of redemption. *One major result was that Judaism always contained a tradition of fierce criticism-from-within, which stretched back to Moses and the early prophets. Such criticisms were a regular and classic feature of Judaism, and their appropriation by John the Baptist and Jesus . . . is paradoxically a sign, not of rejection of Judaism and all that it stood for, but of fidelity to one of Judaism's central traditions.*[120]

This last remark is of great importance for Wright's approach to matters, because he will argue that Jesus, however radical his teaching and life, must be seen as engaging in an in-house discussion with other Jews about the restoration of Israel, not attempting to call Jews away from their monotheistic, covenantal, eschatological faith in the biblical God.

The issue of forgiveness of sins is also an important one, for with the land occupied and Israel sinful, the issue was primarily not that of one or another private individual's sins being dealt with but rather the remission of the *nation's sins.* How was this to be accomplished? "Repentance and sacrifice were part of the means by which Jews *maintained* their status as the covenant people. . . . There is no suggestion that either of them was seen, by Jews, as the means of entry into the covenant people. That was effected by birth and (for males) by circumcision."[121] This overlooks, of course, the fact that proselytes came into Judaism by other means and also fails to deal with the question of whether the Baptist was calling even pious Israelites to see themselves as so apostate that, like a proselyte, they must start afresh with God by means of baptism. It is true, however, that various Jews believed that though Israel would pass through intense suffering as payment for national sin, afterward they would be forgiven and the world would be healed (cf., e.g., Ezek 38:20; Hos 4:3; Zeph 1:3; Dan 12:1).[122]

Of great importance in understanding Wright's views is that he, like Borg, accepts the eschatological views of his mentor George B. Caird that neither Jesus nor other early Jews (or most Christians) were talking about the *end of the world* writ large, but only the end of a particular, more narrowly defined, world order. This was true even when they used the dramatic apocalyptic language of cosmic cataclysm (stars falling, moon turned to blood, etc.) to describe such events. In particular Wright stresses that the coming of the kingdom of God has nothing to do with the end of the world itself. God's "restoration of Israel remained within . . . the this-worldly ambit."[123]

We are not to imagine early Jews expecting the space-time continuum to come to a full stop in the near future. What they were expecting was a radical renovation of the present world order, involving Torah, temple, territory, race, economy and justice. They were not looking to escape this world into heavenly bliss, but rather they looked forward to life again on this earth after the resurrection.[124]

Up to a point I am in agreement with Wright on this matter. My uncertainty has to do with the upshot of his view. Would he deny that Jesus and others believed that at the end of human history there would indeed be cosmic events, a literal return of Christ, a final judgment and a new heaven as well as a new earth? Apparently not, but he is not clear on what Jesus thought and taught about these matters.[125] It is clear enough that Borg does not think these sorts of end-time events were very important in Jesus' eschatology.[126] It does not appear that Wright entirely agrees with Borg, but more clarification will hopefully come forth in the next volume of his work. Furthermore, if indeed the prophecies did fully come to pass, it would most certainly entail a major upheaval of world governments and world order. It would not merely amount to a human renewal movement begun by the man from Nazareth with direct impact on only a minority of human beings.

Wright's interpretation of representation within Israel prepares the way for his discussion of early Jewish messianism and salvation, and Wright agrees that in general "salvation spoken of in the Jewish sources of this period has to do with rescue from the national enemies, restoration of the national symbols, and a state of *shalom* in which every man will sit under his vine or fig tree. Salvation encapsulates the entire future hope."[127] In short, salvation to early Jews would imply liberation from Rome by some means, restoration of the true temple worship and freedom to live in one's own land according to the covenant. It would not be a purely spiritual or otherworldly matter. This is especially because God is the Creator God and aims to redeem, not destroy, creation—"that would simply contradict creational monotheism, implying that the created order was residually evil, and simply to be destroyed."[128]

As Wright acknowledges, there was no single, monolithic messianic expectation in early Judaism. Furthermore, the texts which speak of a particular royal messianic figure are few and far between (but cf. *Pss. Sol.* 17—18; 4Q174). It was not then a matter of Jesus or early Christians appearing on the scene and reacting to a dominant model of what Messiah must be and do. Rather the "early Christians seem to have done . . . what Herod had done: they took a vague general idea of the Messiah, and redrew it around a new fixed point, in this case Jesus, thereby giving it precision and direction."[129] We cannot say for sure what the average common Jew believed about a coming Messiah, for there were a variety of hopes, with no one clearly dominant. What is reasonably clear from the Maccabean experiences and literature is that the one who builds the temple (e.g. Herod) means to legitimate himself as king.[130]

If Jesus did indeed make some sort of promise about a new temple as well as the destruction of the old, he was at least implicitly making royal claims. Indeed, even a "cleansing" of the temple, with the authority that it implied of reordering things, probably carried such an implication. Wright properly rejects the attempt by Horsley and others to dismiss the social or political component of the coming Messiah's role in texts like *Rule of Benediction* (1QSb 5:23-29). There was indeed an expectation of an earthly Messiah who would change earthly realms and power structures.

Wright is able to show that Josephus reflects the fact that the material in Daniel 1—12 was being seen in a messianic light in the first century A.D. (cf. *Wars* 6.312-15 to *Ant.* 10.206-9).[131] In particular, the combining of insights from Daniel 9:24-27 and 2:35, 44-45 seems to have led to an individualized reading of Daniel 7:13-14. This potentially could tell us a lot about Jesus' use of the Son of Man phrase.[132] Wright agrees that the rereading of the Daniel 7 material in 4 *Ezra* 13:3-13 involves an interpretation of the Son of Man figure as the Messiah,[133] but he argues that in Daniel itself Son of Man refers to the group—the saints of the Most High (Dan 7:18, 27). I am unconvinced of this latter conclusion. The Son of Man even in Daniel 7 originally represents rather than is synonymous with, the saints of the Most High.

In any case Wright agrees that at the turn of the era there was already a somewhat clear messianic and Davidic hope and that the phrase *Son of Man* had come to have definite associations with it.[134] He is also convinced that this figure was expected to be a human figure, not a transcendent one, and furthermore it was not expected that this messianic figure would come and suffer. If Jesus said something along these lines, it would have been a new message.

In regard to resurrection, Wright carefully documents the spread of this belief in early Judaism and how it is consistent with a belief in a Creator God determined to renew his creation.

> Resurrection would be, in one and the same moment, the reaffirmation of the covenant and the reaffirmation of creation. . . . Monotheism and election, taken together, demand eschatology. Creational/covenantal monotheism, taken together with the tension between election and exile, demands resurrection and a new world.[135]

Wright's belief that early Christians (and Jesus) looked forward to a future resurrection means that he does believe they looked for radical change in the future, though it did not, in his view, amount to the end of the world.

Speaking of Jesus

Wright is convinced that the atmosphere in the age of Jesus and afterward was volatile and ripe for messianic hopes and claims. In such a time of crisis it was a matter of making extra effort to stay in covenant with God, especially when there might be a risk of finding oneself on the outside looking in when God finally acted to redeem his people. This is why stringent sectarian groups were both so appealing and so demanding—it was critical to be sure that one was in and properly relating to the key symbols of Torah, temple and territory within a proper monotheistic framework.[136] Justification would be both present and future, and would definitely take place because of God's faithfulness to his covenant promises and people, not simply because of the people's fidelity. In this sort of atmosphere, Jesus appeared, claiming that Israel's God was becoming

King even as he, and because he, spoke. "We should not be surprised at what happened next."[137]

We learn a bit more about Wright's view of Jesus from his concluding remarks in his popular book *Who Was Jesus?* Here Wright is quite clear that the Gospels are, as he calls them, reflective or tendential biographies, like other Greco-Roman biographies of the day.[138] This conclusion can be strengthened on the basis of Richard A. Burridge's recent work,[139] but there are problems in applying this conclusion to Luke, especially in view of the two-volume nature of Luke's work.

The vast majority of scholars are not convinced that Acts can be seen as a type of Greco-Roman biography, whether of Paul or of the Christian movement. I share this skepticism, and in a future work I plan to show at length the problems of concluding that Luke's Gospel is biography, including the introduction in Luke 1:1-4, the use of synchronisms, the failure to introduce the main character in the first chapter and other considerations.[140] The case for the biographical character of the other three Gospels is considerably stronger and more convincing.

1. Parabolic Speech and Acts. Wright argues that if we had been Jewish peasants listening to the parables and aphorisms of Jesus, we would have understood that he was announcing that God was at last becoming King among and for his people, that his kingdom was concrete and real and substantial, not a mere state of mind or of inner peace, that Israel at last would be rescued from oppression and that Jesus was some kind of messianic prophet.[141]

One of the probable reasons Jesus used parables, in Wright's estimation, is that Jesus had a radical message—the kingdom was certainly coming, but when "Israel's God acts, the Gentiles will benefit as well! When Israel's God brings in his new world, some of Israel's cherished traditions (like the food laws) will be swept away, no longer needed in the worldwide family!"[142] The announcing of the kingdom would at the same time subvert Israel's national institutions.[143]

> Jesus was saying—in his actions as much as in his words—that you didn't have to observe every last bit of the Torah before you would count as a real member of Israel. He was saying that you didn't have to make the journey to Jerusalem, offer sacrifice, and go through purity rituals in order to be regarded as clean, forgiven, restored as a member of Israel. You could be healed, restored, and forgiven right here, where Jesus was.[144]

This approach would undoubtedly have infuriated the pressure groups demanding an intensified keeping of Torah.[145]

2. *Jesus and the Future of Israel.* Wright believes that Jesus applied the Son of Man material to himself, believing that the kingdom was being redefined around himself. Furthermore, Jesus believed, as Albert Schweitzer rightly saw, that it was his task to go out before Israel and take the judgment of God upon himself in the place of Israel.[146] Jesus believed that through his life, death and resurrection Israel would fulfill its destiny and the world would be saved and renewed. Like the Maccabees, he believed that those who died as martyrs would be raised physically, bodily. "If the Maccabean martyrs could think that, then so could Jesus."[147]

Two carefully written essays further expound these ideas and their corollaries.[148] In his essay on the cross, Wright reiterates the fact that Jesus warned of imminent judgment on Israel—not the end of the world but the end of the present sociopolitical order, including the temple and its hierarchy. His action in the temple was not a cleansing but a symbolic depiction of this coming judgment, which is also referred to in numerous sayings and narratives such as the fig tree narrative.[149] Political action and theology are seen as merging in that Jesus believes that the Romans will come and destroy the heart of Israel and that *their* action will be the form that God's wrath will take. Instead of God judging the Romans, the Romans will be God's instrument of judgment on Israel, as Luke 17:37 suggests, with its reference to the Roman eagles coming and picking over Israel's corpse.[150]

Wright distinguishes his understanding of Jesus from that of Sanders by saying that Jesus was an advocate of reconstitution, not merely restoration theology.[151] Jesus wanted to reconstitute Israel around himself, and his followers would constitute the new people of God. Wright also argues that they could be the new Israel because Jesus saw himself as Israel and believed he was intended by God to undergo God's judgment on Israel so that Israel would not have to undergo it.[152] He further suggests that Jesus saw himself as the temple of God (and his followers also as this temple by extension), the place where God's presence was incarnated on earth. This is yet another reason why Jesus sought to reconstitute Israel around himself.

One may well ask for evidence to justify the conclusions, especially the latter. Wright points to several texts to bolster his views. First, he argues that the Last Supper traditions in the Synoptics suggest that Jesus on the cross was "to become the place of sacrifice."[153] But one objection to this is that the words "this is my body broken" and "this is my blood shed" suggest the sacrifice itself and not the place of sacrifice (i.e., temple). Wright also points to the controversial material in Matthew 16:17-19, arguing that it means, "Blessed are you, Simon, for your confession of me as Messiah: and I tell you, you are the foundation stone of the new temple, and the gates of hell will not prevail against it." Even if this interpretation is correct, it does not suggest that Jesus is the temple, but that Peter and perhaps Jesus' other followers are that temple and that Jesus is its builder.

Wright also points to the gathering of the Twelve as proof that Jesus was seeking to reconstitute Israel around himself. I would agree in part, but I would point out that the gathering of the Twelve suggests, since *Jesus was not one of the Twelve*, that Jesus saw himself not *as* Israel but as the one sent to gather Israel, even the lost sheep, into a new people of God.

Furthermore, if, as Wright argues, Jesus' death is seen as the *climactic* expression of God's wrath on Israel, satisfying the need for divine justice and judgment on a sinful people, with Jesus playing the role of Israel, what sense then can be made of the traditions in Mark 13 and elsewhere that go on to predict the destruction of Jerusalem and the temple sometime later as a form of God's wrath on Israel? It is far easier to argue that Jesus saw himself as God's agent and Israel's representative, not as Israel itself.[154]

I would argue that Jesus did not come to be Israel but rather to free Israel and that this was also the role of the Twelve. They themselves did not constitute the new Israel in toto or even in miniature, but rather they were the ones sent out as missionaries to bring in the twelve tribes. They were but the starting point and agents ("apostles") of Jesus who were meant to gather the new community, a community built on people who had faith in Jesus.

Some of Wright's conclusions are in part dependent on a doubtful interpretation of key texts such as Mark 14:62 and 13:26.[155] He argues that these texts are not about the parousia of the Son of Man but rather about his vindication by God after death, at which point he will be taken up into heaven. This in turn is partly based on a particular reading of Daniel 7.[156] But as Maurice Casey has pointed out at length, the place where God's judgment on Israel and the world takes place and where the kingdom finally comes is earth, not heaven, according to various prophetic texts. Thus it is highly probable that the one like a son of man coming "with the clouds of heaven" in Daniel 7:13-14 involves, if anything, a descent from, not an ascent to, the throne of the Ancient of Days.[157] It seems certain that this is how Paul understood the text when he wrote 1 Thessalonians 4:16-17 and other similar Pauline texts that speak of the parousia and draw on the imagery found in Daniel 7.[158]

3. Messiah, Monotheism and the People of God. More plausible are Wright's arguments that "if Jesus did *not* want to be thought of as in any way as Messiah, the Entry and the action in the Temple were extremely unwise things to undertake."[159] He also presents a convincing argument that Jesus' table fellowship with sinners would have been seen by at least the *ḥᵃ*ḇērîm among the Pharisees as a provocative antitype of their own table fellowship. They sought to restore Israel on the basis of the holiness code and by applying the priestly rules to all, while Jesus sought to reconstitute Israel on the basis of the Old Testament mercy code. In Jesus' mind forgiveness could be had apart from the temple and sacrifices by accepting him and what he offered and becoming his disciple. "If one was with Jesus, one did not need the restoration into covenant membership which was normally attained by going to Jerusalem and offering sacrifices in the temple."[160]

At the conclusion of his short study *Who Was Jesus?* Wright affirms that Jesus could have foreseen and planned for a community of his followers to continue his work after his departure. Indeed he goes much further in the last questions he raises—if Jesus believed he was fulfilling tasks only God could do, such as bringing in the kingdom and rescuing and forgiving God's people, "Why should such a person, a good first-century Jewish monotheist, not also come to hold the strange and risky belief that the one true God, the God of Israel, was somehow present and active in him and even *as* him?"[161]

With this last question, we have of course gone well beyond what almost all of the authors studied in this work would be willing to affirm about how the historical Jesus viewed himself, except perhaps Meier and myself.[162] The point is, however, that Wright has presented a contextual, historical case in which such a view was possible, though of course no one can prove it to be certainly true using the historical-critical method. What Wright's work shows, however, even short of its completion, is that we should not limit the options of how Jesus viewed himself to terms like *teacher,* or *prophet,* or *man of the Spirit,* or *Messiah* or even some combination of all of these. These terms likely have some validity, but neither alone nor in combination do they describe fully how Jesus presented and viewed himself. There is more that needs to be said.

CONCLUSIONS

As we have seen in this chapter, there are New Testament scholars, including Meier and Wright, who hold views of the historical Jesus that more nearly approximate those of the early Christians. This is not to say that either Meier or Wright are precritical in their approach to Jesus or that they are guilty of reading their views into the texts. Rather, the options for understanding what the historical Jesus may actually have been like are not few but many. He was indeed the man who fits no one formula, as Eduard Schweizer has said, and thus something may be learned from many different portraits of Jesus.[163]

The work of Meier and Wright also shows that neither on historical nor on methodological grounds can various of the early church's views about Jesus be ruled to be without basis in the person and work of Jesus himself. This is an important finding, for as I have argued in the previous chapter, it is not satisfactory to radically distinguish the Christ of faith from the Jesus of history. To do that is to create an unexplainable chasm or gulf, when in fact there was some sort of historical continuum. The church and its Christology were not created from nothing. Meier and Wright have set us on the right path in showing that substantially more needs to be said about the historical Jesus, his words and deeds, than the more radical and highly publicized depictions of Jesus would allow.

Finally, we have seen in the work of Meier an attempt to portray Jesus as some sort of special eschatological prophet, perhaps like Elijah, and in the work of Wright the attempt to see Jesus as a type of messianic figure, but also as something more. How much more is a subject the Third Quest may never fully discover because its focus lies on the human face of Jesus, on what is recoverable using the historical-critical method.

CHAPTER 9

THE JOURNEY'S END
SYNOPSIS, CONCLUSIONS, CONJECTURES

AFTER A BRIEF REVIEW OF THE FIRST TWO QUESTS FOR THE HISTORICAL JESUS, the first chapter was devoted to discussing the social setting of Jesus' ministry. It was seen that Jesus lived in a politically volatile climate, though in his own day there seems to have been little sign of open revolt. Small farmers and those who practiced a trade may have felt increasingly marginalized during the period of Jesus' adult life, with the rise of several new cities in the area and the taking over of large tracts of land by the elites, coupled with the ongoing tax burden. There was, however, little need or occasion to express anger against imperial powers in Galilee, because it was not under *direct* Roman rule during Jesus' lifetime, and there is no evidence of any significant Roman presence stationed there. Whatever hostility may have been felt against the elite would have been focused on Herod Antipas and his Hellenized retainers.

Not accidentally, neither John nor Jesus are recorded as having said anything that was clearly against Rome or the emperor while they ministered in Galilee or the region of the River Jordan, but both seem to have criticized either directly or implicitly Antipas and his immoral ways. In general, it appears that Jesus associated primarily with those who lived in the small towns and villages of Galilee and perhaps those in rural areas and farm settings, and seems to have avoided the new Hellenized cities of Sepphoris and Tiberias, which were largely controlled by Herod's retainers. The parables of Jesus are illuminated by the social setting in which Jesus operated.

The religious environment in which Jesus was raised involved Galileans who were quite loyal to the symbolic pillars of early Judaism—Torah, temple and territory—but they were not necessarily able or concerned to pursue the ritual law in the manner and to the extent the Pharisees advocated. In particular, day laborers, small farmers and artisans, of whom Jesus was one, would not always be able to observe an expanded set of rules regulating ritual cleanness.

Social-scientific concepts such as honor and shame, dyadic personality and limited good provide a window on why Jesus and his followers might have thought and acted as they did on a number of occasions. In particular, Jesus' presentation of himself as the Son of Man and the disciples' concern to relate Jesus to previous holy men and Jewish institutions reflect a way of thinking that is foreign to most moderns. The group defined the individual, or to put it the other way around, the individual's self-understanding arose out of the group of which he or she was a part.

There is also evidence that Jesus set out to change certain notions not only about clean and unclean but also about honor and shame, particularly as it applied to male-female relationships. He also seems to have rejected certain understandings of limited good, offering places in God's Dominion to all who would follow him and rejecting the inevitability implied in the concept of limited good by speaking of the eschatological reversal of the fortunes of the poor and oppressed.

The structure of the traditional Jewish extended family was under severe stress during Jesus' day. Jesus' teaching about the primacy of the family of faith and the opportunity for both men and women to follow him in his itinerant ministry would only have exacerbated this trend, as would his teaching about singleness for the sake of the kingdom of God. There is no denying the social implications of a good deal of his teaching, but there is also no denying that Jesus believed that in his own ministry God's saving activity was present in power among the chosen people. There is no evidence that Jesus set about to reorganize local villages or towns according to a social program, much less that he directly confronted local authorities in order to precipitate change, with the sole possible exception that Jesus spent time with toll collectors. These men, however, were not in control of the levers of power in their society. They were low-level functionaries of the elites.

The review of the social setting of Jesus produced no evidence that Jesus sought to lead a resistance movement against the imperial hierarchy of Rome, or even against Herod Antipas. His social critique of Herod seems to have been limited. Jesus chose to be proactive rather than reactive and to call people to follow a new vision of the community of God. His action in the temple may be taken as either a critique of the religious corruption of his day, which would have had social and political implications, *or* a prophetic sign-act meant to foreshadow the coming judgment of God on a corrupt institution. The latter explanation is more probable. The chief action Jesus spoke of was the direct saving and judging action of God.

Jesus in the Seminar

The second chapter consists of a critique of the Jesus Seminar. It was argued that the seminar is made up of a narrow selection of New Testament scholars and that it seems to have many crucial flaws in its methodology. These include an overemphasis on some of the criteria to establish historical authenticity at the expense of others, uncritical optimism regarding the *Gospel of Thomas* as a source for Jesus's actual sayings, a strange tendency of concluding that something is inauthentic even when a distinct minority of scholars have voted it to be such (i.e., voting "black") and a habit of treating sayings apart from their narrative and, in some cases, their historical context. The Jesus Seminar combines an unrepresentative participation with a seemingly democratic method of voting on the sayings material. For all its pretense of objectivity, the charge of bias cannot be avoided. Moreover, it is a strongly and peculiarly North American enterprise.

Jesus the Cynic

In the third chapter we turned our attention to one of the main figures in the Jesus Seminar, John Dominic Crossan, whose work on the historical Jesus has received more publicity and reaction than that of all of the other contributors to the Third Quest put together. Like the Jesus Seminar, Crossan shows a predilection for a non- or realized-eschatological Jesus. He sees Jesus as a Jewish Cynic peasant who chose to itinerate throughout lower Galilee, never staying long in one place in order not to become a broker or mediator between God and his audience. At the heart of Crossan's view is a vision of Jesus as a radical advocate of egalitarianism, adamantly opposed to various sorts of hierarchies, including that of parents over children. By the practice of "open commensality" (eating with anyone and everyone) and by performing what appeared to be miracles, Jesus set about to establish a society free of the structures of domination. Jesus was noted for his aphorisms and parables and never said much about the Son of Man or other apocalyptic themes.

In order to arrive at this picture of Jesus, Crossan must pursue what can only be called a peculiar methodology. For one thing, he allows only material that is multiply attested to be considered likely to have originated with the historical Jesus, and then not even all of that material can be counted as authentic (e.g., *abba*, "your kingdom come" and the Twelve are arbitrarily ruled out). In addition, Crossan repeatedly overvalues a variety of extracanonical works such as the *Secret Gospel of Mark*, the *Gospel of Peter* and the *Gospel of Thomas*, while largely dismissing the evidence found in the passion narratives of the Synoptic Gospels.

Then, too, Crossan continually supposes that the Gospel material passed through a very long period of transmission, undergoing major alterations at various points along the way. This supposition and methodology allows him to cast a net with large holes into the Synoptic ocean, drawing in very few big fish, while casting a very fine-meshed net into the extracanonical sea and retrieving a good deal of "historical" material. Both the methodology and the results of this exercise are problematic at numerous points.

In short, Crossan is not able to demonstrate either that Jesus was a peasant or a Cynic, and while he retains the view that Jesus was Jewish, he certainly is depicted as being unlike any of his Jewish contemporaries on such crucial issues as family, Torah, temple, territory and eschatology. When we are told that Jesus was like a hippie among Augustan yuppies, we have a right to suggest that Crossan is guilty of anachronism and wishful thinking about the historical Jesus.

Jesus the Charismatic Figure

In chapter four we analyzed the views of Marcus Borg, Geza Vermes and Graham Twelftree, who in various ways have presented us with a portrait of Jesus as a charismatic figure. When we speak of a person's charisma we are in essence referring to the effect a person has on others. It is Borg's view that one of the essential things we can say about Jesus is that he not merely believed in God, he experienced God and had what we would call visionary or mystical experiences. As a result of these experiences Jesus became a conduit through whom the power of God flowed into our world and into human lives. Borg believes that such experiences are genuine and have occurred down through the ages in the lives of many saintly individuals. Borg realizes that this portrait only captures a portion of the truth about Jesus, and so he also argues that Jesus should be seen as a sage and a prophet.

The major problems with Borg's approach are that he makes too much out of too little data and, methodologically, he tries to radically separate religious experience from religious belief. Jesus had concerns about issues of moral purity as well as future eschatological emphases that Borg either underplays or fails to come to grips with altogether. Perhaps the least convincing aspect of his approach is that while he admits Jesus set out to reform Judaism, was a mediator of the Spirit to this world, sought to do away with Torah-sanctioned approaches to holiness by means of ritual purity and performed a cleansing of the temple, yet this suggests nothing about Jesus having an exalted self-consciousness. Still, Borg has helpfully shown the significance of understanding Jesus' experience and the realm of the Spirit in interpreting the historical Jesus.

The work of Geza Vermes centers on the suggestion that Jesus was a *ḥāsîd*, a charismatic Galilean holy man who performed remarkable acts of healing and had a very intimate relationship with God. As we saw, while there is something to the suggestion that Jesus stood in the tradition of Elijah, Elisha and other Galilean prophets, this has little to do with the later concept of the *ḥāsîd*, a person extremely scrupulous in the observance of the law.

Jesus' use of *abba* and sonship language in prayer differs from the way it is used in the traditions about *hasids* Honi and Hanina. Furthermore, the historical associations of either of these latter figures with Galilee is tenuous at best. Then too, Honi and Hanina were mighty prayer warriors, not miracle workers per se in the sense that Jesus was. At the end of the day, the category *hasid* does not really add anything to our understanding of the historical Jesus that could not have already been gathered from a close analysis of the Elijah and Elisha traditions.

In the concluding portion of chapter four, we reviewed Graham Twelftree's specialized work on Jesus as an exorcist. This work was helpful in showing the close connection between Jesus' eschatology and various of his acts of healing, and it serves as a corrective to some of the conclusions of Crossan and Borg, which underplay the eschatological and even messianic dimensions of these acts. Twelftree also shows that while Jesus was widely recognized as an exorcist, there was no attempt on the part of Christians who passed along these traditions to expand the exorcist traditions in any significant ways or to create new ones. Furthermore, he shows that there was no tendency to characterize Jesus as a magician, even though he was noted for his miracles.

Jesus the Eschatological Prophet

The important and influential work of E. P. Sanders and the similar approach of Maurice Casey were discussed in chapter five, and in both cases we saw portraits of Jesus as an eschatological prophet. Sanders in part revives the older Schweitzerian view of a Jesus who expected the eschatological climax of human history in his lifetime or immediately thereafter. In his various works Sanders has continued to emphasize the facts of Jesus' life as revealing a good deal about him, including his baptism by John, his calling of disciples, especially the Twelve, his confining of his activity to within Israel, his preaching of the kingdom of God, his celebration of Passover with his disciples and his engaging in a controversy over the temple that eventually led to his death.

It is to Sanders's great credit that he recognizes it is not enough to simply establish this or that fact about Jesus' life and realizes that lines of causal connection must be traced between his life, his death and the beginning of the Christian movement. Sanders is unconvinced that Jesus had major controversies with the Pharisees in Galilee over the sabbath and purity laws, something Casey would allow for, and he is very skeptical of the view that Jesus was a Cynic or a social reformer. Jesus, in Sanders's mind, was an advocate of restoration eschatology, and, somewhat like the Qumran community, he believed that judgment by God on the temple was near and would be a prelude to the restoration. In preparation for these eschatological events Jesus was offering unconditional forgiveness to Jews, including even the wicked and the lost (i.e., "the sinners"), and this last action was one of the more radical aspects of his ministry. Casey differs from Sanders at this point in that he thinks the sinners were simply lapsed Jews, not necessarily the notoriously wicked, and he believes that Jesus, like John, called Israel to repentance. Both Sanders and Casey are wary of ascribing any of the traditional titles to Jesus as a reflection of his historical consciousness, though Sanders is willing to go as far as calling Jesus God's last envoy or viceroy. Casey for his part speculates that Jesus set out to fulfill John the Baptist's prophecy about the Coming One.

Sanders tends to give rationalistic explanations to Jesus' miracles, and Casey does not really address the issue. But Sanders is helpful in pointing out the differences between Jesus and ancient magicians. Only the latter followed certain rules and recipes, acted as isolated professionals without disciples and believed in the great Chain of Being that links lesser things (e.g., grass) to God, so that the greater can be manipulated by the proper handling of the lesser.

Neither Sanders nor Casey gives adequate attention to Jesus' parables and the social implications of his teaching. They both seem to assume that Jesus' eschatology of imminence rules out the idea that he had intentions of working social change in society. The fact that Jesus was not a social revolutionary does not, however, rule out that his teaching had some immediate social implications and effects.

Jesus the Social Prophet

Chapter six focused on several of the more important attempts to depict Jesus as a prophet of social change. The work of Gerd Theissen was given attention first, not least because it has influenced a wide variety of the other proposals we have studied, including those of Crossan, Horsley and Fiorenza. It was Theissen who first vigorously advanced the proposal that Jesus was a radical charismatic itinerant preacher. It was also Theissen who first distinguished between the traveling followers of Jesus who embraced a stringent ethic and lifestyle involving homelessness and vulnerability and the local sympathizers, who in the strict sense were not seen as disciples but rather provided hospitality and material support for Jesus and his entourage.

In Theissen's view, Jesus and his movement were the peace party that advocated an ethic of nonretaliation among the various Jewish reform movements of the day. Itinerancy was embraced in part because it was a means of staying out of harm's way. Theissen believes that the real authority figures and producers of the earliest Jesus traditions were the traveling charismatics and that local authorities and the traditions associated with them developed only later.

Theissen also affirms that Jesus' movement was made up of socially rootless or already homeless people. This last suggestion conflicts with the Gospel traditions, which indicate that Jesus called people away from their trades (fishing, toll collecting) and homes. The traditions in which Peter and others stress how much they gave up to follow Jesus show that they were not totally marginalized peasants to begin with but rather had some assets to sacrifice (cf. Mk 10:28-31). Thus Theissen in the end must even correct himself and suggest that the marginal middle class may have supplied Jesus' main followers. It should also be stressed that Theissen underestimates the ease with which Jesus could have come and gone from a base in Capernaum, which probably suggests that not even all of Jesus' traveling disciples need have embraced an ethic of radical homelessness and abandonment of family. Theissen's sharp distinction between Jesus' traveling and localized supporters is overdrawn, not least because figures like Mary and Martha are depicted as disciples in more than one source.

Theissen helpfully points out that various renewal movements, including the Jesus movement, were alienated from and partially defined in reaction to the Hellenization of their culture and thus in reaction to the Hellenistic cities within their land (e.g., Sepphoris and Tiberias). Jesus, like the Zealots, was involved in a theocratic movement; but unlike the Zealots, the Jesus movement focused on Jesus and his actions rather than on the actions of a group. Theissen subscribes to the same Schweitzerian eschatology we saw resurrected by Sanders, believing that Jesus thought the end was necessarily imminent and must be prepared for, as it would involve a radical reversal of fortunes of the greatest and the least, the weak and the strong. Since God would soon act, revolutionary initiatives against the entrenched powers were unnecessary.

In his most recent work Theissen seeks to rewrite the history of the development of the Synoptic tradition. If even some of his arguments for the early formation (the 40s) of the passion narrative and sayings tradition are cogent, he has undermined the arguments of scholars who assume a long development of the Gospel tradition. In Theissen also we find an attempt to integrate the religious and social dimensions of Jesus' ministry. This is a more balanced approach than we find in the work of Richard A. Horsley.

Horsley argues that Jesus chose to be a social revolutionary, siding with the poor and oppressed and taking on the power elites. It is his view that Jesus sought to reorganize village life in Galilee along more egalitarian and nonpatriarchal lines and that his essential teaching was addressed to such settings, not to traveling disciples. This attempt to see Jesus as a reconstructor of Galilean village life seems to be based on doubtful evidence and even more dubious interpretations of one or two key sayings. Even loving one's enemies is taken to mean establishing relationships of solidarity within one's community!

While Horsley is critical of the proposal that Jesus was a Cynic, his attempt to substitute the idea of Jesus as instigator of class struggle is equally implausible, not least because the whole terminology of classes does not suit Jesus' Galilean society. His attempt to reduce future eschatological expectations about what would happen in the kingdom to contemporary social programs in the villages where food, family, forgiveness and lands were already being received by Jesus' followers during his ministry is an exercise in reductionism, as is his handling of the question of whether there were any messianic components to Jesus' ministry. When messianic figures are reduced to either social reformers or mere bandits, it becomes clear that the social agenda of the author is dictating how the exegesis will turn out.

Horsley's analysis of the Zealot movement and his attempt to argue it out of existence prior to the late 60s fails to come to grips with the polemical and apologetic character of Josephus's *Jewish Wars.* Perhaps the greatest weakness of Horsley's analysis is that if indeed Jesus' ministry was a failed attempt at social reform in Galilee, it is difficult if not impossible to explain the rise of early Christianity as a form of messianic Judaism.

The work of R. David Kaylor is in many ways dependent on that of Horsley and Theissen and so reflects the same flaws and some of the same helpful insights. He differs from the others in seeing Jesus as an advocate of the renewal of Israel who wanted to return to the Old Testament covenant traditions that would produce justice and peace. He believes Jesus was political in the same way that the preexilic prophets were political, though of course there was also a religious component in his message, since God is the prime rectifier of society's ills.

Kaylor's analysis labors under the notion that premonarchical Jewish agricultural society was in some sense egalitarian. Rather, it was simply a different sort of less centralized patriarchal society, with hierarchy based on family and tribal lines. It is a mistake to confuse systems of barter or community of goods with modern ideas about egalitarian societies. Kaylor admits that Jesus probably chose the Twelve but fails to draw the logical conclusion that Jesus was concerned to set up some kind of hierarchical arrangement for his movement.

Kaylor also overplays the Roman factor in Galilee. There were no Roman legions in Galilee during Jesus' ministry, and Galilee was not overrun with Roman authorities or institutions. Outside the more Hellenized larger cities, the ethos was much as it had long been in Jewish society. Thus Jesus was surely not basically reacting against the Roman presence.

Kaylor omits any meaningful discussion of the Son of Man traditions, and his attempt to eliminate the future eschatological elements in Jesus' kingdom teaching fails to convince. Kaylor is, however, right in arguing that Jesus' parabolic teaching had some clear social implications and applications, though these did not supplant its future eschatological dimension. For example, the Beatitudes are not likely to have been addressed to the power elites of Jesus' day, but rather they served as promises for the oppressed and marginalized that things would be reversed when God brought the kingdom in its fullness.

Jesus—Prophet of Sophia or Jesus the Sage?

In chapter seven the work of Elisabeth Schüssler Fiorenza portraying Jesus as prophet of Sophia was explored. It is Fiorenza's view that Jesus saw God as Sophia, not as Abba, and that he was a part of a Jewish wisdom resistance movement that opposed the domination systems in place in his land. Jesus himself should be seen as a radical prophet, liberating women and the marginalized from oppressive patriarchal structures.

In Fiorenza's view, these facts have been largely and deliberately obscured in the course of the later Christian handling of the Jesus traditions, for the tradents were not really interested in preservation but in persuasion. This assumption, coupled with her view that the Gospel traditions underwent a very lengthy period of editing and modification, allows her to choose a very few passages as the only ones representative of what Jesus actually said, did and was like. This tendentious procedure leads to the dismissal of many traditions about family, marriage, divorce, the Twelve and a host of other subjects, even though they are better attested using conventional historical-critical criteria than are the few on which she bases her conclusions.

Fiorenza has in essence modernized Jesus, making him an advocate of politically correct forms of egalitarianism. We might agree that Jesus sought to reform the patriarchal structures of his day in the context of his own community of followers so that women could assume a variety of roles as disciples. But the evidence that he took more radical measures than this and founded a movement involving direct resistance against Rome, or against Jewish authorities in Israel, is lacking.

Fiorenza, however, is quite right that Jesus was involved in starting a movement intended to renew Israel in the light of the inbreaking kingdom of God and that he sought to define holiness in noncultic ways. I would add that this set him at odds with some of the aims and views of both Pharisees and Sadducees. But the evidence that Fiorenza presents for arguing that Jesus was following in an egalitarian stream of Judaism is weak at best. *Judith*, to which she appeals, is no egalitarian document. Also, her argument that the christological garb of the Gospels was only later draped over Jesus does not make sense of the way Jesus' life ended (e.g., the placard on the cross) or of the fact that his earliest followers after Easter were the same people who had followed him during his earthly ministry.

The traditions about the Twelve, though well attested, are lightly dismissed by Fiorenza, and, it is even more important to note, her conclusion that Jesus saw God as Sophia is based on controversial interpretations of two or three difficult texts. The concept of the discipleship of equals is a valuable one, but it does not rule out the idea that Jesus saw himself as a servant leader with authority over his followers or that he might have singled out one or more of his followers for other leadership roles. Furthermore, the concept of the kingdom of God has an inherently hierarchical component, as it involves a theocratic vision of life.

While it is true that there was a liberating character to Jesus' teaching and healing, the evidence is slim, if not nonexistent, that Jesus was opposing Roman imperial domination. This is due no doubt to the fact that Jesus' ministry was mainly in Galilee, where there was no significant Roman presence.[1] In any case the message of Jesus seems to have focused on nonresistance rather than resistance.

Fiorenza's idea that Jesus was opposed to any and all sorts of hierarchical structures founders on the abundant evidence that Jesus chose the Twelve, that he said various things that supported the nuclear family and that he spoke about leadership and its exercise in service to others and about God's kingdom or rulership, the ultimate form of hierarchy. If by the discipleship of equals one means that all were equally valued, whatever their role or status in the world, certainly Jesus affirmed this; but this is a rather different notion from modern egalitarian concepts.

Fiorenza's argument about Jesus viewing God as Sophia was seen to rely, even in her most recent work, on the debatable interpretation of two or three passages, bolstered with an equally tenuous view that the hypothetical Q community continued the emphases of Jesus while other early Christian groups distorted his teaching. Compared to this line of argument, the evidence that Jesus and his earliest followers saw and addressed God as *abba* seems strong.

The last half of chapter seven was devoted to my own proposal that Jesus saw himself as One greater than Solomon who was not merely a prophetic Jewish sage but the embodiment of God's Wisdom, Wisdom come in the flesh. The chief value of this view lies in the host of conundrums it explains about the Jesus tradition and the earliest Christian reflection on Jesus.

For instance, it explains the form of Jesus' teaching, namely his parables, aphorisms, riddles and beatitudes. It also explains some of the key elements in Jesus' teaching: his emphasis on the kingdom, Son of Man, God as Father, creation theology, the lack of halakic material, the absence of any "thus says the Lord" formulas and the stress on justice and the reversal of fortunes. Jesus' sayings about the yoke, about being like a mother bird rejected by her chicks and about Wisdom's deeds, all make better sense in light of the insight that he saw himself as God's Wisdom. Furthermore, it explains why in the early christological hymns that emerged within a decade or so of Jesus' death Christians were applying Wisdom motifs to Jesus (cf. Prov 8—9; Sir 24; Wis 8—9 with Phil 2:6-11; Col 1:15-20, Heb 1:1-4). It also helps explain why in the 50s Paul sought to emphasize God as Abba and Jesus as Wisdom (cf. Rom 8—11; 1 Cor 1—4; Gal 3—4). In short, it explains the transition from sapiential messianology in the teaching of Jesus to early high Christology in the church.

Finally, I stressed that this proposal to see Jesus as sage and Wisdom should not be taken in isolation from the helpful insights to be gained from seeing Jesus as prophet, Spirit person and messianic teacher. No one descriptive term or title adequately encompasses the "man who fits no one formula." While the historical-critical study of Jesus of Nazareth is essentially the study of his human face, we have seen that in these matters history cannot be neatly severed from theology, and this means that we must come to grips with the possibility that Jesus had an exalted self-understanding involving a variety of theologically profound concepts.

Jesus the Messiah

Chapter eight investigates what from one perspective might be called more traditional approaches to the historical Jesus, and it concentrates on the work of John P. Meier and N. T. Wright. Both of these scholars are involved in lengthy detailed studies of the historical Jesus, and since these studies are works in progress, evaluation was necessarily partial and tentative. Meier and Wright are also similar in that both pursue the historical Jesus using more traditional methodologies and conventional presuppositions than some of the other Third Questers.

Meier argues that Jesus should be seen as a Jew living at the margins of Jewish society who chose to pursue a marginalized lifestyle as an itinerant preacher and healer and whose teaching and actions were in many ways not in accord with the views and practices of the majority of early Jews.

Meier proceeds carefully to build up a detailed picture of what Jesus' teaching and deeds were like, sticking almost entirely to the canonical data. In order to understand his portrait, however, it must be recognized that Meier seeks to distinguish the Jesus of history from the Christ of faith. This is a problematic approach if there was a theological component to the historical Jesus' words, deeds and self-understanding.

After a review of some brief studies by a variety of scholars who continue to view Jesus in a messianic light, the balance of chapter eight was devoted to examining the approach of N. T. Wright. It is his conviction that the way to get at the historical Jesus is to move forward from a portrait of early Judaism but also to move backward from the Gospels. He believes the Gospels are like other ancient biographical works and deserve to be evaluated accordingly.

Wright spends considerable time reconstructing what Israel's hope was before and during the age of Jesus. He shows that it involved a variety of messianic beliefs that included the expectation of the restoration of God's people to faithfulness to Torah, the restoration of the temple to its proper state of holiness and the restoration of the land to its rightful rulers, Jews. Especially crucial for Wright is the view that the temple was seen as the heart of Judaism and yet Israel was under foreign or unsatisfactory client-king rule. Thus restoration must involve the cleansing of both land and temple from pollution, even if it meant the destruction and replacement of the latter. By and large, Jews looked to God to rectify these problems, though some Zealots were prepared to take matters into their own hands.

It is Wright's view that both Jesus and Paul set about to radically redefine the Jewish worldview and its core beliefs so that they would center
around Jesus. Like Borg, Wright is not convinced that Jesus foresaw the
near end of the world, but rather thinks that Jesus expected that when
God intervened he would bring to an end a certain world order. Equally
important for Wright's portrayal is that he believes Jews operated with
a concept of corporate personality and thus that Jesus could present himself as the one who embodied Israel, indeed even as the new temple, the
new focus of true religion. There are various problems with these views
and also with the way Wright interpreted Daniel 7.

Nevertheless, in our judgment Wright is correct to locate Jesus within
the stream of early Judaism that had certain concrete messianic hopes.
Jesus used parables because he had a radical message about God's salvation coming through his messianic ministry to surprising people—not just
to the lost sheep of Israel but perhaps even to Gentiles. Wright even goes
so far as to suggest that Jesus, even as a good Jewish monotheist, may
have seen himself as one in whom God dwelt and through whom God
acted. Indeed, he conjectures that Jesus could have thought that "the God
of Israel was somehow present and active . . . as him."[2]

The Journey Toward Jesus
What course will the Third Quest take in the future? Conjecturing about
its future is a risky business. Yet it seems likely that after a series of more
radical "lives" of Jesus, the pendulum is poised to swing in a more conventional direction. I say this for several reasons.

First, the recent magisterial work by Raymond E. Brown, *The Death of
the Messiah*, will have to be reckoned with.[3] This work argues at length that
there is historical substance to our earliest passion narrative, the Markan.
Furthermore, the church did not develop a sudden amnesia regarding
what happened to Jesus during the last week of his life, not least because
there were probably some friendly witnesses of the end of Jesus' life,
including his burial. Brown also argues that later works such as the *Gospel
of Peter* do not really help us reconstruct what happened at the climax of
Jesus' ministry. The impact of Brown's thorough study is likely to bring
the final week of Jesus' life back to center stage in discussions about the
character and meaning of the historical Jesus.

Second, the works of both Meier and Wright promise future discussion
of the close of Jesus' life, and this too will add to the impetus provided

by Brown's work. I suspect it will become less and less plausible to present a portrait of Jesus that does not adequately integrate Jesus' death with his ministry and self-understanding. Among other things, this means that scholars like Crossan and Borg and Fiorenza, who want to reconstruct a Jesus and a Jesus movement that by and large bypasses the cross and its significance, or interprets it in purely political terms, will have increasing difficulties in convincing the majority of New Testament scholars that this does justice to all the relevant data.

Third, nothing is as fleeting as many of the latest trends in New Testament scholarship, including studies of the historical Jesus. This is easily seen simply by reviewing the trends and impact of the Second Quest for the historical Jesus, which offered us, among other things, an existentialist Jesus.[4] The historical Jesus and the Jesus that can be reconstructed by the historical-critical method are not one and the same. More to the point, the Jesus that is reconstructed by an idiosyncratic use of the historical-critical method or is based on reducing the field of focus to a few passages may have only minimal connections with the real Jesus.

If we ask the question, What is the common thread that binds together the works of the Third Quest and distinguishes it from the previous two quests? a few things rise to the surface. First, of course, the search for a common object, knowledge about an ancient historical person, using all the available historical and critical tools obviously connects these works, even though the tools are evaluated and used in various ways with varied results. This is somewhat different from previous efforts, not only because we have more knowledge about Jesus' milieu, but also because new methodologies such as social-scientific criticism are being applied to the data.

Second, it is probable that the attempt to place Jesus more firmly in his social and economic setting and to focus on the social aspects of his life, ministry and teaching will be seen as a distinguishing feature of the Third Quest.

Third, the desire to say something new and fresh characterizes almost all of the works examined in this study, sometimes to the extreme of preferring the new over the probable. It is interesting that the more radical proposals come up with less Jewish images of Jesus, while the less radical ones come up with more Jewish and traditional images of him. This could lead to some interesting speculation about just how much (or how little) of a departure from Jesus' Jewish character is to be found in the familiar early Christian images of Jesus as Christ, Lord and the like.[5]

As always, the historical Jesus remains elusive. But some roads, even if less traveled, may provide the keys to fruitful further discussions of what Jesus was actually like. I suspect that when scholars finally come to grips with Jesus the prophetic and messianic sage, the embodiment of Wisdom, they will have a clearer understanding not only of Jesus of Nazareth, but also of why his movement developed as it did. If this is the outcome of the Third Quest, it will be well worth the many twists and turns the journey has taken along the way.

EPILOGUE

THE DEATH OF THE MESSIAH

One of the most neglected aspects of Jesus in the Third Quest has been the important events that make up the last days of Jesus' life. However, the two-volume work of Raymond Brown *The Death of the Messiah*[1] is a brilliant exception to this charge. It is a work of such weight and importance that it deserves mention, even if briefly.

While I doubt Brown and Meier are having a contest to see who can produce the largest books on Jesus to be published by Doubleday, the similarities of the two massive multivolume works are worth noting: (1) both are characterized by painstakingly detailed exegesis of crucial texts, unlike some of the Third Quest books, where exegesis is neglected and global theories are mounted on the backs of a select few texts, trotted out to bolster the argument; (2) both reflect long study, extensive reading and research, and, in Brown's case, a whole career devoted to Gospel studies; (3) both make for demanding reading because they are encyclopedic and comprehensive treatments of their subjects. As such they are more easily accessed as reference works on particular topics.

Brown tells us from the outset that he aims to study in detail what the Evangelists intended to convey to their audiences about Jesus' passion, starting with the arrest and surveying the trials, the death and finally the burial of Jesus. In other words, this study is, in the main, not intended as a contribution to the Third Quest but is rather a study of the redactional work and theological interests of the Evangelists as shown by the different ways they portray these events. Brown is asking and answering the question, How do the different Evangelists portray these foundational events and what were they trying to convey to their respective audiences? Because Brown's study is primarily intended to be an exercise in redaction and narrative criticism, and a study of the Evangelists' theologies, it is very different from Meier's, and this is why I have placed these comments in an epilogue. It must also be kept in mind that Brown believes that the Gospel traditions passed through various stages and hands, and thus that it is necessary to work through several layers of tradition if one wants to discern the historical kernel of a text, if any is to be found.

Yet it would be a mistake to overlook Brown's many comments and side excursions along the way that say a great deal about the historical Jesus and the close of his life. Indeed, so much is this the case that one could put together a helpful book on this subject simply by ferreting out these passages from the work.[2] This, however, would be a disservice and a dismembering of an important work, and Brown has complained that in some cases, because he put historical reflections in appendices to his earlier work *The Birth of the Messiah*, some people only read the appendices! He has made such a sidestepping maneuver difficult in this book, and rightly so. He has given us both profound analyses of the interpretations of Jesus' passion *and* helpful insights into the events and circumstances that led to such interpretations. We should be grateful for both. For the purposes of this present book, however, it is important to briefly chronicle Brown's historical conclusions.

First of all, Brown's historical reflections are not limited to just the big questions. He also comments on things like the shape of the cross, what type of wine Jesus drank, who Pilate was and where he stayed when in Jerusalem, whether there really was a Jewish trial and a variety of other matters. Brown is convinced that a basic skeletal outline of what happened to Jesus can be discerned by a careful critical sifting of the Gospel materials, especially of Mark, which he believes, as do most scholars, to be the earliest Gospel and the one used by Luke and Matthew in their passion narratives. Brown also believes that the Fourth Gospel is a basically independent witness and is not devoid of some independent historical substance, though its author uses some of the same traditions as Mark and the other Evangelists.[3]

Brown is convinced that it was Jesus' action in the temple that prompted his arrest and that it was the Jewish religious authorities who were pursuing this course of action. Brown does not think Jesus intended the temple action as a symbolic cleansing but rather as a prophetic depiction of the coming destruction of the temple, which Jesus believed would be superseded by another temple in the final age.

This being the case, Brown sees Jesus' action as not merely an attempt to urge reform or to tinker with the existing system, but rather to foreshadow its downfall. This Brown apparently takes as a sign of Jesus' messianic vision and agenda. Also pointing in a messianic direction is the fact that Brown believes that the Jewish authorities charged Jesus with making some sort of religious claims.

This means Brown also thinks, unlike various scholars, that there really was at least a hearing before the high priest, if not a formal trial before the Jewish high council or Sanhedrin.[4] The final responsibility for Jesus' execution lies with the Romans, in particular Pontius Pilate, though he was probably reluctant to do it. Joseph of Arimathea probably was responsible for the burial of Jesus, which probably was indeed at the site of the present-day Church of the Holy Sepulchre.

It will be seen from even this very brief sketch that Brown does not believe that the early Christians all suffered from total amnesia regarding the events surrounding the end of Jesus' life, nor did later handlers of the tradition lack all historical curiosity about what actually happened to Jesus. This rules out any theory that has a very tenuous basis in the Gospel text, particularly if it neglects Mark.[5]

Readers will discern that in much of this Brown is rather old-fashioned, which is frankly refreshing after reading some of the major Third Quest books. To come to his historical conclusions on various matters, Brown uses Mark as his basic guide for the historical bedrock on most matters, a rather different approach than those who overemphasize the Q sayings material to the neglect of the passion material. In other words, we see once again how one's choice of methodology and preferred criteria for testing authenticity strongly affect what conclusions are likely or even possible.

The initial reactions to this book in the scholarly guild have been rather favorable. At the November 1994 Society of Biblical Literature meeting there was a panel review consisting of Donald Senior, E. P. Sanders and James D. G. Dunn. Though Sanders probably had the most reservations about the work in regard to its implications about early Judaism (e.g., the existence of the Sanhedrin), his basic judgment was that Brown always writes books that are at least as good as they are long, which is saying a lot for a two-volume work like this one. Dunn even wanted Brown to say more, about Mark 14:58-61!

In his response to the reviews Brown pointed out that had Jesus simply been a revolutionary,[6] the Romans would have sent out the troops and had him dealt with peremptorily prior to and without any Jewish involvement. Furthermore, they would have been unlikely to leave his followers alone then or thereafter. The presence of James still in Jerusalem much later than Jesus' death reveals something of both the Roman and the Jewish assessment of Jesus.

I have given these brief remarks in hopes of encouraging the reader to go and read at least portions of this important work for themselves. Though I am no prophet, I would suggest that if this book has the impact it deserves, in the future scholars engaged in the Third Quest will feel it necessary to come to grips with the passion material in order to understand who Jesus really was and how he viewed himself. If *The Death of the Messiah* has no other effect than this, it will still be enormously important, for it will have forced scholars to take seriously the linkage between the life, teaching, travels, friends, foes *and death* of Jesus of Nazareth.

POSTSCRIPT

THE CONTINUING SAGA
OF THE JESUS QUEST

SINCE I FIRST WROTE *THE JESUS QUEST*, MUCH MORE HAS BEEN WRITTEN ABOUT JESUS, and there is no end in sight. John P. Meier's much anticipated third volume *A Marginal Jew: Rethinking the Historical Jesus* is on the horizon as well as several others.[1] In this postscript I intend to critically evaluate seven titles that have appeared since my work on the first edition was complete. We will begin with two more popularly written books and work our way to the more technical works, although John Dominic Crossan's work could be said to be written at a popular level as well. *Jesus at 2000*, the collection of essays edited by Marcus Borg, will be considered first.[2]

Jesus at 2000

Jesus at 2000 assembles an interesting variety of essays and provides the modified texts of lectures given in early 1996 as a part of a national forum at Oregon State University for the discussion of Jesus. Downlinked by satellite to 312 other sites, the forum included questions from the audiences and responses by the scholars, which also have been reproduced. Only the essays of Borg (two essays), Crossan and Alan Segal in this volume really focus on the issue of the historical Jesus, and so we will interact with just these four.

In his introduction to the volume, Marcus Borg makes what is for him a fundamental distinction between what the historical Jesus was and what "Jesus had become in the experience of those who followed him."[3] In Borg's view, the historical Jesus was not divine, nor did he make any notable messianic claims or rise from the dead, if by that we mean that something supernatural happened to Jesus' body after he was crucified. Yet Borg affirms what he calls the resurrection, saying the "post-Easter Jesus of Christian experience refers to the fact that Jesus continued to be experienced after his death as a living reality, from the first century to the present."[4]

That various people throughout the last 2000 years have believed they continue to experience Jesus as a living reality is uncontroversial. The question is whether the way Jesus is experienced today is identical with the way the very first followers of Jesus experienced him during the days between his resurrection and his ascension into heaven, as recorded in the Gospels. The answer is no. Neither can we eqaute the event of Jesus' resurrection with the experiences Christians had during their encounters with the risen Lord.

Borg clearly denies that resurrection involves the same thing as the resuscitations of the dead handed down in the tradition concerning Jesus' ministry. I would agree that resurrection involves more than what is said to have happened to Lazarus or others, but whether in the case of Jesus or others, we are talking about a transformation that affected the corpse of a deceased person. This is how the earliest Christians understood the concept of resurrection, not as some subjective visionary experience such as we find in the book of Revelation. Nowhere in the New Testament are visions or dreams called resurrection, and visionary experiences of the risen Lord such as John the seer had (or perhaps Paul had) are not to be equated with resurrection.

Even in the earliest Jewish texts which speak about resurrection we hear about the rising up of *bodies*. Consider Daniel 12:2, which says, "Many of those who sleep in the dust of the earth shall awake, some to everlasting life, and some to shame and everlasting contempt." Now compare this to our earliest New Testament source that speaks at length on this subject, 1 Corinthians 15:35-38: "But someone will ask 'How are the dead raised? With what kind of body do they come? . . . But God gives it a body as he has chosen, and to each kind of seed its own body." What early Jews meant by resurrection is something that would happen to a person's *body* after death. The debate in early Judaism between the Pharisees and the Sadducees was not a debate between those who held a materialistic view of resurrection and those who did not. The Sadducees simply didn't believe in resurrection, while the Pharisees did. One might ask what kind of body was involved, but the discussion was about bodies.

Consider also the creedal fragment found in a text written before any of the

Gospels and within about 22-23 years of Jesus' death: "For I handed on to you as of first importance what I in turn had received: that Christ died for our sins in accordance with the scriptures, and that he was buried, and that he was raised on the third day in accordance with the scriptures" (1 Cor 15:3-4). Now when a former Pharisee speaks of Jesus dying, being buried and then rising, he undoubtedly is speaking about something that he believes has happened to Jesus' body. This is confirmed by his further discussion in 1 Corinthians 15:35ff. The earliest Christians clearly believed that something happened to Jesus, not just to themselves at Easter. Again, visions and dreams are not called resurrection in the New Testament or in the relevant early Jewish sources. This means that either Borg must argue that the earliest Christians misunderstood what really happened to Jesus and his body or he must admit to defining resurrection in a way different from how the earliest Christians would have understood the term, for they were all, with the possible exception of Luke, Jews.

This leads to the related issue of whether, on the one hand, texts like the Emmaus road story in Luke 24 are parables or symbolic allegories of continuing Christian experience or even prophecy historicized or whether, on the other hand, they are intended to make claims about things that actually happened or were believed to have happened to Jesus and his disciples shortly after the crucifixion. Borg here follows Crossan in suggesting that "Emmaus road never happened, Emmaus road always happens." The problem with this suggestion is that from a form critical point of view there is nothing to distinguish this text from various other disclosure texts in the Gospels and elsewhere in the Bible where it is reasonably clear that we are not talking about prophecy historicized or a parable or allegory. Indeed, from a form critical standpoint this narrative is little different from many Lukan and Synoptic narratives about the pre-Easter period.

Only the disappearance of Jesus at the end of the story makes the narrative stand out at all. We must ask too why, if Luke was creating symbolic tales, he didn't bother to make up some about more familiar and paradigmatic disciples like Peter or James or John or members of Jesus' family (whom Luke is certainly interested in—see Acts 1:14). Why should he mention Cleopas and an un-named other disciple? Why portray them in the unflattering way he does? The Emmaus road story is no allegory of continuing Christian experience, any more than the story of Jesus' visit with Mary and Martha in Bethany or the raising of the son of the widow of Nain is. If the problem is the miraculous, then almost all of the Synoptic narrative material is problematic. The resurrec-

tion narratives are not unique in this regard and do not deserve to be treated
as a special genre of literature different from the pre-Easter narratives.

Three final remarks are in order about Borg's approach. First, it is one thing
to speak about the significance Jesus has had for Christians down through the
ages; it is quite another to speak of the meaning of these foundational texts.
Jesus and these texts certainly have taken on a larger significance that goes
beyond these rather succinct stories, but these stories claim to be about what
Jesus was, not merely what Jesus is. A very reasonable case has been made by
Richard Burridge that the Gospels should be seen as ancient biographies, that
is, as lives of an important historical figure—Jesus.[5] If this is so, one must not
minimize the concentration in these works on what Jesus was. It is of course
also true that these foundational texts seek to claim that there is some sort of
profound continuity between the historical Jesus and the living Christ. In other
words, significance grows out of meaning and historical claims.

Second, the big bang theory of Easter, so far as Christology is concerned,
stretches credulity to the breaking point. This is especially so if Easter is based
on subjective visions. And when we know that there were various messianic
pretenders in the Holy Land during the first half of the first century A.D., why
should not Jesus have been one of those who directly or indirectly made
christological claims? It is quite another matter to ask and answer whether one
believes such claims are true.

Third, I find it very strange that, on the one hand, Borg is willing to allow
that all sorts of spiritual and visionary experiences are possible, and even that
Jesus and the early Christians had such experiences, but, on the other hand,
he seems to deny that any of these experiences might involve any enduring
objective content, any true and definitive revelation from God about the divine
nature. Why is the concept of God's true self-disclosure to humans through
words and concepts and not just through emotional experiences so hard to
accept?[6]

John Dominic Crossan's essay is to a large extent a condensation of what
he says in his previous books. There are a few new remarks, including an
interesting and helpful discussion of the relevance of the *Didache* to understanding early Christianity.

At one point he suggests that criteria and methodology are everything and
that the author of *The Jesus Quest* approaches historical Jesus research without
using either to distinguish earlier and later traditions about Jesus.[7] Either
Crossan has not read my *Christology of Jesus* and *Jesus the Sage*, or he has ignored
the detailed discussion of methodology and criteria at the beginning of the

first of these two works. This brings to light a significant problem. Evangelicals who use the historical-critical method tend to read all of the significant literature on the subject, and their writings reflect this familiarity with the relevant scholarly literature written by people of all sorts of faith and of none at all. There are, however, a large number of mainline scholars who continue to simply ignore the work of critical evangelicals, as if it were not scholarly work, or in some cases they appear ignorant of its existence. Neither oversight nor benign neglect is helpful if discourse on the historical Jesus is going to advance beyond the caricaturing of one another's positions.

Some of Crossan's suggestions are interesting and fresh, though they are mixed with much that is questionable:

1. On the basis of the Emmaus road story combined with 1 Corinthians 9:5 Crossan suggests[8] there were women evangelists traveling with men evangelists, who, to prevent scandal, were called "sister wives," even though they were not really married. In other words there was an egalitarian thrust to the community's outreach from the outset. I would not quarrel with the idea that there were Christian women evangelists from an early date, but it is not clear that the person with Cleopas was a woman (though it is quite possible), nor is anything said in this story about their being evangelists. Furthermore, it is far from clear that Paul is talking about anything other than a person's actual wife in 1 Corinthians 9:5, especially since the discussion in 1 Corinthians 7 predisposes one to think in that direction. This is all the more likely given what we know of couples like Priscilla and Aquila who fulfilled the sort of roles Crossan is discussing.

2. Crossan's attempt to minimize or deny the likelihood of Jesus' choosing twelve males as his disciples is not convincing,[9] especially in light of early traditions like 1 Corinthians 15:5 and also Acts 1. By the criterion of multiple attestation the idea of the Twelve should stand as it is found in very different traditions in Mark, Paul and Acts. The fact that they are not mentioned in Thomas or Q is not compelling evidence. Absence of evidence is not the same as evidence of absence. Crossan also does not accept the idea that the mission of the Twelve as a group was to Israel, and that this is why, in an increasingly Gentile church, our later sources do not place any stress on this group, focusing rather on apostles. Crossan simply dismisses a plausible explanation at this point.

3. More promising is Crossan's study of the *Didache*.[10] Here he suggests that this document is early (between A.D. 50 and 100) and that it reflects the viewpoint of the more sedentary or located groups of Christians who were

trying to discern how to deal with Christianity's itinerant prophets, teachers and apostles, especially in regard to their support. On this point I think Crossan is correct, but we cannot simply project these conditions back into the ministry of Jesus wholesale. Crossan has not proved his case in arguing that the Jesus movement may have always involved these two groups of persons—itinerants and householders—with the latter being seen as the domesticators of the Jesus tradition.

4. Crossan continues to maintain that Jesus was simply itinerant, though he provides no new or compelling evidence. I find this picture of Jesus very questionable, particularly if Jesus' ministry went on for several years and involved not only Galilee but perhaps also Judea. The Judean tradition presents, for example, Jesus staying at the home of Mary, Martha and Lazarus. We must also remember, as J. Andrew Overman has pointed out, that with Capernaum as a base, one could travel to and from almost any destination in lower Galilee within a day or so. Crossan is sill trying to avoid the notion of Jesus being a broker of the kingdom, for in his view any kind of a hierarchy, even apparently a divinely ordained one, is a part of the problem and no help to needy human beings.

5. The disciples' dependence on their Near Eastern cultural system of standing hospitality is by no means the same as re-creating peasant society in an egalitarian mode. But I quite agree with Crossan that the meals Jesus himself shared with his own disciples and with the outcasts of Jewish society suggested a reform in a more open direction.

One of the great ironies of *Jesus at 2000* is that the Jewish contributor to the discussion, Alan F. Segal, comes closest to representing the Protestant scholarly position that has dominated twentieth-century discussion of Jesus from the time of Albert Schweitzer until the 1980s: Jesus was a millennialist prophet, an apocalyptic Jew, not a sage or a wisdom teacher. He also argues that the apocalyptic character of earliest Christianity is inexplicable if Jesus himself did not hold these sorts of eschatological views.

A further difference from both Borg and Crossan is seen in Segal's stress on the criterion of dissimilarity and how various apocalyptic remarks attributed to Jesus in the Gospels pass this stringent test of authenticity. He goes further than Borg in saying, "I feel sure that the earliest Christians experienced the continued presence of Jesus in their lives not in some vague form but exactly in the form that combined a resurrected messiah, angel of the Lord, and Son of Man who was enthroned next to God."[11] He adds, "No one actually saw him arise, but evidently his disciples almost immediately felt that he had."[12]

In other words, the disciples believed something happened to Jesus, not just to his first followers at and after Easter. It is both an oddity and an irony that we find Segal far closer than either Borg or Crossan to what conservative and even many mainline Christian scholars continue to say about Jesus—namely, that a non-Jewish, noneschatological, nonapocalyptic, nonprophetic and in some senses a nonmessianic Jesus makes no sense of the origins or character of either early Christianity or of the Jesus tradition after the criterion of dissimilarity has been applied to it.

Luke Timothy Johnson

Luke Timothy Johnson's polemical broadside against the Jesus Seminar entitled *The Real Jesus* can be dealt with succinctly.[13] Many of Johnson's criticisms of the Jesus Seminar are telling in terms of his analysis of agendas, methodology and results, but I agree with N. T. Wright's analysis of Johnson's approach, that it is quite impossible to place history and theology,[14] history and the real, or fact and meaning[15] in entirely separate categories—or even history and religion when the subject is first-century Jewish life (see further on regarding Richard Horsley). It is also quite impossible to insist on a radical disjunction between history as events and history as written, and yet Johnson appears to wish to confine the term *history* to that which is written about the past rather than that which happened in the past.[16] Johnson in some respects ends up sounding like Borg in his Martin Kähler-like distinction between the historical Jesus and the historic or real or post-Easter biblical Christ. He appears to be willing to give up the historical hunt in order to preserve theology and Christology intact.

This, however, will not do, because the New Testament, for better or worse, does make theological and historical claims about the historical Jesus, not just about the post-Easter risen Lord. It is right to say that the historically reconstructed Jesus is not identical with the historical Jesus, Jesus as he actually was. It is right to say that the historical, or "real," Jesus can never be fully known through historical inquiry. It is right to say that all written history is facts plus interpretation. It is, however, wrong to deny that through historical inquiry we might come up with accurate glimpses and indeed even fresh glimpses of the historical Jesus. The historically reconstructed Jesus can indeed be a subset of what was true of the historical Jesus if the work is done carefully and well. If the real Jesus does not include, as part of the picture, the historical Jesus as he was during his human existence, then docetism reigns supreme.[17] To give but one example, if Jesus did not die on the cross, then all the early Christian theological claims in the world about his atoning for sins or providing cleansing from sin go for naught. I would also argue, with Paul, that the same can be said about the resurrection of Jesus from the grave and Christian faith (1 Cor 15:13-14).

It appears to me that the New Testament writers believe that history is inherently theological in character (because they believe God is working in history), and they also believe that much of theology is historical in substance. They do not believe that it is merely a matter of pasting a theological interpretation on secular historical events or mythologizing the mundane. Therefore, the historical substance of the story of Jesus is of the utmost importance to them and to us, and Christian faith in a real sense stands or falls on that substance. What it does not stand or fall on of course is the ever changing historical reconstructions of Jesus which are always at best partial reconstructions and approximations of the truth about Jesus. Oddly, in the end Johnson sounds very much like Borg, of whom he is so critical, in his appeal to Christian experience and life as the touchstone of the final validity and basis for faith.[18]

Like so many others in the Third Quest, Johnson is an example of someone who is right about much of what he affirms about Jesus and the limits of the historical-critical method, but wrong in what he denies about the importance of history and historical inquiry for theology, Christian experience and the Christian faith in general. History is not a *donum super additum* or the frosting on the cake, much less a dispensable ingredient in it. It is the most essential ingredient with which any Christian theological cake must be made and baked, or else the claims about the nourishing and life-giving properties of that cake are highly overrated if not simply false. "Historically less filling but still tastes great" was not the motto of the earliest Christians when they evaluated their experiences. Why should it be that of Christians today?

Richard Horsley

Richard Horsley has provided us with two detailed and intriguing studies about the social realities and situation in first-century Galilee. The first, *Galilee: History, Politics, People*,[19] appeared toward the end of 1995; the second, *Archaeology, History and Society in Galilee*,[20] appeared a year later. We will evaluate each in turn, as they deserve careful attention. Imagine a history of Galilee from about the third century B.C. to about the third century A.D. that takes no significant account of the crucial role played by religion in Galilean life and deliberately says very little about the Jesus movement. If you can imagine such a book, which dwells on matters of economics and politics and social life in general without grappling with the integration of these factors with what we know of early Jewish religious life, you will have a general picture of what you will find in this book. In spite of this deliberate neglect or trivialization of the religious character of early Judaism, this book has much to commend it.

For one thing, Horsley has read extensively, in some cases almost exhaustively, on his subject. He has interacted with detailed archaeological reports and the primary source material in Josephus and the Mishnah and occasionally, but only occasionally, with materials in the New Testament, as well as with the work of social scientists, economists and political historians. The book is a wealth of detailed data that Horsley is to be commended for assembling. It helps in giving a thicker description of the social matrix out of which both early Judaism and early Christianity arose in Galilee, and this is one of the major aims and accomplishments of the book.

For another thing, Horsley brings a sophistication to the discussion, which includes a realization that all the sources, both ancient and modern, must be evaluated critically. He does not simply endorse a modern social model as a tool to evaluate the ancient data, though he does seem overly enamored with the works of J. H. Kautsky, G. E. Lenski and J. C. Scott (none of whom are experts in ancient Near Eastern culture), as well as with the older Marxist economic and class struggle theories, when it comes to evaluating the relationship of the governed to the governors in what Horsley calls a peasant society in Galilee. Evidence must be weighed and sifted, whether it is from a modern archaeological report or an ancient literary source. Horsley is usually a careful sifter, and his efforts produce some interesting results, not the least of which is the conclusion not only that Galilee was a mixed-language milieu and a mixed cultural milieu, but also that it continued to draw on ancient Israelite traditions and ideas. This becomes evident when one evaluates some of the periods of social unrest and banditry in the midst of which, among other things, popular kingship movements sometimes arose.

Horsley is tempted to draw an analogy between the Jesus movement and popular kingship movements in Galilee,[21] but he refrains or perhaps defers the task to another day. What he suggests that he would say, however, is that Jesus was interested in reforming local village life in Galilee. This does not differ from what Horsley has argued in the past (e.g., in *Jesus and the Spiral of Violence*), and he still does not come to grips with the various traditions that suggest that Jesus' aim was to form out of his diverse group of followers a family of faith bound together by their allegiance and discipleship to himself (see, e.g., Mk 3:31-35).

Horsley continues to be unpersuaded by the arguments of Martin Hengel and others about the Zealots, despite the critiques of his views. His view remains that throughout the period of the Herods there was no continuous revolutionary or Zealot movement. In his view Zealots, properly speaking, do not show up until the revolt in A.D. 66-70. Of Saul of Tarsus Horsley has virtually nothing to say. But if one really wanted to evaluate whether there were religious Zealots around during our period who were prepared to do violence in the service of Torah piety, Saul and his persecutions of early Christians would call for examination.

Horsley also continues to argue that there were no synagogues in first-century Galilee. This he maintains in spite of the fact that he allows that Galilee may have been something like a diaspora setting (where there were synagogues) in its everyday religious and social life, and in spite of the fact that the evidence of both the New Testament and Josephus (our two primary literary sources) suggest otherwise, as may also some of the recent archaeological data. Horsley is clearly correct that lower Galilee was a frontier area, well removed from the religious center in Jerusalem. This factor should lead him to a more serious reflection on how Jewish religious life was likely to have appeared in such a setting.

Some of the other major assumptions of this work may be summarized briefly:

1. Horsley operates with the assumption that there was an enormous tax burden laid on Galileans during most of the era he is discussing. This he maintains despite the fact that E. P. Sanders has shown that this cannot have amounted to more than about fifteen to twenty percent of a peasant farmer's assets, even when both the Romans and the Jewish temple authorities were taking their cuts.[22]

2. Horsley continues to lump almost all nonrulers in Galilee into the category of peasants, even though this description does not suit a variety of nonrulers such as the artisans, into which class Jesus of Nazareth fell.

3. Horsley assumes that Herod Antipas was turning Galilean peasants into debt slaves by first demanding tribute, then taking their land when they could not pay. But as Sanders says, if Antipas was looking for funds for his building projects, he would be far more likely to either draw on the considerable resources he already had or plunder those who had wealth within his domain, rather than rely primarily on funds or property gathered from indebted peasants.[23] It is unlikely he could have produced the enormous sum of 200 talents a year that way.

4. Horsley argues that the first-century village economy in Galilee was not a market economy and was not becoming one. He may be mostly right about this, and certainly he is right that modern notions about capitalism do not help us much in evaluating ancient economic conditions in Galilee.

5. Horsley argues that the Pharisees may well have been active in Galilee from time to time during the first century, but not as an independent religious group. Rather they are to be seen as retainers of the Jerusalem priestly hierarchy, coming to impose southern agendas (and revenue demands) on the north. This is perhaps partly true, but it underestimates the religious dimension of the Pharisaic agenda.

6. Horsley tends to assume that what was the case in Sepphoris and Tiberias probably does not inform us very much about Galilean village life elsewhere (e.g., even in Nazareth, a few miles away), because there was not regular social interaction, because in turn there was no market economy or reason for the villagers to go to the big city. He is probably right about this.

Horsley has written an important and stimulating book that gathers together much relevant and helpful data about Galilee. Throughout this work, Horsley uses the work of Sean Freyne[24] as the main point of departure for his own discussion, because he disagrees with Freyne on many, if not most, of the major issues. One would do well to read these two books in tandem. Together they remind us that evaluating the Galilee of the first century A.D. and earlier is a complex matter. An integrative approach that does justice to religion, politics, economy, history and social life and that pays attention to both literary and archaeological data is likely to help us gain a better picture. A purely religious reading of the data will not do, but neither will an underestimation or reductionist approach to the religious factors. Somewhere between these two extremes lies the historical truth about Galilee and its Galileans.

The second of Horsley's books, *Archaeology, History and Society in Galilee*, is equally stimulating. It reflects the same critical acumen and gives even more attention to the details of recent archaeological work in Galilee. It is much more accessible for the general reader, and his first chapter on the history of Galilee is in some ways a nice summary of most of the previous book. The person interested in the New Testament and the historical Jesus will still be frustrated with the lack of attention to the religious factor and to the New Testament data, but Horsley says more about Jesus here than in *Galilee: History, Politics, People*, particularly in his concluding remarks.[25] The following points are important:

1. Horsley provides more evidence for the importance of realizing regional differences, including religious differences, between lower Galilee and other

parts of the Holy Land. Galilee was not Judea, and kingship or messianic movements that arose in Galilee would likely look different and be responding to some conditions different from those in Judea.

2. Horsley's discussion about the language situation in Galilee is illuminating, especially his conclusions that Aramaic was likely the dominant spoken language there, notably among the nonelite, and his discussions of diglossia (a dominant spoken language and a secondary language used mostly for writing and commerce and interelite communication by the few who were literate and part of the ruling class) as opposed to multilingualism are helpful.

3. Horsley's critique of the Cynic Jesus view is telling. Ordinary people in Galilee did not know enough Greek and were not familiar enough with Greek ideas to find a Cynic Jesus either interesting or understandable, for "there may have been little more than a thin veneer of cosmopolitan culture even in the cities of lower Galilee in the early first century C.E. Even more problematic for a Cynic-like Jesus is the failure of its advocates to consider extra-Gospel evidence for how Galilean villagers may have responded to 'influences' upon them from the newly rebuilt Sepphoris."[26]

4. Horsley continues to insist that there were no synagogues in Galilee during Jesus' era but does not deal in any detail with the relevant Gospel texts. He simply dismisses them as retrojections.[27] Even if he were correct that there were no purpose-built religious buildings in Galilee in Jesus' day, only multipurpose assembly buildings which sometimes were used for religious functions, it is not at all clear how this distinction makes much historical difference (except of course to provide grist for Horsley's mill that wishes to grind up any purely religious reading of the historical data). Horsley discusses the archaeological evidence from Galilee of two examples of "Moses' seat"—a chair in the synagogue on which the one expounding the Torah would sit. In both instances he sees them dating from the post-New Testament era. But this discussion does not adequately explain Matthew 23:2.[28] In insisting on the late dating of evidence for "Moses' seat," Horsley implies that it was not an earlier practice. But why then would Matthew refer to the practice of Pharisees and scribes sitting in such chairs if such a social practice did not exist at least in his own day, if not in Jesus' lifetime?

5. Horsley puts a considerable dent in the suggestion that there was any real Christian presence in Galilee during the last two-thirds of the first century A.D., especially after the Jewish War. He thereby undermines the hypothesis of some sort of Galilean Q community which maintained different and more egalitarian views than Christian communities elsewhere. He is especially

critical of the theory that "Peter's house" in Capernaum provides historical evidence of an ongoing presence of Christians in the area after the time of Jesus.

6. In Horsley's view, the advocates of Gerd Theissen's hypothesis of a wandering charismatic Jesus, including Crossan and Borg, have been significantly misled. Jesus was probably not by and large an itinerant, rather he was one who was trying to strengthen and renew village communities that were under stress from the overlords. This he did by "a renewal of the Mosaic covenantal cooperation and reciprocity."[29] This concern stood behind his teachings about marriage, debt forgiveness and the like.

7. Horsley is surely right to reject Sanders's view that there was likely no conflict between Jesus and Pharisees in Galilee. This is especially the case if Pharisees were retainers of the Jerusalem authorities, sent to socialize Galilee and check up on disturbers of the religious peace.

8. Equally helpful is his critique of those who denude Jesus' sayings of their literary and social contexts and then reconstruct them to support a portrait of a largely non-Jewish, noneschatological Jesus.[30]

In short, there is both much to commend and much to debate in these two books from Horsley. They are in some ways the mirror opposites of Johnson's *The Real Jesus*, for they say on every page that history matters greatly in our reconstruction of the "real" Jesus. This large gain must be balanced against a certain disdain for things theological and for Christian devotion expressed in the form of buildings at the holy sites (which he calls Christian debris[31]). When I read Horsley, whose work I admire greatly, I am nonetheless reminded of a remark by Crossan, "A historical reconstruction that is anti-dogmatic is even more silly than one is pro-dogmatic. In both cases, the researcher is trapped in somebody else's agenda."[32] This is an appropriate point at which to turn to the book from which that quote comes.

John Dominic Crossan

Who Killed Jesus? is Dominic Crossan's revision of some of the basic arguments of his earlier work *The Cross That Spoke*.[33] But the arguments have been updated so that they may provide a response in popular form to Raymond Brown's *The Death of the Messiah* (Doubleday, 1994).[34] Crossan characterizes his work in comparison to that of Brown as follows—Crossan's own view is that the passion narratives are 80 percent prophecy historicized and only 20 percent history remembered, while Brown's work is seen as holding the mirror opposite view.[35] Actually, if one reads the entire book, of the 20 percent Crossan thinks is not prophecy historicized, a fair portion of that he thinks is simply

Christian propaganda (e.g., the burial stories). As I said in the first edition of *The Jesus Quest*, the Third Quest has needed desperately to turn to discussing Jesus' death. There was some discussion of this previously—for instance, in Sanders's work—but now in the studies of Brown, Crossan and N. T. Wright this shortcoming is being remedied.

First, we must summarize what Crossan thinks is historical. He accepts that Jesus was crucified in part because of the action he took in the temple, and he accepts that both some of the Jewish authorities and Pontius Pilate were responsible for this execution, primarily on the testimony of Josephus rather than that of the New Testament. He accepts that there was a disciple named Judas who betrayed Jesus, even though he doesn't believe there was an inner circle of disciples called the Twelve. He does not think there were any trials, nor any burial of Jesus by disciples or friends, nor any bodily resurrection.

On this last subject he says the "resurrection means for me that the human empowerment that some people experienced in lower Galilee at the start of the first century in and through Jesus [even before Easter] is now available to any person in any place who finds God in and through that same Jesus."[36] Interestingly, he rejects a rather popular view of resurrection (see above) in the process—the "risen apparitions in the gospels have nothing whatsoever to do with ecstatic experiences or entranced revelations. Those are found in all the world's religions, and there may well have been many of them in earliest Christianity [e.g., in Paul's case]. But that is not what is described in those last chapters of the gospels. It is questions of authority that are under discussion there."[37] In other words, these are stories concocted to support the developing power structures of early Christianity.

One of the impressions one gains from reading through this book carefully is that Crossan comes at the text not as a historian, asking historical questions of plausibility and possibility, but as a literary archaeologist. Where others see whole edifices or edifices with ornamental decorations and fresh paint but still edifices, he constantly sees layers and layers of literary bricks, laid on top of each other over a considerable period of time. In other words, he approaches the narrative material in the Gospels in the same way as he approaches the literary fictions he earlier spent so much time on—namely, the parables and aphorisms of Jesus. He never pauses to consider that this approach might be inappropriate, especially if the authors had as one of their main purposes to convey a certain amount of historical information. He never asks the historical questions first; he is too busy drawing up charts of literary relationships, some more plausible than others.

Ironically, his weakest argument is in the chapter about "Abuse," where he tries to chart a literary development explaining the reed motif in the passion narratives (cf. Mk 15:19; Mt 27:29). He calls this the central chapter of the book where the validity of his theory about prophecy historicized is supposed to be most evident.[38] His chain of literary logic goes from scapegoat ritual and Old Testament texts about it to passion prophecy such as we find in *Epistle of Barnabas* 7 to passion narrative in the *Gospel of Peter* 3:6-9 (helped by notions of abuse found in Philo *Flacc.* 32-39), finally to canonical passion narratives. He pursues this tortuous argument even though, on the one hand, no canonical Gospel says anything about Jesus being nudged by reeds (pierced by a spear is hardly the same thing) and, on the other hand, the idea of even the scapegoat being nudged by reeds is, as Crossan says, not found in the Jewish sources. It is just his hunch that this is what the scapegoat ritual involved.[39]

Why does he go through such a convoluted exercise? Because he wants to maintain at all costs the theory that the *Gospel of Peter* is the earliest form of the passion narrative and the basis of all other forms, and it mentions Jesus' being "nudged by reeds" (*Gos. Pet.* 3:9). This is of course a theory that only a small minority of other New Testament scholars find in any way plausible, but Crossan is unfazed by the criticisms that were leveled against this theory when it was published in *The Cross That Spoke*. He recycles this theory here with some fresh arguments.

This means that we must ask again what we know for sure about the *Gospel of Peter*, and the earlier so-called *Cross Gospel*, which Crossan thinks it contains. Reference to this text, as Crossan himself admits,[40] first surfaces in western Syria at the end of the second century, and fragments of this text have been found in two places in Egypt—one dated to the late second or early third century and containing only *Gospel of Peter* 2:3-5a (P. Oxy. 2949), the other dated from somewhere between the seventh and ninth centuries, containing larger fragments, including one which begins in the midst of Jesus' trial and breaks off during what appears to be a resurrection appearance involving Peter. It needs to be realized that no text simply presents what Crossan calls the *Cross Gospel*. This is his literary extraction from the *Gospel of Peter*, based on his judgments about what must be later accretions. Interestingly, Crossan assigns *Gospel of Peter* 2:3-5a to the latest redactional strain of this material, even though the earliest extant text of the *Gospel of Peter* we have includes this fragment.

We have no evidence whatsoever that the writers of any of the early extracanonical documents knew of the *Cross Gospel* or the *Gospel of Peter*. There is nothing in the *Didache,* nothing in Hermas, nothing in Ignatius, nothing in Justin Martyr, nothing in Clement, and the list could go on. The case for its earliness hinges then on Crossan's ability to show a literary relationship of some sort between the *Cross Gospel* and the canonical Gospels, or at least with Mark, the earliest canonical Gospel, since Crossan thinks even John uses Mark. The arguments in the abuse chapter, which are supposed to be strong ones, do not inspire confidence that such a case can be made.

I say this especially because when one scrutinizes Crossan's reconstruction of the *Cross Gospel,* what he sees as the earliest stratum reads in part like something from second-century pious Christian fiction of the order of John and the Bedbugs or Paul and the Talking Baptized Lion. Consider *Gospel of Peter* 10:39-42:

> And while they were relating what they had seen, they saw again three men come out from the sepulchre, and two of them sustaining the other, and a cross following them, and the heads of the two reaching to heaven, but that of him who was led by them by the hand overpassed the heavens. And they heard a voice out of the heavens crying "Hast thou preached to them that sleep?" And from the cross there was heard the answer "Yes."

Crossan is aware this passage is a liability to his case for the earliness of the *Cross Gospel,* and he tries to deflect criticism by rather lamely suggesting that the word *cross* here refers to a group of people that Christ has liberated from Sheol.[41] This he suggests in spite of the fact that the previous use of the phrase "the cross" in the *Cross Gospel* refers to the instrument of Jesus' execution (see *Gos. Pet.* 4.11). Needless to say there is nothing in the canonical passion narratives like talking crosses or, for that matter, talking animals.

But another rather sure indication that this passage comes from the second century and not the first is the reference to preaching to those who sleep. The development of this tradition is well known, especially in its late stages when it becomes part of the Symbol or Apostles' Creed ("he descended into hell"). It is important to note that scholarly work on texts in the canon such as Jude 6, 1 Peter 3:19-20 and 2 Peter 2:4 (cf., e.g., the work of W. J. Dalton and the commentary on Jude and 2 Peter by R. J. Bauckham) shows that these texts are about the fallen angels believed to be referred to in Genesis 6, not about sleeping human beings. The latter interpretation of this tradition does not come from the first half of the first century but, at the earliest, from the end of that century or the beginning of the second century depending on how we date the *Odes of Solomon* (42:11-20). In short, the *Cross Gospel,* if it ever was separate from the *Gospel of Peter,* does not appear to be an early first-century document at all.

Here we must give a few brief responses to Crossan's other major arguments. Crossan maintains that the *Gospel of Peter* represents earlier material than that found in, say, Matthew, which can be seen in the *Gospel of Peter*'s less anti-Jewish character, at least in its view of the Jewish people's willingness to respond in lament after the death of Jesus ("Woe on our sins, judgment has arrived and with it the end of Jerusalem"—*Gos. Pet.* 7:25). Surely the explanation lies in an apologetic motive, an attempt to win the favor of the Jews. But this motive can be attributed just as well to a writer of the second century as one of the first. It is a caricature to suggest that all Christians in the second and third century had given up hope of converting Jews and were simply engaging in polemics against them. A lack of anti-Jewish tone is no sure indicator of an early date.

Is it plausible to argue that we have evidence of a *Sitz im Leben* in the 40s for the *Cross Gospel* because of the pro-Roman authority, anti-Jewish authority and pro-Jewish people attitude in this document? The first and the last of these attitudes existed at various points in early Christianity and were views held by various Christians throughout the first through third centuries. But it is worthwhile to point out that Claudius's likely expulsion of Jews and Christians from Rome in the early 40s (see Acts 18) does not encourage us to think of the 40s as an especially likely time for the creation of Christian documents reflecting sentiments in favor of Roman authority. As for attitudes against Jewish authority, these are in evidence throughout the first through third centuries because of the probable role of the Jewish authorities in Jesus' death (a probability Crossan affirms).

How do we explain that the *Gospel of Peter* seems to be familiar with distinctive traditions found separately in the four canonical Gospels (especially from Matthew), but does not seem to quote from or show a clear literary relationship with any one of the canonical Gospels in particular?[42] There are several possible answers to this question. Brown suggests it is due to the author's memory of the Gospels rather than his perusing Gospel manuscripts. Another possibility, and perhaps more plausible, is that the author had access to something like Tatian's *Diatesseron*, a harmony of the Gospels which dates to the second century.

Another live possibility has been raised by G. N. Stanton in his August 1996 Society of New Testament Studies presidential address in Strasbourg entitled "The Fourfold Gospel." By the mid-second century collections of the fourfold Gospel or at least multi-Gospel collections may have been circulating. Pointing in this direction are (1) the prefixes attached to the Gospels in the early second

century ("according to" which suggests several Gospels that require distinguishing); (2) Irenaeus's references to the fourfold Gospel at the end of the
century; (3) the Muratorian fragment's reference to the Fourth Gospel; (4) early
multiple or fourfold Gospel codices (e.g., p^{45}, which may date to the end of the
second century, and p^{64}, p^{67} and p^4, which certainly does and includes Matthew
and Luke); and most importantly, (5) evidence of the use of a fourfold Gospel
codex in Justin Martyr's catechetical school in A.D. 150. In short, the author of
the *Gospel of Peter* likely had access to or had been taught by someone using
such a collection, or at least had heard readings from it. This explanation is
surely more plausible than Crossan's argument that the canonical Gospel
writers chose separate and distinct units to copy from the *Cross Gospel*.[43] (When
challenged about this, Crossan simply responds, "It just happened that way.")

Crossan also appeals to some of the distinctive aspects of the *Gospel of Peter*
as evidence that it reflects early traditions. But distinctive traditions are no
clear sign of early date, and in this case they may well be signs of creativity on
the part of the author. If there is one thing we know about the author of the
Cross Gospel within the *Gospel of Peter*, it is that he had a fertile imagination, as
is shown by his mention of a talking cross.

What is to be made of Crossan's argument that the earliest Christians did
not know what happened to Jesus after he was arrested and crucified? Crossan
dismisses all appeals to the traditions about women being witnesses at the
cross, at the burial, at the empty tomb, and probably being the first witnesses
of the risen Jesus. In part Crossan is able to argue this way because he
maintains that even the Fourth Gospel is dependent on Mark, something a
majority of Johannine scholars are either unsure of or deny.

One thing seems quite clear, though. The tradition in John 20 of Mary
Magdalene's being present at the empty tomb and seeing Christ is certainly
not created out of either Synoptic or Peter traditions. It could be a creation of
the Fourth Evangelist,[44] but why would the author want to make a woman the
first witness to both the empty tomb and the risen Christ? We would have
expected a special episode of the Beloved Disciple being the first to find the
tomb and seeing Christ. The witness list in 1 Corinthians 15 (in present form
dating from the 50s, but surely going back further), which focuses clearly on
the men, must be taken as strong evidence that the early church was not likely
to make up empty-tomb and resurrection stories involving women disciples.

No, there were disciples who knew and cared what happened to Jesus'
body, and initially they were horrified to find an empty tomb, as the Gospels
freely admit. The testimony of the women should not be dismissed on the

strength of very questionable theories about the *Cross Gospel's* early date, including the theory that it was silent about women at the tomb. In view of where the fragmentary document begins (at the beginning of the fragment of *Gospel of Peter*), we simply do not know this to be the case for the *Gospel of Peter* or the *Cross Gospel.*

None of the above criticisms is meant to deny the need for careful literary criticism of the Gospels. It is impossible to deny the differences between the canonical accounts of the passion and resurrection or that various of these differences are the result of the theological editing and creative shaping by the Evangelists of some of their source material. No one can deny that the accounts have been written up to try and make clear that these surprising events fulfilled Scripture. It was, however, these surprising events which caused the searching of the Scriptures, not the other way around.

Since Crossan insists that the historical questions should not be dodged—a point on which we strongly agree—I suggest that the data needs to be evaluated first and foremost with a historian's eye, not on the basis of dubious theories of literary linkage. For example, is it really historically likely that Pilate would crucify a known movement leader at Passover and hang a *titulus* on the cross reading "the King of the Jews" *without* due process of some sort of trial? Pilate was anti-Semitic, but he was not entirely stupid, especially when the issue impinged on his self-preservation. Again, is it historically likely that none of Jesus' family and none of his female disciples were at the cross or at the tomb? Or again, is it really true that there is only one witness to the empty tomb, the singular interdependent Gospel tradition? What about 1 Corinthians 15:1-5, which surely implies an empty tomb? More questions of this sort could be raised, but suffice it to say that Crossan has written a stimulating book which shows his skills in literary analysis, but reflects at point after point a failure to exercise good critical, historical thinking about the data.

In some ways this is not surprising, since Crossan thinks nothing much is at stake for Christian faith if one takes the route of historical minimalism. In his view the Gospel writers (notwithstanding Luke's preface in Luke 1:1-4) were not intending to write a history or biography of Jesus; they were interested in apologetics and polemics and doing theology, and in creating artful literary pieces that reflected their faith and piety, with little attention to the historical facts. Consider a revealing quote in Crossan's epilogue: "Reason and revelation, or history and faith, or historical reconstruction and credal articulation cannot contradict each other unless we are misreading one or both of them. I try to hold them always in tensile dialectic, for although in theory revelation is superior to reason, in practice reason is usually the final judge."[45] What this means in practice is that faith must be constantly redefined according to the latest historical reconstruction of the facts.

Robert Funk

Our next port of call is Robert Funk's latest offering, *Honest to Jesus*.[46] This book's title is indebted to Bishop John A. T. Robinson's controversial book of a generation ago—*Honest to God*. Like almost all of the books being discussed here, the author spends a good half of the work laying out a methodology and justifying certain assumptions and presuppositions. This is no doubt necessary since the author wishes to dismiss most of the narrative material in all of the Gospels as later Christian fiction imposed on or used to create a frame for the authentic Jesus tradition.

Like several other prominent members of the Jesus Seminar, Funk subscribes to the dictum "In the beginning was the parable or aphorism." For him this means that the earliest window on Jesus is to be found in the hypothetically reconstructed Q (and in particular its earliest strata) and in the earliest form of the *Gospel of Thomas*, both of which date to the 50s.

Now in fact we have no objective evidence or even hard literary data that justifies this assumption. The only things we can say with some assurance is that (1) the canonical Gospels do not appear to reflect a knowledge of the Thomas material and (2) the First and Third Gospels reflect a knowledge of Q. On Funk's own showing[47] this need mean no more than that there were sayings collections by the 70s, since he wants to date Matthew and Luke to the last twenty years of the first century. Of the absence of the Q or Thomas material in the earliest Gospel, Mark, he provides no real explanation. Nor does he explain why nowhere in the New Testament is the term *gospel* applied to a collection of Jesus' sayings.

Rather, both in Mark and in Paul, which are almost universally agreed to be our earliest sources on this matter, the term *gospel* describes a story, a narrative of the actions and words of Jesus, with the stronger stress on the deeds, especially in Paul (but see 1 Cor 7; Rom 14). Unfortunately, Paul's use of the Jesus tradition in places like Romans 14, or James's use of it,[48] is basically ignored in the attempt to reconstruct the authentic voice of Jesus. This is more than strange in a book which rightly and repeatedly insists that all our sources, both canonical and extracanonical, must be combed for traces of the authentic Jesus tradition.

One of the most serious deficiencies of this work is its failure to draw on one of the major contributions of the Third Quest, namely, detailed social and archaeological analysis of first- century Galilee—Jesus' primary social context. Especially notable is the absence of any interaction with the material that Horsley has painstakingly brought to light (see above). This material would have prevented mistaken assumptions such as the notion that the Galilee of Jesus' day was semipagan,[49] or that Jesus likely made his public proclamations in Greek,[50] or that Galilean villages (i.e., not the cities constructed by Herod Antipas during the same era) were probably significantly Hellenized, or that Galileans were to any real extent of mixed stock—semipagan (Assyrian?) and semi-Jewish and perhaps even familiar with pagan wisdom. The social and archaeological reports do not support this reconstruction of the context of Jesus' ministry. The Galileans had their own Israelite heritage going back to the Mosaic covenant. Jesus operated in places that had a thoroughly Jewish ethos, and that his words were remembered suggests he spoke in a manner understandable by Jews. Neither he nor his audience was likely to have known more than a smattering of Greek, pidgin Greek for business purposes or brief exchanges with foreigners.

Funk's positive portrait of what Jesus was like says next to nothing about his deeds and concentrates instead on his parables and aphorisms.[51] Here we learn that Jesus was a wordsmith, a comic savant, a man of celebrations and well acquainted with quips—in short, an Oscar Wilde without some of the moral drawbacks. He "did not develop major themes on the basis of the Hebrew Scriptures. He did not cite and interpret Scripture. For the most part he did not interpret fine points in the Law, and when he did, he tended to parody the legal process. He rarely spoke directly about the temple, the priests, and the sacred ceremonies. His parables and aphorisms did not recount the epic events of Israel's past. He did not borrow concepts from the world of ideas. There are no theological statements and no philosophical generalizations among his formulations."[52]

In Funk's view, Jesus offered a message for the theologically challenged. However, Funk wants to make clear that Jesus did not go around offering jejune maxims ("an apple a day . . . ") or even concrete advice in story form. Jesus' language was highly figurative, polyvalent and deliberately vague, or at least it had a studied ambiguity to it. It was also indirect and given to hyperbole and comic exaggeration. "Jesus steadily refuses to be explicit."[53] His teaching was meant to "tease people in to active thought," to borrow a phrase from C. H. Dodd. The question is, thought about what? The answer seems to be God's domain, but Funk does not think that Jesus had in mind an eschatological realm to be entered at some future time. "Jesus' parables and aphorisms are doors opening on an alternate construal of reality. . . . [I]n God's domain, people and things do not behave in expected ways."[54]

Since Funk believes Jesus lived his dream of kingdom come, he takes him to be a social deviant, one who was subversive of common sense, one who thought there was already another reality present and happening which ordinary people could not see, unless they really opened their eyes ("the furniture of the world had already been rearranged. God's estate was present everywhere; it was just difficult to detect"[55]). Jesus deliberately crossed social boundaries (eating with tax collectors, women of ill repute, sinners), violated purity taboos (the rules of clean and unclean) and redefined what was appropriate behavior on the sabbath. He was something of a party animal. The kingdom was a way of living and relating here and now that broke down barriers between people and between people and God. It led to surprising conclusions about the "in crowd" being "out" and the "out crowd" being "in," the first being last and the last being first in the kingdom. Jesus' message was a message of fruit basket turnover, of reversal of social fortunes.

Much of this analysis on target. It errs primarily in what it fails to say, and it especially errs in what it fails to say this message implies about Jesus himself. Jesus did not just proclaim the kingdom, he sought to bring it in, and he believed it had an already and a not-yet dimension, just as he had an already and not-yet role to play in that kingdom.

Funk holds that while Jesus began with John the Baptist, he soon left the Baptist's apocalyptic and eschatological message behind, replacing it with a way of living dangerously in the here and now. Never mind that there are various sayings which pass the stringent tests of the criterion of dissimilarity or of multiple attestation or of offensiveness to later church sensibilities about timing ("there are some standing here who will not taste death until they see that the kingdom of God has come with power"—Mk 9:1), all of which show that Jesus said something about the future of God's reign and activity. Never mind that, as Funk admits, Jesus was likely crucified for doing some sort of symbolic action in the temple, a prophetic sign act which suggested the temple would be destroyed. Jesus nevertheless was not an eschatological prophet, he was simply a pungent pundit ("irreligious, irreverent, and impious"[56]).

About the passion and resurrection narratives, Funk is in some ways more radical and in some ways more conservative than Crossan. He does not think Judas was a historical person,[57] but on the other hand he is not convinced that the more mythical account of Jesus' death and resurrection in the *Gospel of Peter* is earlier than Mark's account.[58] Mark invented the passion narrative, which is almost entirely a narrative fiction.[59] Oddly, he recognizes there were other messianic pretenders in Jesus' day ("in Jesus' day the wilderness was a hotbed of messianic activity"[60]) who performed symbolic prophetic actions like that of Jesus in the temple. But while he thinks this reveals something about Theudas and the Egyptian, he does not think it tells us anything about Jesus' messianic self-understanding.[61] At all costs a messianic Jesus must be avoided.

Funk ends by claiming that scholars are hopelessly divided on the origins of the passion narrative.[62] This is not quite true, as any reader of Raymond Brown's review of the literature in *The Death of the Messiah* will know.[63] Most scholars think the passion narrative was the earliest material to take concrete form from the Jesus traditions, and most think it has more historical substance than Funk or Crossan allows. Unfortunately this conflicts with the dictum which urges the aphorism as the alpha and omega of what we can know about Jesus.

Funk repeats the dictum that we have no early empty-tomb traditions prior to Mark, but he nowhere wrestles with the implications of 1 Corinthians 15:1-5. This is somewhat odd because elsewhere in his book Funk is careful not to ignore Paul and to say that Paul reflects early knowledge about Jesus' last meal and Jesus' radical social agenda, breaking down ethnic and purity barriers.[64] In these circumstances, why then do we not have to take seriously the idea that the early creedal statements Paul quotes in 1 Corinthians 15:1-5 stand close to what the original Gospel material and kerygma focused on? Building on the suggestions of James M. Robinson and Reginald H. Fuller, Funk argues that the early appearances were revelatory encounters with luminous apparitions.[65] This argument is strange since neither Matthew 28, nor Luke 24, nor John 20—21 says anything about Jesus' glowing in the dark or his appearing in risen form like shining angels or as he did on the Mount of Transfiguration. Moreover, the recurring motif of tangibility in each of these accounts must count against the vision theory. Funk does not wrestle with the historical improbability of early Christians fabricating appearance stories that relied first and foremost on the testimony of women at the tomb.

One of the more revealing aspects of *Honest to Jesus* can be found in the remarks that Funk makes about himself. He tells us repeatedly that the old dogmas of the past about Jesus are no longer credible and that he himself found it necessary to jettison his former neo-orthodox faith. He had to part company with Barth and Bultmann[66] and to exorcise his own troubling demons—especially the demons of what he had learned in his youth, in Bible college, in ministry, in seminary and even in secular universities.[67] Funk says this book is about setting Jesus free from his dogmatic and ecclesiastical cages,[68] but it sounds more like Funk's effort to free himself from those "cages."

I agree, however, with Funk's sometimes poignant cry for honesty about what we can and can't know about the historical Jesus, and I also agree with him that when it comes to Jesus, it is impossible to hermetically seal off theological matters from historical matters even when we are dealing with the resurrection of Jesus ("there has been a tendency to privilege faith statements: since they are not subject to scientific review, they can be made on the strength of private or community conviction. Privileging the resurrection is a way of blocking access to the popular heart of Christianity"[69]). Funk should be given credit for often asking the right questions and for a commitment to getting at the historical substance of the Jesus material, even if he, like Crossan, pursues it more as a literary archaeologist than as a historian. What is needed is someone who will come at the task with a more global approach, and perhaps that someone is our next author, N. T. Wright.

N. T. Wright

Wright's latest work, *Jesus and the Victory of God*, is part of his larger multivolume work entitled *Christian Origins and the Question of God*,[70] with a third and subsequent volumes forthcoming. This volume, however, deals with a great deal of the Jesus material, including the passion narratives, and so we should be able to get a clear fix on Wright's view of Jesus. If dealing with some of the previous works mentioned in this postscript could be said to be like breathing rarefied air, this book is like diving into a mikvah. Here we have a Jewish Jesus in bold relief. This is a Jesus who was constantly thinking of things in terms of Torah, temple and territory (contrast Funk), and who was constantly speaking and debating on Jewish terms. Here we have a Jesus who saw himself as a leadership prophet, and indeed even as the Jewish Messiah. This Jesus' ministry and understanding was shaped by deep reflection on key prophetic texts like Isaiah 40—55, Daniel 7, Zechariah 9—14 and the Psalms.

In substance, Wright's approach is a form of Schweitzer's argument (Jesus the Jewish prophetic advocate of imminent or consistent eschatology), nuanced and revised in the light of the work of G. B. Caird and C. H. Dodd, among others. This leads to some surprising results. For example, nowhere in the Synoptics (apparently), and certainly not in the authentic material, are there texts which speak about a "second coming." Instead, all such texts are about the return of Yahweh to Zion in the person of the Son of Man in his *exaltation* to God's right hand, rather than in his descent from God's right hand.[71] We are left to assume that some early Christian like Paul conjured up the notion of a parousia.

Wright also argues that Jesus' apocalyptic language must be interpreted to refer to events on the near horizon, including his death on the cross and the fall of Jerusalem within a generation of that death. Mark 13 goes back to Jesus, but it does not go forward to "the end of the world." Indeed, apocalyptic language, as early Jews used it, is said to *not* be about the end of the space-time continuum at all. This of course is a drastic revision of Schweitzer, without jettisoning Schweitzer's insistence on an eschatological Jesus.

Wright's approach in this volume, already announced in the first volume, is to analyze Jesus in terms of story, symbol and praxis, aims and beliefs. He approaches the task as a historian by offering a major thesis, and then seeking to verify or falsify it. He seeks to locate Jesus within the plausibility structure of early Judaism and speaks often of applying the criterion of what he calls "double similarity" and "double dissimilarity" when compared with both Judaism and early Christianity. In other words, Jesus was just similar enough to both Judaism and Christianity that he and his message would have been plausible in early Judaism and early Christianity, without being identical or nearly identical with the message and lifestyle of other Jewish prophets and messianic figures of that age and location, or identical with the message and ministries of early Christians. Jesus differed just enough from how early Christians thought of him that we can see how Christianity developed out of Jesus' ministry without being forced to the conclusion that the church invented the christological Jesus.

In terms of a reading of Jesus in light of the great corpus of Old Testament and early Jewish texts, there is hardly another study of this kind, and certainly not in the Third Quest. In this regard this work is without peer. Not only so, but Wright does not soundbyte the prophetic texts. He insists on reading them in context and shows at point after point how the echoes of these texts in the words and ministry of Jesus are only properly explained as part of the larger storied world in which early Jews lived. If one wishes to dispute Wright's interpretation, one had better come prepared to deal with a plethora of Old Testament texts and early Jewish evidence. Dismissals with a wave of the hand will not do, for as this book rolls on (741 pages in all), the arguments Wright presents gather force and mass such that by the end of the book either one is going to be convinced, convicted and converted to Wright's approach, if not to all his proposals, or one must prepare oneself to offer a very long argument in great detail to refute it. Debunking Wright's interpretation of this or that particular text will not slow down the momentum of the argument. He offers a plethora of converging lines of argument, dependent on no one text or even kinds of text to show that Jesus may and must be read in light of early Jewish hopes and dreams about the kingdom fed by the Hebrew Scriptures.

Jesus is seen as a monotheistic Jew who focused on eschatology and election, on God's people, on God's actions in the present and how God was bringing to a climax in Jesus' own ministry what he had in mind for his people—both redemption and judgment:

> His beliefs were those of a first-century Jew *who believed that the kingdom was coming in and through his own work.* His loyalty to Israel's cherished beliefs therefore took the form of critique and renovation from within; of challenge to traditions and institutions whose true purpose he believed . . . had been grievously corrupted and distorted; and of new proposals which, though without precedent, were never mere innovation. They always claimed the high ground: fulfillment, completion, consummation.[72]

Jesus is also seen as the anti-Zealot, the one who thinks that violence only breeds more violence and that trying to fight Roman fire with fire only produces more Jewish burn victims. This is not to say that we have a nonpolitical image of Jesus. To the contrary, Jesus is seen as one who offers subversive wisdom, counterorder parables and aphorisms, one who performs politically charged prophetic sign acts like riding into Jerusalem on a donkey at Passover, or symbolically indicates that the temple will soon be destroyed. The politics of this Jesus is the politics of killing them with kindness, of loving one's enemies, of breaking down the middle wall of partition between Jew and Gentile rather than reinforcing it. Israel's destiny was to be a light to the world, not a light to itself. Israel was not merely to be a holy presence but one that sanctifies what surrounds it. Now that the kingdom was breaking in, those boundary-marker aspects of the Mosaic Law were transcended in the eschatological moment, not because they represented something shoddy or wrong, but simply because they had had their day and ceased to be. The candle had been eclipsed by the greater light of the sun. Wright stresses that this in no way is to be seen as anti-Semitic, rather it is seen as Jesus' proclaiming and believing that he was enacting the fulfillment of Jewish hopes and dreams.

Jesus is seen, like many other early Jews such as John the Baptist and the sectarians of Qumran, as extremely critical of the present temple regime, seeing Jewish leadership as hopelessly corrupt and about to face judgment. On this score he agreed with the Zealots. But he endorsed neither appeasement nor zealotry, choosing rather the transformation that was being brought about through his ministry and that would be brought to climax in his death. The spiral of violence was to be stopped in its tracks by suffering and so absorbing and deflecting its effects from God's people.

Jesus was redefining Israel around himself in preparation for the coming climax. In this he was more than a prophet, more like a messianic king who had come to claim or reclaim his own. More than this, in the end Wright concurs with the notion that Jesus saw himself as called upon to fulfill tasks that in the Old Testament only Yahweh is said to fulfill:

> Forget the "titles" of Jesus. . . . Focus, instead, on a young Jewish prophet telling a story about YHWH returning to Zion as judge and redeemer, and then embodying it by riding into the city in tears, symbolizing the Temple's destruction and celebrating the final exodus. I propose, as a matter of history, that Jesus of Nazareth was conscious of a vocation: a vocation, given him by one he knew as "father," to enact in himself what, in Israel's scriptures, God had promised to accomplish all by himself. He would be the pillar of cloud and of fire for the people of the new exodus. He would embody in himself the returning and redeeming action of the covenant God.[73]

If the strength of this approach is its deep and rich knowledge and use of early Jewish sources, and its breadth is its focusing on words, deeds, symbols, praxis and beliefs, its weakness or Achilles' heel is in the area of critical methodology. Relying on the suggestions of K. E. Bailey and others, he repeatedly dodges the critical bullet by asserting that Jesus must have said substantially the same things in a variety of ways during his ministry such that variants in the Synoptic traditions can largely be explained in this way.[74] This suggestion, while very plausible at the level of history, fails to deal with the selectivity of the accounts of the Gospel writers. There are as often differences in the accounts of a singular event (e.g., Jesus' entrance into Jerusalem on a donkey) as there are in parables where multiple tellings could explain some things. The failure to deal with issues of form and redaction criticism, especially the latter where it can be shown that differences are often part of a pattern of editorial changes of source material made by an Evangelist, will mean unfortunately that Wright risks being written off by some who most need to hear his arguments.

This is especially so since Wright is not interested in simply preaching to those already converted to his point of view. This is not to say that Wright takes a precritical approach to the issues or that he does not make some excellent points about weaknesses in critical theories (see, e.g., the remarks on Q people[75] or frequent critiques of the Jesus Seminar), it is just that in the Third Quest, failure to deal directly with the Synoptic Problem and the issues raised by form and redaction critics will cause some, who have ears, to fail to hear a great deal of what Wright so compellingly argues.

Notably, Wright, unlike Meier, does not spend as much time on the miracles of Jesus as he could and should have done,[76] which would have provided more grist for his mill. A bit less on Jesus the wordsmith and sign giver and a bit more on Jesus' mighty works and relationships would have provided more balance. I also do not think that Wright has made his case that Jesus had no end-of-the-world eschatology, but he is quite right that more texts can be explained by the imminent eschatological approach than is usually thought.[77] To be sure, the major emphasis in the ministry of Jesus was on the kingdom being "at hand," but one can only press the "future is now" button so many times. The theory of purely imminent eschatology does not explain a text like Mark 13:32-37 or the similarities between Mark 14:62 and 1 Thessalonians 4:16-17. It also does not explain texts which discuss a future messianic banquet, or the judging of the twelve tribes by the Twelve in the kingdom.

None of these remarks should take away from the fact that I think this is the most revealing and telling study of Jesus yet written during the Third Quest. Wright has made it quite clear that anyone who still wants to argue for a rather non-Jewish, noneschatological, nonprophetic and nonmessianic Jesus will have to be prepared to argue long into the night. Even where Wright may be wrong, it will take much to show this is so, and I would suggest that he has managed to shift the burden of proof on those who want to argue for a nonmessianic Jesus. We may look forward to the third volume in this series[78] in which, I take it from personal conversation, we will hear about matters ranging from resurrection to Paul and justification. It is a consummation devoutly to be wished, as it is an oddity that of these seven Jesus books, those which you would expect to say more about the resurrection say less, and those which you would expect to say less in fact say more (see, e.g., Borg's work). In any event, these seven books prove that the Third Quest is still alive and well, and remains fertile, not futile.

Notes

Preface

[1]For a detailed review of how the New Testament, including the Gospels, has been interpreted by scholars in the modern era, see Stephen Neill and Tom Wright, *The Interpretation of the New Testament, 1861-1986*, rev. ed. (Oxford: Oxford University Press, 1988). Wright's reference in this work to "the Third Quest" (cf. p. 379 and n. 3) may be the first use of this title for the present movement.

[2]Some of the similarities between what happened during this period of New Testament scholarship and what has been happening in the last dozen or so years, with increasingly bizarre portraits of Jesus emerging, should be noted. We have been down this road before, and the first time the journey ended in a cul-de-sac.

[3]Notice J. Andrew Overman, "Deciphering the Origins of Christianity," a review of *A Myth of Innocence: Mark and Christian Origins*, by Burton Mack, *Interpretation* 44 (April 1990): 193-95, here p. 195: "It will be for scholars to decide if in this renewed quest Mack has looked down the well of history and seen his own reflection. There is something disturbingly familiar about a mildly reforming, sagacious teacher, who is gifted in repartee, only utters things of this world, and does not use language and imagery that promises the reversal of the rulers of the world." Much the same could be said about John Dominic Crossan's bestseller, *The Historical Jesus: The Life of a Mediterranean Jewish Peasant* (San Francisco: Harper-SanFrancisco, 1991), which shares certain similarities in viewpoint with Mack's work.

[4]Most moderns of course do not know Schweitzer in his early period as a New Testament scholar and the factors that led to his abandoning the scholarly world for mission work in Africa.

[5]Bultmann's oft-quoted conclusion, "I do indeed think that we can now know almost nothing concerning the life and personality of Jesus, since the early Christian sources show no interest in either, are moreover fragmentary and often legendary; and other sources about Jesus do not exist," did not prevent him from claiming Christian faith to the end of his life, precisely because of his bifurcating approach to faith and historical inquiry. The quote is conveniently found in his *Jesus and the Word* (New York: Scribner's, 1934), p. 14. One of the major differences between Bultmann and some of the radical third questers like Crossan and Mack is that the latter do indeed believe we have sources other than the canonical Gospels that reveal what the historical Jesus was really like—in particular the *Gospel of Thomas*. Bultmann did not share this confidence in the historical worth of such sources. It should also be noted that some of the more sensational claims made about Jesus on the basis of purported new evidence from Qumran fragments also depend on the assumption that we both need and have found crucial evidence about Jesus outside the canonical

Gospels. Nothing I have seen or heard of the new Qumran data leads me to think we must radically reevaluate Jesus or assume he was a member of the Dead Sea Community.

My own view is that if one is going to do serious historical research, one must be open to all possible sources of data, but all such data must be evaluated critically. When the critical searchlight is applied to the *Gospel of Thomas*, most scholars have concluded that it is written later than the canonical Gospels, is probably largely dependent on those Gospels and, many would say, gives its subject matter a Gnostic interpretation the original data did not warrant. This does not mean it may not occasionally preserve an early authentic saying not found in the canonical Gospels.

⁶Found in translation in Ernst Käsemann, *Essays on New Testament Themes* (London: SCM, 1964).

⁷Günther Bornkamm, *Jesus of Nazareth* (New York: Harper, 1960), p. 24.

⁸I remember well from my college days at the beginning of the 1970s the enthusiasm for reading Kierkegaard, the great Christian existentialist theologian, an enthusiasm which seemed to have diminished notably by the time I graduated in 1974.

⁹For a helpful brief review of all the quests see Colin Brown, "Historical Jesus, Quest of," in *Dictionary of Jesus and the Gospels*, ed. Joel B. Green, Scot McKnight and I. Howard Marshall (Downers Grove, Ill.: InterVarsity Press, 1992), pp. 326-41. For a good introductory review of the Third Quest see Charlesworth's article "Jesus Research Expands with Chaotic Creativity," in *Images of Jesus Today*, ed. James H. Charlesworth and Walter P. Weaver (Valley Forge, Penn.: Trinity, 1994), pp. 1-41, and see also John P. Meier, "Reflections on Jesus-of-History Research Today," in *Jesus' Jewishness: Exploring the Place of Jesus in Early Judaism*, ed. James H. Charlesworth (New York: Crossroad, 1991), pp. 84-107, and Marcus Borg, *Jesus in Contemporary Scholarship* (Valley Forge, Penn.: Trinity, 1994).

There were also several important preliminary works which helped reignite the quest for the historical Jesus, including Ben F. Meyer, *The Aims of Jesus* (London: SCM, 1979), and Anthony E. Harvey, *Jesus and the Constraints of History* (Philadelphia: Westminster, 1982).

Chapter 1: Galilee and the Galilean
¹L. P. Hartley, *The Go-Between* (New York: Stein and Day, 1953).

²John K. Riches, *The World of Jesus: First-Century Judaism in Crisis* (Cambridge: Cambridge University Press, 1990), p. 4. Of the many works that introduce the social milieu of Jesus, this is one of the better and easier to read ones.

³Sean Freyne, "The Geography, Politics and Economics of Galilee," in *Studying the Historical Jesus: Evaluations of the State of Current Research*, ed. Bruce Chilton and Craig A. Evans (Leiden: Brill, 1994), pp. 75-121, here p. 76.

⁴For the serious student who wishes to do historical Jesus research, there are two vital annotated bibliographic tools that one may use as a guide, both by Craig A. Evans: (1) *Jesus* (Grand Rapids, Mich.: Baker, 1992) and (2) the more detailed *Life of Jesus Research: An Annotated Bibliography* (Leiden: Brill, 1989).

⁵On this important point I agree with John Dominic Crossan, *The Historical Jesus* (San Francisco: HarperSanFrancisco, 1991), p. 102, in saying that when Tacitus stresses *sub Tiberio quies*, all he means is that the Roman legions stationed in Syria did not need to be called upon between A.D. 14 and 37 in order to intervene in the problems in Palestine. Rather the local auxiliaries under prefects such as Pilate and the client ruler Herod Antipas were adequate to handle whatever problems arose. Such problems are seen as minor by Tacitus because they are of no immediate significance for the Roman history he is writing, the history of the activities of Roman emperors and legions.

⁶The frequent remark that the revolts against Rome invariably took place in Judea and centered on Jerusalem is not entirely correct. As Martin Goodman, *The Ruling Class of Judea* (Cambridge: Cambridge University Press, 1987), p. 10, points out, even as early as 55 B.C. a certain Pitholaus led a revolt in Galilee against Roman authority. While it is right to caution against overestimating the revolutionary potential of Galilee during the early first century, it would also be wrong to underestimate the hostility toward Rome that resided just beneath the surface in both Galilee and Judea. I would suggest that the reason why there were not more overt attacks on Romans in Galilee during the period 37 B.C. to A.D. 66 is that there were not that many Romans around. There were no Roman legions in Galilee during this time, and, furthermore, Galilee did not experience direct Roman rule as did Judea. Cf. Uriel Rappoport, "How Anti-Roman Was the Galilee?" in *The Galilee in Late Antiquity*, ed. Lee I. Levine (New York: Jewish Theological Seminary, 1992), pp. 95-102.

⁷See Ben Witherington III, *The Christology of Jesus* (Philadelphia: Fortress, 1990), pp. 90-96.

⁸See Richard A. Horsley and John S. Hanson, *Bandits, Prophets and Messiahs: Popular Movements at the Time of Jesus* (Minneapolis: Winston, 1985).

⁹It is true that the Romans during the early empire did not tend to mix their politico-cultural colonialism with any explicit religious imperialism (see Crossan, *Historical Jesus*, pp. 209-10), but Jews did not separate these things. The temple itself was both a political and a religious institution, serving among other things as the treasury, or bank, for the nation.

¹⁰On all of this cf. James D. Newsome, *Greeks, Romans, Jews: Currents of Culture and Belief in the New Testament World* (Philadelphia: Trinity, 1992) pp. 294-97.

¹¹Fergus G. B. Millar, *The Roman Near East 31 B.C.-A.D. 337* (Cambridge: Harvard University Press, 1993), pp. 44ff.

¹²E. P. Sanders, *The Historical Figure of Jesus* (London: Penguin, 1993), p. 18.

¹³Herod died about 4 B.C., which means of course Jesus was born before this time (cf. Mt 1—2). The mistake in the reckoning of the calendar can be attributed to a sixth-century monk, Dionysius Exiguus, whose mathematical calculations were a bit off when he originated the system of B.C. and A.D.

¹⁴Newsome, *Greeks, Romans, Jews*, p. 285.

¹⁵Goodman, *Ruling Class*, p. 1.

¹⁶Ibid., p. 3, points for example to Caesarea Maritima, the Greco-Roman port city that Herod the Great built, as one of his showpieces, demonstrating that he was a ruler in the grand Roman style.

¹⁷Sanders, *Historical Figure*, pp. 28-30, is right to emphasize that Romans were not setting about to Romanize Galilee in terms of education, religious practices or civil institutions, but we must not overlook the Hellenizing and market agenda of Antipas that was seen as antagonistic to traditional values.

¹⁸Goodman, *Ruling Class*, p. 40, emphasis mine.

¹⁹Herod Agrippa could perhaps be seen as an exception to this rule, but he only really enters the picture in important ways after the lifetime of Jesus.

²⁰E. P. Sanders, *Judaism: Practice and Belief 63 B.C.E.-66 C.E.* (Philadelphia: Trinity, 1992), pp. 159-68, rightly warns that we must not exaggerate the tax burden, although it was certainly bad enough, because the Roman system took into account Jewish taxes, so that it is not quite correct to speak of Jews paying double taxes. In his November 1994 Society of Biblical Literature (SBL) lecture on Herod's temple economics, Sanders reiterated these points and stressed that religious taxes were not like taxes of a monarchy which supported a government and its military forces. The religious taxes supported religious institutions, in particular the temple, which was an institution that created thousands of jobs. It is also

worth noting that Herod the Great remitted taxes at least four times.

[21]Goodman, *Ruling Class*, p. 10.

[22]Many scholars have now concluded that Jesus is referring to toll collectors and not those who were involved in tax collecting in the whole province, but I am not yet fully convinced. Cf. Freyne, "Geography, Politics and Economics of Galilee," pp. 100-103.

[23]*Life* 375, 384, 392. Sean Freyne, "The Galileans in Light of Josephus' *Vita*," *New Testament Studies* 26 (1979-80): 397-413.

[24]Freyne, "Geography, Politics and Economics of Galilee," pp. 75-121. In his November 1994 Society of Biblical Literature lecture on urbanization in Galilee, Freyne stressed that Hellenization and Romanization are two different though related forms of urbanization. It is not clear how profoundly the changes in Galilee had affected Galilean peasants, village people and others not living in Sepphoris or Tiberias.

[25]Sanders, *Historical Figure*, p. 21.

[26]See Freyne, "Geography, Politics and Economics of Galilee," p. 121. Freyne continues to stress that Jesus' revision of the traditional categories of Torah, temple and territory undermined the centrality of the temple and the unqualified loyalty to it that even rural Galileans tended to show.

[27]The clear evidence that Jesus drew his disciples from farming peasants or small landowners is notably lacking, but he certainly addresses their situation in various parables. Cf. Freyne, "Geography, Politics and Economics of Galilee," p. 111. It is equally interesting that Jesus does not seem to have had much contact or confrontation with local Herodian officials and retainers, except for the tax collectors. Perhaps he was setting out to gather his new community and did not wish to divert his focus by confronting the brokers of other economic systems and communities.

[28]Goodman, *Ruling Class*, p. 44.

[29]Ibid.

[30]Ibid., p. 46.

[31]Witherington, *Christology of Jesus*, p. 56.

[32]See Ellis Rivkin, "Pharisees," in *Interpreter's Dictionary of the Bible, Supplementary Volume*, ed. Keith R. Crim et al. (Nashville: Abingdon, 1976), pp. 657-63.

[33]Witherington, *Christology of Jesus*, p. 59.

[34]Cf. Luke 7:36-50, where Simon the Pharisee does not offer the customary Jewish acts of hospitality exemplified by the washing of feet but does dine in Greco-Roman fashion by reclining at table.

[35]Of course the Pharisees' views had some political ramifications, but my point is that it is a mistake to see the Pharisees as mainly or simply having a political agenda. The "politics of holiness" are indirect in that they reform society, not governmental structures. The one exception seems to be that the priests in the temple felt they must sacrifice in the manner the Pharisees required in order to keep the peace.

[36]Cf. Sanders, *Historical Figure*, p. 40, and my fuller critique of his views in Witherington, *Christology of Jesus*, pp. 56-81.

[37]See discussion in Witherington, *Christology of Jesus*, pp. 124-26. It is my view that the Twelve were not chosen by Jesus as a new version of Israel, that is, to be Israel, but rather to free Israel, to be Jesus' ministers to the least, the last and the lost.

[38]Sanders, *Historical Figure*, p. 38, is right to point out that what distinguished Judaism from other religions is that it elevated moral values and laws to the same level of importance as ritual customs and rules. Jesus then would be going one step further in the direction away from the Greco-Roman approach to religion which focused on perfection of the

performance, or execution, of rituals.

[39]Witherington, *Christology of Jesus*, p. 59.

[40]Eric M. Meyers, "Galilean Regionalism as a Factor in Historical Reconstruction," *Bulletin of the American Schools of Oriental Research* 221 (1976): 95. The one qualification I would add to this statement is that recent archaeological digs have suggested that upper Galilee was open to influences from the north, from places like Tyre and Sidon.

[41]See pp. 58-92.

[42]See the careful discussion in John P. Meier, *A Marginal Jew: Rethinking the Historical Jesus* (New York: Doubleday, 1991), pp. 255-68, and Stanley E. Porter, "Jesus and the Use of Greek in Galilee," in *Studying the Historical Jesus*, ed. Bruce Chilton and Craig A. Evans (Leiden: Brill, 1994), pp. 123-54. I tend to agree with Porter that there were likely some occasions when Jesus used Greek, for instance in his exchanges with Pilate, or with Gentiles such as a Roman centurion.

[43]Goodman, *Ruling Class*, p. 51.

[44]Ibid., p. 61.

[45]See discussion in Ben Witherington III, *Women in the Ministry of Jesus* (Cambridge: Cambridge University Press, 1984), pp. 11ff.

[46]Freyne, "Geography, Politics and Economics of Galilee," p. 96.

[47]Goodman, *Ruling Class*, p. 65.

[48]Crossan has argued in various of his works that Jesus in this Beatitude is referring to the destitute rather than just the marginalized poor, but this conclusion is far from certain and cannot be decided just on the basis of a word study *in Greek*, since Jesus mainly spoke Aramaic.

[49]See Douglas R. Edwards, "The Socio-economic and Cultural Ethos in the First Century: Implications for the Nascent Jesus Movement," in *The Galilee in Late Antiquity*, ed. Lee I. Levine (New York: Jewish Theological Seminary, 1992), pp. 53-73. What this means is that the cities were not simply parasites but had something to offer in exchange to the smaller villages in Galilee.

[50]Ibid., p. 61.

[51]See Riches, *The World of Jesus*, pp. 16-17: "Contemporary Western society is divided into classes that are largely though not entirely defined by reference to their position within an industrial economy: workers/management; shareholders/wage earners; employed/self-employed/unemployed. Although some of these distinctions would have applied in first-century societies, other distinctions were more important." For example, the distinction between slave and free person has no equivalent counterpart in our society today. Crossan's continued use of class terminology is not helpful at this point.

[52]Goodman, *Ruling Class*, p. 67.

[53]Sean Freyne, "Urban-Rural Relations in First Century Galilee," in *The Galilee in Late Antiquity*, ed. Lee I. Levine (New York: Jewish Theological Seminary, 1992), p. 85.

[54]See Freyne, "Geography, Politics and Economics of Galilee," pp. 82-83.

[55]Edwards, "Socio-economic and Cultural Ethos," p. 71.

[56]See the discussion by Marcus Borg, "The Palestinian Background for a Life of Jesus," in *The Search for Jesus: Modern Scholarship Looks at the Gospels*, ed. Hershel Shanks (Washington, D.C.: Biblical Archaeology Review, 1994), pp. 37-54.

[57]Riches, *The World of Jesus*, p. 25.

[58]See Howard Clark Kee, "The Transformation of the Synagogue After 70 C.E.: Its Import for Early Christianity," *New Testament Studies* 36 (1990): 1-24; Richard E. Oster, "Supposed Anachronism in Luke-Acts' Use of *Sunagoge*: A Rejoinder to H. C. Kee," *New Testament Studies*

39 (1993): 178-208; and Howard Clark Kee, "The Changing Meaning of Synagogue: A Response to Richard Oster," *New Testament Studies* 40 (1992): 281-83.

[59]See Ben Witherington III, *Conflict and Community in Corinth: A Socio-rhetorical Commentary on 1 and 2 Corinthians* (Grand Rapids, Mich.: Eerdmans, 1995), pp. 24ff.

[60]On all this see Oster, "Anachronism," p. 195.

[61]Lee I. Levine, "The Second Temple Synagogue: The Formative Years," in *The Synagogue in Late Antiquity*, ed. Lee I. Levine (Philadelphia: American Schools of Oriental Research, 1987), pp. 7-31. The arguments of Howard Clark Kee are not compelling, neither the one that the famous Theodotus synagogue inscription in Jerusalem dates to much later than the first century nor the one that Luke's use of the term *synagōgē* for a place where Jews met weekly for religious services is anachronistic. The Theodotus synagogue inscription refers to a leader and builder of a synagogue and was found at the bottom of a cistern in Jerusalem. It is generally dated to the first century because of the type of script in which it is written. But cf. Kee, "Early Christianity in the Galilee," in *The Galilee in Late Antiquity*, ed. Lee I. Levine (New York: Jewish Theological Seminary, 1992), pp. 3-22, here pp. 4-6.

[62]More debatable, however, is when the term *synagōgē* became almost a technical term for a religious meeting place, and here it is right to point out that in Philo and elsewhere in the first century the term can be used to refer to something other than a Jewish place of worship. It can, for instance, refer to the people who have assembled for that purpose. Cf. the evidence in Kee, "The Changing Meaning," pp. 281-82. On Galilean synagogues, including the earliest ones which go back to the first century A.D., cf. G. Foerster, "The Ancient Synagogues of Galilee," in *The Galilee in Late Antiquity*, ed. Lee I. Levine (New York: Jewish Theological Seminary, 1992), pp. 289-319.

[63]See Witherington, *Women in the Ministry of Jesus*, pp. 2ff.

[64]Goodman, *Ruling Class*, p. 61.

[65]Bruce Malina, *The New Testament World: Insights from Cultural Anthropology*, rev. ed. (Louisville, Ky.: Westminster/John Knox 1993), p. 54.

[66]See Witherington, *Christology of Jesus*, pp. 61-66, and *Women in the Ministry of Jesus*, pp. 12ff.

[67]We can see immediately how this would get someone like Jesus into trouble if his father was unknown, or if he was referred to by the probably pejorative label "son of Mary" (Mk 6:3).

[68]Consider for example the story of Mary and Jesus' siblings going out to bring him home because they had heard and believed what others were saying about him—that he was a bit touched in the head (Mk 3:21). In that society people cared deeply about what the neighbors or relatives would think or say.

[69]Malina, *New Testament World*, p. 63.

[70]Notice how Jesus asks his disciples who others say that he is (Mk 8:27). Could his reticence to state directly his identity in public be a reflection of his knowledge of how such individualism would be viewed negatively in his world?

[71]Malina, *New Testament World*, p. 64.

[72]Ibid., p. 95. A friend has pointed out to me how this notion of limited good still exists today in various parts of the world. For instance, a National Public Radio broadcast recently chronicled how there are many people in Russia today who do not believe wealth can be "created." Thus, if you see someone with a Mercedes Benz and you want one, you do not conclude that you must work harder but rather that you must either steal one or do without!

[73]Ibid., p. 101. It is easy to see in a world where the operative principle is "there is no free lunch" or "you scratch my back and I'll scratch yours" how difficult the concept of grace,

or unmerited and nonreciprocal favor, would be.

[74]Ibid., p. 97.

[75]See ibid., pp. 158-66.

[76]Cf. Meier, *A Marginal Jew*, pp. 277-78.

[77]Ibid., p. 277. Cf. Sean Freyne, *Galilee from Alexander the Great to Hadrian* (Wilmington, Del.: Glazier, 1980), pp. 259-343, and his *Galilee, Jesus and the Gospels* (Philadelphia: Fortress, 1988), pp. 176-218; Rainer Riesner, *Jesus als Lehrer* (Tübingen: Mohr, 1981), pp. 208-9.

[78]See Freyne, *Galilee, Jesus and the Gospels*, pp. 201ff. The caricature of Galileans as nonobservant Jews is based on later rabbinic sources, and what seems to be meant is that they were not observant in a way that would have been fully satisfactory to Pharisees, especially those who shaped post-A.D. 70 Judaism.

[79]Alan F. Segal, "Conversion and Messianism," in *The Messiah*, ed. James H. Charlesworth (Minneapolis: Fortress, 1992), p. 298.

[80]Cf. ibid., pp. 303-5.

[81]Some of the more conservative ḥªbērîm among the Pharisees may have made such a demand.

[82]On the Son of Man see Witherington, *Christology of Jesus*, pp. 233-62, and on Jesus as God's Wisdom in the flesh see Ben Witherington III, *Jesus the Sage: The Pilgrimage of Wisdom* (Minneapolis: Fortress, 1994).

[83]I will say a great deal more about this later in this study. See pp. 185-96.

[84]Segal, "Conversion and Messianism," p. 319.

[85]I have adopted and modified the list given by Riches, *The World of Jesus*, p. 51.

[86]See the discussion in ibid., pp. 55-57.

Chapter 2: Jesus the Talking Head

[1]I owe to Richard Hays the epithet "Jesus the talking head," from his evaluation of the sort of Jesus the Jesus Seminar has depicted.

[2]One of its earlier publications, edited by Robert W. Funk, Bernard Brandon Scott and J. R. Butts, entitled *The Parables of Jesus: Red Letter Edition* (Sonoma, Calif.: Polebridge, 1988), here pp. 93-94.

[3]I count only two names from countries other than the United States or Canada, though the editors speak of European members (plural) who have participated by mail. Only one, Benno Schroeder of West Germany, is listed in the 1988 listing. Later listings are not much more impressive for their global inclusiveness.

[4]Richard B. Hays, "The Corrected Jesus," *First Things* 43 (May 94): 44.

[5]In other words a token number that could not possibly affect the overall outcome of the voting unless it was exceedingly close on a particular saying.

[6]Published as an appendix to *The Five Gospels: The Search for the Authentic Words of Jesus*, ed. Robert W. Funk and Roy W. Hoover (New York: Macmillan, 1993). During the course of things, some scholars withdrew from the Jesus Seminar. The listing in the parables volume included 96 names, in *The Five Gospels* only 74. I have personally been told that some withdrew due to the theological agendas of the founders of the group.

[7]Hays, "The Corrected Jesus," p. 47.

[8]Hays also notes that if one examines where the participating scholars got their doctorates, the two institutions most heavily represented are Claremont and Harvard, both well known to be leading liberal institutions.

[9]Robert W. Funk, Bernard Brandon Scott and J. R. Butts, eds., *The Parables of Jesus* (Sonoma, Calif.: Polebridge, 1988), p. 94.

[10]Ibid.

[11]It would seem to be implied though not stated by this remark that scholars who teach Sunday school or write for Sunday-school audiences have lost their credibility as critical scholars, at least if they do so in a way that is consonant with traditional portraits of Jesus.

[12]Hays, "The Corrected Jesus," p. 47.

[13]While spending time in Europe doing research and at SNTS meetings, overall I got the impression that many Continental scholars found the Jesus Seminar and its whole approach flawed and rather humorous. One remark was, "This is the kind of thing that could only happen in the U.S. where democratic procedures are assumed to make clear and settle even issues of truth. It is assumed that what 'the majority' believes must be so."

[14]In the *Parables of Jesus*, pp. 54-55.

[15]I say "apparently" because it is always possible that more evidence yet to be discovered about early Judaism or early Christianity could prove that one or another saying or idea was not in fact without parallel.

[16]On the use of historical-critical criteria see Ben Witherington III, *The Christology of Jesus* (Philadelphia: Fortress, 1990), pp. 22-31.

[17]Ben F. Meyer, *The Aims of Jesus* (London: SCM, 1979), p. 84.

[18]So Hays, "The Corrected Jesus," p. 45.

[19]Ibid., p. 49.

[20]While I would not agree with Sanders in going to the other extreme and focusing almost solely on the *events* in Jesus' life as a way of recovering the historical Jesus, I quite agree with him that these things must also be taken into account in any serious quest for the historical Jesus. Cf. E. P. Sanders, *Jesus and Judaism* (Philadelphia: Fortress, 1985).

[21]The promise to go on at this juncture and deal with the deeds of Jesus is not in itself helpful, since the point is that the two things must be compared and related to each other.

[22]James D. G. Dunn, "Messianic Ideas and Their Influence on the Jesus of History," in *The Messiah*, ed. James H. Charlesworth (Minneapolis: Fortress, 1992), pp. 371-72.

[23]It is striking to me that almost without exception Jewish scholars such as David Flusser, Samuel Sandmel or Geza Vermes who have spent considerable time dealing with the Jesus tradition basically agree with this conclusion. It is necessary not only to understand Jesus in his Jewish context but also to understand the handing on of his teachings in this context for at least the period leading up to A.D. 70.

[24]See the discussion in Ben Witherington III, *Jesus the Sage: The Pilgrimage of Wisdom* (Minneapolis: Fortress, 1994), pp. 212-13.

[25]By Stephen J. Patterson, published in 1993, with a promise of his red-letter edition of *Thomas* to come forth from Polebridge soon.

[26]See John S. Kloppenborg et al., *Q—Thomas Reader: The Gospels Before the Gospels* (Sonoma, Calif.: Polebridge, 1990), p. 80.

[27]Richard J. Bauckham, "Gospels (Apocryphal)," in *Dictionary of Jesus and the Gospels*, ed. Joel B. Green, Scot McKnight and I. Howard Marshall (Downers Grove, Ill.: InterVarsity Press, 1992), pp. 286-91. The emphasis is mine.

[28]See pp. 197-211.

[29]See pp. 175-76 on Q, the non-Markan material, which Matthew and Luke share in common. Q, like *Thomas*, consists mostly of sayings of Jesus. Some scholars, in order to account for Q as a source, have posited a community in which this document arose and where it served as an authoritative anthology of the sayings of Jesus.

[30]We must also remember that while the existence of sayings collections even earlier than the *Gospel of Thomas* seems likely, for otherwise it is very difficult to explain the similarities

in order and form of various material in Matthew and Luke, no one has yet found a copy of Q.

[31]I would not rule out that *Thomas* may have originally been composed in the late first century, but if in fact it proves to be dependent on the Synoptics at various points, it would have to be very late indeed.

[32]Q is a resource embedded within the Synoptics. Crossan's argument (cf. *Historical Jesus*, pp. xxx-xxxii and 425-26) that our earliest manuscripts of the canonical Gospels are relatively late and thus not necessarily more reliable than noncanonical material overlooks a very important point. There are clear traces of Jesus' sayings material both in Paul's letters (cf. 1 Cor 7 and 11 and Rom 13—15) and in the homily attributed to James (i.e., parallels with the Sermon on the Mount; cf. Witherington, *Jesus the Sage*, pp. 211-47), but there are *not* clear traces in the canonical books of the *Thomas* forms of Synoptic sayings nor any traces of the sayings found only in *Thomas*.

[33]The saying in Mark 13:21-23 escapes the ax apparently because it is also found in *Thomas* 113.2-4. Nothing of Mark 10:1-16 falls into either the red or pink category except some version of Mark 10:14, which gets a pink rating. In the later portion of the chapter only Mark 10:23, 25 in its Markan form is in pink.

[34]See Robert W. Funk with Mahlon H. Smith, *The Gospel of Mark: Red Letter Edition* (Sonoma, Calif.: Polebridge, 1991), pp. 11ff.

[35]See the discussion by Funk in *The Five Gospels*, in the introductory material.

[36]Hays, "The Corrected Jesus," pp. 44-45.

[37]See Joseph A. Fitzmyer, *The Gospel of Luke I—IX*, vol. 28, Anchor Bible (New York: Doubleday, 1981), pp. 231ff.

[38]These conclusions are found in various of the red-letter editions, but I am following *The Gospel of Mark*, pp. 30-34.

[39]Pronouncement stories are those narratives which end with a dramatic pronouncement that sums up the significance of the story. (Cf., e.g., Mk 2:23-27 or 28.)

[40]See Sanders, *Jesus and Judaism*, passim.

[41]See Witherington, *Jesus the Sage*.

[42]See Ben Witherington III, *Jesus, Paul and the End of the World* (Downers Grove, Ill.: InterVarsity Press, 1992), and *Christology of Jesus*.

[43]On Sanders see pp. 118-32 below.

[44]See the preface.

Chapter 3: Jesus the Itinerant Cynic Philosopher

[1]The full title for Crossan's book is *The Historical Jesus: The Life of a Mediterranean Jewish Peasant* (San Francisco: HarperSanFrancisco, 1991).

[2]John Dominic Crossan, *Jesus: A Revolutionary Biography* (San Francisco: HarperSanFrancisco, 1994).

[3]I owe this reference to Hans Dieter Betz from an essay he presented at the 1993 meeting of the Society for New Testament Studies meeting in Chicago, in which he traced the modern attempt to portray Jesus as a Cynic to the influence of Nietzsche.

[4]They were said to be famous for their *anaideia*, shamelessness.

[5]Crossan, *Historical Jesus*, pp. 72-88.

[6]Burton Mack, *A Myth of Innocence: Mark and Christian Origins* (Philadelphia: Fortress, 1988), p. 73.

[7]In his Society for New Testament Studies lecture, Hans Dieter Betz, "Jesus and the Cynics: Survey and Analysis of a Hypothesis." The Syrophoenician woman story (Mk 7:24-30)

says that Jesus visited the region of Tyre once, but it does not say he ever entered the city. Even if the story recorded in Mark 5:1-13 does refer to Gadara, which is textually debatable (it could be Gerasa, or even Gergasa), it should be noticed that Jesus never enters the town and immediately returns across the lake to Galilee.

[8]Ben Witherington III, *Jesus the Sage: The Pilgrimage of Wisdom* (Minneapolis: Fortress, 1994), p. 123.

[9]Most recently, see F. Gerald Downing, *Christ and the Cynics: Jesus and Other Radical Preachers in First Century Tradition* (Sheffield, U.K.: Sheffield Academic Press, 1988), but see also, among other books by Downing, *Jesus and the Threat of Violence* (London: SCM, 1987). I have argued at some length against the Cynic proposal as it has been developed by Downing in Witherington, *Jesus the Sage*, pp. 117-45.

[10]Of course it could be argued that Mark is covering up the Cynic background of Jesus, but if this is the case and he was deliberately arguing against a Cynic view, we might expect him to present the mission charge and Jesus' own itinerary in a rather different light.

[11]So rightly Bernard Brandon Scott, "Jesus as Sage: An Innovating Voice in Common Wisdom," in *The Sage in Israel and the Ancient Near East*, ed. John G. Gammie and Leo G. Purdue (Winona Lake, Ind.: Eisenbrauns, 1990), pp. 399-415, here p. 401.

[12]Everett Ferguson, *Backgrounds of Early Christianity* (Grand Rapids, Mich.: Eerdmans, 1987), p. 276.

[13]Borg, "Portraits," in *The Search for Jesus: Modern Scholarship Looks at the Gospels*, ed. Hershel Shanks (Washington, D.C.: Biblical Archaeology Review, 1994), p. 92.

[14]For those unfamiliar with Crossan's work, this is a pun on the title of one of his earlier works, John Dominic Crossan, *The Cross That Spoke* (San Francisco: Harper and Row, 1988).

[15]Crossan, *Historical Jesus*, p. xi.

[16]See Ben Witherington III, *The Christology of Jesus* (Philadelphia: Fortress, 1990), pp. 42-46.

[17]See Crossan, *Historical Jesus*, pp. 236-37.

[18]Ibid., p. 238.

[19]Ibid., pp. 240-59.

[20]Ibid., pp. 259-60.

[21]Ibid., p. 248.

[22]Ibid., p. 259.

[23]The first discussion of this comes at Crossan, *Historical Jesus*, pp. 261-64, and it appears again on pp. 332-48.

[24]See Ben Witherington III, *Women in the Ministry of Jesus* (Cambridge: Cambridge University Press, 1984), pp. 11ff.

[25]Crossan, *Historical Jesus*, p. 300.

[26]If, as Crossan allows, Jesus really did say, "Render unto Caesar," and the saying is not totally ironic, this would seem to imply that Jesus did not advocate pure theocracy (the rule of God alone over humankind), as did the Zealots, and thus did not totally reject human hierarchies. One may also wonder about stories such as when Jesus tells a man who has been healed and cleansed to go and show himself to the local priest. This would imply some sort of respect for a hierarchy, in this case a religious and patriarchal one (cf. Mk 1:44).

[27]Crossan, *Historical Jesus*, pp. 293-94.

[28]See Witherington, *Women in the Ministry of Jesus*, pp. 3ff.

[29]Crossan, *Historical Jesus*, pp. 270-74.

[30]Ibid., p. 281.

[31]See the discussion in Ben Witherington III, *Jesus, Paul and the End of the World* (Downers

Grove, Ill.: InterVarsity Press, 1992), pp. 51-58.

[32]Crossan, *Historical Jesus*, p. 304.

[33]I will discuss in the next chapter the work of Graham H. Twelftree, *Jesus the Exorcist* (Tübingen: J. C. B. Mohr, 1993), who argues that Jesus did on occasion use techniques recognizable to his contemporaries and yet was never categorized as a magician.

[34]On this whole subject see Witherington, *Christology of Jesus*, pp. 155-60.

[35]I, however, agree with Crossan, *Historical Jesus*, pp. 305-10, that it is wrong to overpress the distinction between miracle as request to God and magic as attempt to coerce God into acting by some means, but there does regularly seem to be, on the part of ancient magicians, the view that God or the gods can be manipulated with the right formula or spell.

[36]Ibid., pp. 313-20.

[37]Ibid., pp. 338-39.

[38]Not the least of which is, as Crossan admits, that Jesus did not share the Cynic's urban strategy but focused on small villages and towns; cf. ibid., p. 340.

[39]Notice the lack of meaningful discussion of the Last Supper in Crossan's *Historical Jesus*.

[40]Unless of course one accepts the remarks in the parallel in Matthew 22:11-12, which speak of the need for a wedding garment, for proper dress to participate in the messianic banquet. Crossan must naturally reject this verse since it conflicts with "open commensality."

[41]Crossan, *Historical Jesus*, p. 349.

[42]Ibid., p. 346.

[43]Ibid., p. 353.

[44]Crossan is, however, careful to say at the end of his book that one must not overemphasize the inclusive aspects of Jesus' teaching at the expense of the exclusive, since too much of either side can cause a person to lose their sense of their identity or religious soul. But I would suggest that Crossan is indeed guilty of overemphasizing the inclusive side of Jesus' teaching at the expense of what some would call the more Jewish and sectarian side.

[45]In John Dominic Crossan, "The Search for Jesus," in *The Search for Jesus: Modern Scholarship Looks at the Gospels*, ed. Hershel Shanks (Washington, D.C.: Biblical Archaeology Review, 1994), pp. 121-23, and the quote is on p. 132.

[46]Crossan, *Historical Jesus*, p. 372, cf. p. 382.

[47]Crossan, "The Search for Jesus," p. 110.

[48]Translation from J. K. Elliott, ed., *The Apocryphal New Testament* (Oxford: Clarendon, 1993), p. 155.

[49]Crossan, *Historical Jesus*, p. 390.

[50]Ibid., pp. 360-67.

[51]I find it ironic that in the popular book *The Search for Jesus*, pp. 131-32, the editor Hershel Shanks, a Jew, suggests it must have taken something like a resurrected figure to get early Christians to write the passion narratives as we have them, but it is Crossan, of Catholic background, who flatly rejects the view that Easter faith created the possibility of the Gospels.

[52]Crossan, *Historical Jesus*, p. xxviii.

[53]Cf., for example, ibid., p. xxi, where there are more quotes from *Thomas* than from the canonical Gospels. Of course those who know Crossan's previous work will not be surprised by this move, for he once wrote a book dedicated to the thesis that *four other Gospels*—the *Gospel of Thomas*, *Secret Mark*, the *Gospel of Peter* and Egerton 2 are in various key ways more original than the four canonical Gospels (cf. John Dominic Crossan, *Four Other Gospels* [Minneapolis: Winston, 1985]). This broader thesis seems to have been narrowed down to a strong advocacy of *Thomas* in the work we are currently evaluating. Perhaps this is

because Raymond E. Brown did a rather good job of demolishing the argument that the Synoptics depended on the *Gospel of Peter* for their passion narrative material (or other material). Cf. Raymond E. Brown, *"The Gospel of Peter* and Canonical Gospel Priority," *New Testament Studies* 3 (1987): 321-43. See also John P. Meier, *A Marginal Jew: Rethinking the Historical Jesus* (New York: Doubleday, 1991), pp. 114-23.

[54]This in part depends on how much creativity one attributes to early Christians who handled and passed along Jesus' sayings.

[55]Crossan, *Historical Jesus*, pp. 424-26.

[56]On which see the previous chapter.

[57]Robert W. Funk, "Beyond Criticism in Quest of Literacy: The Parable of the Leaven," *Interpretation* 25 (1971): 149-70, here p. 151.

[58]Richard A. Burridge, *What Are the Gospels? A Comparison with Greco-Roman Biography* (Cambridge: Cambridge University Press, 1992). I find his arguments about Matthew, Mark and John compelling, but not those about Luke, which appears to me to be deliberately cast as the first volume of a two-volume historical monograph in the Greco-Roman mold. I will say more on this in my forthcoming commentary on Acts.

[59]Some may think this is plenty of time for all sorts of creative handling of this material, but one must remember that prior to Paul and the undertaking of the Gentile mission in earnest in the 40s and 50s, this material was in the hands of Jews who had definite and conservative traditions about how to handle the teachings of important Jewish sages and prophets. One must also reckon with the ongoing existence and probable influence of at least some eyewitnesses so long as the church continued to be centered in Jerusalem.

[60]Crossan, *Historical Jesus*, p. xxxi.

[61]On this whole matter cf. Witherington, *Christology of Jesus*, pp. 3-22.

[62]Crossan, *Historical Jesus*, pp. 328-32.

[63]Robin A. Scroggs, review of *The Historical Jesus*, by John Dominic Crossan, *Interpretation* 47 (1993): 301.

[64]Crossan, *Historical Jesus*, p. xxxiv.

[65]Reader-response theory involves the notion that meaning comes from the reader's creative encounter with the text or even that meaning lies in the eyes of the beholder. In short, meaning does not lie in the text itself, and the search for an author's intended meaning is futile. Thus, one is left with multiple creative subjective readings or appropriations of the text. I have critiqued this radically subjective epistemology and its antihistorical character in *Jesus the Sage*, pp. 147-55.

[66]See Ben F. Meyer's review in *Catholic Biblical Quarterly* 55 (1993): 575-76.

[67]See now N. T. Wright's satirical review and response to Crossan's work, deliberately done in a postmodernist mode. Cf. "Taking the Text with Her Pleasure: A Post-Modernist Response to J. Dominic Crossan, *The Historical Jesus: The Life of a Mediterranean Jewish Peasant,"* *Theology* 96 (1993): 303-10. It includes the aphorism: "There will come a man called Dominic who will claim that most Jesus-material comes from Thomas; and he will be opposed by a man called Thomas [Wright] who will claim that most Jesus-material is Dominical" (p. 305).

[68]Crossan, *Historical Jesus*, p. xxix. In this regard Crossan sounds little different from various of the Second Questers, or from Bultmann.

[69]Ibid., p. 7.

[70]Cf. pp. 14-20.

[71]On Corinth and patronage see Ben Witherington III, *Conflict and Community in Corinth* (Grand Rapids, Mich.: Eerdmans, 1995).

[72]See Witherington, *Jesus the Sage*, chapters 4—5, and Craig A. Evans, *Jesus and His Contemporaries: Comparative Studies*, Arbeiten zur Geschichte des antiken Judentums und des Urchristentums 25 (Leiden: Brill, 1995).

[73]Crossan, *Historical Jesus*, p. 16.

[74]It is no more than about a day's walk in any direction to any spot since we are only talking about an area about 15 miles by 25 miles.

[75]Indeed, as I have shown in *Conflict and Community*, it is also not how artisans and merchants viewed themselves in the larger Greco-Roman world. On Jewish views of work see Sanders, *Judaism: Practice and Belief*, passim.

[76]See pp. 27-30 above.

[77]See Crossan, *Historical Jesus*, p. 178.

[78]Scroggs, review of *Historical Jesus*, p. 301.

[79]I am equally wary of Crossan's reliance on Gerhard E. Lenski's class categorizations, since we cannot really talk about "classes" of people in ancient Jewish society. See above on Goodman's evaluation, p. 29.

[80]Diogenes was seen as the founder of the Cynic movement well before Jesus' day, and Dio after Jesus' time was certainly influenced by Cynic notions.

[81]Crossan, *Historical Jesus*, pp. 125-27.

[82]Crossan is even willing to say that Jesus and his followers are like hippies in a world of Augustan yuppies! Ibid., p. 421.

[83]Ibid., pp. 124-25.

[84]See above pp. 26-31 on the social milieu of Galilee.

[85]Cf. pp. 145-51.

[86]It is really quite incredible that Hengel's detailed work on Hellenism and Hellenization in Palestine, as well as his work on the Zealots, is completely ignored by Crossan. They do not even appear anywhere in his bibliography! Cf. Martin Hengel, *Judaism and Hellenism*, 2 vols. (Philadelphia: Fortress, 1974); *The Hellenization of Judea in the First Century After Christ* (Philadelphia: Trinity, 1989); and *Die Zeloten*, 2nd ed. (Leiden: Brill, 1976).

[87]See by contrast the balanced discussion in John K. Riches, *The World of Jesus: First-Century Judaism in Crisis* (Cambridge: Cambridge University Press, 1990), pp. 57ff. In Crossan's view the Zealots only show up about A.D. 67, after the Jewish revolt has begun, and represent a coalition of various bandit groups in Jerusalem. While I would agree that the specific and immediate conditions which could have prompted revolution seem to have been absent in Jesus' day in Galilee, though the potential was present, and it may be better not to speak of a Zealot *party* before the Jewish War, nonetheless the ideals of the Maccabees and Judas the Galilean were surely alive and well, and the attempt to reduce the holders of such ideals to mere social bandits and to make social problems (rather than religious and nationalist causes) the only or most crucial issue in Jesus' Galilee is a mistake.

I agree with Crossan that Josephus must indeed be read critically, not least because *Antiquities* and *Wars* can contradict each other. I do not, however, entirely subscribe to the notion of an evolutionary reading of the two documents, which often overvalues one or another of the works depending on the issue. It must be remembered that the *Jewish Wars* is an example of the rhetoric of defense, aimed at a non-Jewish audience. In this early work Josephus is especially looking for scapegoats, and he seeks to avoid highlighting the Pharisees so as to protect the group with which he most identified. He is more candid about their importance and about his own pro-Jewish and anti-Samaritan feelings in his later works, including *Antiquities*. On the whole, the later work, which is less of a polemic in most regards, deserves more credence. Josephus always had his biases, as Crossan insists, but to completely dismiss him at key points (such as in regard to the Zealots and the ongoing resistance movement) and to construct one's own theory *based on silence* is a perilous procedure at best.

88See the discussion in Crossan, *Historical Jesus*, pp. 138-67, and consider Mark 8:28.

89Crossan, *Jesus: A Revolutionary Biography*, p. xiv.

90Ibid., pp. 11-15.

91See ibid., pp. 62-64. For a critique of this notion see pp. 68-69 above.

92Ibid., pp. 24-25, where he draws on the discussions of Ramsay MacMullen about Roman social relationships, not Jewish ones. But as MacMullen points out, the inscriptional evidence shows that artisans did not regard their vocation as shameful. See discussion in Witherington, *Conflict and Community in Corinth*, pp. 204ff.

93See Crossan, *Jesus: A Revolutionary Biography*, p. 25.

94Ibid., pp. 96-98.

95It is telling to me that few of Jesus' parables can really be said to focus on problems of patronage or clientage, with the possible exception of the parable of the wicked servant. We do not hear stories of people going to the cities looking for a dole from a patron and offering to support him in his endeavors. Instead we hear of day laborers waiting in the marketplace to be hired, a very different social system. To suggest that Jesus was radically itinerant in order to offer a counterblast to systems of patronage is based on various false assumptions about what Jesus was reacting against.

96Ibid., pp. 122, 121.

97Ibid., pp. 118-19.

98Ibid., p. 108.

99See now Raymond E. Brown, *The Death of the Messiah*, 2 vols. (New York: Doubleday, 1994).

100See Crossan, *Jesus: A Revolutionary Biography*, pp. 59-60.

101Ibid., pp. 127-33.

102Ibid., pp. 177-78. One suspects that Crossan's real problem with miracles is that he has capitulated to a thoroughly modern mindset about the nature of reality and what can be known. Parker J. Palmer, in *To Know As We Are Known: Education as Spiritual Journey* (San Francisco: HarperSanFrancisco, 1993), p. 12, describes such a person: "More subtly, the self creates the world by forcing it into the limits of its own capacity to know. If we can know only what is available to our senses and our logic, then reality is reduced to those narrow terms." What is ironic about such a "scientific" viewpoint is that many scientists now find this limited worldview passé.

103Crossan, *Jesus: A Revolutionary Biography*, p. 101.

104Ibid., p. 17.

105Ibid., p. 95.

106Ibid., p. 85. Crossan understands exorcism as a process whereby one is delivered from a state of social dysfunctionality or perhaps multiple personality disorder.

107Ibid., p. 82.

108Remembering the words of Shakespeare, "Who can minister to a mind diseased?"

109Crossan, *Jesus: A Revolutionary Biography*, p. 190.

110Ibid., pp. 163-65.

111Or perhaps we should think of a Thomas community instead?

112Crossan, *Jesus: A Revolutionary Biography*, p. 190.

113Leander E. Keck, "The Second Coming of the Liberal Jesus?" *Christian Century* 111, no. 24 (1994): 784-87, here p. 785. As Keck goes on to stress (p. 786), for Crossan, Jesus' social location is far more important than his religious location, and the omission of almost all discussion of Jesus' relationship to Mosaic law and customs is telling, revealing that both Crossan and, to a lesser extent, Borg seem intent on distancing Jesus from some of the central aspects of early Judaism. Theology, including futurist eschatology, is collapsed into sociology or the experience of the Spirit world in the present.

[114]For one thing, why give women such prominent roles as witnesses in these stories if one is really trying to create tales that justify male leadership in the church?

Chapter 4: Jesus, Man of the Spirit

[1]Marcus Borg's major works are *Conflict, Holiness and Politics in the Teachings of Jesus* (Lewiston, N.Y.: Mellen, 1984); *Jesus: A New Vision* (San Francisco: Harper, 1987); *Meeting Jesus Again for the First Time* (San Francisco: Harper, 1994); and *Jesus in Contemporary Scholarship* (Valley Forge, Penn.: Trinity, 1994). There are some similarities between Borg's proposal and earlier suggestions by James D. G. Dunn in *Jesus and the Spirit* (Philadelphia: Westminster 1975), though Dunn's proposal amounts to something closer to calling Jesus a "charismatic" in the modern sense of the term, while Borg's proposal places Jesus in the more transcultural category of a person in close touch with the sacred.

[2]Geza Vermes has produced a trilogy of important works: *Jesus the Jew: A Historian's Reading of the Gospels*, 2nd ed. (New York: Macmillan, 1983); *Jesus and the World of Judaism* (Philadelphia: Fortress, 1984), which includes ten previously published articles; and *The Religion of Jesus the Jew* (Minneapolis: Fortress, 1993).

[3]Graham H. Twelftree, *Jesus the Exorcist* (Tübingen: Mohr, 1993).

[4]See Marcus Borg, "Portraits of Jesus," in *The Search for Jesus: Modern Scholarship Looks at the Gospels*, ed. Hershel Shanks (Washington, D.C.: Biblical Archaeology Review, 1994), pp. 83-103, which is a very helpful introduction to the discussion of the various proposals of Third Questers about Jesus.

[5]On which, see the preface.

[6]Marcus Borg, "An Orthodoxy Reconsidered: 'The End-of-the-World-Jesus,' " in *The Glory of Christ in the New Testament*, ed. Lincoln D. Hurst and N. T. Wright (Oxford: Clarendon, 1987), pp. 207-18.

[7]Marcus Borg, "Jesus and Eschatology: A Reassessment," in *Images of Jesus Today*, ed. James H. Charlesworth and Walter P. Weaver (Valley Forge, Penn.: Trinity Press International, 1994), pp. 42-67.

[8]See George B. Caird, *The Language and Imagery of the Bible* (Philadelphia: Westminster, 1980).

[9]I have sought to deal with this stereotype in Ben Witherington III, *Jesus, Paul and the End of the World* (Downers Grove, Ill.: InterVarsity Press, 1992).

[10]On which, see pp. 137-55.

[11]Borg, "An Orthodoxy Reconsidered," pp. 210-11.

[12]On the dating of this Enoch material cf. Ben Witherington III, *The Christology of Jesus* (Philadelphia: Fortress, 1990), pp. 234-36.

[13]Cf. Witherington, *Jesus, Paul and the End of the World*, pp. 36-48.

[14]See Witherington, *Christology of Jesus*, pp. 238-43.

[15]Borg adds nothing to his argument for a noneschatological Jesus in "Jesus and Eschatology," pp. 50ff., but it is intriguing that in this essay, particularly on pp. 60-61, he seems more cautious, saying that one needs to define what is meant by eschatology and then going on to affirm that Jesus had a cosmic eschatology involving final judgment. This is true enough, and it shows Borg knows it will not do to simply assume that Schweitzerian eschatology is the only form Jesus might have had. What Borg seems now to assert is that Jesus does not say much about eschatology and that it does not define him nor is it at the

heart of his teaching. I would disagree even with this retrenchment of his argument.

[16]*Webster's New World Dictionary,* ed. D. B. Guralnik, 2nd coll. ed., s.v. "charisma."

[17]See for example the discussion in Crossan, *The Historical Jesus* (San Francisco: Harper, 1991), p. 196.

[18]Here I am simply following Borg's own recent summary of his position in "Portraits of Jesus," pp. 96-97.

[19]That is, dreams or visions are taken to reflect inner reality in the subconscious of the individual, not some objective otherworldly outer reality, and miracles are taken as examples of psychosomatic process, the "healing" of illnesses that were engendered or real only in the mind of the sick person.

[20]Borg, *Jesus: A New Vision,* pp. 33-34.

[21]On which see pp. 124-25.

[22]See my discussion of these texts in Witherington, *Christology of Jesus,* pp. 146-55.

[23]I would want to stress at this point that whatever else one may wish to add, Jesus led his life as a human being drawing on the resources of God's Word, the power of the Spirit and his deep intimacy with the one he called *Abba.* In other words, he lived in a fashion in which his followers could also live and thus set them an example. Even Jesus' miracles seem in large measure to be portrayed as things he accomplished by the power of the Spirit (cf. Mt 12:28/Lk 11:20).

[24]N. T. Wright, *Who Was Jesus?* (Grand Rapids, Mich.: Eerdmans, 1992), pp. 15-16.

[25]On Jesus' relationship to the Pharisees see pp. 124-26. Jesus no doubt would have had conflict with the Qumran community and their radical approach of equating ritual purity with holiness as well. But there is no real evidence for Jesus' contact with the Qumran sectarians. John the Baptist, however, may have originally come out of the Qumran community. Cf. Witherington, *Christology of Jesus,* pp. 34-36.

[26]See his admission of this in "Jesus and Eschatology," pp. 60-61.

[27]Borg, "Portraits of Jesus," p. 87.

[28]See pp. 137ff. and pp. 161ff.

[29]See *Antiquities* 18.4.1 for the Samaritan, *Antiquities* 20.5.1 (cf. Acts 5:36) for Theudas, and *Antiquities* 20.8.6 and *Wars* 2.13.5 (cf. Acts 21:38) for the Egyptian.

[30]See Witherington, *Christology of Jesus,* pp. 90-91.

[31]Borg, *Meeting Jesus,* p. 11.

[32]On which see Witherington, *Christology of Jesus,* pp. 221-28.

[33]Borg, *Meeting Jesus,* p. 59.

[34]One begins to suspect that in various of these radical portrayals of Jesus, especially those of Crossan and Borg, nothing must be allowed to interfere with a politically correct Jesus. He must be egalitarian to a fault, open and accepting of all people as they are, and furthermore he must be something of a universalist. This sounds suspiciously like a Jesus taken captive by modern Western agendas and not Jesus the Jew from Nazareth.

[35]For a discussion of the meaning of this saying and its authenticity, see Ben Witherington III, *Women in the Ministry of Jesus* (Cambridge: Cambridge University Press, 1984), pp. 28-32. The saying stands in contrast with other teachings in early Judaism about the obligation to marry and procreate unless one was a eunuch.

[36]Borg, *Meeting Jesus,* p. 62.

[37]See E. P. Sanders, *The Historical Figure of Jesus* (London: Penguin, 1993), pp. 198-204.

[38]Since Sanders disputes this, I will say more in the following chapter when I evaluate his work.

[39]For example, Simon the Pharisee certainly would not have entertained Jesus in his own

home if Jesus had suggested that sinners did not need to be reformed or change their behavior (cf. Lk 7:36-50, which speaks of the need for forgiveness of sins). One significant trend in radical Jesus scholarship is the favoring of the Lukan (including Luke's form of Q) portrait of Jesus over any other. Yet even so, there is great selectivity in this favoritism, for it involves neglecting Lukan teaching such as Luke 16:18. If Luke 16:18 has a higher claim to authenticity than Luke 6:36, then even those who favor Luke's version of things need to come to grips with Jesus' purity demands.

[40]Borg, *Meeting Jesus*, pp. 81-82.

[41]On the authenticity of this material see Witherington, *Women in the Ministry of Jesus*, pp. 11ff.

[42]Cf. Witherington, *Christology of Jesus*, pp. 215-21.

[43]On this subject cf. Bruce Malina, *Calling Jesus Names* (Sonoma, Calif.: Polebridge, 1993). It is hardly believable that Mark would have invented a saying like Mark 10:17, which might be taken to suggest that Jesus saw himself as neither good in any absolute or divine sense, nor God.

[44]See Borg, *Meeting Jesus*, pp. 83-85.

[45]Ibid., p. 14.

[46]Ibid.

[47]It is telling that elsewhere in the book he admits that his notions of Jesus as a Spirit person and as mediator of the sacred (rather than conveyor of some specific revelation about a personal being known as Yahweh) came from the study of cultural anthropology and non-Western religions. See ibid., p. 32.

[48]Compare ibid. p. 17 with p. 137.

[49]See ibid., pp. 96-111. I will say more about Borg's statements about Jesus and Wisdom in chapter seven.

[50]And if he was, what possible or compelling reasons could there be for wanting to "meet him again for the first time"?

[51]Perhaps at the end of the day, the real root of Borg's insistence that one can separate faith in Jesus (as relationship and experience) from beliefs about Jesus and the things he required, and of his pitting compassion against "conventional wisdom" about holiness, faithfulness, duty and the like, arises from the Lutheran ethos of dramatically setting grace over against works, even over faith as a work. The pitfall is that the notion of *sola gratia* swallows up the rest of the gospel.

[52]See Hershel Shanks's interview with Vermes entitled "Escape and Rescue," *Bible Review*, June 1994, pp. 30-37.

[53]For a short, clear presentation of his argument see Vermes's essay "Jesus the Jew" in *Jesus' Jewishness: Exploring the Place of Jesus in Early Judaism*, ed. James H. Charlesworth (New York: Crossroad, 1991), pp. 108-22.

[54]See the discussion in Crossan, *Historical Jesus*, pp. 142-58. Crossan insists on using the term *magic* for what these early Jews did, but in our modern context the term connotes legerdemain, sleight of hand, the creating of illusions and the like, and it should be avoided. See pp. 70-72 on the differences between Jesus' miracles and magic.

[55]See Witherington, *Christology of Jesus*, p. 153.

[56]See Vermes, *Jesus the Jew*, pp. 210ff.; *World of Judaism*, pp. 41-43.

[57]Witherington, *Christology of Jesus*, p. 217, cf. p. 216. In *b. Ta'an.* 23b, which involves Hanin ha Nehba, the grandson of Honi, there is a play on words: he is called *abba* by children, and in turn alludes to God as the *abba* who truly can answer the plea for rain. Note that Hanin does not address God here as *abba* but as "Master of the World."

[58]The evidence produced by James D. J. Dunn, *Christology in the Making* (Philadephia: West-

minster, 1980), p. 27, from *Wisdom of Solomon* 14:3; *Sirach* 23:1, 4; 51:10; 3 Maccabees 6:3, 8, is not directly relevant to this discussion. The only one of these sources which is in Hebrew is the material in *Sirach* 23:1, 4 and 51:10, but there God is addressed as *abi*, "my Father," not as *abba*, "dearest Father." This evidence shows that especially in intertestamental Wisdom literature the term *Father* was being increasingly used of God. See discussion in Ben Witherington III, *Jesus the Sage: The Pilgrimage of Wisdom* (Minneapolis: Fortress, 1994), pp. 106, 315.

[59]Vermes, "Jesus the Jew," p. 116.

[60]Ibid., p. 115.

[61]Twelftree, *Jesus the Exorcist*, p. 211.

[62]*B. Pes.* 112b is interesting, but it does not involve an exorcism per se. Here Hanina encounters the queen of demons, Agrath, and forbids her to pass through an inhabited place. The cleansing of a person who has an unclean spirit is not involved in this story.

[63]See Vermes, "Jesus the Jew," p. 118.

[64]John P. Meier, *A Marginal Jew*, vol. 2, *Mentor, Message, Miracle* (New York: Doubleday, 1994), pp. 581-88, and notes on pp. 605-9.

[65]Ibid., 584.

[66]Ibid.

[67]Ibid., 585-86.

[68]Ibid., 587.

[69]Ibid., 587-88.

[70]Ibid., 581.

[71]See the discussion of Jesus' miracles in Witherington, *Christology of Jesus*, pp. 155-61.

[72]See Twelftree, *Jesus the Exorcist*, pp. 157-65.

[73]See pp. 185-96.

[74]Twelftree, *Jesus the Exorcist*, p. 226.

[75]Ibid., p. 227.

[76]Ibid., pp. 217-24.

[77]Ibid., p. 228. Cf. Luke 10:18.

[78]In later Christian tradition, of course, Jesus' miracles were attributed to his own divine nature, but it is notable that this is not how they are portrayed in the earliest Gospel material.

[79]Twelftree, *Jesus the Exorcist*, p. 218.

Chapter 5: Jesus the Eschatological Prophet

[1]R. David Kaylor, *Jesus the Prophet: His Vision of the Kingdom on Earth* (Louisville, Ky.: Westminster/John Knox, 1994), p. 211.

[2]One could also put Crossan, and to a lesser extent Borg, in this camp, though *prophet* is not the main label they might choose for Jesus.

[3]E. P. Sanders, *Jesus and Judaism* (Philadelphia: Fortress, 1985).

[4]It is interesting, however, that some of the major reviews in the more notable journals were not all that enthusiastic. Cf. Reginald H. Fuller's review, "Searching for the Historical Jesus," *Interpretation* 41 (1987): 301-3; Donald Senior's review in *Catholic Biblical Quarterly* 48 (1986): 569-71; and, in a bit more laudatory vein, Bruce Chilton in *Journal of Biblical Literature* 106 (1987): 537-39. James D. G. Dunn in his review in *Journal of Theological Studies* 37 (1986): 510-13 is one of the more critical, thinking Sanders has pushed the pendulum too far in the wrong direction by suggesting Jesus had no major quarrel with the Pharisees.

[5]E. P. Sanders, *The Historical Figure of Jesus* (London: Penguin, 1993), now released and dis-

tributed by Viking in the United States.

⁶E. P. Sanders, *Paul and Palestinian Judaism: A Comparison of Patterns of Religion* (Philadelphia: Fortress, 1977); *Paul, the Law and the Jewish People* (Philadelphia: Fortress, 1983); *Jewish Law from Jesus to the Mishnah: Five Studies* (Philadelphia: Trinity Press International, 1990); *Judaism: Practice and Belief 63 BCE-66 CE* (Philadelphia: Trinity Press International, 1992).

⁷Sanders, *Historical Figure*, p. 54. Here he is dealing with the particular issue of dates during which Jesus lived, but this sentence I think aptly sums up his general view of the Gospels—that they should be believed unless there are strong reasons to think they are not trustworthy on some matter. It is also important to note Sanders's judgment on the material in the *Gospel of Thomas* and other apocryphal documents: "I share the general scholarly view that very, very little in the apocryphal gospels could conceivably go back to the time of Jesus. They are legendary and mythological. . . . only some of the sayings in the *Gospel of Thomas* are worth consideration" (p. 64). With this judgment I concur. On Crossan's more radical view see pp. 77-82, and on *Thomas* in general see pp. 48-50.

⁸I will abbreviate the *Historical Figure* volume as *HF* and the *Jesus and Judaism* volume as *JJ*.

⁹Not listed but clearly discussed and affirmed in *Historical Figure*, pp. 185-87.

¹⁰These lists can be found in *Jesus and Judaism*, p. 11, and in *Historical Figure*, pp. 10-11.

¹¹Sanders, *Jesus and Judaism*, p. 22.

¹²Why did he attract so many followers, both male and female, and yet choose the Twelve as his inner circle, and why was he never taken captive or interrogated by Herod during his ministry if he really was a radical egalitarian social prophet?

¹³Ibid., p. 55.

¹⁴Ibid., pp. 61-90.

¹⁵Ibid., pp. 84-85. He sees Revelation 21:22 as polemic against the normal early Jewish view.

¹⁶Ibid., p. 90.

¹⁷Ibid., p. 98.

¹⁸Ibid., p. 104.

¹⁹See Ben Witherington III, *Christology of Jesus* (Philadelphia: Fortress, 1990), pp. 126-32.

²⁰Cf. Sanders, *Jesus and Judaism*, p. 116.

²¹Ibid., pp. 118-19.

²²Ibid., p. 127.

²³Ibid., p. 152.

²⁴Ibid., p. 153.

²⁵Ibid., p. 156.

²⁶Ibid., p. 164.

²⁷Ibid., p. 172.

²⁸Ibid., p. 173.

²⁹See the discussion pp. 112-14 above on Jesus the exorcist.

³⁰Sanders, *Historical Figure*, p. 136.

³¹Ibid., p. 159. Cf. Crossan's views pp. 70-71 above.

³²For example, scientists who accept the big bang theory about the origins of the universe are confronted with the fact that at some point one must posit a first cause that itself has no natural cause. Some try to get around this fact, but it always ends up sounding like they are affirming something they do not want to affirm—the eternality of matter and the universe.

³³Unlike Crossan, who regularly asserts that *magic* is just an opponent's term for someone else's miracle. See pp. 70-71 above.

³⁴Sanders, *Historical Figure*, p. 140.

35Sanders, *Jesus and Judaism*, p. 177.

36Ibid., p. 199.

37Ibid., p. 203.

38Ibid., p. 204.

39Ibid., p. 207.

40I suspect that this was also in part what galled John the Baptist's opponents. He too was offering repentance and forgiveness through baptism and apart from the usual cultic means of sacrifice and the like, centered in Jerusalem.

41Sanders, *Historical Figure*, p. 232-37.

42See ibid., pp. 234-37.

43Ibid., p. 234.

44Ibid., p. 226.

45On which see the analysis of Vermes's views on Jesus (pp. 108-12).

46See chapter four, pp. 93-100.

47See the review by Donald Senior, p. 571.

48See my earlier arguments in Witherington, *Christology of Jesus*, pp. 73-81, where I was more inclined to dispute Sanders on his equation of "sinners" with "wicked."

49Here let me mention one small further indicator of Jesus' approach to the purity laws. As Sanders admits, the normal preparation for the Passover included being sprinkled on the tenth and fourteenth of Nisan, bathing and taking a lamb to the temple (cf. *Historical Figure*, pp. 250-51). The Gospels say absolutely nothing about Jesus or his followers performing such rites. How do we read this silence? Sanders suggests the silence implies that Jesus and the disciples did do these things, since not to do them would have caused remark. I suggest to the contrary that, at least in regard to the purification ritual, we have no reason to think Jesus and his followers kept it, especially in light of a text like Mark 7:15. Furthermore, a Jesus who was willing to reinterpret the very elements and symbols of Passover may certainly also have "passed over" some parts of the ritual he saw as no longer to the point or necessary in view of the kingdom breaking in.

50Sanders, *Jesus and Judaism*, p. 220.

51Sanders, *Historical Figure*, p. 192.

52Ibid., pp. 50, 68, 84, 153, 238-39.

53Ibid., pp. 239, 242; cf. Sanders, *Jesus and Judaism*, p. 235.

54Sanders, *Jesus and Judaism*, p. 240.

55Sanders, *Historical Figure*, pp. 241-42.

56Sanders, *Jesus and Judaism*, p. 318.

57Sanders, *Historical Figure*, p. 21.

58See chapter one, pp. 26-30.

59Sanders, *Historical Figure*, p. 176.

60Ibid., p. 177.

61Ibid., p. 178.

62Ibid., p. 179.

63Ibid., p. 178.

64See ibid., p. 188. As Senior, p. 571, asks: "Are there not other ways Jesus might have envisioned political transformation [than] . . . armed revolt against the Romans?"

65See Maurice Casey, *Son of Man: The Interpretation and Influence of Daniel* (London: S.P.C.K., 1980), *From Jewish Prophet to Gentile God: The Origins and Development of New Testament Christology* (Louisville, Ky.: Westminster/John Knox, 1991), and articles cited in this latter volume.

66See Casey, *From Jewish Prophet*, p. 57: "I have also assumed that both Mark and Q contain a large quantity of authentic source material, much of which was written down in Aramaic by Jews long before the writing of the Gospels, and which can therefore be properly understood only if we apply to it the assumptions of Jewish culture."

[67]Ibid.

[68]Ibid., p. 59.

[69]Ibid.

[70]See discussion in Witherington, *Jesus, Paul and the End of the World* (Downers Grove, Ill.: InterVarsity Press, 1992), pp. 42-43.

[71]Casey, *From Jewish Prophet*, p. 60.

[72]This is Casey's term, ibid., p. 63.

[73]Ibid., p. 62.

[74]For instance, Mark 7:15 is interpreted only to mean that Jesus rejected the requirement of the washing of hands prior to eating to avoid uncleanness of food caused by unclean hands (cf. Casey, *From Jewish Prophet*, p. 71). I seriously doubt this verse will bear this interpretation. Casey repeats the usual argument that stories like Acts 10—11 about Peter's vision show that Jesus had never taught that all food was clean. This overlooks two important considerations: (1) Mark assumes that Jesus' metaphorical saying about what enters the body requires interpretation and explanation. In its original setting it may have been like many of Jesus' other aphorisms, left in a form that forced the hearer to puzzle out its meaning, and the disciples failed to get the point. (2) Peter, to judge from Galatians 2, was not notably quick to understand the practical and social implications of the gospel and may have needed a vision to straighten him out about food.

[75]Casey, *From Jewish Prophet*, p. 61.

[76]Ibid., p. 65. Contrast what Sanders has to say, pp. 130-32 below.

[77]Ibid., pp. 64-65.

[78]Ibid., p. 65.

[79]Ibid., p. 67.

[80]Ibid., pp. 48-54.

Chapter 6: Jesus the Prophet of Social Change

[1]See especially Gerd Theissen, *Sociology of Early Palestinian Christianity* (Philadelphia: Fortress, 1978); *The Gospels in Context: Social and Political History in the Synoptic Tradition* (Edinburgh: T & T Clark, 1992); and the novelistic *The Shadow of the Galilean: The Quest of the Historical Jesus in Narrative Form* (Philadelphia: Fortress, 1987). There are other important articles in German and French by Theissen, but many have not yet been translated into English.

[2]See Marcus Borg, *Jesus in Contemporary Scholarship* (Valley Forge, Penn.: Trinity Press International, 1994), who mentions Theissen in only six scattered references (pp. 16, 39, 41, 48, 61, 96) but treats Theissen's disciples Crossan and Horsley as major figures in the ongoing discussion.

[3]Notice how Horsley in his *Sociology and the Jesus Movement* (New York: Crossroad, 1989) not only partially echoes the title of Theissen's earlier work (see note 1 above) but spends the first third of his book analyzing and critiquing Theissen's seminal work well over a decade after it first appeared in English.

[4]Theissen, *Sociology*, pp. 10-16.

[5]Theissen uses the phrase "under the surface it's still seething" (*Shadow*, p. 63) to describe the situation, and he also leaves the impression that Roman authority was directly involved through spies and informants in Galilee, which was Herod Antipas's domain.

[6]Theissen, *Sociology*, p. 20.

[7]See ibid., pp. 36-37.

[8]We are talking about an area that is only a little more than 50 miles from the Mediterranean coast at its *easternmost* point. In a given day Jesus could have traveled from Capernaum to Magdala and Chorazin and back to Capernaum by nightfall, or traveled from Nazareth through Cana to Capernaum and back in about a day.

[9]Notice the assumption by Theissen that "all the renewal movements within Judaism . . . drew their recruits from those who had no roots in society" (*Sociology*, p. 37). Again I would stress that material renunciation requires that one must first have some worldly goods. It is another matter that Jesus was highly critical of the rich and of obtaining wealth for one's own benefit. This latter is true, but it appears that most of Jesus' followers were in the position of neither the rich young ruler nor the poor beggar on the side of the road. That Jesus treats people like Mary and Martha as both friends and disciples, without apparently requiring them to give up their home and abilities to be hospitable, says something about Jesus (cf. Lk 10:38-42 and Ben Witherington III, *Women in the Ministry of Jesus* [Cambridge: Cambridge University Press, 1984], pp. 100-103).

[10]Theissen, *Sociology*, p. 46.

[11]Ibid., p. 50.

[12]See the discussion in chapter one, pp. 29-31.

[13]Theissen, *Sociology*, pp. 62-63.

[14]Ibid., p. 64.

[15]Ibid., p. 79.

[16]Ibid., p. 80.

[17]Ibid., p. 87.

[18]See ibid., pp. 92-93.

[19]Ibid., p. 105.

[20]See Ben Witherington III, *The Christology of Jesus* (Philadelphia: Fortress, 1990), pp. 140-43.

[21]Much of what follows appears in a different form in my review of this book in *The Journal of Ecclesiastical History* 44, no. 2 (1993): 289-92.

[22]Examples of these would be accurate information about local geography, customs, rulers and incidents that one would not expect in traditions formed far from the locale in which the events are said to have happened, and formed perhaps by those who did not know such minutiae and had little or no personal experience of the region.

[23]E.g., Burton Mack, *The Myth of Innocence: Mark and Christian Origins* (Philadelphia: Fortress, 1988), or John Dominic Crossan, *The Historical Jesus* (San Francisco: HarperSanFrancisco, 1991). The impasse I am referring to is that few scholars still believe that the early church settings Rudolf Bultmann and Martin Dibelius originally thought provided the matrix in which certain types of tradition were created are in fact the points of origin of these traditions (e.g., pronouncement stories).

[24]Marcus Borg, *Jesus in Contemporary Scholarship* (Valley Forge, Penn.: Trinity, 1994), p. 28.

[25]He has published a series of important studies, chiefly, Richard A. Horsley and John S. Hanson, *Bandits, Prophets and Messiahs: Popular Movements at the Time of Jesus* (Minneapolis: Winston, 1985), and three other books which he authored alone, especially the influential *Jesus and the Spiral of Violence* (San Francisco: Harper, 1987), but also *Sociology and the Jesus Movement* (New York: Crossroad, 1989) and *The Liberation of Christmas: The Infancy Narratives in Social Context* (New York: Crossroad, 1989).

[26]Horsley, *Spiral of Violence*, p. 287.

[27]Ibid., pp. 255-73.

[28]Ibid., pp. 170-72, 190-92 and 207.

29Ibid., p. 322.

30Cf. Horsley and Hanson, *Bandits, Prophets and Messiahs.*

31Horsley, *Spiral of Violence*, pp. 227-28.

32Against the Cynic proposal see Horsley, *Spiral of Violence*, pp. 230-31. His criticisms are much the same as those I have made above, pp. 61-63.

33Horsley, *Spiral of Violence*, p. 231.

34Ibid., pp. 240-45.

35See Horsley, "Like One of the Prophets of Old: Two Types of Popular Prophets at the Time of Jesus," *Catholic Biblical Quarterly* 47 (1985): 435-63.

36Ibid., p. 435.

37See ibid., pp. 439-441.

38Ibid., p. 443.

39Witherington, *Christology of Jesus*, pp. 80-88.

40See Horsley, "Like One of the Prophets," pp. 454-57.

41This sort of prophet has also been called a sign prophet. Cf. Paul W. Barnett, "The Jewish Sign Prophets, A.D. 40-70: Their Intentions and Origin," *New Testament Studies* 27 (1981): 679-97.

42See pp. 108-12 above on Geza Vermes.

43See chapter one, p. 29.

44On the degree of such control in Galilee cf. chapter one, pp. 17-19.

45R. David Kaylor, *Jesus the Prophet: His Vision of the Kingdom on Earth* (Louisville, Ky.: Westminster/John Knox, 1994), p. 213.

46On the problems with Brandon's proposal see Witherington, *Christology of Jesus*, pp. 96-100.

47Kaylor, *Jesus the Prophet*, p. 3.

48Ibid., p. 4.

49See pp. 20-22 above.

50This is a repeated assertion throughout the volume. Cf., e.g., p. 32.

51Kaylor, *Jesus the Prophet*, pp. 37-38, emphasis mine.

52See, e.g., ibid., p. 44.

53There was in fact a pattern of this sort of behavior when power was shifting from one ruler to the next. James the Just, Jesus' brother, was killed by the high priest during a period when one Roman governor had left Judea and another was on the way to replace him.

54See above on Crossan, chapter three, pp. 58ff.

55Kaylor, *Jesus the Prophet*, pp. 60ff.

56See ibid., pp. 63-69.

57Ibid., p. 64.

58See my argument in Witherington, *Christology of Jesus*, pp. 101-4.

59Horsley, *Spiral of Violence*, pp. 311-13.

60Kaylor, *Jesus the Prophet*, p. 132.

61See Ben Witherington III, *Conflict and Community in Corinth* (Grand Rapids, Mich.: Eerdmans, 1995), pp. 414-19. This same problem of reading clientage into the parable may be observed in Kaylor's interpretation of Matthew 18:23-35 (Kaylor, *Jesus the Prophet*, pp. 152-54). This parable is about slaves, whom it is doubtful one can call clients of their owner, and the lesser slave is not really a client of the greater one. The social context is the lending of money or aid directly and not any developed system of patronage.

62See Kaylor, *Jesus the Prophet*, p. 77.

63Ibid., p. 89.

64Ibid., p. 90.

[65]Ibid., pp. 194-97.

[66]Ibid., p. 99.

[67]Ibid., p. 103.

[68]Ibid., p. 119, suggests that Jesus may have seen himself as greater than Moses or perhaps as the prophet of whom Moses spoke in Deuteronomy 18:15, 18.

[69]Ibid., pp. 114-15. He says, rightly in my judgment, "To take the specific examples as laws can lead to reducing the all-encompassing nature of his teachings to carefully circumscribed areas given in the illustrations" (p. 117).

[70]Ibid., p. 122: "Jesus' parables contain a reflection of existing conditions under Roman rule, while they also create a vision of renewed relationships among the people and advocate a new way of seeing society, the self and others so that God's rule can transform social relationships."

[71]See pp. 190-92 below.

[72]Kaylor, *Jesus the Prophet*, pp. 142-43.

[73]Ibid., pp. 153.

[74]Ibid., pp. 179-80.

Chapter 7: Jesus the Sage: The Wisdom of God

[1]I have here deleted the portions of the passage that the vast majority of scholars, Christian or Jewish, take to be Christian interpolations. For detailed arguments for the authenticity of the portion of the text I have quoted see the superb treatment of the matter in John P. Meier, *A Marginal Jew: Rethinking the Historical Jesus* (New York: Doubleday, 1991), pp. 56-88.

[2]Since it appears that Josephus originally wrote his material, or dictated it, in Aramaic or Hebrew and had help in translating it into Greek, it is possible that he used the term *ḥākām* of Jesus, "sage." We cannot be certain about this, however, because while Josephus admits that he used collaborators to translate his earlier work *Jewish Wars* from Aramaic into good Greek (cf. *Ag. Ap.* 1.9), he seems to claim that by the time *Antiquities* was written he knew enough Greek grammar and vocabulary to compose it in Greek himself (cf. *Ant.* 20.12.1). Whether or not we accept that claim for this lengthy work, *ḥākām* is surely the Semitic equivalent he *would have* used for Jesus.

[3]See *"sophos,"* in *A Patristic Lexicon*, ed. G. W. H. Lampe (Oxford: Clarendon, 1961).

[4]It is interesting that this sort of evaluation of Jesus by non-Christians existed not only among non-Christian Jews but also among pagans, even in the second century A.D. As is widely known, Lucian of Samosata, writing in the latter half of the second century, composed a work entitled *The Passing of Peregrinus*, in which Peregrinus is depicted as one who converts to Christianity and then relapses to his old ways. What is important for our purposes is that he calls Jesus "that crucified sophist" (chap. 13; the key word is *sophisten*, which in this case probably connotes a wordsmith or rhetor, with a pejorative overtone).

[5]See pp. 58ff.

[6]Taken together, the last two chapters and the first portion of this chapter provide impressive evidence that Jesus was seen, and at least in part viewed himself, as some sort of prophet of social change, and the strong case made by Sanders and Fiorenza makes it unlikely that we can dismiss the idea that Jesus' teaching had an eschatological flavor. It is noteworthy that in none of these treatments of Jesus as prophet or liberator is there any concerted effort to come to grips with the Son of Man traditions or the idea of Jesus as some sort of messianic figure. The approaches taken in these two chapters provide at best only partial insights into what the historical Jesus was probably like.

⁷The academic debate about the historical Jesus in all three quests has been and continues to be, by and large, a debate among Europeans and North Americans, or scholars trained by institutions in those parts of the world. So for the most part it is true to say that the "interest of [Third World] liberation theologians in the historical Jesus separates them from scholars who are involved in the so-called quest of the historical Jesus. Liberation theologians are not on a quest to establish objective data to recover precisely what Jesus said and did. Rather, they want to understand the relevance of the historical Jesus for their own . . . context." (P. Pope-Levison and J. R. Levison, *Jesus in Global Contexts* [Louisville, Ky.: Westminster/John Knox, 1993], p. 31. This book is a helpful introduction to the field.)

This fact has led many scholars to simply dismiss, or fail to examine, what various Latin American, Asian and African scholars have been saying about the historical Jesus. This is a mistake, not least because many liberation theologians are able exegetes in their own right. Furthermore, many of them have been heavily influenced by European presentations of the historical Jesus, especially those of Joachim Jeremias and Günther Bornkamm. In other words, they reflect the use of the European discussion of the historical Jesus as applied to a very different setting, and their perspectives could add a great deal to the discussion. But I will not here undertake the task of surveying the work of Third World liberation theologians on Jesus, in part because I have not read enough of the primary source literature to do an adequate evaluation of it and in part because I agree with the comment of the Levisons, quoted above, about the general lack of interest among liberation theologians in the academic recovery of data about the historical Jesus using the historical-critical method.

⁸See the brief review of her work in Marcus Borg, *Jesus in Contemporary Scholarship* (Valley Forge, Penn.: Trinity, 1994), pp. 23-26.

⁹See pp. 58-65.

¹⁰Elisabeth Schüssler Fiorenza's major contribution to the discussion of Jesus comes in her influential book *In Memory of Her: A Feminist Theological Reconstruction of Christian Origins* (New York: Crossroad, 1984), pp. 99-159, now available in a new second edition (1994). In a more recent monograph, *Jesus: Miriam's Child, Sophia's Prophet: Critical Issues in Feminist Christology* (New York: Continuum, 1994), she further develops her argument along the same lines. Though the book is two hundred pages long, it deals as much with methodological issues as with Jesus, with the result that we still do not have an adequate full study of the historical Jesus by a feminist scholar.

¹¹There are of course other female New Testament scholars who have said similar things, such as Elizabeth A. Johnson or Luise Schottroff, but to date their work has not been as influential as Fiorenza's. Not only has no feminist New Testament scholar yet produced a full monograph on Jesus, the same can be said of African-American female New Testament scholars such as Clarice J. Martin, who takes a womanist and African-American rather than a feminist approach to these issues. Cf. Luise Schottroff, "Women as Followers of Jesus in New Testament Times," in *The Bible and Liberation: Political and Social Hermeneutics*, ed. Norman K. Gottwald and Richard A. Horsley, rev. ed. (Maryknoll, N.Y.: Orbis, 1993), pp. 453-61; Elizabeth A. Johnson, "Jesus the Wisdom of God: A Biblical Basis for a Non-androcentric Christology," *Ephemerides theologicae lovanienses* 61 (1985): 261-94; and Clarice J. Martin, "A Chamberlain's Journey and the Challenge of Interpretation for Liberation," in *The Bible and Liberation: Political and Social Hermeneutics*, ed. Norman K. Gottwald and Richard A. Horsley, rev. ed. (Maryknoll, N.Y.: Orbis, 1993), pp. 485-503. Johnson takes a somewhat different tack from Fiorenza in using the Sophia language to speak about Jesus rather than

the God to whom Jesus prayed, which is nearer the mark. Cf. Ben Witherington III, *Jesus the Sage: The Pilgrimage of Wisdom* (Minneapolis: Augsburg, Fortress, 1994).

[12]Fiorenza, *In Memory*, pp. 99-100.

[13]Ibid., pp. 101-2.

[14]Ibid., p. 102.

[15]See pp. 143-46.

[16]Almost all of the more radical proposals about Jesus have as their presupposition the assumption that there was a long and convoluted process of the transmission of the Jesus tradition, with considerable distortion along the way. This leads to the conclusion that much of the tradition must simply be rejected as later theologizing about Jesus that does not represent how the historical Jesus really spoke and acted, and that only in a distinct minority of passages do we see the real Jesus shining through, though of course no two scholars would agree on exactly which passages these are. See Fiorenza, *Jesus*, p. 79, where she reiterates her view that there was considerable distortion of the Jesus tradition as it was passed down.

[17]Judith Plaskow, "Blaming Jews for Inventing Patriarchy," *Lilith* 7 (1980): 11-12. The question is what one means by *radical*. If reforming existing views of marriage, divorce and singleness, and seeing as obsolescent laws about clean and unclean, and accepting women as disciples are radical, then Jesus was radical.

[18]See Ben Witherington III, *Women in the Ministry of Jesus* (Cambridge: Cambridge University Press, 1984).

[19]There is an attempt on the part of some radical scholars to "up the ante" and make Jesus appear more radical than he was, in the desire to make him "relevant" to today's world and forms of oppression.

[20]Fiorenza, *In Memory*, pp. 105-6.

[21]Ibid., p. 107.

[22]One may distinguish this from texts which specifically argue for a particular patriarchal point of view, such as Sirach 25:13—26:18, where women are stereotyped as either sluts or saints.

[23]Fiorenza, *In Memory*, pp. 108-9.

[24]Sometimes the feminist argument goes something like this: (1) there was a subculture in Israel that gave greater roles to women, and after the Exile this subculture even brought to the fore a form of goddess worship in Palestine, under the influence of Egyptian Wisdom (Ma'at, Isis) material; (2) this subculture, however, has by and large left no texts, and so we must argue that portions of Proverbs and other Wisdom texts reflect a repression of such a feminist strain, or a sanitizing of its content, conforming it to Yahwism; (3) Jesus revived or continued this feminist tradition.

The problem with this kind of argument is that it requires a lot of mirror-reading, by which I mean that when one sees polemics in the text, one then assumes that the opposite view was being espoused by someone in that context. It also requires reading between the lines of patriarchal texts and is otherwise largely an argument from silence. This is too tenuous a foundation on which to base a whole theory of the development of early Jewish culture. See chapter one of Witherington, *Jesus the Sage*.

[25]Fiorenza, *In Memory*, p. 113.

[26]See Ben Witherington III, *Women in the Earliest Churches* (Cambridge: Cambridge University Press, 1988), chap. 1.

[27]As Craig A. Evans suggests, the provenance of the book of Judith seems to be Palestinian and may reflect the period of the Maccabees, in which case it may even come from the

second century B.C. Cf. Evans, *Non-canonical Writings and New Testament Interpretation* (Peabody, Mass.: Hendrickson, 1992), p. 12.

[28]Notice that Judith is scrupulous in keeping the food laws (Judith 12:2).

[29]Fiorenza, *In Memory*, p. 118.

[30]Ibid., p. 119.

[31]Compare ibid., pp. 120-21.

[32]This text is so important for her argument that she uses it several times. Ibid., p. 121 and pp. 143-45.

[33]See discussion in Witherington, *Women in the Ministry of Jesus*, pp. 32-35.

[34]Cf. Fiorenza, *In Memory*, p. 143.

[35]The relevant commentaries refer to this practice as *beena* marriage, a practice known in antiquity.

[36]In a way Crossan does not; cf. pp. 68-70 above.

[37]Fiorenza, *In Memory*, p. 145.

[38]See pp. 16ff. above on Jesus' travels in Galilee.

[39]Cf. Fiorenza, *In Memory*, p. 146.

[40]Ibid.

[41]Ibid., p. 147.

[42]See Elisabeth Schüssler Fiorenza, "You Are Not to Be Called Father," in *The Bible and Liberation: Political and Social Hermeneutics*, ed. Norman K. Gottwald and Richard A. Horsley, rev. ed. (Maryknoll, N.Y.: Orbis, 1993), pp. 462-84.

[43]Fiorenza, *In Memory*, p. 150.

[44]Ibid., p. 151.

[45]There is simply no plausibility in the argument that this material could be late. For one thing the Corban matter presupposes the existence of the temple on an ongoing basis. For another, we have no evidence whatsoever that early Christians were interested in the Corban issue. This material must surely go back to Jesus. Cf. Witherington, *Women in the Ministry of Jesus*, pp. 12-13. There is another text that shows Jesus affirms this part of the Ten Commandments, Mark 10:19 and parallels, always of course with the proviso that the family of faith comes first and is primary.

[46]Fiorenza, *In Memory*, p. 148.

[47]Ibid.

[48]See Witherington, *Jesus the Sage*, chap. 1.

[49]Fiorenza, *In Memory*, p. 132.

[50]It is possible that this saying also refers to Jesus, especially in view of the reference to sending the apostles out.

[51]See pp. 145-51 on Horsley.

[52]Elisabeth Schüssler Fiorenza, *Jesus: Miriam's Child, Sophia's Prophet: Critical Issues in Feminist Christology* (New York: Continuum, 1994). In an interview at the time of publication, Fiorenza expressed displeasure with the fact that the publisher insisted on having Jesus as the leading word in the title, whereas she wanted to place the emphasis on his roles as child and prophet, with the stress on God as Sophia.

[53]Fiorenza, *Jesus*, p. 79.

[54]See pp. 58ff. above.

[55]Something Fiorenza wrongly accuses me of denying. See Fiorenza, *Jesus*, pp. 80-81.

[56]Ibid., pp. 158-59, and the notes to these pages.

[57]See the presentation of John Meier's views on Thomas, pp. 199-202.

[58]See Fiorenza, *Jesus*, pp. 139-43, especially p. 143 and the notes.

59Ibid., p. 161.

60Ibid.

61Ibid., p. 162, on "our own experiences and theological struggles."

62See my discussion of this matter in Ben Witherington III, "Three Modern Faces of Wisdom," *Ashland Theological Seminary Journal* 25 (1993): 96-122. It is notable that Fiorenza endorses various modern attempts at sophialogies, in particular those in *Wisdom's Feast*, which I have critiqued in the article just cited.

63Fiorenza, *Jesus*, p. 157, emphasis mine, and p. 162.

64Ibid., p. 86.

65Ibid., pp. 87-88.

66Ibid., p. 90.

67Ibid., p. 89.

68Ibid., p. 91.

69Ibid., pp. 92-93. Here she is partially following the logic of the Jewish scholar Ellis Rivkin. See his article "What Crucified Jesus?" in *Jesus' Jewishness: Exploring the Place of Jesus in Early Judaism*, ed. James H. Charlesworth (New York: Crossroad, 1991), pp. 226-57.

70See Ben Witherington III, *The Christology of Jesus* (Philadelphia: Fortress, 1990), pp. 101-4.

71Fiorenza, *Jesus*, p. 96.

72I would quite agree that Jesus did not intend to institute a gender-based hierarchical structure of leadership among his followers, but this does not mean that he was an advocate of modern egalitarianism.

73Fiorenza, *Jesus*, p. 133.

74Ibid., pp. 134-39.

75Ibid., p. 135.

76Ibid., p. 137.

77Ibid., p. 135.

78"The theological discourses on Sophia speak positively about Israel's God in the language of their own Egyptian-Hellenistic culture." Ibid., p. 137.

79Ibid., p. 139.

80See my discussion in Witherington, *Jesus the Sage*, pp. 249-333, on both these sources.

81Fiorenza, *Jesus*, pp. 140-43.

82It may be true, as Fiorenza urges, following Horsley, that this is a lament of Galilean people against the corrupt governing authorities in Jerusalem (*Jesus*, p. 142), but that would necessarily include and may especially refer to the Jewish authorities.

83See my discussion, pp. 185-94 below.

84See Witherington, *Christology of Jesus*, pp. 49-50.

85See Bruce M. Metzger's *A Textual Commentary on the Greek New Testament* (New York: United Bible Societies, 1971), p. 30.

86Fiorenza, *Jesus*, p. 143.

87Ibid., pp. 145-46, following the "Isis-gesis" of S. Schroer.

88See Fiorenza, *Jesus*, pp. 145-46.

89The reader wanting a more detailed presentation of this proposal should see Witherington, *Jesus the Sage*, pp. 117-208.

90For example, in the sapiential work of Ben Sira, the sage says he will pour out his teaching like prophecy (24:33) and will draw on prophetic material (39:1). In Wisdom of Solomon 7:27 the Spirit of Wisdom is said to make a person a prophet when it passes into a human soul. There is also the later Talmudic saying that God took prophecy from the prophets and gave it to the sages (*b. B. Bat.* 12a).

91See pp. 180-81 above.

92On Sanders, Horsley, Fiorenza and others see pp. 116-70.

93See discussion in Witherington, *Christology of Jesus*, pp. 49-50.

94See pp. 185ff.

95See Witherington, *Christology of Jesus*, pp. 227-28.

96Cf. pp. 187-88.

97See discussion in Witherington, *Jesus the Sage*, pp. 52-74.

98Ibid., pp. 3-74.

99See Larry W. Hurtado, *One God, One Lord: Early Christian Devotion and Ancient Jewish Monotheism* (Philadelphia: Fortress, 1988), pp. 17-92.

100Witherington, *Jesus the Sage*.

101Witherington, *Christology of Jesus*, pp. 221-28.

102Note that even in Daniel 7 the phrase *kingdom of God* does not occur as it does in Wisdom of Solomon 10:10.

103See Witherington, *Jesus the Sage*, pp. 143-45.

104See p. 174 for other suggestions.

105A more detailed and lengthy presentation of this proposal may be seen in Witherington, *Jesus the Sage*, pp. 1-208. There also I hope I have laid to rest the suggestion that Jesus should be seen as a Gentile-like (Cynic) sage.

Chapter 8: Jesus: Marginal Jew or Jewish Messiah?

1Markus Bockmuehl, *This Jesus: Martyr, Lord, Messiah* (Edinburgh: T & T Clark, 1994), pp. 5-6.

2I am referring to Evan Powell's novel approach in *The Unfinished Gospel: Notes on the Quest for the Historical Jesus* (Westlake Village, Calif.: Symposium Books, 1994). Perhaps the strongest of his arguments is the case he makes for Matthew being the latest of the Gospels, and some of his arguments against the existence of Q deserve careful scrutiny.

3John P. Meier, *A Marginal Jew: Rethinking the Historical Jesus*, vol. 1, *The Roots of the Problem and Person* (New York: Doubleday, 1991); N. T. Wright, *Christian Origins and the Question of God*, vol. 1, *The New Testament and the People of God* (Minneapolis: Fortress, 1992). As we shall see, Meier's discussion of prolegomena issues provides fewer surprises than Wright's in some respects. Both, however, are quite convinced that it is possible through careful study to get at the historical Jesus and properly locate him in his historical, social and theological context.

4See Marion L. Soards's review, "Recent Works in New Testament Studies," *Circuit Rider* 18, no. 7 (1994): 11-12. See also the appreciative review of Meier's first volume as well as of my *Jesus the Sage* by Robert W. Yarbrough, "Modern Wise Men Encounter Jesus," *Christianity Today* 38 (December 12, 1994): 38-45.

5Meier, *Marginal Jew*, 1:7.

6Ibid., p. 8.

7Ibid.

8Ibid., p. 9.

9Ibid., pp. 24-25.

10See ibid., pp. 26-27.

11See ibid., p. 45.

12Ibid., p. 43.

13See discussion in Ben Witherington III, *The Christology of Jesus* (Philadelphia: Fortress, 1990), pp. 3-7.

14Meier admits that Paul did not feel free to create teachings of Jesus and put them in his mouth (Meier, *Marginal Jew*, 1:46). But if one as creative and as much of a charismatic authority figure as Paul did not feel free to do this, even though he claimed to be a prophet and to have the Spirit of God within him (cf. 1 Cor 7:40; 14:19, 31, 32, 37), it is difficult to believe that other early Christians felt they had such freedom.

[15]See Meier, *Marginal Jew*, 1:60-61.

[16]Ibid., pp. 89-111.

[17]Ibid., pp. 116-66.

[18]Ibid., p. 118.

[19]Ibid., pp. 126-30. Especially notable is the hermeneutic in *Thomas* whereby anything in the Jesus tradition that is too clear or univocal or with too particular an application is omitted, since *Thomas* is meant to be a collection of Jesus' secret, esoteric and eternal teachings. So ibid., p. 133. Meier's comments on *Thomas* continue throughout the two volumes; cf. for example 1:140-41 and 2:206 n. 117.

[20]Meier, *Marginal Jew*, 1:134-37.

[21]Ibid., pp. 167-95.

[22]Ibid., p. 173.

[23]Ibid., p. 177.

[24]Ibid., pp. 198-99.

[25]Interestingly, even so conservative a Protestant New Testament scholar as George E. Ladd believed that Jesus had already ascended prior to the resurrection appearances. This in turn meant that the event that came to be called the ascension was simply a phenomenological occurrence as a concession to the disciples' perspective. Cf. George E. Ladd, *A Theology of the New Testament* (Grand Rapids, Mich.: Eerdmans, 1974).

[26]See Witherington, *Christology of Jesus*, passim.

[27]The third volume is not yet finished as I write.

[28]Already we have over 1,500 pages in just the first two volumes. The conclusions are most conveniently found in *Marginal Jew*, 2:1039-47.

[29]Like many scholars, Meier does not find a lot of historical substance in the birth narratives in regard to the place of Jesus' birth and its attendant circumstances.

[30]Meier, *Marginal Jew*, 2:1039.

[31]This is the juncture at which the first volume concludes.

[32]Meier, *Marginal Jew*, 2:1041.

[33]Ibid.

[34]Ibid., p. 1042.

[35]Ibid., p. 1043.

[36]Ibid., p. 1045.

[37]Ibid., p. 1046.

[38]This is especially clear from his final footnote in ibid., p. 1049 n. 8.

[39]On all this see Meier, *Marginal Jew*, 1:372-433.

[40]See ibid., p. 402.

[41]On all this, cf. Harold W. Hoehner, *Chronological Aspects of the Life of Christ* (Grand Rapids, Mich.: Zondervan, 1977).

[42]Meier, *Marginal Jew*, 2:3.

[43]See ibid., pp. 291-317.

[44]Ibid., pp. 34-36.

[45]Ibid., p. 124.

[46]Cf. ibid., p. 150, and my discussion in Witherington, *Christology of Jesus*, pp. 73-81.

[47]Meier, *Marginal Jew*, 2:147. I have argued for this in *Jesus the Sage: The Pilgrimage of Wisdom*

(Minneapolis: Fortress, 1994), pp. 155-201.

48See Meier, *Marginal Jew*, 2:153.

49Ibid., p. 179.

50See ibid., p. 269.

51Ibid., p. 287. Meier, however, offers a critique of other aspects of Chilton's approach.

52Ibid., p. 331.

53Ibid., p. 337.

54Ibid., pp. 338-39.

55Ibid., p. 6 and pp. 336-51 and the notes there.

56See Ben Witherington III, *Jesus, Paul and the End of the World* (Downers Grove, Ill.: InterVarsity Press, 1992), pp. 36-48 and notes, and my article "Transfigured Understanding: A Critical Note on Mk. 9:2-13 as a Parousia View," *Ashland Theological Seminary Journal* 24 (1992): 88-91.

57See Meier, *Marginal Jew*, 2:344-48.

58See E. P. Sanders, *Jewish Law from Jesus to the Mishnah* (Philadelphia: Trinity, 1990), pp. 21ff.

59See Meier, *Marginal Jew*, 2:731-33, n. 20-24.

60Ibid.

61Ibid., 2:11.

62See the lengthy discussions in ibid., pp. 509-1038, a good half of the book.

63Ibid., pp. 537-52 and the notes that follow.

64See discussion in Witherington, *Christology of Jesus*, pp. 156-60.

65See Meier, *Marginal Jew*, 2:546-47.

66Ibid., pp. 550.

67One of the problems with Twelftree's analysis (cf. pp. 112-14 above) is that he thinks it is necessary to associate Jewish exorcisms with magic and therefore sees Jesus using some "magical" conventions in the exorcism stories.

68See Witherington, *Christology of Jesus*, pp. 157-67.

69Meier has said that volume three is, in all likelihood, some time off from being published.

70On the use of the term *Christ* in the Gospels see Larry W. Hurtado, "Christ," in *Dictionary of Jesus and the Gospels*, ed. Joel B. Green, Scot McKnight and I. Howard Marshall (Downers Grove, Ill.: InterVarsity Press, 1992), pp. 106-17, and Ben Witherington III, "Christ," in *Dictionary of Paul and His Letters*, ed. Gerald F. Hawthorne, Ralph P. Martin and Daniel G. Reid (Downers Grove, Ill.: InterVarsity Press, 1993), pp. 95-100.

71See James H. Charlesworth, "From Messianology to Christology: Problems and Prospects," in *The Messiah*, ed. James H. Charlesworth (Minneapolis: Fortress, 1992), pp. 3-35.

72Jacob Neusner, William S. Green and Ernest Frerichs, eds., *Judaisms and Their Messiahs at the Turn of the Era* (Cambridge: Cambridge University Press, 1987).

73See Marinus de Jonge, "The Use of the Word 'Anointed' in the Time of Jesus," *Novum Testamentum* 8 (1966): 132-48, and "The Earliest Christian Use of *Christos*: Some Suggestions," *New Testament Studies* 32 (1986): 321-43.

74All of this is laid out in Charlesworth, "From Messianology to Christology."

75See his article, " 'Messianic' Figures and Movements in First-Century Palestine," in *The Messiah*, ed. James H. Charlesworth (Minneapolis: Fortress, 1992), pp. 276-95, here pp. 276-77. It is Horsley's view that Jesus was not much, if at all, interested in eschatology, nor does he think most other early Jews were either. This radical view hardly explains texts like *Psalms of Solomon* or *1 Enoch*, or some of the material from Qumran where eschatology was a lively part of the discussion. See Charlesworth, "From Messianology to Christology," pp. 7ff.

76Peter Stuhlmacher, *Jesus of Nazareth—Christ of Faith* (Peabody, Mass.: Hendrickson, 1993), pp.

6-7.

[77]See above pp. 119-200. It does appear, from my conversations with Meier, that he will argue in his third volume that Jesus did at least implicitly claim some of the things the church later acclaimed him to be.

[78]Stuhlmacher, *Jesus of Nazareth*, pp. 12-13.

[79]Ibid., pp. 19-21.

[80]Ibid., pp. 22-23.

[81]See especially Otto Betz, *Jesus: Der Messias Israels: Aufsätze zur biblischen Theologie* (Tübingen: J. C. B. Mohr, 1987).

[82]I. Howard Marshall, *The Origins of New Testament Christology* (Downers Grove, Ill.: InterVarsity Press, 1976) pp. 63-96; Petr Pokorný, *The Genesis of Christology* (Edinburgh: T & T Clark, 1987), pp. 38-59.

[83]See Dunn's helpful article "Messianic Ideas and Their Influence on the Jesus of History," in *The Messiah*, ed. James H. Charlesworth (Minneapolis: Fortress, 1992), pp. 365-81.

[84]Ibid., p. 367. Having examined Old Testament prophecies, the Qumran data (such as 1QSa 2.12, 14, 20 and 1QS 9.11) and *Pss. of Sol.* 17—18, Dunn says: "We may conclude that these passages must have nurtured a fairly vigorous and sustained hope of a royal messiah within several at least of the various subgroups of Israel at the time of Jesus, and that that hope was probably fairly widespread at the popular level (such being the symbolic power of kingship in most societies then and since)."

[85]Ibid., p. 373.

[86]Ibid., p. 375.

[87]Ibid., pp. 376-81.

[88]Ibid., pp. 380-81.

[89]See pp. 197ff. above.

[90]Marinus de Jonge, *Jesus, the Servant Messiah* (New Haven, Conn.: Yale University Press, 1991).

[91]Ibid., p. 67.

[92]Ibid., p. 72.

[93]Ibid. This is a rather pointed rebuttal of the view that makes too much of the resurrection appearances and not enough of the ministry and (implicit) claims of Jesus.

[94]Ibid., pp. 74-75.

[95]See Witherington, *Christology of Jesus*, pp. 221-28, and pp. 185ff. above.

[96]De Jonge, *Jesus, the Servant Messiah*, p. 75.

[97]Bockmuehl, *This Jesus*, p. 1.

[98]See ibid., pp. 42-59 and pp. 164-65.

[99]N. T. Wright, *Who Was Jesus?* (Grand Rapids, Mich.: Eerdmans, 1992).

[100]Ibid., p. 95.

[101]Wright, *New Testament and the People of God*.

[102]Wright's critique of form criticism is also significant, as is his insistence on critical realism. Both of these factors lead him to take a different approach from Crossan and others who see a multilayered Gospel text and are skeptical about the possibility of any sort of objectivity. Cf. chapter 14 of Wright, *New Testament and the People of God*.

[103]See ibid., p. 225.

[104]Ibid.

[105]Ibid., p. 226.

[106]Ibid.

[107]Ibid., p. 227.

[108]So ibid., p. 243.

[109]Ibid., p. 246.
[110]Ibid., pp. 252-59.
[111]Ibid., p. 259.
[112]See the discussion of my work in chapter seven.
[113]Wright, *New Testament and the People of God*, p. 259.
[114]Ibid., p. 260.
[115]Ibid., pp. 262-63.
[116]Ibid., p. 265.
[117]The notion of corporate personality goes beyond the idea of someone who is a representative or agent of a group. Thus, for instance, Wright will talk about Jesus acting as Israel, not merely acting for Israel. In the notion of corporate personality the many are included in or incorporated into the one. So, for instance, with Adam the idea would be that the seed of Adam are (seminally) present in Adam so that when Adam acts, his descendants have also acted. This idea has rightly been questioned by various scholars, especially Old Testament scholars such as J. Rogerson. It seems to involve a reading of the idea of "being in Christ" (i.e., believers incorporated into the divine and omnipresent Christ) back into Old Testament notions about Israel and its representatives or agents.
[118]Wright, *New Testament and the People of God*, p. 268.
[119]Ibid., p. 269.
[120]Ibid., p. 272, emphasis mine.
[121]Ibid., p. 275, emphasis mine.
[122]Ibid., p. 278.
[123]Ibid., p. 285.
[124]Ibid., pp. 285-86.
[125]See N. T. Wright, "Putting Paul Together Again," in *Pauline Theology*, ed. Jouette M. Bassler (Minneapolis: Fortress, 1991), 1:183-211.
[126]See pp. 93ff.
[127]Wright, *New Testament and the People of God*, p. 300.
[128]Ibid.
[129]Ibid., p. 310.
[130]Ibid., p. 309.
[131]Ibid., pp. 312-314.
[132]See my discussion in Witherington, *Christology of Jesus*, pp. 236-43.
[133]Wright, *New Testament and the People of God*, pp. 315-16.
[134]So ibid., p. 319, following W. Horbury.
[135]Ibid., p. 332.
[136]See ibid., pp. 335-36.
[137]Ibid., p. 338.
[138]Wright, *Who Was Jesus?* p. 96.
[139]Richard A. Burridge, *What Are the Gospels? A Comparison with Greco-Roman Biography* (Cambridge: Cambridge University Press, 1992).
[140]See my forthcoming commentary on Acts, due to be published by Eerdmans in 1997.
[141]Wright, *Who Was Jesus?* p. 97.
[142]Ibid., p. 98.
[143]Ibid., p. 99.
[144]Ibid.
[145]Ibid. This would presumably include the Pharisees in particular.
[146]Ibid., p. 101.

147Ibid., p. 102.

148N. T. Wright, "Jesus, Israel and the Cross," in *Society of Biblical Literature 1985 Seminar Papers*, ed. Kent Harold Richards (Atlanta: Scholars Press, 1985), pp. 75-95; and "Jerusalem in the New Testament," in *Jerusalem Past and Present in the Purposes of God*, ed. P. W. L. Walker (Cambridge: Tyndale House, 1992), pp. 53-77.

149See Wright, "Jesus, Israel and the Cross," pp. 78-81.

150See Wright, "Jerusalem," p. 60.

151Wright, "Jesus, Israel and the Cross," p. 84.

152See Wright, "Jerusalem," p. 63: "So Jesus went to his death, convinced within his own first-century Jewish worldview that Israel's destiny had devolved upon him and that he represented the true Israel in the eyes of God. His death would therefore be the means of drawing to a climax the wrath of God against the nation, forging a way through wrath and out the other side; as a result, all who wanted to do so could follow his way, be joined to his people, and find rescue from the great and imminent disaster."

153Ibid.

154Wright even suggests that Jesus identifies himself with sinful Israel and so contracts her uncleanness by fellowshiping with the likes of Zacchaeus, and later identifies himself with the Zealots or revolutionaries by dying with two of them on crosses outside Jerusalem. Cf. Wright, "Jesus, Israel and the Cross," pp. 83ff. Later, however, in the same essay (p. 93) he suggests that Jesus died as Israel's representative "believing that if Israel's death could be died by her representative she might not need to die it herself."

155Ibid., p. 88.

156Cf. Wright, "Jerusalem," p. 60.

157See at length Maurice Casey, *Son of Man: The Interpretation and Influence of Daniel 7* (London: S.P.C.K., 1979).

158See Witherington, *Jesus, Paul and the End of the World*, pp. 152-69. Equally creative but questionable is Wright's suggestion that Jesus saw Daniel's fourth beast as Jerusalem and the temple hierarchy taking on the role of Babylon, Edom and Antiochus Epiphanes (with Caiaphas playing the starring role). See Wright's "Jerusalem," p. 62.

159Wright, "Jesus, Israel and the Cross," p. 87.

160Wright, "Jerusalem," p. 58. Wright is following Borg here to some degree. In these table-fellowship activities Jesus is seen by Wright as acting as the replacement of the temple. This raises an interesting point, for if this was true of Jesus, why could it not equally be said of the Baptist, who seems to have offered forgiveness with baptism, and without going to Jerusalem and sacrificing? It seems better to argue that while both John and Jesus saw coming judgment on Israel and the destruction of the temple, they saw something else other than another temple and its activities as replacing the Herodian temple. Perhaps it was the coming One who would bring the final word. It seems plausible to say as Wright does that Jesus as a Galilean saw in the downfall of Jerusalem and the temple the downfall of both the Judean domination of Judaism and the aristocratic rich (including Sadducees) who benefited from the temple cultus and its trade.

161Wright, *Who Was Jesus?* p. 103.

162See pp. 185ff. and pp. 197ff.

163See Eduard Schweizer, *Jesus Christ: The Man from Nazareth and the Exalted Lord* (Macon, Ga.: Mercer University Press, 1987), p. 86.

Chapter 9: The Journey's End
1See pp. 19ff. above.

[2]N. T. Wright, *Who Was Jesus?* (Grand Rapids, Mich.: Eerdmans, 1992), p. 271.

[3]Raymond E. Brown, *The Death of the Messiah*, 2 vols. (New York: Doubleday, 1994), and see the review by Donald Senior, "Jesus' Passion and the Message of the Gospels," *Christian Century,* October 5, 1994, pp. 900-904. A bit more will be said about this in the epilogue, pp. 249ff.

[4]See pp. 95ff.

[5]For further discussion see Ben Witherington III, *The Christology of Jesus* (Philadelphia: Fortress, 1990), and *Jesus the Sage: The Pilgrimage of Wisdom* (Minneapolis: Fortress, 1994).

Epilogue

[1]Raymond E. Brown, *The Death of the Messiah*, 2 vols. (New York: Doubleday, 1994).

[2]Notice the direction of Donald Senior's review, "Jesus' Passion and the Message of the Gospels," *Christian Century,* October 5, 1994, pp. 900-904, which focuses mainly on the comments on the historical data.

[3]Brown also believes that in many cases one cannot trace back a tradition to a situation in the life of Jesus.

[4]Brown's final judgment seems to be that what was a hearing in actuality is narrated as a more formal trial in the Gospels.

[5]For instance as Crossan and various Q scholars do.

[6]For example, of the sort Horsely has in mind, cf. pp. 145ff. above.

Postscript

[1]Including my own *Jesus the Seer and the Progress of Prophecy*, forthcoming from Fortress.

[2]Marcus Borg, ed., *Jesus at 2000* (Boulder, Colo.: Westview Press, 1996).

[3]Marcus Borg, "From Galilean Jew to the Face of God: The Pre-Easter and Post-Easter Jesus," in *Jesus at 2000*, p. 5.

[4]Borg, "From Galilean Jew," p. 8.

[5]Richard A. Burridge, *What Are the Gospels? A Comparison with Greco-Roman Biography* (Cambridge: Cambridge University Press, 1992).

[6]We might also ask why Borg claims that the notion of original sin does not show up until the fourth century A.D. (p. 19). Surely the roots and a good deal of the substance of the idea can be found in the Pauline epistles, especially Romans 1—7, and particularly in Romans 5:12-21. It is, however, characteristic of Borg and Crossan that they wish to bracket out Paul from their discussions of what earliest Christianity and what Christ were really like.

[7]John Dominic Crossan, "Jesus and the Kingdom: Itinerants and Householders in Earliest Christianity," in *Jesus at 2000*, p. 32.

[8]Ibid., pp. 39-40.

[9]Ibid., pp. 40-41.

[10]Ibid., pp. 46-48.

[11]Alan F. Segal, "Jesus and First Century Judaism," in *Jesus at 2000*, p. 59.

[12]Ibid., p. 57.

[13]Luke Timothy Johnson, *The Real Jesus: The Misguided Quest for the Historical Jesus and the Truth of the Traditional Gospels* (San Francisco: HarperSanFrancisco, 1996).

[14]See ibid., p. 69.

[15]See ibid., p. 160.

[16]See N. T. Wright, *Jesus and the Victory of God* (Minneapolis: Fortress, 1996), p. 9 n. 16.

[17]See ibid., p. 89 n. 24.

[18]Johnson, *Real Jesus*, pp. 175-77.

[19]Richard A. Horsley, *Galilee: History, Politics, People* (Valley Forge, Penn.: Trinity Press International, 1995).

[20]Richard A. Horsley, *Archaeology, History and Society in Galilee: The Social Context of Jesus and the Rabbis* (Valley Forge, Penn.: Trinity Press International, 1996).

[21]Horsley, *Galilee*, pp. 271-82.

[22]E. P. Sanders, *Judaism: Practice and Belief* (Philadelphia: Trinity Press International, 1992), pp. 166-67.

[23]Ibid., pp. 166-78.

[24]Sean Freyne, *Galilee from Alexander the Great to Hadrian* (Wilmington, Del.: Michael Glazier, 1980).

[25]Horsley, *Archaeology*, pp. 176-85.

[26]Ibid., p. 179.

[27]Ibid., p. 147.

[28]Ibid., pp. 142-49.

[29]Ibid., p. 181.

[30]Ibid., pp. 6-7.

[31]Ibid., p. 112.

[32]John Dominic Crossan, *Who Killed Jesus? Exposing the Roots of Anti-Semitism in the Gospel Story of the Death of Jesus* (San Francisco: HarperSanFrancisco, 1995), p. 214.

[33]John Dominic Crossan, *The Cross That Spoke* (San Francisco: Harper & Row, 1988).

[34]See the prologue and epilogue of this book.

[35]Crossan, *Who Killed Jesus?* p. 1.

[36]Ibid., p. 216.

[37]Ibid., p. 208.

[38]Ibid., p. 119: "If I can't persuade you in this chapter, I doubt if I can do it elsewhere."

[39]Ibid., p. 129.

[40]Ibid., p. 23.

[41]Ibid., pp. 196-97.

[42]Ibid., pp. 138-39.

[43]Ibid., p. 138.

[44]But see Ben Witherington, *John's Wisdom: A Commentary on the Fourth Gospel* (Louisville: Westminster John Knox, 1995), pp. 328-33.

[45]Crossan, *Who Killed Jesus?* p. 214.

[46]Robert W. Funk, *Honest to Jesus: Jesus for a New Millennium* (San Francisco: HarperSanFrancisco, 1996). It was a big year for Harper Jesus books.

[47]Ibid., p. 125.

[48]See Ben Witherington III, *Jesus the Sage: The Pilgrimage of Wisdom* (Minneapolis: Fortress, 1994), pp. 236-47.

[49]Funk, *Honest to Jesus*, p. 33.

[50]Ibid., p. 79.

[51]Ibid., pp. 143-216.

[52]Ibid., pp. 149-50.

[53]Ibid., p. 160.

[54]Ibid., p. 165.

[55]Ibid., p. 167.

[56]Ibid., p. 302.

[57]Ibid., p. 234.
[58]Ibid., p. 239.
[59]Ibid., p. 240.
[60]Ibid., p. 227.
[61]Ibid., pp. 226-30.
[62]Ibid., p. 238.
[63]Raymond Brown, *The Death of the Messiah*, 2 vols. (New York: Doubleday, 1994).
[64]Funk, *Honest to Jesus*, pp. 206, 273-74.
[65]Ibid., pp. 268-71.
[66]Ibid., p. 304.
[67]Ibid., pp. 3-6.
[68]Ibid., p. 300.
[69]Ibid., p. 258.
[70]On volume one, *The New Testament and the People of God*, see pp. 219-27 above.
[71]See, Wright, *Jesus and the Victory*, e.g, p. 361.
[72]Ibid., p. 652.
[73]Ibid., p. 653.
[74]See ibid., e.g., p. 170, p. 240 n. 159.
[75]Ibid., p. 281.
[76]But see ibid., pp. 186-96.
[77]See Ben Witherington III, *Jesus, Paul and the End of the World: A Comparative Study in New Testament Eschatology* (Downers Grove, Ill.: InterVarsity Press, 1992).
[78]See Wright, *Jesus and the Victory*, p. 280.

Bibliography

Bauckham, Richard. "Gospels (Apocryphal)." In *Dictionary of Jesus and the Gospels*, pp. 286-91. Edited by Joel B. Green, Scot McKnight and I. Howard Marshall. Downers Grove, Ill.: InterVarsity Press, 1992.

Betz, Otto. *Jesus: Der Messias Israels: Aufsätze zur biblischen Theologie*. Tübingen: Mohr, 1987.

Bockmuehl, Markus. *This Jesus: Martyr, Lord, Messiah*. Edinburgh: T & T Clark, 1994.

Borg, Marcus. *Conflict, Holiness and Politics in the Teachings of Jesus*. Lewiston, N.Y.: Mellen, 1984.

———. *Jesus: A New Vision*. San Francisco: HarperSanFrancisco, 1987.

———. "Jesus and Eschatology: A Reassessment." In *Images of Jesus Today*, pp. 42-67. Edited by James H. Charlesworth and W. P. Weaver. Valley Forge, Penn.: Trinity, 1994.

———. *Jesus in Contemporary Scholarship*. Valley Forge, Penn.: Trinity, 1994.

———. *Meeting Jesus Again for the First Time*. San Francisco: HarperSanFrancisco, 1994.

———. "An Orthodoxy Reconsidered: The-End-of-the-World-Jesus." In *The Glory of Christ in the New Testament*, pp. 207-17. Edited by L. D. Hurst and N. T. Wright. Oxford: Clarendon, 1987.

———. "The Palestinian Background for a Life of Jesus." In *The Search for Jesus: Modern Scholarship Looks at the Gospels*, pp. 37-57. Edited by Hershel Shanks. Washington, D.C.: Biblical Archaeology Review, 1994.

———. "Portraits of Jesus." In *The Search for Jesus: Modern Scholarship Looks at the Gospels*, pp. 83-103. Edited by Hershel Shanks. Washington, D.C.: Biblical Archaeology Review, 1994.

———, ed. *Jesus at 2000*. Boulder, Colo.: Westview Press, 1996.

Bornkamm, Günther. *Jesus of Nazareth*. New York: Harper, 1960.

Brown, Colin. "Historical Jesus, Quest of." In *Dictionary of Jesus and the Gospels*, pp. 326-41. Edited by Joel B. Green, Scot McKnight and I. Howard Marshall. Downers Grove, Ill.: InterVarsity Press, 1992.

Brown, Raymond E. *The Death of the Messiah*. 2 vols. New York: Doubleday, 1994.

———. "*The Gospel of Peter* and Canonical Gospel Priority." *New Testament Studies* 3

(1987): 321-43.

Bultmann, Rudolf. *Jesus and the Word.* New York: Scribner's, 1934.

Burridge, Richard A. *What Are the Gospels? A Comparison with Greco-Roman Biography.* Cambridge: Cambridge University Press, 1992.

Caird, George B. *Language and Imagery of the Bible.* Philadelphia: Westminster, 1980.

Casey, Maurice. *From Jewish Prophet to Gentile God: The Origins and Development of New Testament Christology.* Louisville, Ky.: Westminster/John Knox, 1991.

————. *Son of Man: The Interpretation and Influence of Daniel.* London: SPCK, 1980.

Charlesworth, James H. "From Messianology to Christology: Problems and Prospects." In *The Messiah,* pp. 3-35. Edited by James H. Charlesworth. Minneapolis: Augsburg Fortress, 1992.

————. "Jesus Research Expands with Chaotic Creativity." In *Images of Jesus Today,* pp. 1-41. Edited by James H. Charlesworth and Walter P. Weaver. Valley Forge, Penn.: Trinity, 1994.

Crossan, John Dominic. *The Cross That Spoke.* San Francisco: Harper & Row, 1988.

————. *Four Other Gospels.* Minneapolis: Winston, 1985.

————. *The Historical Jesus: The Life of a Mediterranean Jewish Peasant.* San Francisco: HarperSanFrancisco, 1991.

————. *Jesus: A Revolutionary Biography.* San Francisco: HarperSanFrancisco, 1994.

————. *Who Killed Jesus? Exposing the Roots of Anti-Semitism in the Gospel Story of the Death of Jesus.* San Francisco: HarperSanFrancisco, 1995.

Downing, F. Gerald. *Christ and the Cynics: Jesus and Other Radical Preachers in First Century Tradition.* Sheffield, U.K.: Sheffield Academic Press, 1988.

————. *Jesus and the Threat of Violence.* London: SCM, 1987.

Dunn, James D. G. *Christology in the Making.* Philadelphia: Westminster, 1980.

————. *Jesus and the Spirit.* Philadelphia: Westminster, 1975.

————. "Messianic Ideas and Their Influence on the Jesus of History." In *The Messiah,* pp. 365-81. Edited by James H. Charlesworth. Minneapolis: Augsburg Fortress, 1992.

Edwards, Douglas R. "The Socio-economic and Cultural Ethos in the First Century: Implications for the Nascent Jesus Movement." In *The Galilee in Late Antiquity,* pp 53-73. Edited by Lee I. Levine. Cambridge: Harvard University Press, 1992.

Evans, Craig A. *Jesus.* Grand Rapids, Mich.: Baker, 1992.

————. *Life of Jesus Research: An Annotated Bibliography.* Leiden: Brill, 1989.

————. *Non-canonical Writings and New Testament Interpretation.* Peabody, Mass.: Hendrickson, 1992.

Ferguson, Everett. *Backgrounds of Early Christianity.* Grand Rapids, Mich.: Eerdmans, 1987.

Fiorenza, Elisabeth Schüssler. *In Memory of Her: A Feminist Theological Reconstruction of Christian Origins.* New York: Crossroad, 1984.

————. *Jesus: Miriam's Child, Sophia's Prophet: Critical Issues in Feminist Christology.* New York: Continuum, 1994.

————. "You Are Not to Be Called Father." In *The Bible and Liberation: Political and Social Hermeneutics*, pp. 462-84. Edited by Norman K. Gottwald and Richard A. Horsley. Rev. ed. Maryknoll, N.Y.: Orbis, 1993.

Fitzmyer, Joseph A. *The Gospel of Luke I-IX*. Anchor Bible 28. New York: Doubleday, 1981.

Foerster, G. "The Ancient Synagogues of Galilee." In *The Galilee in Late Antiquity*, pp. 289-319. Edited by Lee I. Levine. Cambridge: Harvard University Press, 1992.

Freyne, Sean. "The Galileans in Light of Josephus' *Vita*." *New Testament Studies* 26 (1979-1980): 397-413.

————. *Galilee from Alexander the Great to Hadrian*. Wilmington, Del.: Glazier, 1980.

————. *Galilee, Jesus and the Gospels*. Philadelphia: Fortress, 1988.

————. "The Geography, Politics and Economics of Galilee." In *Studying the Historical Jesus: Evaluations of the State of Current Research*, pp. 75-122. Edited by Bruce Chilton and Craig A. Evans. Leiden: Brill, 1994.

————. "Urban-Rural Relationships in First Century Galilee." In *The Galilee in Late Antiquity*, pp. 75-94. Edited by Lee I. Levine. Cambridge: Harvard University Press, 1992.

Funk, Robert W. "Beyond Criticism in Quest of Literacy: The Parable of the Leaven." *Interpretation* 25 (1971): 149-70.

————. *Honest to Jesus: Jesus for a New Millennium*. San Francisco: HarperSanFrancisco, 1996.

Funk, Robert W., and Roy W. Hoover, eds. *The Five Gospels: The Search for the Authentic Words of Jesus*. New York: Macmillan, 1993.

Funk, Robert W., Bernard Brandon Scott and J. R. Butts, eds. *The Parables of Jesus: Red Letter Edition*. Sonoma, Calif.: Polebridge, 1988.

Funk, Robert W., and Mahlon H. Smith, eds. *The Gospel of Mark: Red Letter Edition*. Sonoma, Calif.: Polebridge, 1991.

Goodman, Martin. *The Ruling Class of Judaea*. Cambridge: Cambridge University Press, 1987.

Hartley, Leslie P. *The Go-Between*. New York: Stein and Day, 1953.

Harvey, Anthony E. *Jesus and the Constraints of History*. Philadelphia: Westminster, 1982.

Hays, Richard B. "The Corrected Jesus." *First Things* 43 (May 1994): 43-48.

Hengel, Martin. *The Hellenization of Judea in the First Century After Christ*. Philadelphia: Trinity, 1989.

————. *Judaism and Hellenism*. 2 vols. Philadelphia: Fortress, 1974.

————. *Die Zeloten*. 2d ed. Leiden: Brill, 1976.

Hoehner, Harold W. *Chronological Aspects of the Life of Christ*. Grand Rapids, Mich.: Zondervan, 1977.

Horsley, Richard A. *Archaeology, History and Society in Galilee: The Social Context of Jesus and the Rabbis*. Valley Forge, Penn.: Trinity Press International, 1996.

————. *Galilee: History, Politics, People*. Valley Forge, Penn.: Trinity Press International,

1995.

———. *Jesus and the Spiral of Violence*. San Francisco: HarperSanFrancisco, 1987.

———. *The Liberation of Christmas: The Infancy Narratives in Social Context*. New York: Crossroad, 1989.

———. "Like One of the Prophets of Old: Two Types of Popular Prophets at the Time of Jesus." *Catholic Biblical Quarterly* 47 (1985): 435-63.

———. " 'Messianic' Figures and Movements in First-Century Palestine." In *The Messiah*, pp. 276-95. Edited by James H. Charlesworth. Minneapolis: Augsburg Fortress, 1992.

———. *Sociology and the Jesus Movement*. New York: Crossroad, 1989.

Horsley, Richard A., and John S. Hanson. *Bandits, Prophets and Messiahs: Popular Movements of the Time of Jesus*. Minneapolis: Winston, 1985.

Hurtado, Larry W. "Christ." In *Dictionary of Jesus and the Gospels*, pp. 106-17. Edited by Joel B. Green, Scot McKnight and I. Howard Marshall. Downers Grove, Ill.: InterVarsity Press, 1992.

———. *One God, One Lord: Early Christian Devotion and Ancient Jewish Monotheism*. Grand Rapids, Mich.: Eerdmans, 1988.

Johnson, Elizabeth A. "Jesus the Wisdom of God: A Biblical Basis for a Non-androcentric Christology." *Ephemerides theologicae lovanienses* 61 (1985): 261-94.

Johnson, Luke Timothy. *The Real Jesus: The Misguided Quest for the Historical Jesus and the Truth of the Traditional Gospels*. San Francisco: HarperSanFrancisco, 1996.

Jonge, Marinus de. "The Earliest Christian Use of *Christos*: Some Suggestions." *New Testament Studies* 32 (1986): 321-43.

———. *Jesus, the Servant Messiah*. New Haven, Conn.: Yale University Press, 1991.

———. "The Use of the Word 'Anointed' in the Time of Jesus." *Novum Testamentum* 8 (1966): 132-48.

Kähler, Martin. *The So-Called Historical Jesus and the Historic Biblical Christ*. Philadelphia: Fortress, 1964.

Käsemann, Ernst. *Essays on New Testament Themes*. London: SCM, 1964.

Kaylor, R. David. *Jesus the Prophet: His Vision of the Kingdom on Earth*. Louisville, Ky.: Westminster/John Knox, 1994.

Keck, Leander E. "The Second Coming of the Liberal Jesus?" *Christian Century* 111, no. 24 (1994): 784-87.

Kee, Howard Clark. "The Changing Meaning of Synagogue: A Response to Richard Oster." *New Testament Studies* 40 (1992): 281-83.

———. "The Transformation of the Synagogue after 70 C.E.: Its Import for Early Christianity." *New Testament Studies* 36 (1990): 1-24.

Kloppenborg, John S., et al. *Q—Thomas Reader: The Gospels Before the Gospels*. Sonoma, Calif.: Polebridge, 1990.

Ladd, George E. *A Theology of the New Testament*. Grand Rapids, Mich.: Eerdmans, 1974.

Lampe, G. W. H. *A Patristic Lexicon*. Oxford: Clarendon, 1961.

Levine, Lee I. "The Second Temple Synagogue: The Formative Years." In *The Synagogue in Late Antiquity*, pp. 201-22. Edited by Lee I. Levine. Philadelphia: American School of Oriental Research, 1987.

Mack, Burton L. *A Myth of Innocence: Mark and Christian Origins*. Philadelphia: Fortress, 1988.

Malina, Bruce. *Calling Jesus Names*. Sonoma, Calif.: Polebridge, 1993.

———. *The New Testament World: Insights from Cultural Anthropology*. Louisville, Ky.: Westminster/John Knox, 1993.

Marshall, I. Howard. *The Origins of New Testament Christology*. Downers Grove, Ill.: InterVarsity Press, 1976.

Meier, John P. *A Marginal Jew: Rethinking the Historical Jesus*. Vol. 1, *Origins of the Problem and the Person*. New York: Doubleday, 1991.

———. *A Marginal Jew: Rethinking the Historical Jesus*. Vol. 2, *Mentor, Message, Miracle*. New York: Doubleday, 1994.

———. "Reflections on Jesus-of-History Research Today." In *Jesus' Jewishness: Exploring the Place of Jesus in Early Judaism*, pp. 84-107. Edited by James H. Charlesworth. New York: Crossroad, 1991.

Metzger, Bruce M. *A Textual Commentary on the Greek New Testament*. New York: United Bible Societies, 1971.

Meyer, Ben F. *The Aims of Jesus*. London: SCM, 1979.

Meyers, Eric M. "Galilean Regionalism as a Factor in Historical Reconstruction." *Bulletin of the American Schools of Oriental Research* 221 (1976): 93-101.

Millar, Fergus G. B. *The Roman Near East 31 B.C.—A.D. 337*. Cambridge: Harvard University Press, 1993.

Neill, Stephen, and Tom Wright. *The Interpretation of the New Testament, 1861-1986*. Rev. ed. Oxford: Oxford University Press, 1988.

Neusner, Jacob, William S. Green and Ernest Frerichs, eds. *Judaisms and Their Messiahs at the Turn of the Era*. Cambridge: Cambridge University Press, 1987.

Newsome, James D. *Greeks, Romans, Jews: Currents of Culture and Belief in the New Testament World*. Philadelphia: Trinity, 1992.

Oster, Richard E. "Supposed Anachronism in Luke-Acts' Use of *Sunagoge*: A Rejoinder to H. C. Kee." *New Testament Studies* 39 (1993): 178-208.

Overman, J. Andrew. "Deciphering the Origins of Christianity." *Interpretation* 44 (April 1990): 193-95.

Palmer, Parker J. *To Know As We Are Known: Education as Spiritual Journey*. San Francisco: HarperSanFrancisco, 1993.

Patterson, Stephen J. *The Gospel of Thomas and Jesus*. Sonoma, Calif.: Polebridge, 1993.

Pokorný, Petr. *The Genesis of Christology*. Edinburgh: T & T Clark, 1987.

Pope-Levison, Priscilla, and John R. Levison. *Jesus in Global Contexts*. Louisville, Ky.: Westminster/John Knox, 1993.

Porter, Stanley E. "Jesus and the Use of Greek in Galilee." In *Studying the Historical Jesus*, pp. 123-54. Edited by Bruce Chilton and Craig A. Evans. Leiden: Brill, 1994.

Powell, Evan. *The Unfinished Gospel: Notes on the Quest for the Historical Jesus.* Westlake Village, Calif.: Symposium Books, 1994.

Rappoport, Uriel. "How Anti-Roman Was the Galilee?" In *The Galilee in Late Antiquity,* pp. 95-102. Edited by Lee I. Levine. New York: Jewish Theological Seminary, 1992.

Riches, John K. *The World of Jesus: First-Century Judaism in Crisis.* Cambridge: Cambridge University Press, 1990.

Riesner, Rainer. *Jesus als Lehrer.* Tübingen: Mohr, 1981.

Rivkin, Ellis. *What Crucified Jesus?* Nashville: Abingdon, 1984.

Robinson, James. M. *A New Quest for the Historical Jesus.* Naperville, Ill.: A. R. Allenson, 1959.

Sanders, E. P. *The Historical Figure of Jesus.* London: Penguin, 1993.

———. *Jesus and Judaism.* Philadelphia: Fortress, 1985.

———. *Jewish Law from Jesus to the Mishnah.* Philadelphia: Trinity, 1990.

———. *Judaism: Practice and Belief 63 B.C.E.—66 C.E.* Philadelphia: Trinity, 1992.

Schottroff, Luise. "Women as Followers of Jesus in New Testament Times." In *The Bible and Liberation: Political and Social Hermeneutics,* pp 453-61. Rev. ed. Edited by Norman K. Gottwald and Richard A. Horsley. Maryknoll, N.Y.: Orbis, 1993.

Schweitzer, Albert. *The Quest of the Historical Jesus: A Critical Study of Its Progress from Reimarus to Wrede.* Rev. ed. New York: Macmillan, 1968.

Scott, Bernard Brandon. "Jesus as Sage: An Innovating Voice in Common Wisdom." In *The Sage in Israel and the Ancient Near East,* pp. 399-415. Edited by John G. Gammie and Leo G. Purdue. Winona Lake, Ind.: Eisenbrauns, 1990.

Segal, Alan F. "Conversion and Messianism." In *The Messiah,* pp. 296-340. Edited by James H. Charlesworth. Minneapolis: Augsburg Fortress, 1992.

Stuhlmacher, Peter. *Jesus of Nazareth—Christ of Faith.* Peabody, Mass.: Hendrickson, 1993.

Theissen, Gerd. *The Gospels in Context: Social and Political History in the Synoptic Tradition.* Minneapolis: Augsburg Fortress, 1991.

———. *The Shadow of the Galilean: The Quest of the Historical Jesus in Narrative Form.* Philadelphia: Fortress, 1987.

———. *Sociology of Early Palestinian Christianity.* Philadelphia: Fortress, 1978.

Twelftree, Graham H. *Jesus the Exorcist.* Tübingen: Mohr, 1993.

Vermes, Geza. "Escape and Rescue." Interview by Hershel Shanks. *Bible Review,* June 1994, pp. 30-37.

———. *Jesus the Jew: A Historian's Reading of the Gospel.* 2d ed. New York: Macmillan, 1983.

———. *Jesus and the World of Judaism.* Philadelphia: Fortress, 1984.

———. *The Religion of Jesus the Jew.* Minneapolis: Augsburg Fortress, 1993.

Witherington, Ben, III. *The Christology of Jesus.* Philadelphia: Fortress, 1990.

———. *Conflict and Community in Corinth: A Socio-rhetorical Commentary on 1 and 2*

Corinthians. Grand Rapids, Mich.: Eerdmans, 1995.

————. *Jesus, Paul and the End of the World*. Downers Grove, Ill.: InterVarsity Press, 1992.

————. *Jesus the Sage: The Pilgrimage of Wisdom*. Minneapolis: Augsburg Fortress, 1994.

————. *John's Wisdom: A Commentary on the Fourth Gospel*. Louisville: Westminster/John Knox, 1995.

————. "Lord." In *Dictionary of Jesus and the Gospels*, pp. 484-92. Edited by Joel B. Green, Scot McKnight and I. Howard Marshall. Downers Grove, Ill.: InterVarsity Press, 1992.

————. "Three Modern Faces of Wisdom." *Ashland Theological Seminary Journal* 25 (1993): 96-122.

————. *Women in the Earliest Churches*. Cambridge: Cambridge University Press, 1988.

————. *Women in the Ministry of Jesus*. Cambridge: Cambridge University Press, 1984.

Wright, N. T. "Jerusalem in the New Testament." In *Jerusalem Past and Present in the Purposes of God*, pp. 53-77. Edited by P. W. L. Walker. Cambridge: Tyndale House, 1992.

————. *Jesus and the Victory of God*. Vol. 2 of *Christian Origins and the Question of God*. Minneapolis: Fortress, 1996.

————. "Jesus, Israel and the Cross." In *Society of Biblical Literatuare 1985 Seminar Papers*, pp. 75-95. Edited by Kent H. Richards. Atlanta: Scholars Press, 1985.

————. *The New Testament and the People of God*. Vol. 1 of *Christian Origins and the Question of God*. Minneapolis: Fortress, 1992.

————. "Putting Paul Together Again." In *Pauline Theology*, Vol. 1: *Thessalonians, Philippians, Galatians, Philemon*, pp. 183-211. Edited by Jouette M. Bassler. Minneapolis: Augsburg Fortress, 1991.

————. "Taking the Text with Her Pleasure: A Post-Post-Modernist Response to J. Dominic Crossan, *The Historical Jesus: The Life of a Mediterranean Jewish Peasant*, T & T Clark, HarperSanFrancisco, 1991." *Theology* 96 (1993): 303-10.

————. *Who Was Jesus?* Grand Rapids, Mich.: Eerdmans, 1992.

Yarbrough, Robert W. "Modern Wise Men Encounter Jesus." *Christianity Today* 18, no. 7 (1994): 38-45.

Index of Subjects

Index of Modern Authors

Index of Scripture and Other Early Literature